Coming for to Carry Me Home

THE AMERICAN CRISIS SERIES
Books on the Civil War Era

Series Editor
Steven E. Woodworth, Professor of History,
Texas Christian University

Coming for to Carry Me Home

Race in America from Abolitionism to Jim Crow

J. Michael Martinez

ROWMAN & LITTLEFIELD PUBLISHERS, INC.
Lanham • Boulder • New York • Toronto • Plymouth, UK

Published by Rowman & Littlefield Publishers, Inc.
A wholly owned subsidiary of The Rowman & Littlefield Publishing Group, Inc.
4501 Forbes Boulevard, Suite 200, Lanham, Maryland 20706
www.rowmanlittlefield.com

Estover Road, Plymouth PL6 7PY, United Kingdom

British Library Cataloguing in Publication Information Available

Library of Congress Cataloging-in-Publication Data

Martinez, J. Michael (James Michael)
   Coming for to carry me home : race in America from abolitionism to Jim Crow /
J. Michael Martinez.
       p. cm. — (The American crisis series)
   Includes bibliographical references and index.
   ISBN 978-1-4422-1498-9 (cloth : alk. paper) — ISBN 978-1-4422-1500-9 (electronic)
   1. United States—Race relations—History—19th century. 2. Race—Political aspects—
United States—History—19th century. 3. Lincoln, Abraham, 1809-1865—Political and
social views. 4. Antislavery movements—United States—History—19th century. 5.
African Americans—Civil rights—History—19th century. 6. Slaves—Emancipation—
United States. 7. United States—Politics and government—19th century. I. Title.
   E185.18.M335 2011
   305.800973—dc23

                                                                      2011039081

♾TM The paper used in this publication meets the minimum requirements of American
National Standard for Information Sciences—Permanence of Paper for Printed Library
Materials, ANSI/NISO Z39.48-1992.

Printed in the United States of America

For Aswad Elisha "Ellie" Woodson—
So he might know the tragedy of the past
and the promise of the future

I looked over Jordan, and what did I see
Coming for to carry me home?
A band of angels coming after me
Coming for to carry me home.

If you get there before I do
Coming for to carry me home
Tell all my friends I'm coming, too,
Coming for to carry me home.

—"Swing Low, Sweet Chariot," Negro spiritual

For perhaps he therefore departed for a season from thee that thou mightest receive him again for ever: Not now as a servant, but instead of a servant, a most dear brother, especially to me: But how much more to thee, both in the flesh and in the Lord? If therefore thou count me a partner, receive him as myself.

—The Epistle of St. Paul to Philemon

As he was of opinion that Vindicius should have his share of the reward, he procured a decree of the people that the freedom of the city should be given him, which was never conferred on a slave before, and that he should be enrolled in what tribe he pleased and given his suffrage with it. . . . The act of enfranchising a slave is to this day called *Vindicta* (we are told) from this Vindicius.

—Plutarch, *Publicola*

Contents

Illustrations

Preface and Acknowledgments

This book began as one thing and ended as another. It began as an examination of President Abraham Lincoln's troubled relationship with the radical members of his party, and it ended as a history of the politics surrounding U.S. race relations during the half century between the rise of the abolitionist movement and the dawn of the Jim Crow era. The evolution of the manuscript occurred because it became clear as I researched and wrote the text that the story of Lincoln and the Radical Republicans could be understood and appreciated only in the broader context of nineteenth-century race relations. To understand how Lincoln and his contemporaries viewed race, one must first delve into the origins of abolitionism and the tumultuous decade of the 1830s, when that generation of political and military leaders came of age. To appreciate the consequences of Lincoln's policy disputes with the Radicals, one must follow the meandering trail through Reconstruction, Redemption, and the beginnings of legal segregation in the 1880s. Just as Orville Vernon Burton wrote of the "age of Lincoln" as an epoch that extended before and after the sixteenth president's tenure in office, this book explores broad issues through a wide lens.[1]

The central question can be stated succinctly: how and why did the concept of race in the United States change from the 1830s, when the abolitionists rose to prominence, until the 1880s, when the Jim Crow regime commenced? Progressive historians argue that the cycles of history inexorably lead toward enlightened policies, and iterative change provides benefits for all mankind. The English historian Robert MacKenzie observed, "Human history is a record of progress—a record of accumulating knowledge and increasing wisdom, of continual advancement from a lower to a higher platform of intelligence and well-being." Even after witnessing the horrors of the twentieth century, Francis Fukuyama contended that "pessimistic lessons about history that our century supposedly taught us need to be rethought from the beginning."[2] Without tackling the question of whether an end to history is desirable, or even possible, I wondered how the promise of eradicating slavery and lurching toward some kind of equality for freed slaves that began with abolitionism could sputter to a halt and yield to legal segregation half a century later. Did the trend represent genuine historical progress or a continued violation of the American creed, albeit in a different manner? A progressive could argue that segregation is preferable to human bondage, and I would begrudgingly concede the point. My rejoinder would be that guarantees of political equality encapsulated in the Thirteenth, Fourteenth, and Fifteenth Amendments to the U.S. Constitution were violated when Americans retreated from commitments made to freed slaves after Appomattox. In my view, historical progress toward equality from the 1830s until the 1860s gave way to retrograde inequality during the 1870s and 1880s.

This book argues that Lincoln and the Radical Republicans were the pivotal actors, albeit not the architects, that influenced this evolution from abolitionism to Jim Crow, a kind of fulcrum between what came before and what came after. The promise of a new era in U.S. race relations reached its nineteenth-century apex in the 1860s and declined after the Radicals passed from the scene.

Reasonable minds can differ on whether we should assign praise, blame, or some combination thereof, to the Civil War generation. To give them their due, these Union men, whatever their mixed motives and however haltingly they sometimes acted, accomplished a stupendous feat that no one who had preceded them had been able to achieve: they abolished the peculiar institution that had bedeviled the nation since its creation. Few observers would deny that this accomplishment altered the course of human history, not only on the North American continent but, because the United States (despite occasional lapses) serves as a symbol of the virtues of democratic government, in far-flung corners of the globe. Save for unreconstructed Southern partisans, subsequent neo-Confederates, and die-hard contrarians, anyone conversant with the goals of consensual self-rule must acknowledge that the abolition of slavery was a monumental epitaph for a generation of American political and military leaders who served the nation during the 1860s, and a giant step toward the eventual creation of a color-blind society.

Yet in some ways, the war that was fought from 1861 until 1865 represented an unfinished revolution. Newly emancipated slaves set forth on a long, arduous journey toward equal justice under the law—a journey they assumed the victorious Union army and a reasonably sympathetic Northern public would assist. Much to their dismay, the freedmen discovered, with some notable exceptions, their traveling companions had abandoned them on the road from freedom to citizenship. Ideally, federal Reconstruction policy was supposed to rebuild the American polity while simultaneously providing a permanent place for the previously enslaved underclass. It was not to be. As discussed within these pages, the many promises made to the freedmen in 1865 were broken within the next decade and a half.

The question naturally arises whether responsibility for the failures of Reconstruction can be laid at the doorstep of the same generation of Northerners that successfully prosecuted a bloody civil war, produced the Emancipation Proclamation, and ratified the Civil War amendments. Perhaps it was too much to ask that one group of leaders break the shackles of past oppression as well as create, virtually from scratch, a blueprint for future equality, followed by vigorous enforcement in the face of alternating protests and indifference from a war-weary populace. Perhaps it was a labor that no single generation could complete.

As for my labors, I realize with each book I write that the endeavor invariably becomes a collaborative effort. Fortunately, I have been assisted by numerous kind souls—far too many to name in the brief space allotted here. Some folks who deserve special mention include the talented (and patient) archivists and research assistants who kept me on the right path, especially Karen Dupell Drickamer, director of special collections and college archivist at the Musselman Library of Gettysburg College; Kristi Finefield in the reference section of the Prints and Photographs Division at the Library of Congress; Kay Peterson of the archives center at the Smithsonian Institution's National Museum of American History; and Stephen T. Robinson and Anne Louise Moore in the special collections and university archives of the W. E. B. Du Bois Library at the University of Massachusetts, Amherst. I also appreciated the marketing assistance I received from my terrific web designer, Liz Kula of webdesignsbyliz.com.

I am deeply indebted to the fine professionals at Rowman & Littlefield, especially Carrie Broadwell-Tkach, associate editor for American history; Niels Aaboe, formerly executive editor; Jehanne Schweitzer, senior production editor; Grace Baumgartner, editorial assistant; and copyeditor Michele Tomiak. In addition, I owe many thanks to Dr. Orville Vernon Burton, a scholar and a gentleman, for reviewing an early version of the manuscript and saving me from making innumerable errors, both major and minor. Moreover, I appreciated the advice and comments I received from the editor of the American Crisis series, Dr. Steven E. Woodworth, a noted Civil War scholar from Texas Christian University. Needless to say (but I will say it anyway), all mistakes of fact or interpretation that remain are my responsibility alone.

Friends and family have endured all manner of disruption and lengthy absences during the years I labored on this project, and their support has not gone unappreciated. I am thankful for support and encouragement from Paula R. Martinez; Loren and Polly Mead; Martha and Dick Pickett; Bob and Peggy Youngblood; the late Charles DuBose and his wife, Glenda; Wallace and Leila Jordan; Dr. William D. Richardson of the University of South Dakota; Keith W. Smith; Cheryl Schmidt; Sheila Traub; Gabriel Wardell; Barbara Wise; Shirley Hardrick; and Chuck and Lisa Redmon. My grandchildren, Brianna Marie Carter, Aswad Elisha Woodson, and Christopher Kainan Carter, have been a delight, as always. Thanks also to family members who are fellow writers—Loren B. Mead (uncle), William W. Mellette (uncle), Walter Russell Mead (cousin), Christopher A. Mead (cousin), Robert Sidney Mellette (cousin), and Jim Wise (cousin)—for setting the bar high. Colleagues at Dart Container Corporation, Kennesaw State University, the University of South Dakota, and the University of Georgia have been supportive as well. I have been blessed to receive such tremendous encouragement throughout the years.

Prologue

"We Have the Wolf by the Ear"

He was a thin, bespectacled, balding man with effeminate features and a slight, fragile frame. To the uninitiated, he looked to be an accountant or a draftsman, perhaps a professor of literature or theology. Whatever he was, he was unassuming and plain, surely a person of no great consequence. He did not stand out in a crowd.

This physically unimposing product of New England, an unlikely prophet portending radical change in American life, hailed from Newburyport, Massachusetts. His father, an itinerant sailor once described as "a seaman with a taste for rum," deserted his family in 1808, when the boy was three years old. Although their family was destitute and the future appeared bleak, his mother was a strong-willed Baptist who refused to succumb to despair despite her lowly station as a cleaning woman. She taught her child the virtues of hard work and righteousness, to say nothing of dedication to a noble cause.

Hard work was his credo from childhood. At the tender age of five, the strong-willed, pious Yankee boy sold homemade molasses candy on the streets to help support his family. It was his introduction to the world of work, and it showed him the meaning and dignity that accompanied an entrepreneurial spirit and the freedom to pursue one's dreams.

In his adolescence, he served as an apprentice in the newspaper business. There, he learned the art and mechanics of publishing as well as the power of words. Following in the footsteps of Benjamin Franklin, another self-made man who rose from humble beginnings as a printer's apprentice to become an outspoken opponent of chattel slavery, this young fellow advanced through the ranks as a writer and editor. At twenty-five, he joined the abolitionist movement and became one of its leading proponents, a controversial, polarizing symbol of antislavery sentiment in the Northern states.[1]

1

**William Lloyd Garrison, pictured here in old age, radical-
ized the slavery issue in the 1830s when he called for
immediate emancipation.**
Courtesy of the Library of Congress.

If William Lloyd Garrison did not impress with his appearance, he was
impressive, nonetheless; his passion and facility with the English language
became the stuff of legend. Throughout his long life, he was "all on fire"
with religious zeal and an unmitigated antipathy for human bondage. His
angry, uncompromising rhetoric reverberated across the decades, indeed the
centuries, to express the moral indignation and outrage that a generation of
nineteenth-century antislavery activists felt toward the "peculiar institution"
that so dominated American life and commerce. In his most famous editorial,
he penned these oft-quoted lines:

> I am aware that many object to the severity of my language; but is there not
> cause for severity? I *will be* as harsh as truth, and as uncompromising as justice.
> On this subject, I do not wish to think, or to speak, or write, with moderation.
> No! no! Tell a man whose house is on fire to give a moderate alarm; tell him
> to moderately rescue his wife from the hands of the ravisher; tell the mother to

gradually extricate her babe from the fire into which it has fallen;—but urge me not to use moderation in a cause like the present. I am in earnest—I will not equivocate—I will not excuse—I will not retreat a single inch—AND I WILL BE HEARD.[2]

Although manumission societies and antislavery sentiment existed as early as the colonial period, abolitionism did not arise as an organized, activist movement until half a century after the ratification of the U.S. Constitution. By the 1830s, the founding generation had disappeared, manufacturing and commerce were rapidly spreading throughout the northeastern United States, immigration was on the rise, and evangelical movements were increasing in many parts of the country. With the invention of the cotton gin, which greatly increased the profitability of cotton production, and westward expansion across the southern territory of the old Louisiana Purchase, allowed under the terms of the Missouri Compromise of 1820, slavery became an ever-more important cornerstone of the white Southern economy. The horrors of what Abraham Lincoln later called "the bondsman's two hundred and fifty years of unrequited toil," which could be ignored by white Northerners while it was hidden away, suddenly were visible for all but the most myopic to see.[3] Autobiographies and polemics such as David Walker's 1829 pamphlet *Walker's Appeal in Four Articles* were published in increasing numbers, and these firsthand accounts provided convincing and excruciating details of the inhumanity of human bondage. The ubiquity of slavery as a topic of articles, books, and conversation and as a feature of economic and social life transformed it into the defining issue of the nineteenth century. Concomitant with the spread and newfound visibility of slavery, a strong current of antislavery activism arose, especially in New England.[4]

Some historians date the birth of the abolitionist movement to the initial publication of Garrison's *Liberator* in Boston on January 1, 1831. As with many events in American history, the story is more complicated than folklore would suggest. Garrison was not the first white public figure to call for Negro emancipation, nor was he the first writer to publish an antislavery newspaper, but he was a cofounder of the American Anti-Slavery Society as well as a pivotal figure in the movement from gradualism to immediate emancipation, as his stirring words published in the inaugural edition of the *Liberator*, above, make clear.[5]

By Thomas Jefferson's tenure as president, emancipation laws had been enacted in every state north of the Mason-Dixon Line. Slavery was the economic engine of the Cotton South, however, which made eradication almost impossible. The antislavery strategy, such as it existed before Garrison's time, was to pursue quiet, gradual change, almost imperceptible in states where human bondage was not an integral feature of the economy. In the North, the Quakers as well as the Moravians had led the push for manumission as far back as the Revolutionary War era. By the early nineteenth century, organized groups such as the Pennsylvania Antislavery Society and the New York Manumission Society were at the vanguard of the antislavery movement, but their influence in the South was virtually nonexistent.[6]

When William Lloyd Garrison arrived on the scene, a permanent schism between North and South was growing. He perceived the futility of gradualism outside of New England and the mid-Atlantic states. If the peculiar institution were to be assaulted, the issue could not wait for Southerners to come to the mountain; the mountain must come to Southerners. In 1835, abolitionists began mailing tracts to individuals and institutions in the slave-holding states. This brazen effort to enlighten the Southern mind so incensed the slaveholding class that abolitionist literature was banned from Southern states. The U.S. Postmaster General refused to deliver abolitionist pamphlets in the South. Northern teachers who preached an antislavery message were exiled. The developing national conversation over the virtues and vices of slavery that had begun in the wake of the Missouri Compromise grew louder during the 1830s, with the voices on each side becoming hysterical and shrill.[7]

If 1831 was significant for Garrison's dramatic entry into the abolitionist crusade, it was also the year that the largest and most infamous slave uprising sent shock waves through the Southern states. Slave uprisings were hardly new—the Stono Rebellion of 1739, Gabriel Prosser's foiled attempt to incite an insurrection in Virginia in 1800, and the free black Denmark Vesey's thwarted conspiracy to unite slaves and former slaves in Charleston in 1822 were well known, especially to Southerners—but the sheer terror and bloodshed associated with the 1831 rebellion were unprecedented.[8]

At 2:00 a.m. on Monday, August 22, Nat Turner, a thirty-year-old slave on the Travis Plantation in Southampton County, Virginia, led six fellow rebels on a killing spree that brought Southerners' ancestral fears of bloody insurrection to life. A self-proclaimed preacher with a messianic personality, Turner claimed to have witnessed a series of visions such as blood on the corn and human figures dancing in the air, prophesies that he interpreted to be instructions for leading a violent revolt. As he later explained, "I saw white spirits and black spirits engaged in battle, and the sun darkened—thunder rolled in the heavens, and blood flowed in the streams."[9]

The bloodletting was especially horrific. Turner's band entered his owners' home under cover of darkness and attacked Joseph and Sally Travis with axes, cutting them down with no compunction before slaughtering the masters' twelve-year-old son as well as a twelve-year-old apprentice. Before leaving the plantation house, the rebels found an infant lying in his cradle and hacked him to pieces.

For his part, Turner killed only one person, a young woman who might have escaped to raise the alarm. He left it to his followers to do the grisly work while he directed events from the rear. The mob seized weapons and roamed the countryside in search of additional victims, raiding plantation homes and showing no mercy for its victims. When all was said and done, Turner's mob numbered sixty. Of the fifty-seven whites killed during the two-day rampage, forty-six were women and children.[10]

A combination of federal troops from the U.S. naval base at Norfolk, state militia troops, and vigilantes eventually quelled the rebellion. Retribution was swift and brutal, not only for Turner's adherents, but for many blacks living in southern Virginia regardless of whether they had participated in the uprising. As for Turner, he eluded capture by hiding under a pile of fence railings until he was apprehended on October 30. Rather than execute him on the spot, authorities bound him over for trial. While he awaited his fate, Turner spoke to a white attorney, Thomas Gray, who later published the story of this fascinating slave preacher as *The Confessions of Nat Turner*.[11]

Predictably, Turner was found guilty and hanged. Immediately following his death, surgeons skinned and dissected the corpse, passing out souvenirs to a crowd of onlookers. For many decades thereafter, trophies of Turner's bones and purses made from his skin could be found in Southern homes. Even worse for blacks living in large slaveholding states, frightened whites exacted vengeance against slaves regardless of whether they had planned or participated in rebellious activities. New laws enacted by state legislatures strengthened authorities' power to punish rebellious slaves and anyone who assisted their efforts.[12]

In the wake of the burgeoning abolitionist movement and the Turner rebellion, it was clear by the early 1830s that slavery was an increasingly important political issue. Although some parties couched the debate as a dispute over federal and state rights and the constitutionality of nullification—South Carolina statesman John C. Calhoun was the most ardent proponent of this view—slavery was the driving factor behind the constitutional niceties.[13] Americans could not agree on how the issue should be resolved, if it could be resolved at all. Garrison may have issued a clarion call for an immediate end to slavery, but the antislavery movement was divided on the efficacy of quick, universal emancipation.[14]

A second faction of abolitionists championed gradual emancipation of the slaves. Although these abolitionists viewed slavery as morally indefensible, they believed that major changes in society could not occur overnight without wreaking havoc on the republic. Any effort to free slaves without providing for their care or compensating their former owners was doomed to failure. Throughout the antebellum years, various emancipation schemes appeared, including a plan to compensate former slave owners as well as a plan for sending slaves to specially created colonies in Africa, Haiti, or South America. Some men who later joined the "Radical" camp during the 1850s and 1860s traced their lineage to this position. All such plans were politically doomed at the outset: they were too slow and plodding for true abolitionists to endorse and too radical and invasive to placate anxious slave owners, who feared their way of life and their property were at risk.[15]

Just outside of the abolitionist camp was a group that considered slavery morally wrong but believed that the peculiar institution was protected by the U.S. Constitution. Had civil war not erupted, members of this group might have left the status quo intact, allowing slavery to exist where it was already legal and focusing instead on preventing its spread to the territories. Historians have debated whether these antislavery men would have evolved to appreciate the potentially ruinous effects of a republic existing half slave and half free, but prior to the 1860s this group was unprepared to risk serious sectional tensions to advance the abolitionist cause.[16]

Although he hoped that slavery eventually would die out, Lincoln was a skilled, pragmatic politician. He dared not travel too far ahead of the citizenry. One reason Garrison and radical abolitionists became so infuriated with Lincoln and other conservative elected officials in the northern United States at midcentury was because the radicals feared they could not push someone who preferred to maintain a stable, even keel to the extreme position of agreeing to the immediate emancipation of all slaves in the United States. Without a radical departure from the current state of affairs, universal emancipation might never occur.[17]

On the other end of the continuum, supporters of slavery generally fell into one of two camps: those who viewed slavery as a necessary evil, and those who viewed slavery as a positive good. The former were owners who recognized that slavery was a pernicious institution but that it had become an integral part of American life, especially in the South. With so much of the economy predicated on the perpetuation and spread of human bondage, destroying the institution would decimate the Southern economy and trigger dire consequences for social and political relations between the races.[18]

The quintessential example of the "slavery as a necessary evil" school of defenders was Thomas Jefferson, who wrestled with the problem through much of his adult life, alternately defending and denouncing the institution. By observing his struggles, Jefferson's progeny (literally and figuratively) can see the myriad perspectives on slavery that characterized the antebellum era. In 1789, he reflected a widely held paternalistic view of slaves when he wrote, "To give liberty to, or rather, to abandon persons whose habits have been formed in slavery is like abandoning children."[19] In query 18 of his book

Notes on the State of Virginia, he recognized the deeply disturbing character of the master-slave relationship: "The whole commerce between master and slave is a perpetual exercise of the most boisterous passions, the most unremitting despotism on the one part, and degrading submissions on the other."[20] His long-running ambivalence was reflected in a famous line he penned to a Massachusetts politician in 1820: "But as it is, we have the wolf by the ear, and we can neither hold him, nor safely let him go. Justice is in one scale, and self-preservation in the other."[21]

To observers who look across the centuries at the blight of slavery on the American landscape, Jefferson and the "slavery as a necessary evil" apologists appear self-serving and foolish, victims and perpetrators of a deliberately myopic and tragic enervation. A man who sees an obvious moral conundrum and shrugs, muttering, "What can you do?" invites opprobrium from good men who refuse to turn a blind eye to a depraved social order. Yet in fairness to Jefferson, to conclude that anyone save a small, radical clique living in the antebellum period could have foreseen the demise of chattel slavery in the nineteenth century is to risk falling prey to presentism, the fallacy of judging the actions and motives of people living in the past through the standards and sensibilities of the present. Presumably, if Jeffersonians had seen a way out of slavery without igniting a conflagration, they would have made different choices.[22]

Some Southerners were not nearly as conflicted or apologetic as Jefferson. They argued that slavery was beneficial to slave owners and slaves alike. Proponents of the polygenesis school of thought were especially vehement in arguing that the black race was innately inferior, not a true descendant of Adam, but akin to a missing link in the chain of what later came to be called evolution. This theory, while serving as a convenient rationale for defending chattel slavery, contradicted the biblical account found in Genesis and therefore presented more problems than it solved for the proslavery faction. Even the most ardent slaveholder was troubled by this explanation, and it eventually lost favor among a vast majority of the Southern planter elite.[23]

Despite the problems associated with polygenesis, slaveholders obviously benefited from having a captive labor force on hand. Even without a formal evolutionary theory, masters contended that slaves benefited from the relationship because the bondsmen were too childlike, simplistic, and stupid to care for themselves. If slave owners did not provide them with food, clothing, and shelter, especially in their old age, blacks probably would starve to death. Emancipation was not kind; it was cruel. It forced a group of simpletons to fend for itself when the laws of nature meant for blacks to be subjugated to whites, much as beasts of burden are cared for and used by man.[24]

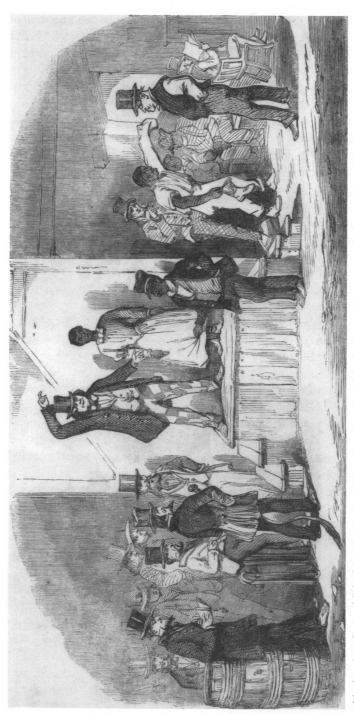

This drawing, first published in *The Illustrated London News* in 1856, depicts a slave woman being auctioned in Richmond, Virginia. Such horrific scenes were all too common in the antebellum South.

This division of opinion about the relative merits of the peculiar institution was the political reality that confronted America's political leaders in the middle of the nineteenth century. Among all the leaders who drove the slavery issue in the U.S. Congress, perhaps none were as vociferous as the so-called Radicals, a faction of the Republican Party that gained prominence in the U.S. Congress during the 1860s. They did not call themselves "radicals"; indeed, from their vantage point, all they asked was equal treatment for all human beings. How could such a seemingly innocuous proposition be deemed "radical," hence dangerous to the polity? That this group was seen as a band of rabble-rousers zealously pursuing a foolhardy policy says more about the tenor of the times than the wisdom of their objective. The group opposed slavery and fervently lobbied for emancipation, a novel position in mid-nineteenth-century America, but they were not abolitionists of the Garrisonian stripe. They were practical politicians who had to stand for election, mollify constituents, and champion public policies that had a reasonable chance of passing into law. Even within the group, the Radicals were not always consistent or in absolute agreement on the preferred means for eradicating slavery. What united them was a shared recognition that something had to be done through the legislative process if the American republic were to survive and remain true to its creed.[25]

When civil war erupted in 1861, the Radical Republicans urged President Lincoln to emancipate the slaves as part of the administration's wartime policy. The president's refusal to adopt the group's agenda convinced the Radicals he was a timid, ineffectual leader who sought to preserve the status quo even at an opportune time in history when the blight of slavery finally could be eradicated. Although some Radical Republicans later supported Lincoln as his position evolved during the course of the conflict, the relationship between the president and the Radical camp remained uneasy, especially after the latter created the Joint Committee on the Conduct of the War to oversee Lincoln's actions.[26]

Slavery, in Lincoln's view, was anathema, but he had sworn an oath to preserve, protect, and defend the Constitution of the United States. The Constitution allowed slavery to exist; the three-fifths clause, part of the compromise between North and South at the founding convention, required that blacks be considered 60 percent as productive as whites for purposes of taxation and representation. Lincoln did not believe he had the power to assail the institution in the normal course of affairs. He was sympathetic to the abolitionists' goals of ending chattel slavery, but he found their bold initiatives dangerous because their radical agenda was too far removed from mainstream public opinion. Thus, when the war began, Lincoln's goal was to preserve the union and leave the institution of slavery untouched despite his personal predilections. As he wrote in a famous public letter to newspaperman Horace Greeley on August 22, 1862, outlining his objectives in prosecuting the war:

I would save the Union. I would save it the shortest way under the Constitution. The sooner the national authority can be restored; the nearer the Union will be "the Union as it was." If there be those who would not save the Union, unless they could at the same time save slavery, I do not agree with them. If there be those who would not save the Union unless they could at the same time destroy slavery, I do not agree with them. My paramount object in this struggle is to save the Union, and is not either to save or to destroy slavery. If I could save the Union without freeing any slave I would do it, and if I could save it by freeing all slaves I would do it; and if I could save it by freeing some and leaving others alone I would also do that. What I do about slavery, and the colored race, I do because I believe it helps to save the Union; and what I forbear, I forbear because I don't believe it would help to save the Union.[27]

Lincoln also added that "I have here stated my purpose according to my view of *official* duty; and I intend no modification of my oft-expressed *personal* wish that all men every where could be free." What he did not say—because the timing was not right—was that he already had resolved to issue the Emancipation Proclamation.[28]

If the Greeley letter seems disingenuous under the circumstances, it can be defended as a method of forestalling critics until a Union victory would allow Lincoln to issue the proclamation without appearing desperate. He recognized a civil war was not a normal course of affairs; his limited goal to preserve the Union had to be modified as the war continued. By the time he responded to Greeley in 1862, the president had come to see that freeing some slaves, at least those in the rebellious states, could advance his war aims. Issuing an emancipation proclamation shortly after a marginal Union victory at the battle of Antietam in September 1862 dissuaded some European nations from recognizing the legitimacy of the Southern Confederacy. The proclamation also led the way toward recruiting black Union soldiers. In addition, Lincoln sought to induce Southerners to lay down their arms and return to the Union before the proclamation went into effect. A state that ceased hostilities before January 1, 1863, would not be affected by the president's edict but, as a practical matter, it was unlikely that the leaders of any Southern state that had sacrificed so much blood and treasure to secede and defend against an invading force would willingly capitulate except under force of arms. Nonetheless, the president could argue that he had provided an opportunity for insurrectionists to recognize the errors of their ways before they were decimated through a policy of total war and unconditional surrender.[29]

The Radicals supported Lincoln's Emancipation Proclamation, although it was too plodding and incomplete for their tastes. If they never quite reconciled their position with Lincoln's ponderous decision-making, his tentative steps toward emancipation, and his lenient reconstruction terms for the traitorous South, they came to realize his virtues. By the standards of the presidents who came before him—and, as some critics would learn to their consternation, those who succeeded him—Lincoln was hardly the ideal chief executive, but at least some of the Radicals' goals were accomplished during his tenure.[30]

After Lincoln fell victim to an assassin's bullet and Andrew Johnson stepped into the presidency, the Radical Republicans demanded severe punishment for the defeated South. Initially, Johnson agreed. His incendiary rhetoric was riddled with the fire-and-brimstone wrath favored by the Radicals and a far cry from Lincoln's conciliatory tone. The new president insisted that the "traitors must be punished and impoverished," a sentiment wholly in keeping with uncompromising measures advocated by the congressional Republicans. Benjamin Wade, a Radical Republican in the U.S. Senate, spoke for many in his party when he told Johnson that he welcomed punitive measures. Lincoln had been far too kindhearted for the rough work ahead. An iron hand was needed "to deal with these damned rebels."[31]

Echoing Wade's desire to "bare the iron hand" against the now-defunct Southern Confederacy, the celebrated novelist Herman Melville, a sometime poet, captured the "passion of the people on the 15th of April, 1865" in his poem "The Martyr":

> He lieth in his blood—
> The father in his face;
> They have killed him, the Forgiver—
> The Avenger takes his place.[32]

In this verse, Lincoln is the Forgiver and Andrew Johnson is the Avenger who will exact vengeance for the terrible deeds of Good Friday 1865. Although no direct evidence tied the assassin to Southern leaders, the rebellious states had created the climate where slavery and murder were practiced with impunity. Melville's angry verse reflected the national mood that someone should have to pay a price for the "rivers of blood" that soaked the national soil.[33]

Yet for all of his tough talk, Johnson fell short of the mark. Among the many events demonstrating that his actions would not live up to his numerous promises to make the South pay for its transgressions, six weeks into his tenure the accidental president issued a proclamation of amnesty pardoning all Southerners, except for the Confederate leadership, for their roles in the rebellion. The Radicals were stunned, but Democrats and Southerners were delighted with this unexpected turn of events. As one historian has written, the proclamation was "so much the essence of the man, and so tone deaf to the political world around him that the policy couldn't help but doom him. Reconstruction was his short road to the ash heap of history."[34]

When it became clear that Johnson would not "bare the iron hand" toward the South, the Radicals confronted him with a series of punitive legislative measures that Johnson vetoed. The Republican-controlled Congress over-rode the vetoes after the Radicals compromised with moderate Republicans to forge an alliance. The tension between the Republicans who felt bitterly betrayed and an obstinate chief executive who would not yield led to a showdown when Congress impeached the embattled president in 1868 for violating the questionably constitutional Tenure of Office Act. Johnson won acquittal by one vote during his Senate trial, but he was destroyed politically, and the Radicals were weakened by the imbroglio as well.[35]

Ulysses S. Grant became president in 1869, and although he was not the zealous defender of the freedmen and the Republican agenda the Radicals would have preferred, his tenure started with great promise. During the for-mer general's first term in the Executive Mansion, he vigorously prosecuted white supremacist groups such as the Ku Klux Klan and did not hesitate to use military authority in keeping the peace. Unfortunately, the president's support for tough Reconstruction policies declined during his second term as his administration was engulfed by scandal and a sluggish economy that fol-lowed the Panic of 1873. By the end of Grant's second term, Reconstruction had ended in all but name. In 1877, Grant's successor, Rutherford B. Hayes, removed federal troops from Southern statehouses, and the Reconstruction era passed into history.[36]

This book examines the period of American history between the rise of the abolitionist movement in the 1830s and the dawn of the Jim Crow re-gime the 1880s, focusing especially on the leading Radical Republicans in Congress, their relationship with Lincoln during the American Civil War, the zenith of their influence during the postbellum era, and the aftermath. The book discusses the three major Radicals in Congress—Thaddeus Stevens, Charles Sumner, and Benjamin Wade—but also explores the thinking of other prominent Radicals and their influence on the course of national affairs in the nineteenth century.

The Radicals championed a variety of crucial issues and legislation dur-ing the 1860s and 1870s, including the Confiscation Acts, emancipation, the enlistment of blacks in the Union army, the ratification of the Civil War amendments to the U.S. Constitution, and various Reconstruction policies.[37] Although Lincoln eventually sided with these members of his party on is-sues such as emancipation, many Radicals opposed his renomination in 1864 primarily owing to differences regarding Reconstruction. It is probably fair to say that had the Radical Republicans not created the extreme position on the left of the political spectrum, Lincoln probably would have had a difficult time justifying his more controversial, far-reaching actions. The Radicals cajoled and pressured Lincoln, always pushing him to be bold and creative; in this manner, they influenced the evolution of the administration's wartime policies. After his death, they relentlessly checked Andrew Johnson's power, refusing to allow him to turn his back on the freedmen. The failure of the Radical Republicans to fulfill the promises of Reconstruction probably says more about the prejudices of nineteenth-century America than it does about the Radicals' commitment to effecting changes in society.[38]

The exploration begins in the 1830s after William Lloyd Garrison's antislavery publication *The Liberator* assailed the peculiar institution and Nat Turner's rebellion struck fear in the hearts of white Southerners. With the passing of the founding generation, the American experiment was still new enough to be novel and innovative but not so stable and well established that it could be said to exist in perpetuity. The nation might yet be broken on a wheel, and that wheel might yet turn on how that nation's leaders addressed the momentous issue of human bondage.

Chapter One

"The Crimes of This Guilty Land Will Never Be Purged Away but with Blood"

By the end of the 1830s, the United States comprised twenty-six states with a population of seventeen million people, more than four times as many denizens as recorded in the first census of 1790. It was a young nation, its constitution dating back but half a century. Its institutional structure, constructed on new theories of political science and faith in the efficacy of republican government, was not yet settled and secure, its political parties not yet stabilized on the bedrock of a two-party system. The standing army by modern standards was nonexistent; the nation's system of militias and local defense was ill equipped and underfunded, not a professional operation in any sense. The continent had not been fully conquered or exhaustively explored, although the storm clouds of Manifest Destiny were visible on the horizon.[1]

In the five decades stretching from the ratification of the U.S. Constitution until the 1830s, national political leaders struggled to establish precedents and procedures that would bind all citizens together as part of a singular country, but numerous divisions persisted. Northeastern states relied on industrial and manufacturing processes while the Southern economy was rooted in agriculture. Eastern states sought to fix territorial boundaries and tame their interior lands while western states pushed for greater exploration to accommodate the growth of an ever-restless and mobile population. The challenge of developing effective domestic and foreign policies for a fledgling nation had marginalized the slavery issue in the early decades of the nineteenth century. This respite would not last; the issue was moribund, temporarily shunted to one side, but never forgotten.

During Andrew Jackson's tenure as president, the bondsman's plight, which had been a part of the American experience for two hundred years, increasingly became a topic of discussion and debate. With the growth of the new nation and the influx of immigrants, labor and property took center stage

15

in crucial public policy considerations. As the abolitionist movement was born and grew to maturity, the decision of whether human bondage should remain a fixture in the American republic could not be ignored.[2]

If Americans of the 1830s were divided by opinions on slavery, they also were physically divided by space. To prosper, they must first overcome vast distances. The lack of what later generations would call an infrastructure presented a challenge to the entrepreneurial American character, but the obstacles were not insurmountable. At the beginning of the decade, steamboats and horse-drawn buggies were the predominant forms of transportation. By the end of the decade, the steam locomotive was poised to spark a revolution. Dramatic improvements in communications were not far behind; the telegraph would soon transform the way nineteenth-century inhabitants passed news and information to one another. Almost as startling was the development and availability of photography. In 1830, a person's likeness could be preserved only through drawings and portraits. By 1839, with the dissemination of a new technology—the daguerreotype, an image preserved on a silver-coated copper plate—a more exact likeness was possible.[3]

The overwhelming majority of Americans still lived on farms and depended on agriculture to scratch out what was often little more than a subsistence living. The average citizen lacked creature comforts, but he was enshrouded in faith—a deep, abiding religious feeling brought on by the Second Great Awakening that spread the Christian gospel through heart and hearth. Unburdened by the traditions that sometimes stifled advances in European society, Americans optimistically looked to a future that seemed limited only by the imagination and tenacity of the country's people.[4]

The United States of the 1830s sometimes has been called the Age of Jackson, and with good reason. The frontier hero ensconced in the Executive Mansion from 1829 until 1837 cast a large shadow across the politics of his epoch. A hero of the Battle of New Orleans in 1815, a dramatic postscript to the War of 1812 (which had ended before the battle was fought), this legendary general-turned-statesman embodied many values that would be heralded as uniquely "American": seemingly self-made, unrefined, hardworking, indefatigable, relentless when he knew he was right, and deferential to no one save his God, his conscience, and the supposed voice of the people.

He was a symbol of the ingenuity that abounded in the new land. Where his predecessors had come of age as members of the landed gentry or sported illustrious pedigrees originating with the fine families of Virginia or scaled the heights of educational achievement based on privilege and intellectual prowess, he was down to earth, coarse, tough, easily provoked to anger if his character were impugned, and reared in the frontier school of hard knocks. He represented a distinct break from the past, for Jackson was the first occupant of the executive office that was not a Founder or, in the case of his immediate predecessor, the son of a Founder. Whether he was championing Indian removal from the Southern states, facing down would-be secessionists in South Carolina during the 1832 nullification crisis, or defending the honor of Peggy Eaton, the embattled wife of his secretary of war, Old Hickory shaped the character of the nation with an indomitable will that would be matched by few heads of state. He became the model of an activist executive for his successors to emulate.[5]

For all of the promise the new nation held, it was nevertheless a troubling time. Indeed, if Jackson reflected the optimism of the era, he also symbolized another, darker side of American life. Mistrustful of banks and financiers and reflecting the racial prejudice of the age, Jackson undermined the Bank of the United States and refused to consider extending the privileges of citizenship to Indians or persons of color. The lack of roads, bridges, and canals made day-to-day life difficult, and an economic downturn in 1837—a "panic," as it was called in that era—exposed the precarious nature of the financial system. Immigration was on the rise, and with it came a xenophobia that threatened to betray the American creed that "all men are created equal." Most troubling of all was the one issue that had lurked beneath the American façade since the colonial period: slavery.[6]

It was an issue that had haunted statesmen for generations, reducing even the most conscientious moral and political philosopher to a mass of inconsistencies and self-serving rationalizations. Many citizens expressed opinions on the benefits and costs associated with the peculiar institution, but few elected leaders could see their way clear to resolve the dilemma without jeopardizing the health and continuation of the republic. The wolf by the ear, indeed: here was a wolf that promised to wriggle free or die trying.

Jackson was not a man given to fretting over slaves. He owned slaves; he believed slavery to be a condition natural to the darker races; he saw no need in, or advantage to, engineering a social, political, and moral upheaval over an institution that had endured for decades and likely would endure for decades to come. Old Hickory would not be drawn into the fight. It probably boded well for his administration that he would not enter the fray; despite his much-lauded strength and power, "King Andrew" did not govern without opposition, nor was the Age of Jackson hegemonic. In the U.S. Congress, three men—Daniel Webster, Henry Clay, and John C. Calhoun, sometimes called the "Great Triumvirate"—towered above the rest, destined to shape national affairs, including the debate over slavery and the perpetuation of the Union, for decades. Each man was a rival to the other, and each objected to, and occasionally supported, President Jackson's policies. Whatever else can be said, the Great Triumvirate kept the chief executive from exercising his will without limits.[7]

Daniel Webster enjoyed a long and illustrious career as a lawyer, legislator, and adviser to presidents. The brilliant New Englander, a graduate of Dartmouth College, was nicknamed "Black Dan" because of his dark complexion, thick, heavy eyebrows, and piercing eyes, which gave him the vaguely menacing countenance reminiscent of a hollow-eyed apparition. First elected to the U.S. House of Representatives representing his home state of New Hampshire, he later moved to Massachusetts, where he served in both the House and the Senate in a career that spanned more than twenty years. He also served as secretary of state under Presidents William Henry Harrison, John Tyler, and Millard Fillmore.

His oratorical gifts were legendary. Mellifluous words, spoken with powerful, emotive force and exactly the right inflection and intonation, flowed from his lips in a seemingly endless torrent of unassailable logic and eloquent rhetoric. With his ramrod-straight posture, sonorous voice, confident, almost haughty manner, and flawless, erudite command of the subject matter, he held his audiences enthralled with a series of dramatic performances, each a veritable tour de force of reasoned persuasion and verbal gymnastics.[8]

Today Webster is best remembered for his reply to South Carolina senator Robert Hayne during a debate over a protective tariff and the growing powers of the federal government, both vehemently opposed by Southern representatives. Reflecting the view of many Southerners, including fellow South Carolinian John C. Calhoun, who was then serving as vice president of the United States, Hayne argued on the floor of the Senate that Northern polices were so onerous to the South that the doctrine of nullification, whereby a state could ignore a law that harmed a state's interests, must be used to prevent the diminution of state rights. The theory of nullification threatened the stability of the fledgling nation. In one of the most stirring speeches ever delivered from the Senate floor, Webster rose to his feet and famously remarked:

When my eyes shall be turned to behold for the last time the sun in heaven, may I not see him shining on the broken and dishonored fragments of a once glorious Union; on States dissevered, discordant, belligerent; on a land rent with civil feuds, or drenched, it may be, in fraternal blood! Let their last feeble and lingering glance rather behold the gorgeous ensign of the republic, now known and honored throughout the earth, still full high advanced, its arms and trophies streaming in their original lustre, not a stripe erased or polluted, not a single star obscured, bearing for its motto, no such miserable interrogatory as "What is all this worth?" nor those other words of delusion and folly, "Liberty first and Union afterwards"; but everywhere, spread all over in characters of living light, blazing on all its sample folds, as they float over the sea and over the land, and in every wind under the whole heavens, that other sentiment, dear to every true American heart,—Liberty *and* Union, now and for ever, one and inseparable![9]

Although not Webster's equal as an orator, Henry Clay of Kentucky surpassed his renowned New England colleague as a parliamentarian and master legislator of the first order. A native of the Old Dominion, Clay found his way to the Kentucky frontier and earned a living practicing law as a young man. He served in the U.S. Senate on two separate occasions, but his greatest achievements occurred in the House of Representatives, where he served several times as Speaker and became known as the "Great Compromiser" for his willingness and ability to negotiate legislative programs that preserved the Union even as slavery tested the resilience of the young republic. At midcareer, he joined the nascent Whig Party and led the charge for "internal improvements," that era's term for government financing of roads, bridges, canals, and other infrastructure development projects designed to unite different parts of the nation. Through his American System, Clay hoped to join the industrial East and the agricultural West in a political alliance that would further his political career. A perennial presidential candidate and opponent of Andrew Jackson, Clay served as secretary of state under John Quincy Adams and distinguished himself as a visionary foreign policy analyst. Late in his career, he brokered a deal that became known as the Compromise of 1850, a figurative bookend to his first major legislative negotiation, the Missouri Compromise of 1820. The earlier legislative maneuver allowed Maine to enter the Union as a free state while Missouri joined as a slave state, thereby preserving the balance between free states (11) and slave states (11) in the Senate (except for Missouri, where slavery was forbidden north of a line designated 36° 30', the northern boundary of Arkansas).[10]

In the Compromise of 1850, the aging Clay once more brought his impressive parliamentary skills to bear. In the resultant legislative package, the U.S. Congress defined the western border of Texas and New Mexico, a requirement in the wake of the war with Mexico. Clay had opposed the war because he thought the addition of new territorial lands would exacerbate the slavery issue, which of course it did. To finesse the matter, his compromise allowed the land ceded by Mexico to the United States to remain open to slavery through popular sovereignty—that is, the right of residents in the those lands to vote on whether slavery should be extended into the territory—and admitted California as a free state. Washington, D.C., abolished the slave trade, although the right to own slaves in the city continued.[11]

The doctrine of popular sovereignty eventually engendered a heated political debate among public figures battling over the spread of slavery into the territories, but the most controversial provision of the Compromise of 1850 in the immediate aftermath of Clay's triumph was the Fugitive Slave Act. The statute was grounded in the U.S. Constitution (Article IV, Section 2, clause 3) and required that citizens refrain from aiding or abetting

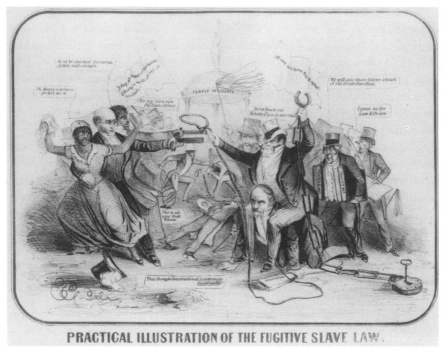

PRACTICAL ILLUSTRATION OF THE FUGITIVE SLAVE LAW.

This caricature (circa 1851) is a "Practical Illustration of the Fugitive Slave Law." At the left, the abolitionist William Lloyd Garrison protects a runaway slave girl from a brutish slave driver who rides on the back of Secretary of State Daniel Webster. Webster clutches a copy of the U.S. Constitution in his hand. A nearby caption reads, "This, though Constitutional, is extremely disagreeable." The Temple of Liberty is visible in the background.
Courtesy of the Library of Congress.

runaway slaves anywhere in the United States on pain of six years in prison and a $1,000 fine. The act infuriated Northerners because, in effect, it made all citizens agents of slaveholders regardless of where they lived or their affinity for the peculiar institution. An abolitionist who discovered a runaway slave hiding in his barn was legally obligated to inform the authorities even if the abolitionist lived in a free state. As odious as this law was for the antislavery faction, Southerners insisted on its inclusion as a sign that the federal government was not colluding with Northern representatives and was not actively encouraging slaves to escape to the North as part of a *de facto* emancipation plot. When a Virginia slave owner traveled to Boston in 1854 and seized his escaped slave, Anthony Burns, with assistance from federal authorities, the episode convinced many Northern men of the wickedness of the Fugitive Slave Act and the long arm of the Slave Power.[12]

No one represented the Slave Power more assiduously than the regal South Carolina statesman John C. Calhoun. Of the triumvirate, Calhoun is the most difficult to understand in the twenty-first century, for much of what he believed and championed has been deposited into the ashbin of history. He was almost a polar opposite of Webster and Clay in his insistence that the interests of the South must be protected without compromise, but he was no less brilliant in his intellectual gifts and driving ambition than these men. As with his brethren in the triumvirate, he enjoyed a long and distinguished career in public service. He was a proponent of federal authority in his early years, but over time he came to see the advantages of a strong state rights position. Calhoun served as a congressman, senator, secretary of war, secretary of state, and vice president. As with the others, the only office of great import denied him was the presidency, a position he longed for but could never capture. Remembered today largely as an apologist for slavery, he also constructed eloquent arguments in support of state rights as a matter of constitutional purity.[13]

The stability of the two-party system waxed and waned in the 1830s, 1840s, and 1850s as Calhoun rose to prominence and slavery moved to the forefront of the national political agenda. Southerners began to speak of nullification as a creative interpretation of the Tenth Amendment to the U.S. Constitution. The concept theoretically allowed states to circumvent federal laws by ignoring, or "nullifying," federal laws not to their liking. This debate was hardly new. Since the founding period, disputes had erupted over the power of the federal government and its relation to state authority. As far back as 1798, Jefferson and Madison in the Virginia and Kentucky Resolutions had defied the Alien and Sedition Acts and, in so doing, had championed the concept of state rights. During the War of 1812, New Englanders had opposed "Mister Madison's War" at the Hartford Convention; they even spoke of secession.[14]

Examining these earlier historical precedents, Calhoun was one of many Southerners before and since his time who argued that an expansion of federal authority would eclipse the states and, with it, the liberty enjoyed by citizens. Unlike Southerners who opposed obdurate, centralized authority without offering a workable alternative apart from simplistic truisms, he was shrewd enough to construct his arguments under the guise of a political philosophy based supposedly on foundational principles discernible from a close textual analysis of the U.S. Constitution and its supporting documentation. According to Calhoun's reading of the foundation documents, the American constitutional system is not designed as a tug-of-war between opposing bastions of power—the decentralized states versus the centralized federal government—but first and foremost it is a protector of individual rights. These rights could be appreciated by examining the importance of "interests." In enacting public policy, the states and the federal government must not allow

a tyranny of the majority to occur whereby one form of government harms
the interests of individuals. This form of constitutional interpretation relies on
"concurrent majorities," which

> regards interests as well as numbers—considering the community as made up
> of different and conflicting interests, as far as the action of government is con-
> cerned—and takes the sense of each through its majority or appropriate organ,
> and the united sense of all as the sense of the entire community. The former of
> these I shall call the numerical or absolute majority, and the latter, the concur-
> rent or constitutional majority.[15]

In this understanding of the U.S. political system, different interests
existed simultaneously. To protect those interests, citizens could be called
upon to determine whether the actions of a larger group, especially actions
undertaken by the federal government, were to be considered constitutionally
valid. As Calhoun explained in *The South Carolina Exposition and Protest*,
a treatise he composed to argue against a high protective tariff in 1828, when
a federal law undermines the U.S. Constitution by harming the interests of
a state, the state can convene a special convention to determine whether the
law is null and void. This erudite apology for nullification represented the
high-water mark of the Tenth Amendment, which states that "the powers not
delegated to the United States by the Constitution, nor prohibited by it to the
States, are reserved to the States respectively, or to the people." Calhoun's
spirited interpretation of the Tenth Amendment's empowerment of states
and people was discredited in the years following the Civil War, but it was
a forceful argument in the antebellum era. The theory transformed Calhoun
into the intellectual father of the state rights position.[16]

The anomalous nature of Calhoun's arguments and his contrarian interpretation of constitutional history were illustrated vividly during a formal dinner
held at the Indian Queen Hotel in Washington, D.C., on April 13, 1830, mark-
ing the late Thomas Jefferson's birthday. On this auspicious occasion, politicians of all stripes mingled and chatted about the weighty issues of the day.
During a round of toasts, President Jackson rose to his feet, held up his glass,
and said, much to the chagrin of the Southern representatives present, "Our
Union—it must be preserved." Coming less than three months after Webster's celebrated reply to Robert Hayne, the message was clear: the president
would brook no dissent on the tariff, nor would he entertain the notion that
states could triumph over the federal government with threats of nullification.

Southerners, including Calhoun, had watched repeated assaults on the
state rights position with alarm. The president's toast was the latest in a long
line of insults to Southern interests and sensibilities. After Jackson returned
to his seat, the vice president stood and, facing his nominal superior, raised

his glass. "The Union—next to our liberty the most dear," he said. If this aphorism were not enough to clarify his position, he added, "May we all remember that it can only be preserved by respecting the rights of the States and distributing equally the benefit and burden of the Union."[17]

Calhoun and his supporters were correct that state rights and especially the peculiar institution were under attack during the antebellum era. The attacks came from many quarters over time, and from various sources. Aside from William Lloyd Garrison and the abolitionists, larger events dictated, to some extent, the nature and scope of the slavery debate.

In 1836, Texas broke away from Mexico and sought annexation by the United States. Serving out the last days of his presidency and anxious to avoid a politically contentious fight in an election year, President Jackson refused to annex the new territory despite the potential boon for slaveholding interests. As a result of Jackson's decision, among other things, the independent Republic of Texas was born. The republic folded within less than a decade, and a new state joined the Union despite warnings from the Mexican government that U.S. annexation could lead to war. After Mexico broke off diplomatic relations, armed conflict seemed almost inevitable, especially in light of Texans' claim to territory north of the Rio Grande River. All that was needed was a spark to ignite the conflagration. President James K. Polk found exactly the spark he needed when a Mexican cavalry unit attacked a small U.S. patrol in disputed territory in April 1846. The United States declared war a month later.[18]

Although slavery was not a major cause of the war, the matter was never far from policy considerations, as illustrated by the Wilmot Proviso. First introduced into the U.S. House of Representatives in 1846 by Congressman David Wilmot of Pennsylvania, the proviso required as "an express and fundamental condition to the acquisition of any territory" that "neither slavery nor involuntary servitude shall ever exist in any part of said territory." The resolution passed the House twice but died in the U.S. Senate.[19]

The end of the war with Mexico and the ratification of the Treaty of Guadalupe Hidalgo, signed on February 2, 1848, reinforced the political divisiveness of the slavery issue. As a victor in the war, the United States gained undisputed control of Texas and established the border at the Rio Grande, which was exactly the position Texans had taken before the war. The United States gained a huge new expanse of territory, including the present-day states of California, Nevada, and Utah as well as portions of Arizona, Colorado, New Mexico, and Wyoming. In return, the United States paid Mexico $15 million, less than half of what the Americans had offered during prewar negotiations, and also assumed \$3.25 million in debts that the Mexican government owed to American citizens.[20]

The addition of a large new territory raised the question of whether slavery would be allowed to expand as the population headed west. To Northern men, President Polk, a Tennessee slaveholder, had engineered the war to acquire more territory for slave owners. To Southerners, meddling abolitionists sought to deny them their constitutionally protected property rights by limiting their ability to travel to the newly acquired lands with slaves in tow.

The slavery issue also highlighted a central weakness within the Whigs, Henry Clay's political party that had formed in 1834 as part of the second political party system in opposition to President Jackson's policies. Comprising former Democratic Republicans and citizens worried about the growth of an imperial presidency, the Whigs named themselves after the English political party that continually criticized the Crown. It was a strange mixture of partners and alliances. The Whigs also included former members of the Anti-Masons, a third party formed in the late 1820s to oppose the secretive Masonic fraternity as well as champion social conservatism and national economic policies. The Whigs generally were united in their call for infrastructure improvements as a means of improving financial prosperity, but a fissure developed that ultimately signaled the party's demise. The so-called Conscience Whigs, or New England wing of the party, believed that slavery was a moral evil and must be opposed fervently while the Cotton Whigs downplayed slavery to avoid alienating the South and thereby missing out on the lucrative cotton trade. The Whigs had been struggling with this schism for years, but the Wilmot Proviso and the Fugitive Slave Act of 1850 revealed an unbridgeable gap that destroyed the party. Some former Whigs joined the American, or Know-Nothing, Party to oppose foreigners and Catholics while others eventually formed the Republican Party to oppose the spread of slavery.[21]

Before former Conscience Whigs could establish the Republican Party, they had to agree that slavery must be resisted, especially in the new territories. During the 1848 and 1852 elections, the antislavery men, mostly from upstate New York, western Massachusetts, and Ohio, created a short-lived third party. Their motto was "'Free Soil, Free Speech, Free Labor and Free Men,' and under it we will fight on and fight ever, until a triumphant victory shall reward our exertions." The Free-Soilers, as they came to be known, contended that slavery was inherently undemocratic because it robbed men of their dignity as human beings, their ability to rise in accordance with their God-given talents, and their ability to labor diligently toward social mobility and economic advancement. In their view, prominent Democrats, including President Franklin Pierce and his successor, James Buchanan, allowed the Slave Power to abuse the Fugitive Slave Act with the imprimatur of the federal government. These Northern men who seemed sympathetic to Southern interests soon earned the derisive appellation "doughfaces" because of their malleability and lack of fixed political principles.[22]

At the Free-Soil Party's convention in Buffalo in 1848, the delegates nominated a former president, Martin Van Buren, as their standard-bearer while Charles Francis Adams, son of John Quincy Adams and grandson of John Adams, became the vice presidential nominee. After serving as secretary of state and later vice president during the Jackson administration, Van Buren, the "Wizard of Kinderhook," was a controversial choice because he was viewed by some antislavery voters as too closely associated with Old Hickory. The Free-Soil Party failed to garner a single electoral vote, but Van Buren's ties to New York pulled enough popular votes away from the Democrats to deliver the state to Whig presidential candidate Zachary Taylor. Both the Whigs and the Democrats had captured less than 50 percent of the popular vote, but winning New York State led to Taylor's narrow victory in the Electoral College. Although the party continued to exist through 1852, Free-Soilers eventually

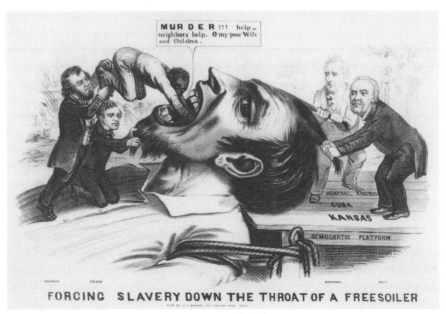

FORCING SLAVERY DOWN THE THROAT OF A FREESOILER

This cartoon, first published during the 1856 presidential campaign, shows prominent Democrats Stephen A. Douglas (a U.S. senator from Illinois), Franklin Pierce (the current president of the United States), James Buchanan (the Democratic Party's presidential candidate), and Lewis Cass (a U.S. senator from Michigan) forcing antislavery Free-Soilers to swallow slavery (as represented by the black man shoved into the mouth of a giant). The image vividly illustrates abolitionist objections to federal protection of the peculiar institution in the 1850s.
Courtesy of the Library of Congress.

joined forces with other disaffected groups, such as the Barnburner faction of the Democratic Party, to create the Republican Party.[23]

The collapse of the Whigs and the failure of the Free-Soil Party to represent the interests of the antislavery advocates undoubtedly contributed to the creation of the Republican Party in time, but the most immediate precipitating event was the Kansas-Nebraska Act. Senator Stephen A. Douglas of Illinois, known as the Little Giant for his diminutive physical stature and large legislative presence, pushed a measure through Congress that called for the creation of the territories of Kansas and Nebraska. This bill reversed decades of legislative initiatives designed to balance the admission of free states and slave states into the Union. Recall that under the Missouri Compromise of 1820, slavery was outlawed north of the 36° 30' line. Missouri was designated a slave state but territory to the north and west of its border was considered free. Thirty years later, Congress, under Henry Clay's leadership, struck a similar balance with the adoption of the Compromise of 1850. The Kansas-Nebraska Act threatened to pull the thread that would unravel the garment.[24]

Douglas's proposal seemed to destroy the Missouri Compromise because it championed the concept of popular sovereignty. Rather than debate arbitrary lines and argue over which states would be free and which would be slave, the senator suggested that residents in the territories could decide for themselves whether they would allow human bondage within their borders. In Douglas's view, popular sovereignty could satisfy all parties. Southerners would be pleased that the rising tide of antislavery legislation had been arrested, and the possibility of slavery's spreading beyond the Cotton South was assured. Northerners would find solace in the likelihood that slavery would not spread to southwestern states, where the dry, arid climate made agriculture, with its heavy dependence on the peculiar institution, a perilous enterprise. What could be more democratic, in theory if not in practice, than to allow residents to determine their sovereign relationships based on the will of a majority of voting citizens?[25]

The Little Giant badly misjudged the mood on both sides. Northerners were outraged that the carefully crafted web of laws and philosophical doctrines that had antedated the Kansas-Nebraska Act would be summarily dismissed, potentially paving the way for the peculiar institution to snake its way farther west. If the institution were to be set on a course of ultimate extinction, kowtowing to a free white citizenry inflamed by white-hot passion and engulfed in racial animosity was a bizarre method of achieving the goal. For their part, Southerners feared the measure disguised an antislavery conspiracy. Because popular sovereignty left open the possibility of limiting slavery through a referendum, an abolitionist cabal conceivably could manipulate the vote and eradicate slavery without fairly providing for the popular will. "Squatter sovereignty," as critics labeled it, was denounced by a large percentage of citizens on both sides of the Mason-Dixon Line as an unworkable compromise because it encouraged all manner of machinations and intrigue. After all, determining residency was a complicated matter open to interpretation and manipulation. In seeking to please all, Douglas had pleased none.[26]

Perhaps the best that could be said of the Kansas-Nebraska Act with the benefit of hindsight is that it brought so many people together, although it was not the way Douglas had intended. Factions that could not agree on anything else agreed that this law was an abomination. Northern Democrats hated it, as did abolitionists and former Whigs. Ministers, some of whom had not been in the vanguard of the abolitionist movement but nonetheless believed the act was not in keeping with Christian principles, used their pulpits to decry the wickedness of the statute. Douglas cobbled together the necessary coalition to push the measure through Congress, and President Franklin Pierce signed it into law, but thereafter the senator's supporters deserted him. Deeply wounded, Douglas recognized that his attempt to be all things to all people had failed. He sardonically observed that "on my return home I traveled from Boston to Chicago in the light of fires in which my own effigies were burning."[27]

Hostile reaction to the Kansas-Nebraska Act led to the formation of the Republican Party in the North and exacerbated the sectional tensions that had been increasing since the 1830s. A group of disaffected Whigs, Democrats, and Free-Soilers met at Ripon, Wisconsin, on February 28, 1854, to create a political party opposing the legislation. During the meeting, participants used the term "Republican Party" for perhaps the first time. A month later, on March 20, the group reconvened. Finally, on July 5, the nascent political party met at Jackson, Michigan, and nominated candidates for state offices. This latter date is the generally accepted starting point of the Republican Party.[28]

Launching a new political party was not simply a matter of organizing like-minded individuals to oppose the Democrats and the Slave Power. With the demise of the Whigs and the rise of multiple third parties, it was no easy task to unify all persons incensed over the deteriorating state of the Union and the advance of a pernicious institution. In particular, the American Party, or the Know-Nothings, siphoned away some would-be Republicans because it appealed to citizens who were worried that Catholics and immigrants were more dangerous to the republic than slavery ever would be.[29]

The Republicans gradually emerged as a logical successor to the Whigs, but the party's ascent was by no means assured. No one knew at the outset whether the new organization could attract and run viable candidates for state and local elective offices, much less the presidency. Although the Republican

Party fielded a bona fide celebrity candidate, the politically well-connected western explorer John C. Fremont, in the 1856 presidential contest, it was 1860 before the party offered a successful nominee in Abraham Lincoln.[30]

—ιιυ—

If the Kansas-Nebraska Act served as a ticking bomb on the question of slavery, a controversial U.S. Supreme Court case, *Dred Scott v. Sandford*, was the detonator.[31] The court was not yet the central political force in American politics it would become during the twentieth century; in fact, for much of its history the high court had been a relatively minor participant in American political life. Alexander Hamilton wrote in "Federalist 78" that "the judiciary, from the nature of its functions, will always be the least dangerous to the political rights of the Constitution; because it will be least in a capacity to annoy or injure them." According to Hamilton, because it could wield neither the power of the purse nor the power of the sword, the judiciary would be a reactive, not proactive, force in influencing national affairs.[32] The *Dred Scott* case was a notable nineteenth-century exception to Hamilton's eighteenth-century rule.[33]

The case originated years earlier when Dr. John Emerson, an army doctor who traveled frequently, transported his slave, Dred Scott, from a slave state to a free state and back. Dr. Emerson resided with his slave at Fort Armstrong, Illinois; Fort Snelling, Wisconsin Territory; Fort Jessup, Louisiana; and St. Louis, Missouri. During these travels, Scott lived for approximately seven years in areas designated as free territory, yet he was unaware of that designation and Dr. Emerson never mentioned it. On the doctor's death, his wife inherited his property. The widow moved to Massachusetts and remarried, leaving the slave in the possession of her brother, John F. Sandford (sometimes spelled "Sanford") in St. Louis.

Before Mrs. Emerson departed from Missouri, Scott attempted to purchase his freedom, a common transaction in the antebellum era. She refused. When abolitionists learned of the situation, they met with the slave and advised him to file a lawsuit contending that he should be released because he had resided in several free states over a period of years. In 1846, with assistance from abolitionist legal advisers, Scott filed suit in state court, thus initiating a convoluted legal process that culminated in a U.S. Supreme Court opinion directly confronting the slavery issue.[34]

Chief Justice Roger B. Taney penned the majority opinion in *Dred Scott*. He has long been excoriated in the pages of history for writing an opinion smacking of unbridled racism, but the chief justice's views on slavery were more complex than they initially appeared. In fact, earlier in his life Taney had not been so accommodating to the slaveholding creed. He was born into a well-to-do Maryland family in 1777 and came of age in a society where slavery was widely accepted as a way of life, but even so he did not mindlessly condone the perpetuation of the institution. A second son, young Taney realized he would not inherit the family fortune; thus, he came to appreciate the virtues of earning a living by the sweat of one's own brow.

To make his way in the world, he chose a career in law and politics. As an up-and-coming lawyer in 1819, he defended an abolitionist minister against charges of inciting a slave insurrection. In a stirring, eloquent summation, Taney won an acquittal from a jury comprising primarily slave owners. "Until the time shall come when we can point without a blush, to the language in the Declaration of Independence," he exclaimed, "every friend of humanity will seek to lighten the galling chain of slavery and better, to the utmost of his power, the wretched condition of the slave." This man, who was once described as possessing a "moonlit mind" that shone with "all of the moon's brightness but none of its glare," even emancipated his own slaves. Later, as a member of the U.S. Supreme Court, he voted to free the slaves on trial in the celebrated *Amistad* case. As astonishing as it may seem, the figure who would become known as a virulent apologist for slavery was known to favor Northern interests in the years leading up to *Dred Scott*.[35]

Taney began his political life as a Federalist but eventually became a Democrat and ardent supporter of Andrew Jackson. Whether this evolution in his sentiments represented a genuine change of heart or a politically expedient adaptation to circumstances remains a point of contention. In any case, in 1831 Taney became Jackson's attorney general and assisted Old Hickory in his battle against authorizing the Second Bank of the United States. To retaliate, the U.S. Senate refused to confirm him as secretary of the treasury after Jackson nominated him for the post in 1834. Later, the Senate blocked his nomination to become an associate justice of the U.S. Supreme Court. These Senate defeats no doubt were humiliating, but Taney enjoyed the last laugh when Jackson successfully appointed him chief justice after John Marshall's death and a change in Senate membership radically altered the political terrain.[36]

Taney was a proponent of original intent, the doctrine that judges and justices should seek to discern what the Founders intended when they drafted the U.S. Constitution in 1787. Based on this standard, the chief justice believed that regardless of his personal beliefs, slavery was enshrined in the nation's laws and constitution. Because the Founders intended to protect the institution, the Supreme Court was duty bound to follow their intent. Moreover, because the Founders were adamant that federalism required a vigorous system of state governments that were sovereign and separate from the federal government, the Supreme Court could not allow the slow, steady encroachment of federal power over state rights to proceed, as his predecessor had done.

Unlike the nationalistic Marshall, Taney mistrusted federal power. The Taney court overturned cases that expanded federal authority in favor of state power in many areas save one. When it came to limiting the rights of slaveholders, Taney did not hesitate to limit state authority. In *Prigg v. the Commonwealth of Pennsylvania* (1842), for example, the Taney court prohibited the State of Pennsylvania from punishing a Maryland man who had crossed state lines to apprehend a former slave and her child without first seeking a court order from the Pennsylvania courts permitting the seizure.[37] Ten years later, Justice Grier, writing for the Taney court in *Moore v. Illinois* (1852), held that a state law "which interrupts, impedes, limits, embarrasses, delays or postpones the right of the owner to the immediate possession of the slave, and the immediate command of his service, is void."[38]

Not surprisingly, the chief justice ruled against the slave Dred Scott. In one sense, however, Taney's opinion was odd. For a man who professed to hold strict constructionist views, his broad ruling that slaves do not possess constitutional rights was a sweeping new doctrine not strictly found in Supreme Court jurisprudence. Taney need not have gone so far. He could have applied the precedent found in a U.S. Supreme Court case, *Strader v. Graham* (1850), which held that states have authority to determine citizenship questions within their borders free from federal interference.[39] Because Dred Scott filed his original lawsuit in Missouri, a slave state, and Missouri did not recognize his right to file suit, a narrowly tailored opinion would have ended the case there. Scott would have remained a slave, and the U.S. Supreme Court would not have intervened directly into a seemingly intractable national debate.[40]

The charitable view is that Taney sought to provide judicial guidance on the question of whether slavery would be allowed in the territories. Perhaps the fierce debate over the 1850 Compromise and the Kansas-Nebraska Act could be put to rest if the U.S. Supreme Court weighed in on the issue definitively. The uncharitable view is that in his dotage Taney had turned his back on his previous antipathy toward slavery and surrendered to the virulent racism of the Jacksonian Democrats he had embraced in the 1830s. Whatever his motives, the chief justice concluded that Congress could regulate only those territories that existed at the time of the founding. Based on his understanding of original intent, he also held that Scott could not sue for his freedom in a court of law. Slaves had not enjoyed citizenship during the founding period and therefore did not enjoy it now.[41]

Taney explained that the "question before us is, whether the class of persons described in the plea in abatement compose a portion of this people, and are constituent members of this sovereignty? We think they are not, and that they are not included, and were not intended to be included, under the word 'citizens' in the Constitution, and can therefore claim none of the rights and privileges which that instrument provides for and secures to citizens of the United States."[42]

Outrage over the *Dred Scott* decision was immediate and fierce. Northerners were convinced it was only a matter of time before slavery metastasized into every state and killed a republican form of government. In this vein, a *New York Times* editorial predicted that "slavery is no longer local; it is national." One Northern editorial denounced the opinion as "no better than what might be obtained in a Washington City bar room fight." William Lloyd Garrison, Wendell Phillips, and other leading abolitionists argued that the opinion was the death knell for the Union, and they were not sorry to see it die. One minister said, "If people obey this decision, they disobey God."[43]

Southerners felt vindicated by the U.S. Supreme Court; finally, an institution of the federal government had responded with a constitutional interpretation that protected their property rights from further encroachment. In a gleeful tone, the *Richmond Enquirer* observed that "abolitionism has been staggered and stunned. Another supporting pillar has been added to our institutions." A leading Southern editorialist praised the decision because it "crushes the life out of that miserable . . . Black Republican organization."[44]

One reaction, notable only with the benefit of hindsight, came from far-off Illinois. Abraham Lincoln read *Dred Scott* and became dismayed by its tortured constitutional interpretation. Although he was prosperous and well known in his adopted hometown of Springfield, on a national level Lincoln had been heretofore undistinguished. After the Kansas-Nebraska Act was enacted into law, he had emerged as an important political leader in his home state. It is difficult today after he has become a mythic character enshrined in American folklore to remember that Lincoln was a curious, sometimes enigmatic figure in his time. When it suited his purposes, he portrayed himself as a country bumpkin unlearned in the corrupting ways of city folk. On other occasions, he cast himself as a man of subtle, nuanced ideas who was not as provincial as he seemed. Tall and lanky, far from handsome, the poorly educated frontiersman initially appeared to be the exact opposite of the typical politician and orator. He spoke in a high, piercing tenor, almost a shriek. One contemporary observer who watched Lincoln speak in 1858 found "his pronunciation is bad, his manners uncouth and his general appearance anything but prepossessing."[45] Stephen A. Douglas, Lincoln's frequent political rival, recognized his opponent's political strengths even if some observers were not impressed. "He is a strong man of the party—full of wit, facts, dates, and the best stump-speaker, with his droll ways and dry jokes, in the West."[46]

If Lincoln seemed to be the antithesis of a nineteenth-century politician, therein lay his appeal. He was a quintessential diamond in the rough. The force of his persuasion rose from the quality of his arguments and the eloquence of his words. He generally did not rely on demagoguery or the accepted hyper-bole that characterized political campaigns then as now—he did not need to employ such silly histrionics or cheap gimmickry except on brief, limited oc-casions—but Lincoln was not above using rhetorical flourishes or *reductio ad absurdum* arguments to make a point or provoke a reaction from an audience. That a political leader with such a subtle mind and a rare gift of self-expression could emerge from the heartland eventually transformed Lincoln into an icon because here was a truly self-made man who could pull himself up by his bootstraps from humble origins to assume the highest office in the land. What would become a cliché for Horatio Alger and later American writers was sim-ply Abraham Lincoln's life as a product of "the short and simple annals of the poor," as he once described his early years.[47]

A lawyer and former one-term congressman from Illinois, Lincoln had been a bit player on the national stage before the mid-1850s. By eloquently criticizing the Kansas-Nebraska Act and *Dred Scott* without wallowing in extreme, emotional language, he gained prominence as a voice of calm, thoughtful moderation. Lincoln was not an abolitionist, nor was he a sup-porter of chattel slavery. Instead, he insisted that slavery was a moral evil that should not be allowed to spread into the territories. He believed that the fed-eral government was required to protect slavery in the states where it already existed because such protections were written into the Constitution, but that the expansion of slavery was not justified.[48]

After serving in the Illinois General Assembly and a single term in the U.S. House of Representatives, Lincoln had retired from office holding, although he remained interested in politics. When the Kansas-Nebraska Act was signed into law, he reemerged in Illinois politics by advising former Whig Richard Yates on Yates's desire to run again for Congress. Lincoln also de-bated his own political future as he struggled to decide whether to take a seat in the General Assembly after his election or refuse to serve so that he could campaign for the U.S. Senate. Because the General Assembly selected U.S. senators, under the Illinois state constitution Lincoln could not campaign for the Senate if he also served as a sitting state legislator. After much agonizing, he chose to run for the Senate. Although Lincoln did not capture the seat, he was back in the political fray for the rest of the 1850s.[49]

Throughout the 1854 campaign season, Lincoln delivered a series of speeches criticizing Douglas's doctrine of popular sovereignty. In a famous speech at Peoria, Illinois, on October 16, he laid out his position in a three-hour talk noted for its logical clarity and antislavery sentiment. "No man is good enough to govern another man, without that other's consent," he remarked. "I say this is the leading principle—the sheet anchor of American republicanism."[50] Senator Douglas's claim that popular sovereignty was a democratic principle was deliberately misleading, in Lincoln's view. Because the doctrine allowed white settlers to determine whether blacks would be held as property in the territories, it violated the basic "self-evident truth" embodied in the U.S. Declaration of Independence that "all men are created equal." Whatever could be said of the U.S. Constitution's proslavery propensities, Lincoln had no doubt that the Declaration of Independence was devoted to a higher principle of individual liberty for all human beings.[51]

In his Peoria speech and in similar orations, Lincoln carved out a middle approach between the abolitionists and supporters of slavery. Although he would later contend that "I have always hated slavery," he was a pragmatic politician who recognized that calls for immediate emancipation would fall on deaf ears and likely hobble his political career. As a middle position, he argued that limiting the spread of slavery into the territories and urging the eventual extinction of the pernicious institution was not tantamount to advocating social equality among the races. Lincoln's measured, careful approach led William Lloyd Garrison later to remark that "if he *is* 6 feet 4 inches high, he is only a dwarf in mind!"[52]

Lincoln also refused to condemn Southerners for supporting the institution of slavery. In a number of speeches he delivered during the 1850s, he argued that Southerners had been shaped partially by their circumstances. Because the region's economy was predominantly based on agriculture and because slavery was an accepted practice, it was little wonder the average white Southerner was wary of changes that would threaten his way of life. In recognizing that institutional and cultural forces shape people's lives, Lincoln did not accept a proslavery rationalization; he understood that outside factors partially influence individual human behavior. One of Lincoln's greatest strengths as a political leader, and as a human being, was his ability to understand opposing points of view and feel compassion toward his political opponents. He believed that the pernicious institution must be put "on the road to ultimate extinction," but that this lofty goal would not be accomplished suddenly without triggering unprecedented social upheaval.[53]

Abolitionists viewed Lincoln's pragmatism and kindness toward white Southerners as misguided and weak. He simply was too gentle a soul for the rough work that lay ahead. Although some abolitionists begrudgingly agreed to support the Lincoln administration's earnest efforts to grapple with emancipation during the Civil War, initially they failed to grasp the virtues in Lincoln's middle approach. Had Lincoln ardently embraced their cause, however, he might never have propelled himself into public office; he would not have been in a position to effect changes in public policy. This assessment, of course, benefits from hindsight and does not adequately consider the passions and political turmoil of the day.[54]

Lincoln's reaction to the *Dred Scott* case was reminiscent of his outrage over the Kansas-Nebraska Act. In this instance, the chief justice's misinterpretation of the Declaration of Independence was especially galling. During one memorable speech in 1857, Lincoln lamented the court's "obvious violence to the plain unmistakable language of the Declaration." The Founders did not accept the polygenesis thesis that blacks were subhuman and therefore excluded from the language of the Declaration that "all men are created equal." At the same time, Lincoln assured his conservative audience that opposition to slaveholding did not mean he supported social equality. He did not want slavery to spread into the western territories, but neither did he believe that blacks were equal to whites in every respect.[55]

The middle approach was not always logically consistent, but it was shrewd politics for an up-and-coming midwestern politician. In 1858, with his political career ascendant, Lincoln accepted the Illinois Republican Party's nomination for the U.S. Senate seat against the author of the popular sovereignty doctrine, his nemesis Stephen A. Douglas. On June 16, before a large assemblage of party leaders crowded into the House of Representatives chamber, Lincoln delivered the most controversial oration of his political career, forever after known as the "House Divided Speech." In renouncing the Kansas-Nebraska Act and the *Dred Scott* decision, he relied on a biblical allusion he had used in previous speeches to lesser effect:

> "A house divided against itself cannot stand." I believe this government cannot endure permanently half slave and half free. I do not expect the Union to be dissolved—I do not expect the house to fall—but I do expect it will cease to be divided. It will become all one thing, or all the other. Either the opponents of slavery will arrest the further spread of it, and place it where the public mind shall rest in the belief that it is in the course of ultimate extinction; or its advocates will push it forward, till it shall become alike lawful in all the States, old as well as new—North as well as South.[56]

In the aftermath of the Civil War, it is tempting to interpret these fiery words as eerily prophetic, proof that Lincoln recognized the bloody conflagration to come years before the firing on Fort Sumter ushered in armed conflict. Such a conclusion imbues Lincoln with a prescience he did not possess. He was careful to state that "I do not expect the house to fall." Nonetheless, the hysteria of the times ensured that his words would be read as an invitation to sectional conflict. Even if Lincoln did not foresee the eruption of a civil war, anyone astute enough to witness the growing schism between North and South could have uttered remarks warning of the dire consequences of slavery and its spread, albeit perhaps not as eloquently. William H. Seward, the New York politician who became Lincoln's rival for the presidency in 1860 and eventually served as his secretary of state, delivered his "irrepressible conflict" speech in opposition to *Dred Scott* in a similar vein, although Seward went further than Lincoln in warning of the bloodshed likely to come. Recognizing the potential for a cataclysm was not noteworthy, but discussing incendiary issues so boldly carried political risks for anyone seeking elective office in the 1850s.[57]

Contemporary Republicans cautioned the usually reserved candidate that he should temper his remarks, but Lincoln assured his supporters and friends before the oration that "the time has come when it should be uttered & if it must be that I go down because of this speech then let me go down linked to the truth—die in the advocacy of what is right & just."[58] In his opinion, his remarks may have been more forthright than his usual speeches, but he was not delivering a new message. He was distinguishing his position from Douglas's position. If slavery spread into the territories, as Douglas's popular sovereignty would allow, the deep chasm between the regions would widen and the nation would be torn apart. The "house divided" rhetoric was stronger than many of Lincoln's stock phrases, but his sentiments were unchanged.[59]

Lincoln's speech was noteworthy for another rhetorical device, specifically the inclusion of a conspiracy theory involving the leading Democratic politicians of the time. He did not genuinely believe that such a conspiracy existed, but it was a deft maneuver, politically astute demagoguery from a man who seldom relied on such chicanery. At one point in the speech, Lincoln acknowledged that no one could prove a conspiracy existed or that the spate of proslavery laws were "the result of preconcert." Nonetheless, it suited his purposes to explain how Stephen A. Douglas, Franklin Pierce, Roger B. Taney, and James Buchanan worked in seeming concert to allow the spread of slavery into new territories. According to Lincoln, the proslavery positions propounded in the Kansas-Nebraska Act and *Dred Scott* were too convenient to be entirely coincidental. Using a house-building analogy, he explained how a conspiracy could be constructed:

We cannot absolutely know that all these exact adaptations are the result of preconcert. But when we see a lot of framed timbers, different portions of which we know have been gotten out at different times and places and by different workmen—Stephen, Franklin, Roger and James, for instance—and when we see these timbers joined together, and see they exactly make the frame of a house or a mill, all the tenons and mortices exactly fitting, and all the lengths and proportions of the different pieces exactly adapted to their respective places, and not a piece too many or too few—not omitting even scaffolding—or, if a single piece be lacking, we see the place in the frame exactly fitted and prepared yet to bring such a piece in—in such a case, we find it impossible not to believe that Stephen and Franklin and Roger and James all understood one another from the beginning, and all worked upon a common plan or draft drawn up before the first blow was struck.[60]

This use of the conspiracy theory and the construction imagery was disingenuous, but it allowed Lincoln to portray himself as a person of good faith laboring against a cabal of proslavery men. "Judge Douglas"—a sarcastic honorific Lincoln applied to his better-known opponent—and his co-conspirators knew or should have known that their words championing the democratic process were empty. Lincoln was assailing popular sovereignty by alleging that it was a hollow doctrine, a placeholder for proslavery forces. Under the cloak of "good government" and democracy in action, the conspirators contended that they would leave it to the citizens of the territories or the Supreme Court to decide the question of slavery. To Lincoln, this "don't care" attitude—the conspirators don't care whether slavery is upheld or struck down in the name of a democratic process—was unfathomable. Even if the conspirators made such claims in good faith, which Lincoln doubted, they would be throwing open a crucial question of American life, namely slavery, to the whims and passions of the day. A "hands-off" attitude was nothing more than a failure of leadership, at best. At worst, the Democratic leaders, under the guise of popular sovereignty, were allowing slaveholders free rein in the territories. If slavery spread, it might not stop at the territories.[61]

The speech provided critics with fodder for months and years to follow. Douglas and many Democrats seized on the intemperate language, castigating Lincoln as an extremist who sought to exacerbate the raw feelings between North and South. For a politician seeking elective office outside of New England in the 1850s, the appellation "abolitionist" was sufficient to destroy a candidacy. In response to the attacks, Lincoln claimed to be astonished that anyone could hear the speech or read his words and infer that he sought to worsen sectional tensions. He was not saying he desired bloodshed or that the nation was inevitably on a path to civil war. Instead, he was arguing against the spread of slavery beyond its already-recognized borders. To friends who chided him for his words, Lincoln remained adamant. "Well, Gentlemen," he declared to several supporters, "you may think that Speech was a mistake, but I never have believed it was, and you will see the day when you will consider it was the wisest thing I ever said."[62]

Lincoln was correct that history would judge his words as wise, but in the context of a hard-fought senatorial campaign in 1858, it frightened some voters into believing he was a dangerous radical. Anxious to correct this misperception, he crisscrossed the state speaking to numerous gatherings. His greatest opportunity and largest audiences came when he challenged Senator Douglas to a series of face-to-face debates. He had been following Douglas and denouncing popular sovereignty already, so a challenge was not surprising, although the idea originated not with Lincoln but with *New York Tribune* editor Horace Greeley, who proposed it in the pages of his newspaper. Douglas accepted the offer.[63]

The strategy of engaging in face-to-face debates presented opportunities and risks for both men. As the incumbent, Douglas was better known than Lincoln, but he did not want to appear fearful of a challenge. He also was weary of Lincoln following him around and rebutting his arguments without affording the senator a chance to respond immediately. Lincoln welcomed a forum to promote his candidacy and continue his attacks on popular sovereignty, but he was pitted against a seasoned campaigner and accomplished legislator who would be sure to capitalize on any mistakes or misstatements.[64]

The duo eventually met seven times, beginning in Ottawa on August 21 and concluding at Alton on October 15. Each candidate spoke for approximately an hour and a half, and each had an opportunity to offer a rebuttal. Large crowds attended the gathering at each stop except for Jonesboro, in the southern half of the state. Newspapers covered the debates extensively, and the speeches, focusing as they did on the paramount issue of the day, drew national attention.[65]

It is almost impossible to imagine the excitement of political stump speeches on the Illinois frontier of the 1850s. Politics was more than a hobby or a passing interest for many citizens. It was entertainment. People rode for miles to experience an event similar to a county fair, a summer picnic, a wedding, or a Fourth of July celebration. Families traveled together, relishing the chance to lay aside their burdens for a day to reminisce with old friends and take part in the grand pageant that was local politics. If nothing else, it was a chance to see two well-known luminaries and marvel at the verbal repartee of polished political raconteurs.[66]

Although Lincoln and Douglas were competing for but one political office in one state, their ongoing conversation centered on the extension of slavery into the territories and therefore had a greater impact on national politics than a senatorial race normally would. Douglas continually championed popular sovereignty and the Kansas-Nebraska Act while Lincoln characterized his opponent's position as little more than a tyranny of the majority and squatter sovereignty. In his rejoinder to Douglas during the last debate in Alton, Lincoln succinctly explained the differences that characterized American political life. "The real issue in this controversy—the one pressing upon my mind—is the sentiment on the part of one class that looks upon the institution of slavery as a wrong, and of another class that does not look upon it as a wrong." In another part of the speech, he compared slavery to a cancer on the body politic, arguing that although the cancer could not be cut out, "surely it is no way to cure it, to engraft it and spread it over your whole body."[67]

In perhaps the most famous exchange between the two candidates, Lincoln asked a rhetorical question during the debate at Freeport: "Can the people of the United States Territory, in any lawful way, against the wish of any citizen of the United States, exclude slavery from its limits prior to the formation of a State Constitution?" This was a crafty method for exposing the contradictions in Douglas's position. The Little Giant had championed popular sovereignty, which left the question of whether slavery would be allowed in the territories to settlers living there, but he also had asked citizens to support Justice Taney's opinion in *Dred Scott*, which seemed to undercut popular sovereignty by concluding that slaves had no rights under the U.S. Constitution no matter what the voters in the territories decided. If popular sovereignty reflected Douglas's position that he was indifferent to the outcome of the settlers' vote on slavery, how could he support *Dred Scott*, which clearly favored the slaveholding position?[68]

Douglas was in a difficult position logically because popular sovereignty and the *Dred Scott* decision were antithetical. Fortunately for him, logic is not a prerequisite for politics. He struggled to reconcile the irreconcilable, arguing that despite appearances, *Dred Scott* did not negate popular sovereignty:

> It matters not what way the Supreme Court may hereafter decide as to the abstract question whether slavery may or may not go into a Territory under the Constitution, the people have the lawful means to introduce it or exclude it as they please, for the reason that slavery cannot exist a day or an hour anywhere, unless it is supported by local police regulations. Those police regulations can only be established by the local legislature; and if the people are opposed to slavery, they will elect representatives to that body who will by unfriendly legislation effectually prevent the introduction of it into their midst. If, on the contrary, they are for it, their legislation will favor its extension. Hence, no matter what the decision of the Supreme Court may be on that abstract question, still the right of the people to make a Slave Territory or a Free Territory is perfect and complete under the Nebraska bill.[69]

In other words, despite the U.S. Supreme Court's ruling on slavery, the issue for territorial representatives was whether they would support slavery through local legislation. If they chose to countenance the spread of slavery, under popular sovereignty they could enact local legislation to that effect. If territorial representatives preferred to oppose the extension of slavery in their territory, they simply need not enact local legislation to allow slavery, despite the "abstract question" decided in *Dred Scott*.[70]

The "Freeport Doctrine," as Douglas's position was later called, infuriated Lincoln because it was a cynical view of the law, to say nothing of circumventing the slavery issue. Douglas argued that popular sovereignty allowed citizens to choose whether they would endorse slavery. In effect, voters were free to ignore an opinion of the U.S. Supreme Court if they did not support the court's conclusion. As much as Lincoln detested the *Dred Scott* proslavery opinion, he did not believe authoritative judicial decisions could be ignored or nullified. In Lincoln's view, a bad law must be changed, not conveniently overlooked. By refusing to confront slavery directly, Douglas, who later campaigned for the presidency, hoped to mollify Southerners because he could argue that the Kansas-Nebraska Act and popular sovereignty never prohibited the extension of slavery into the territories. He could argue to antislavery forces that he never condoned slavery, either.[71]

If Douglas sought to attract Southerners to his candidacy for president in 1860, it was far too late for that. The Little Giant had already broken with the Democratic Party leadership in opposing the Lecompton constitution, the second of four proposed constitutions for the Kansas Territory. As Congress and the citizenry struggled to decide whether Kansas would be admitted to the Union as a slave state or a free state, political leaders battled over competing state constitutions. President James Buchanan, a Northerner who supported slavery—thus earning him the appellation "doughface," a derogatory term suggesting his political principles were far too malleable—had championed the proslavery Lecompton constitution, but Douglas was worried that the constitution did not specify who was eligible to vote for statehood and therefore could lead to widespread fraud. As a result of his opposition to Lecompton, Douglas alienated Southerners and split the Democratic Party, ironically helping Lincoln to win the presidency in 1860. In attempting to have his cake and eat it, too, Douglas pleased no one; he was a pariah among slave owners and among antislavery forces.[72]

On Election Day, the Democrats won a small majority of seats in the Illinois General Assembly. Because state legislatures picked U.S. senators until the Seventeenth Amendment was ratified in 1913, the Democratic victory in the General Assembly ensured that Douglas would win the Senate seat even though Lincoln garnered more popular votes. Despite the loss, Lincoln's stature grew; he was well positioned to capture the Republican presidential nomination in 1860. Legend has it the senatorial defeat did not bother Lincoln because, as he supposedly said, "I am killing larger game"—obliquely referring to his quest for the presidency—but most accounts portray a melancholy Lincoln who was not altogether sure he had a political future. Only time would tell.[73]

While Lincoln was staking out the middle ground in Illinois, the abolitionists were growing in power throughout the northeastern United States, notably in

New England. William Lloyd Garrison became the focal point for Southern anger toward antislavery forces that threatened the peculiar institution, but he was not the only abolitionist to speak out, nor did he speak for all abolitionists. With assistance from a prominent evangelical minister, Theodore Weld, and a free black man, Robert Purvis, Garrison formed the Anti-Slavery Society in 1833. The group welcomed blacks into its ranks and sponsored speeches by former slaves Frederick Douglass, Sojourner Truth, and William Wells Brown. Their talks featured firsthand accounts of the horrors of human bondage and proved to be especially effective in representing the antislavery position.[74]

Despite these high-profile efforts, only a small group of dedicated activists participated in the abolitionist movement, and even they could not always agree on strategy and tactics. After 1840, they split into liberal and conservative forces that fought almost as much with each other as they did against proslavery proponents. In many towns and communities in the North, abolitionists were as reviled as they were in the South and often faced violence from mobs and vigilantes.[75]

Aside from Garrison, Wendell Phillips was perhaps the most renowned, and reviled, white abolitionist of his time. Phillips and Garrison were friends as well as colleagues, but they arose from markedly different backgrounds. Unlike Garrison, whose impecunious upbringing afforded him a firsthand view of the indignities suffered by the unfortunate masses, Phillips sported a refined pedigree. As the son of the first mayor of Boston and a Harvard graduate, he was a Boston Brahmin, trained in the law and expected to ascend through the ranks of the bar to take his rightful place at the top of the legal and political hierarchy of New England. His plans changed when he witnessed an attack on Garrison by a lynch mob that nearly hanged the abolitionist one evening in October 1835. A year later, Phillips formally joined the cause.[76]

Although he did not share Garrison's antipathy for organized religion, and they later parted company over support for Abraham Lincoln in the 1864 presidential election—with Garrison favoring the president despite opposition by abolitionists, including Phillips, who thought the Great Emancipator's commitment to fighting chattel slavery was too timid—Phillips initially looked up to Garrison as a mentor. Phillips proved to be a gifted orator who eschewed the flowery rhetoric of Daniel Webster in favor of plain, direct language that sometimes infuriated listeners because it was so blunt and uncompromising.[77]

Phillips was once described as an expert "at the art of political agitation," and this proved to be an apt characterization.[78] Unlike Lincoln and mainstream politicians, Phillips and the radical abolitionists were not satisfied to work within the context of a flawed political system to improve public policy

Wendell Phillips became one of the most influential and uncompromising abolitionists of the antebellum era.
Courtesy of the Library of Congress.

through incremental reform. They demanded immediate, uncompromising, undiluted change. Phillips provoked outrage when he suggested that the most venerated document in American history, the U.S. Constitution, should be understood as the Founders understood it, namely as a proslavery document that must be rejected because it was fatally flawed. To prove this assertion, he analyzed the debates during the Philadelphia convention and pointed to numerous sections in the Constitution that protected human bondage although the word *slavery* was not used. The three most prominent examples included Article I, Section 2, clause 3, which stated that "Representatives and direct Taxes shall be apportioned among the several States which may be included within this Union, according to their respective Numbers, which shall be determined by adding to the whole Number of free Persons, including those bound to Service for a Term of Years, and excluding Indians not taxed, three fifths of all other Persons." The three-fifths clause, in effect, institutionalized the idea that slaves were subhuman beasts of burden. Article I, Section 9, clause 1 stated: "The Migration or Importation of such Persons as any of the States now existing shall think proper to admit, shall not be prohibited by the Congress prior to the Year one thousand eight hundred and eight, but a Tax or duty may be imposed on such Importation, not exceeding ten dollars for each Person." By waiting to eliminate the importation of slaves until two decades after the ratification of the Constitution and by refusing to address the domestic slave trade, the Founders ensured the growth of the peculiar institution as a cancer on the body politic. Finally, Article IV, Section 2, clause 3 stated: "No Person held to Service or Labour in one State, under the Laws thereof, escaping into another, shall, in Consequence of any Law or Regulation therein, be discharged from such Service or Labour, but shall be delivered up on Claim of the Party to whom such Service or Labour may be due." This objectionable provision laid the foundation for the Fugitive Slave Act of 1850, one of the worst legislative enactments in the nation's history.[79]

In the introduction to his analysis of the constitutional debates, Phillips penned these provocative words, every bit as fiery and uncompromising as his friend William Lloyd Garrison's incendiary rhetoric appearing in the pages of *The Liberator*:

> If, then, the Constitution be, what these Debates show that our fathers intended to make it, and what, too, their descendants, this nation, say they did make it and agree to uphold, then we affirm that it is "a covenant with death and an agreement with hell," and ought to be immediately annulled. No abolitionist can consistently take office under it, or swear to support it. . . . To continue this disastrous alliance longer is madness. The trial of fifty years with the best of men and the best of Constitutions, on this supposition, only proves that it is impossible for free and slave States to unite on any terms, without all becoming partners in the guilt, and responsible for the sin of slavery. We dare not prolong the experiment, and with double earnestness we repeat our demand upon every honest man to join in the outcry of the American Anti-Slavery Society,—NO UNION WITH SLAVEHOLDERS![80]

As uncompromising as Garrison, Phillips, and members of the American Anti-Slavery Society were, they still did not know firsthand the terrible burden of slavery. They could walk away from the battle for emancipation if they were so inclined, but blacks, even those freed through purchase, could never escape the stigma of the society in which they lived. In the quest for self-respect, free blacks realized they could not rely on paternalism to end their oppression, nor were they content to leave the abolitionist movement to whites. In some cases, white abolitionists were racially biased or insulting to slaves and former slaves, although most abolitionists valiantly struggled to transcend their prejudices. Black abolitionists such as Frederick Douglass recognized that they would gain respect and a measure of control over the movement if they actively participated in freeing their brethren—even if their participation caused rifts in the abolitionist ranks. Aside from speeches and writings by prominent black activists, many ordinary free blacks, especially those who worked as boatmen and dock workers, assisted the cause by volunteering to transfer escaped slaves along the celebrated Underground Railroad.[81]

The Underground Railroad has assumed mythic stature in the annals of American slavery, although only a few thousand bondsmen successfully escaped using this system of hideouts and meeting points. What it lacked in practical effects, the railroad more than compensated for in symbolic value. The knowledge that a series of safe houses, called "stations" in railroad jargon, existed where they could rest and seek assistance from conductors—that is, willing volunteers who would assist "passengers" in moving along the rails, or escape routes—gave hope to bondsmen who might otherwise have become despondent. For many years, historians viewed this system predominantly as a system of assistance, but twenty-first-century scholarship suggests that the railroad succeeded in large measure because slaves and former slaves took an active role in maintaining the Underground Railroad and communicating the possibility of escape.[82]

Despite the yearning for freedom that virtually all slaves felt, the decision to run away from captivity was never made lightly. A successful escape required advance planning, knowledge of roadways and conditions, food and water, and the stamina to persevere under arduous circumstances. It also meant that slaves would leave behind loved ones as well as the relative security of the only home they might ever have known. In addition, an escaped slave who was apprehended could expect severe reprisals. As horrible as a life in slavery was, the old adage "'Tis better to accept the devil you know than the devil you don't know" prevented some less adventurous souls from fleeing. For those intrepid slaves who risked everything to escape, the railroad was designed to improve the odds that they could make it to safety in Canada or elsewhere in the North.[83]

Only strong, cunning escapees could entertain a reasonable chance of success, but stories abound of elderly or disabled slaves who found safety through a combination of luck, chicanery, and assistance from skilled conductors. Harriet Tubman and William Still were the most storied Underground conductors. Between them, they assisted hundreds of fugitives in moving to a better life outside the Upper South. Tubman, in particular, became famous for her adventures. She was fearless and uncompromising. After escaping from slavery in eastern Maryland in 1849 and traveling to Philadelphia, she returned to the Upper South many times to rescue family members and others held in bondage. A petite woman of unremarkable appearance, to bounty hunters in search of fugitive slaves this unprepossessing Negress did not appear to constitute a threat. No one imagined she was the legendary Harriet Tubman, the Underground Railroad conductor with a price on her head. William Still once commented that "in point of courage, shrewdness, and disinterested exertions to rescue her fellowman, she was without equal."[84]

Still knew whereof he spoke. He is sometimes called the father of the Underground Railroad for his efforts to organize and preserve meticulous records of the escapes he engineered. During more than fourteen years, he assisted and interviewed more than six hundred escaped slaves as they fled from their masters. Still eventually published his records so that posterity could document the work of the Underground Railroad.[85]

The most famous black abolitionist of the nineteenth century was the inimitable Frederick Douglass. Born into slavery in Maryland, he escaped from an abusive overseer in 1838 while still in his early twenties. After performing odd jobs to survive, he came to the attention of the Massachusetts Antislavery Society. Douglass was the embodiment of everything the abolitionists were arguing for in denouncing the peculiar institution. He was intelligent, well spoken, and wholly committed to publicizing the degradation of slavery. The group hired Douglass to travel throughout the Northern states lecturing and sharing his firsthand experiences as a slave. His talks were exceptionally well received and effective. In 1845, he published *Narrative of the Life of Frederick Douglass*, a powerful window into the slave experience. Worried that his former master might track him down after publication of the autobiography, Douglass fled to England until his friends purchased his freedom. Returning to the United States, he traveled extensively, espousing what has been labeled "fraternal communitarianism."[86]

Douglass argued that every human being, regardless of race, is a member of the brotherhood of man. Individuals must exercise responsibility for their fellow human beings and not merely embrace self-interest or a classical liberal creed of "that government is best which governs least." The problem with the slaveholding system was that it undermined human brotherhood and convinced slaveholders that their self-interest was advanced by owning other human beings. In one typical speech, he told his audience that emancipation was required by "the heavenly teachings of Christianity, which everywhere teaches that God is our Father, and man, however degraded, is our brother."[87]

For many Americans of the antebellum era, William Lloyd Garrison, Wendell Phillips, and Frederick Douglass were antagonistic, frightening public figures dedicated to destroying the American way of life. Abolitionism was a radical position to be feared with its intemperate language and calls for wholesale, immediate change. Frederick Douglass especially, for all of his eloquence and obvious intelligence, forced middle-class Americans to confront issues that were too painful and abrasive to contemplate. During the mid-nineteenth century, candidates for elective office everywhere except small enclaves of New England feared being branded an "abolitionist"; the label tarnished many a public servant and destroyed many a campaign. If attitudes about the blight of slavery were to change, they must be changed in some other manner. Even if they had witnessed the abuses of slavery firsthand and did not countenance the institution, a large number of nonslaveholding whites remained blind or indifferent to the plight of the bondsmen in their midst. The average citizen simply had too many challenges and problems of his own in scratching out a living to worry about the vicissitudes of the invisible slave.[88]

—⋙—

Although most Americans north of the Mason-Dixon Line remained indifferent to the tribulations of slaves well into the 1850s, they were jolted from their moral stupor with the publication of a remarkable book by a remarkable woman. Titled *Uncle Tom's Cabin; Or Life Among the Lowly*, the novel depicted the horrors of a life in bondage and became the most popular book of the nineteenth century, selling three million copies between its publication and the outbreak of the Civil War nine years later. During the rest of the century, it outsold every other book in the United States, rivaling the Christian Bible. Unlike abolitionist tracts and speeches that frightened their audiences or alienated them with a morally righteous, indignant tone, *Uncle Tom's Cabin* told a story in simple, evocative language that connected with a mass audience unlike anything that had been written previously. The book did not lecture the reader; it presented a series of vignettes that allowed anyone to empathize with characters that were similar to one's own family.[89]

The author, Harriet Beecher Stowe, was shrewd. *Uncle Tom's Cabin* was not merely a mawkish romance or a tale of adventure, although it was those things as well. The book transcended the genre of most sentimental fiction because the prose was simple and direct, yet under the surface was a sophisticated morality tale. Stowe realized she had to grab the reader's attention before she could slip in an antislavery message.

That a woman wrote this groundbreaking work was not surprising, for women's fiction was on the rise. That this particular woman wrote the work was not surprising. Harriet Beecher Stowe was the seventh child in a prominent family of Christian ministers, educators, and political activists. She was raised in an abolitionist household, albeit not as radical as the Garrison or Phillips home. Lyman Beecher, the patriarch, was an influential Protestant clergyman and president of Lane Theological Seminary. His sons included

Henry Ward Beecher, arguably the most famous minister of the age, and Edward Beecher, the first president of Illinois College, the oldest college in the state and a bastion of abolitionism.[90]

Stowe married a widower and eventually bore him seven children. Before the publication of *Uncle Tom's Cabin*, her writing career was unremarkable. She typically penned sentimental, highly romanticized stories depicting the virtues of Christian living and hard work. When she concocted the story of Uncle Tom and Simon Legree as a serial in the pages of the *National Era* beginning in the summer of 1851, Stowe was so desperate for funds to support her family and so unsure of the appeal of the story that she entertained

Harriet Beecher Stowe, author of the best-selling 1852 novel *Uncle Tom's Cabin*, described the evils of slavery for a mass audience. Her work was so popular that, upon meeting her for the first time, President Lincoln supposedly remarked, "So this is the little lady who made this big war?"
Courtesy of the National Archives & Records Administration.

only the modest hope of earning enough money to buy a new silk dress. Her publisher, John Jewett, recognized the virtues of the work and persuaded her to collect the stories and publish them as a novel the following year.[91]

Stowe later explained that she based much of the book on real events involving a former slave named Josiah Henson. In 1830, Henson escaped from a plantation in Maryland and fled to Canada. In *Uncle Tom's Cabin*, the title character modeled on Henson was not so fortunate. Uncle Tom was sold to a ruthless slave owner, Simon Legree, a transplanted Yankee who owned a Louisiana plantation. Legree eventually ordered his overseers to whip Uncle Tom to death because the slave would not succumb to Legree's wishes.[92]

During the twentieth century, *Uncle Tom's Cabin* was bitterly criticized for its offensive portrayal of blacks. The "happy darky," the black "mammy," the "pickaninny" characterization of black children, and especially the eager-to-please, obsequious "Uncle Tom" character became ingrained in American culture as demeaning stereotypes, part of the ongoing debasement of blacks. While it is true these characters and descriptions violated the sensibilities of a later age, the impact of the novel as an abolitionist tool in the antebellum era should not be forgotten. For the thousands of Americans who read for the first time of the brutality and abject humiliation of slavery, it was an eye-opening, transformative experience. Harriett Beecher Stowe put a human face on the peculiar institution.[93]

Uncle Tom's Cabin was a nonviolent antislavery tool, but not all abolitionists were content to rely on peaceful forms of protest against the pernicious institution. Perhaps the best-known episode of violent protest, aside from insurrections led by the slaves themselves, involved an episode spearheaded by the messianic white abolitionist John Brown. Twice married and the father of twenty children, this fiercely antislavery man grew increasingly distraught over the spread of slavery in the antebellum years. After learning that a mob had attacked and killed abolitionist newspaper editor Elijah P. Lovejoy in Illinois in 1837, Brown vowed, "Here, before God, in the presence of these witnesses, from this time, I consecrate my life to the destruction of slavery!" He honored his pledge.[94]

Brown's life apart from his abolitionist zeal and religious fervor was undistinguished. He lived in several Northern states and struggled to earn a living tanning hides and trading cattle as well as breeding horses and sheep. Eventually, he slipped into bankruptcy and even served a jail term. One hesitates to attach too much importance to Brown's financial reverses as motivation for his subsequent activities, but clearly his private life left something to be desired.[95]

In 1855, he set out for the Kansas Territory after he learned from his sons that antislavery forces needed help to fend off slaveholders anxious to bring Kansas into the Union as a slave state. During his journey, Brown contacted abolitionists to support his plans for a violent confrontation with slave owners. The challenge he presented would divide antislavery forces for the rest of the decade: should violence be used to halt the spread of slavery into the territories? Part of the abolitionist strategy was to take the moral high ground, arguing, among other things, that slavery degraded the human condition and should be resisted based on immutable moral principles. If abolitionists condoned the use of violence, they risked dividing the movement and losing their moral force—to say nothing of the wrath they would incur from slaveholders already outraged at the abolitionist position. Eventually, Brown persuaded six wealthy abolitionists—Thomas Wentworth Higginson, Samuel Howe, Theodore Parker, Franklin Benjamin Sanborn, Gerrit Smith, and George Luther Stearns—to finance his operations. The financiers, some of whom were black, became known as the "Secret Six," and they suffered reprisals in the aftermath of Brown's subsequent misadventures.[96]

Whatever the reaction of mainstream abolitionists, Brown was not a man beset by doubts; his righteous indignation and religious piety drove him relentlessly. After settling in the Kansas Territory at Osawatomie—the home of two abolitionist Christian missionaries, Brown's half sister, Florella, and her husband, the Reverend Samuel Adair—he devoted his energies in 1855 and 1856 toward preventing proslavery border ruffians from terrorizing antislavery forces. The Browns were a close-knit family devoted to the abolitionist cause; John depended heavily on his sons to aid in his schemes.[97]

May 1856 was a momentous time for the antislavery struggle and for Brown personally. His beloved father died on May 8. As he struggled with his grief, Brown learned that proslavery forces, including some of his neighbors, had targeted him and his family for retribution. Even as these revelations came to light, Brown's enemies struck a blow. On May 21, some one thousand proslavery men, led by the local sheriff, attacked a well-known antislavery town, Lawrence, Kansas. Although only one person was killed in the ensuing melee, the posse destroyed several printing presses and a landmark hotel. The "sacking of Lawrence," as it came to be known, was a symbolic blow against the antislavery men in "Bleeding Kansas," but an even more aggressive act occurred the following day.[98] South Carolina congressman Preston S. Brooks charged into the U.S. Senate and attacked Massachusetts senator Charles Sumner with his cane for insults the senator made in a speech denouncing Brooks's cousin, Andrew Butler.[99]

Inflamed with passion and convinced he must act against the Slave Power before it acted against him, Brown and his sons launched a preemptive strike on the evening of May 24. Rousting five proslavery settlers from their homes in Pottawatomie Creek, the Browns chopped them to pieces with broadswords. This episode initiated a series of frontier skirmishes between Brown's forces and proslavery men. His son Frederick was killed during one assault. The old man and his ragtag army valiantly fought against overwhelming odds to save his frontier village. Although unsuccessful, he earned the sobriquet "Osawatomie Brown" for his valor. Skirmishes such as the sacking of Lawrence and the bloody exchange at Osawatomie presaged the bloody guerrilla warfare that would occur in border states during the Civil War.[100]

In the years following Brown's engagements in Kansas, he traveled throughout the eastern United States and parts of Canada soliciting funds and support for an antislavery army he hoped to build. Brown believed that he could strike a blow at the economy of the South if he compelled a mass exodus of slaves from plantations. His detractors later argued that he sought to trigger a massive slave insurrection by distributing weapons and providing leadership to plantation slaves in the Upper South. The vision of rebellious slaves rising en masse to slaughter their masters—echoes of Nat Turner's rebellion—touched a raw nerve among Southerners. Their ancestral fears would be realized if armed slaves revolted and exacted vengeance for the long years of abuse and humiliation.[101]

The Southern reaction to Brown and his tactics revealed an inherent contradiction in the region's position on slavery, long recognized by Southern leaders but seldom discussed in the light of day. If slaves were docile and happy, satisfied with their limited station in life because they were unable to care for themselves, as many Southerners claimed, why was the fear of slave insurrection so potent? Presumably, if Southerners were correct that most slaves would not abandon the peculiar institution even if offered an opportunity, a poorly planned and executed would-be slave insurrection would be an inconvenience, no doubt, and a temporary breakdown of law and order, but hardly cause for concern that the social compact would be severely jeopardized. Yet much of the incendiary Southern rhetoric that followed Brown's raid focused on the strong possibility of dissolving the Union in the face of an impending slave revolt.[102]

It is difficult to say with precision whether John Brown desired a bloody slave insurrection or saw himself as a latter-day Moses for a race held down in bondage, fighting only in self-defense and limiting bloodshed whenever possible. Whatever the details of his plot, here was a man who embraced William Lloyd Garrison's call for immediate emancipation in literal terms. Rather than wait for an incremental resolution to be hammered out between antislavery and proslavery forces locked in an increasingly stalemated policy process, Brown would arm slaves so that they could rise up against their sea of troubles and, by opposing, end them.[103]

In retrospect, the idea that slaves who had been brutalized for generations would flee their homes or overwhelm their masters in large numbers
seems astonishingly naïve. Nat Turner's rebellion, the most successful of the
nineteenth-century slave uprisings, had ended in ignominious defeat and an
excruciating death for Turner and harsh reprisals for blacks throughout the
South. Although Turner's revolt had sparked hope in many a bondsman's
breast and fear in many a slaveholder's heart, the days when symbolic acts
of violence would accomplish anything apart from exacerbating sectional
tensions were dwindling. If Brown honestly believed that arming a multitude
of slaves was possible or that a popular uprising would alter the balance of
power between antislavery and proslavery forces, he was deluded. To this
day, the clarity of his thinking and the motivations for his actions are points
of contention.[104]

Whatever his reasoning, on October 16, 1859, Brown launched his most
ambitious enterprise. He led a band of nineteen men against the federal armory at Harpers Ferry, Virginia (now West Virginia). Dividing his forces,
he left three conspirators at the base of operations, a nearby farmhouse, to
act as sentries. The plan was to break into the arsenal, liberate the weaponry,
and march through the countryside calling for slaves to join Brown's band of
brothers. To succeed, the scheme depended on swift action; if they absconded
with the weapons before the alarm was sent to Washington, D.C., the rebels
could avoid a protracted battle with U.S. military forces. To ensure they
would not be interrupted, Brown directed his troops to cut the telegraph lines
near Harpers Ferry.[105]

The group met almost no resistance at the outset, but the plan went awry
after a Baltimore & Ohio train escaped Brown's clutches and the conductor
sent out an alarm by telegraph. Ironically, a free black baggage porter for
the railroad, Heyward Shepherd, was the first casualty, shot and killed when
he tried to escape from the raiding party. The assault rapidly spiraled out of
control.[106]

Responding to the threat with alacrity, local militia pinned Brown's "piti-
fully small 'army'" inside the armory long enough for a contingent of U.S.
marines to arrive. In another of history's ironies, Colonel Robert E. Lee commanded the federal forces that arrived at Harpers Ferry that day. Lieutenant J.
E. B. Stuart was at his side. Stuart approached the arsenal under a flag of truce
and demanded that Brown and his men surrender or face the consequences.
When Brown refused to yield, the denouement was predictable. A shoot-out
followed after the marines battered down the door and rushed inside. Ten
of Brown's raiders were killed or mortally wounded, including two of his
sons. Brown was injured when he was struck across the head and neck with
a saber.[107]

Although the attacks involved federal property, Brown and his surviving coconspirators were held for trial in a state court on charges of engaging in treason against Virginia. After much legal maneuvering and a weeklong trial, Brown was found guilty and sentenced to be hanged.[108] The outcome of the proceeding was never in doubt, nor was the public reaction. Abolitionists hailed Brown as a hero whose name would live in the pages of history. The transcendentalist Ralph Waldo Emerson famously remarked that Brown "will make the gallows glorious like the Cross." Louisa May Alcott christened him "Saint John the Just."[109] Henry David Thoreau later called Brown "a crucified hero."[110] Northern political figures outside the abolitionist camp, including Abraham Lincoln, agreed that slavery was a terrible blight on the land, but they could not condone the use of violence in the service of any cause, regardless of how noble it appeared to some citizens. "It was a violation of law and it was, as all such attacks must be, futile as far as any effect it might have on the extinction of a great evil," Lincoln said in a speech in Elmwood, Kansas, after he learned of the raid. His cautious language toward the abolitionist movement would do much to further his political career, but the abolitionists and Radical Republicans would later find fault with what they saw as Lincoln's timid approach to eradicating slavery and ensuring emancipation.[111]

Southerners hailed Brown's sentence as an act of justice for crimes against their property rights and, by extension, their liberty as American citizens acting under the protections afforded by the U.S. Constitution. They began to speak of secession as though it were inevitable. From the floor of the U.S. Senate, an angry Jefferson Davis asked rhetorically, "Have we no right to allege that to secure our rights and protect our honor we will dissever the ties that bind us together, even if it rushes us into a sea of blood?" "The day of compromise is passed," a Southern newspaper, the *Charleston Mercury*, declared. "The South must control its own destinies or perish."[112] According to the influential *De Bow's Review*, Brown's bloody revolt was made possible by the people of the North who "sanctioned and applauded theft, murder, treason," and the episode raised the question of whether Southerners could continue "to live under a government, the majority of whose subjects or citizens regard John Brown as a martyr and a hero."[113]

Brown was as resolute in his hour of defeat as he had been in the years leading to the assault of Harpers Ferry, refusing to repudiate his cause or beg for mercy. By all accounts, he faced his death with grace and courage. Shortly before he marched to the gallows on December 2, 1859, he wrote, "I, John Brown, am now quite certain that the crimes of this guilty land will never be purged away but with blood. I had, as I now think, vainly flattered

myself that without very much bloodshed it might be done." Brown realized
he was speaking to history, and history responded with the bloodshed he
prophesied.[114]

While these dramatic events unfolded during the 1830s, 1840s, and 1850s,
life went on for most slaves as it had always gone on; time seemed to have
no beginning or end. Slaves did not see a great civil war or emancipation
on the horizon any more than did whites on either side of the Mason-Dixon
Line. When a person in bondage is forced to eke out a day-to-day existence,
the philosophical debates between slavery and antislavery forces have little
practical effect. African slavery had existed in North America since the seventeenth century; few whites in positions of power saw a need for the institution to change markedly after more than two hundred years.

**The messianic John Brown was a violent opponent of slavery.
His 1859 attack on Harpers Ferry and subsequent hanging
transformed him into a martyr for the abolitionist cause.**
Courtesy of the National Archives & Records Administration.

By the mid-nineteenth century, the generation of slaves that had endured the Middle Passage—transportation from Africa's Gold Coast to the new continent—had died out except for the illegal transatlantic slave trade that still flourished in some pockets of the Americas. The domestic trade continued to expand in the Southern states. From the age of Jackson to the age of Lincoln, slavery remained a stable institution with its own set of rules and rhythms of daily life. The conditions under which slaves live and worked depended on time and place, but some general characteristics existed.

As the slavery debate unfolded on a grand, national stage, proslavery proponents shrewdly couched their arguments in the language of federalism and constitutional interpretation. Aside from a small group that argued slaves were happy living in bondage because it was their natural condition, most proslavery adherents simply ignored the human toll. When the institution was considered up close and personal, at a level where human suffering could be witnessed on a daily basis, justifying the perpetuation of legal bondage became problematic. If confronted squarely, absent convoluted talk of human ownership as a natural, God-given condition and the constitutional protection of slaveholders' rights, it was impossible to rationalize the sexual exploitation of women who bore their masters' children as the next generation of the labor force, the heart-wrenching tales of families torn apart by the slave auction, or the brutish treatment of disobedient slaves broken with the lash. Sophisticated slavery apologists knew this. Proslavery forces were on sure ground when they stayed away from the human beings tossed about at the center of the tempest. If the debate could be cast in abstract terms of federal versus state power, the human toll could be passed over without a backward glance.[115]

It is left to history to take account of the human costs. As memories of life in Africa were lost to the mists of time, slaves were forced to fashion new lives as best they could. Their art, music, culture, folklore, and religion retained some features of their original heritage, but it mixed with an increasing array of distinctly American components. Bits and pieces of African languages continued to exist, but gradually they mixed with English and were transformed into pidgin dialects such as Gullah. Ever vigilant, lest slaves develop a secret language or means to communicate incendiary messages, slaveholders discouraged the use of unknown languages and symbols, although obviously masters could never completely eradicate all forms of surreptitious, potentially disruptive communication.[116]

Even in the most desperate circumstances imaginable, slaves carved out a family life. Slave marriages were not legally recognized, but owners were aware of such pairings; they understood that threats to disrupt family life could be used as a tool for social control. Anxious to protect a spouse and children, a slave could be kept docile and easy to control. Detached young males with visions of freedom and dignity, no familial ties, and little to lose caused the greatest consternation for the white community.[117]

Because many bondsmen had been ripped from their families at a young age and did not enjoy the luxury of an extended family network, they developed fictive kin relationships that augmented bloodlines. Older male slaves often were awarded the appellation "uncle" as an honorific term and a mark of affection. Members of a slave community looked out for their younger brethren, upbraiding them and teaching them ways to survive their predicament even if the children were not their progeny. Consanguinity was not a luxury enjoyed by most slaves; their relationships depended on choices, acts of faith, and affection.[118]

Class distinctions arose based on a slave's position. A house slave lived inside the master's home and was not forced to engage in the backbreaking agricultural work that caused untold suffering and cut short the lives of so many field hands. The food was better, and a house slave might be adorned in a master's hand-me-down clothes as opposed to the rough, homespun cloth supplied to those who worked in the yard. For all its advantages, however, house slaves were subjected to the wrath of sadistic owners or the sexual advances of white males who would not be denied. Living in proximity to the family carried risk; who better to brutalize in times of crisis than the familiar figure lurking in the corner of the room? In all cases, humiliation and degradation were the order of the day, for no one forgot who was master and who was slave.[119]

Women in bondage faced an untenable situation. Forced to submit to their masters' desires, invariably some female slaves gave birth to mulatto sons, thereby increasing the plantation's store of property. They also enraged the master's wife, who felt powerless to protest to her husband but who could vent her displeasure and frustration toward the offending slave woman.[120]

Outside the main house, most field slaves awoke to the sound of a bell. They were expected to work from sunup to sundown. Except for small breaks for lunch, to drink water, or to relieve themselves, they labored steadily throughout the day. Permission would have to be sought and granted for even minor deviations to the routine. Sometimes slaves feigned illness or stupidity to avoid particularly unpleasant tasks. On other occasions, they intentionally broke their tools or mistreated draft animals to secure a respite, but such actions were dangerous. A slave who became known as a troublemaker or a rebel would be marked for special scrutiny and might face brutal punishment for even minor infractions of the rules.[121]

Religion was a large part of a slave's life, and with little wonder. Although not all slaves were Christians, especially prior to the nineteenth century, the Christian faith offered a measure of hope, no matter how dire one's circumstances. The promise of the meek inheriting the earth or a greater glory in the next life nurtured many a broken soul. It also served the slaveholders' interests since the New Testament's emphasis on turning the other check and the redemptive power of suffering could be used as an instrument of social control.[122]

The black minister became a figure of respect and power in the world of the slave during Reconstruction and in the Jim Crow era, long after the peculiar institution was abolished. For many slaves, the minister was a man of wisdom and justice; he had attained his status because he understood the ways of the world and of God far better than they. Slaveholders encouraged this development as long as the minister served as an avuncular figure, functioning as a palliative force in the slave community. No one, black or white, forgot the power of a preacher man when he became infused with too much religious zeal. Nat Turner had claimed to be an instrument of God in leading his Virginia rebellion, and the scars from that wound did not soon heal.[123]

The larger the plantation, the better the treatment a slave could expect to receive. Mammoth plantations existed as small, self-sufficient villages with virtually everything a plantation owner needed to lead a comfortable, prosperous life. On a large plantation, a well-developed hierarchy existed and everyone knew his or her place. Disruptions were to be avoided whenever possible. Brutal treatment led to unhappy slaves, and unhappy slaves potentially disrupted the social order.[124]

Treatment also varied according to the attitude of the overseer and the slave driver. The former was usually white; he served as a foreman ensuring that the slaves were at their posts working efficiently and not engaging in mischief or attempting to escape. The slave driver, by contrast, usually was an older male slave who had ascended through the ranks to become a leader among the other slaves. He had to walk a fine line. The overseer needed to regard the slave driver as diligent and conscientious, but at the same time the slave driver could not be seen by other slaves as brutal or heartless. Today the term *slave driver* is used derisively to describe a person who drives himself or his subordinates relentlessly. A wise slave driver, in contrast, was a leader on the plantation. He had to be seen as firm but fair. He settled minor disagreements, doled out advice on living in bondage, and ensured stability and order in the community for his masters.[125]

This hierarchical arrangement sounds neat and tidy, which was exactly what the proslavery propaganda suggested. Yet large plantations were the exception rather than the rule. Available figures indicate that about 88 percent of the nation's slave owners held twenty slaves or fewer in 1860. In that same year, about four million black slaves belonged to four hundred thousand slaveholders, mostly in the Southern states. The "orderly" nature of slave life was far less structured and orderly on smaller homesteads.[126]

Through it all, individual slaves and former slaves struggled not to be victims under the yoke of the white man, for nothing is as powerless as a victim. The determination to escape victimization and be fully free and human compelled Frederick Douglass, William Wells Brown, and Sojourner Truth to travel the lecture circuit awakening a slumbering American populace to the horrors of the peculiar institution. The unquenchable zeal to help others know the freedom they knew is why Harriet Tubman and William Still risked life and limb as conductors on the Underground Railroad. The burning desire to escape from a life of continuing degradation compelled Henry "Box" Brown to ship himself from Richmond, Virginia, to Philadelphia inside a crate—a desperate, audacious (and successful) escape attempt. Many other acts of resistance restored a semblance of dignity and self-respect to those who had been robbed of it by a vicious master class.[127]

For all these individual acts of dignity and self-empowerment, however, many hundreds of thousands of nameless men, women, and children labored in silence. Despite their best efforts, they were victims of a cruel stereotype. Because it was illegal to teach slaves to read, most slaves were functionally illiterate, a fact that led whites to dismiss slaves as stupid and inferior. Except in rare instances, slaves were seldom allowed to bathe or practice sanitary personal hygiene. As a result, whites dismissed them as foul-smelling brutes that were unwilling to clean their bodies. The vicious cycle of exploitation and victimization continued as long as the peculiar institution endured—but it could not, and would not, endure forever.

Chapter Two

"Mr. President, You Are Murdering Your Country by Inches"

And so war came.

With it came a new generation of American political leaders, men of enormous ability and intellect, directly focused, unlike so many of their predecessors, on slavery. The peculiar institution had confounded the Founders, but in the grand tradition of legislators the world over they had successfully sloughed it off for future generations to tackle. By the dawn of the 1860s, the framers of the republic had been gone for many decades; power had changed hands across the generations. Old Hickory had been in his grave almost sixteen years when Southern forces fired on Fort Sumter. The Great Triumvirate of the U.S. Congress at midcentury—Daniel Webster, Henry Clay, and John C. Calhoun—passed from the scene early in the 1850s. Presidents Millard Fillmore, Franklin Pierce, and James Buchanan had fretted their tumultuous hours upon the national stage, exacerbating sectional tensions and floundering ineffectually before exiting the Executive Mansion for a gradual descent into well-deserved obscurity.[1]

Looking back over that troubled period from the 1830s until the 1860s, perhaps the most surprising fact was not that war erupted between North and South but that it erupted so late in the life of the republic. Unresolved questions of slavery and federalism had lurked beneath the surface of political debates since the founding period. War had seemed imminent more than once. A careless act, a slew of incendiary words, a symbolic misstep—all might have triggered a violent civil insurrection, beginning with the Missouri Compromise and extending to the inception of the Lincoln presidency. Had it not been for the legislative compromises and deal brokering of Henry Clay and his congressional progeny spanning nearly four decades, nineteenth-century American history would have been markedly different.[2]

Of the new generation of political leaders, Abraham Lincoln seemed the least likely to ascend to the heights of high federal office. Despite his newfound prominence during the 1858 senatorial contest with Stephen A. Douglas, he remained a dark horse candidate for the 1860 Republican presidential nomination. The party was less than a decade old, but it had attracted many capable candidates far better known and seemingly more qualified than homely, coarse, undereducated Abraham Lincoln. William H. Seward, the former New York governor and longtime senator from the Empire State, was most often mentioned as a serious contender, as to a lesser extent was Salmon P. Chase, a former governor and senator from Ohio. Senator Simon Cameron of Pennsylvania, while perhaps not as well known as Seward and Chase, also

Lincoln reputedly said this photograph—taken by the legendary photographer Mathew Brady on February 27, 1860—along with the famous Cooper Institute address "made me president."
Courtesy of the Library of Congress.

enjoyed better presidential prospects than Lincoln as 1860 dawned, despite Cameron's reputation for cronyism and corruption. Even Republican politicos such as Edward Bates of Missouri and Ben Wade of Ohio appeared more promising presidential timber than Lincoln.[3]

Therein lay his strength. Lincoln had always been underestimated, one of the few men in public life who delivered more than he promised. In his own reserved, inimitable way, he had used his time between the 1858 Senate contest and the 1860 presidential election wisely, traveling through midwestern and northern states to speak on the importance of foreclosing the territories to slavery. In this manner, he quietly positioned himself for the presidency.[4]

On February 27, 1860, Lincoln delivered his most important oration of the prewar years at the Cooper Institute (later called Cooper Union) before a crowd of fifteen hundred influential New Yorkers. The seven-thousand-word speech, which required an hour to deliver, featured a detailed history of the peculiar institution and described the Founders' intention to regulate and limit the spread of slavery, despite Southerners' insistence to the contrary. Lincoln's reputation as a rube did not survive the night; he emerged from the Cooper Institute as an up-and-coming politician with gravitas. The photograph carefully arranged (and retouched) by famed photographer Mathew Brady earlier that same day showed a confident, poised statesman on the cusp of a storied political career.[5]

Lincoln and his political advisers manipulated his image and background to suit their purposes. Sometimes he appeared as a straight-shooting, plain-talking, common-sense-wielding man of the people. His image as the "Rail Splitter" dates from this era. His supporters also portrayed him as "Honest Abe," the country fellow who was simply dressed and not especially polished or formal in his manner but who was as honest and trustworthy as his legs were long. Even Lincoln's tall, gangly frame was used to good advantage during the campaign as many drawings and posters showed the candidate sprinting past his vertically challenged rivals. At other times, Lincoln appeared as a sophisticated, thoughtful, articulate, "presidential" candidate. He carefully used the Cooper Union photograph and similar images to portray himself as someone competent and savvy enough to serve effectively in the nation's highest executive office.[6]

The advantage of a dark horse candidate, then as now, is novelty. If familiarity breeds contempt, a novice enjoys a decided advantage. Lincoln's rivals had amassed long track records in politics, which also meant they had acquired long lists of enemies. Because he was relatively new to national politics, he was not the primary target of the slander and innuendo so common in hardball politics. Illinois Democrats remembered his "House Divided" speech and would use his words against him after Lincoln snagged the Republican presidential nomination, but in the early days he was not the front-runner. Hence he avoided the harsh limelight that destroyed other candidacies.

During the nineteenth century, a candidate for elective office, especially a presidential aspirant, was forced to walk a fine line. He must not appear too eager to step into high office, for a covetous man was judged far too self-interested and therefore not to be trusted with the people's business. Yet he must not be too aloof and disdainful of elective politics or he would not cultivate the requisite political contacts and establish the necessary relationships to carry him through a long campaign. Perhaps nowhere was this strange arrangement as visible as in presidential politics. Because it was deemed unseemly to attend the nominating convention, presidential hopefuls dispatched proxies in their stead. A smart candidate would select an agent devious enough to garner delegate support through deft wheeling and dealing without locking his principal into a series of untenable bargains and false promises.[7]

As expected, William H. Seward sent his longtime political adviser Thurlow Weed to Chicago as his surrogate. To his supporters, Weed was a master politician who understood the machinations necessary to secure victory. To his detractors, Weed was an unscrupulous political boss of the Machiavellian school: the ends justified the means and nothing was beyond the pale. Everyone agreed that whatever his character faults, Weed proved remarkably adept at assessing his candidate's political fortunes and responding accordingly. The old boss was confident heading into the 1860 Republican presidential convention that he could easily garner a third of the requisite 233 votes for Seward to capture the nomination. The question was whether he could devise a strategy to reach the prize. To most observers, Seward's national stature and Weed's political prowess ensured the nomination was Seward's to lose.[8]

In the normal course of affairs, Weed probably would have been correct in his assessment that his candidate was an unstoppable juggernaut; however, 1860 was not the normal course of affairs. Seward was unquestionably the man to beat, but the party was not united with storm clouds of civil war visible on the horizon. Moreover, the New Yorker's gruff ways and reputation for intemperate language and extremist views proved to be problematic. Desperate to appeal to moderates in the general election, some of the party faithful believed that Seward's comments about an "irrepressible conflict" would poison the well and frighten off potential supporters for fear of the candidate's zealotry—to say nothing of the possible backlash his nomination would trigger in the Southern states. The Republicans thus were caught in gridlock. No other potential nominee, even Salmon P. Chase, possessed the votes to slip past Seward and win the nomination, yet Seward could not secure the requisite votes to claim his prize. The factions coalescing around the respective candidates had the votes to deter Seward, but that was all. De-railing a candidate was not difficult; finding an acceptable candidate was the challenge. A would-be nominee whose operatives could devise a way to cut the Gordian knot would prevail.[9]

The Republican Party of 1860 was home to an eclectic, uneasy alliance of men who opposed the Democrats for one reason or another but who did not find solace in the company of like-minded individuals inside the party. United by the loose principle that "the enemy of my enemy is my friend," the multitude of politically ambitious individuals calling themselves Republicans encompassed western farmers, eastern manufacturers, antislavery men who eschewed party labels, former Conscience Whigs and Free-Soilers, moder-ates seeking to arrest the spread of slavery in the territories, radicals pushing to enact legislation that would bring about social upheaval, and abolitionists infected with religious piety and ideological zeal.[10]

Delay and disharmony were the order of the day as Republican delegates anxious to stop Seward launched a campaign to deny the senator a first-ballot victory. Although the convention occurred well before the age of the modern media, the breakdown of party discipline was widely reported. Everyone knew press reports of the party's divisiveness did not portend well for the fall campaign, but no one knew how to resolve the fractiousness. As this drama unfolded, Lincoln's representatives David Davis and Norman Judd pursued a sophisticated course to end the stalemate. They maneuvered to make Lincoln the second choice of delegates when the better-known candidates locked horns after Seward failed to win on the first ballot. The location of the con-vention in Chicago also proved to be a benefit as Davis and Judd arranged for cheering crowds to create an impression of unity and enthusiasm for the state's favorite son. It was a shrewd strategy. When the party could not agree on a nominee after three days of balloting, Lincoln emerged as a suitable compromise. Although he had cautioned Davis and Judd to "make no deals that bind me," Lincoln arguably owed several cabinet appointments to his Republican rivals when the convention ended with his victory.[11]

The story of Lincoln's improbable rise to become the Republican nominee was dramatic, but it was not the only drama of 1860. As the nation unrav-eled, Lincoln still had to win the presidency and devise a plan to govern a potentially ungovernable nation. Two images from 1860 tell remarkably dif-ferent stories of this unusual presidential contest. The first image is found on a campaign poster showing the tousle-haired nominee flanked by two iconic figures, Justice and Liberty. Lincoln sat for many portraits during the years leading up to his presidential campaign. In most sittings, he appeared solemn and dignified, as was typical for politicians of that time. In one well-known photograph—the model used for the poster—Lincoln deliberately ruffled his

ABRAHAM LINCOLN,

REPUBLICAN CANDIDATE FOR PRESIDENT OF THE UNITED STATES.

This 1860 campaign poster depicts a tousle-haired Abraham Lincoln as a man of the people, pledged to protect justice and liberty while safeguarding the American republic. Courtesy of the Library of Congress.

hair, presumably to present himself as the quintessential "average man" who did not "put on airs." The figure of Justice appears at the left, holding scales in one hand and a sword in the other. At the right, Liberty cradles a copy of the U.S. Constitution and holds a staff topped with a Phrygian cap, a symbol of liberty since antiquity. An American eagle is perched atop the roundel and surrounded by American flags. At the bottom of the roundel to the left is a parchment representing "The Union," and to the right is a fasces, a bundle of white birch rods tied together with a bronze axe. The fasces represents "strength through unity," a sentiment associated with the Roman Republic. The poster's message was clear: a vote for Lincoln was a vote for a man of the people who would protect justice and liberty by ensuring the perpetuation of the American Union.[12]

A second image showed Lincoln in a less flattering light and highlighted a fissure between Lincoln and the Radical wing of the Republican Party.

SHAKY.

DARING TRANSIT ON THE PERILOUS RAIL, · · · · · · · · · · Mr. Abraham Blondin De Lave Lincoln.

For all of his personal antipathy toward slavery, presidential candidate Lincoln had to tread carefully toward the middle of the political spectrum lest he alienate moderate voters. In this cartoon, a Radical Republican, Horace Greeley, urges a "shaky" Lincoln not to forsake blacks in the quest to win the election.

Courtesy of the Special Collections Department, Musselman Library, Gettysburg College.

The image, a cartoon published in the June 9, 1860, edition of *Vanity Fair* magazine, depicts Lincoln as a circus performer crossing a cracking, unstable log with a black child nervously perched inside a bag. Behind him, *New York Tribune* publisher Horace Greeley calls out to the Republican nominee, "Don't drop the carpet bag." The cartoon was meant to show the difficulties Lincoln experienced as a candidate in 1860 as he tried to appeal to a wide array of voters, many of whom were not in favor of emancipation, while Radical Republicans such as Greeley urged the candidate to address slavery as a key campaign issue.[13]

Divisions within the Republican Party mirrored divisions within the country. A breakdown of civility between the sections triggered an electoral schism in 1860 that helped Lincoln win the presidency. The Democratic Party split into a Southern faction and a Northern faction, with the former nominating President Buchanan's vice president, John C. Breckinridge of Kentucky, and the latter nominating Lincoln's old adversary, Senator Stephen A. Douglas of Illinois. The Constitutional Union Party, a third party created in 1859 and pledged to preserve the Union at all costs, nominated John Bell, a former Speaker of the U.S. House of Representatives and senator from Tennessee as well as secretary of war under Presidents Harrison and Tyler. The election was complicated by the fact that Lincoln's name did not appear on the ballot in the Southern states.[14]

Breckinridge performed well the South, but he lost the border states to Douglas and Bell. Lincoln performed well in the North and in some border states, but he lost the South. Douglas campaigned throughout the South, but his support for the Lecompton constitution and his opposition to President Buchanan were not forgotten or forgiven. Although he won 29.5 percent of the popular vote—second only to Lincoln—Douglas captured but 12 electoral votes. When all was said and done, Breckinridge won 72 electoral votes (18.1 percent of the popular vote) and Bell won 39 electoral votes (12.9 percent of the popular vote). Lincoln won more electoral votes (180, or 59.4 percent) than all other candidates combined—28 more than he needed to win—although the four-way race ensured that the best he could muster in the popular vote was a plurality (39.82 percent).[15]

Elected in November 1860, he was not scheduled to be sworn in as president for four long months. During the interregnum, Lincoln deliberately remained silent in public as he met with party faithful, considered cabinet appointments, and wrote draft after draft of his inaugural address. During that period, seven Southern states claimed to secede from the Union, beginning with South Carolina on December 20. Early in the new year, Mississippi, Florida, Alabama, Georgia, Louisiana, and Texas followed suit. By the time Lincoln swore the oath of office on March 4, 1861, almost one-fifth of the states in the nation had announced their intention to band together as a separate confederacy. An ironic photograph of the period shows the U.S. Capitol dome still under construction, an unintentional metaphor for the unfinished work that lay before Lincoln and the generation of leaders facing the daunting task of preserving the Union.[16]

—m—

In the face of the growing crisis of the Union, Lincoln did not enjoy a honeymoon period in office. Even within his own party, factions threatened to undermine his presidency at the outset. A group of men emerged as leading critics of their new party leader; they passed down in history with the designation "Radical Republicans" or, in some volumes, the "Jacobins," a reference to the radicals of the French Revolution. The Radical Republicans harbored deep reservations about the Rail Splitter from the beginning. To these men, deeply committed to confronting the peculiar institution directly and unequivocally, anyone who did not share their zeal was suspect. Caution is in order when discussing the Radical position. Not all of these men described themselves as "Radicals," nor did they caucus as such. Moreover, a Radical Republican was not necessarily a staunch abolitionist. Although a few Radicals properly can be labeled "abolitionist," even within their ranks the term is misleading. One man's radical was another man's moderate. Some Radicals called for an immediate end to chattel slavery and the consequences be damned; others focused on practical questions such as the means by which newly freed slaves would be inculcated into society. For all of their ardor and vehemence, most Radicals were elected officials who had to consider their constituents and deliver on promises uttered during the last campaign. As a result, while they were united by their passionate desire to eradicate the peculiar institution, they were not an impenetrable union. They generally agreed on the ends but often quarreled over the means.[17]

The Radical Republicans reached the pinnacle of their fame and power during the 1860s. Congressman Thaddeus Stevens of Pennsylvania, influential chairman of the House Ways and Means Committee; Senator Charles Sumner of Massachusetts, chairman of the Senate Foreign Relations Committee; and Senator Benjamin Wade of Ohio, president pro tempore of the Senate during the Johnson administration, were among the more prominent and influential members of the group. Another Radical, Galusha A. Grow of Pennsylvania, briefly served as Speaker of the House until he was defeated in his 1862 reelection bid. Radical Illinois congressman Owen Lovejoy, brother of murdered abolitionist Elijah Lovejoy, was a persistent, vehement advocate for emancipation. Joshua Giddings, formerly an Ohio congressman for two decades during the antebellum era, was no longer a member of

Congress when Lincoln became president, but he remained a powerful voice for Radical policies. Giddings's son-in-law, George W. Julian, served as an Indiana congressman and was daring enough to support women's suffrage long before the issue garnered wide popular support. Senator Henry Wilson of Massachusetts, another prominent Radical, later served as vice president under Ulysses S. Grant in 1873–1875. New Hampshire senator John P. Hale, formerly a presidential candidate under the Free-Soil Party, also supported the Radical cause. Senator Zachariah Chandler of Michigan, a stern critic of the Lincoln administration, emerged as a leading Radical when he wrote a letter to Michigan governor Austin Blair early in 1861 declaring that the war was a positive development because it would resolve the schism between North and South. "Without a little blood-letting, this Union will not, in my estimation, be worth a rush," he explained in a postscript.[18]

These men were among the most powerful and able legislators to serve in Congress during the latter half of the nineteenth century, although their effectiveness often was compromised by external events as well as their own self-righteousness and unwillingness to compromise. The Radicals, these men of little faith, mistrusted leading moderates such as Lincoln and his friend Orville Browning of Illinois along with Jacob Collamer of Vermont and James Doolittle of Wisconsin.[19] The moderates favored gradual, compensated emancipation, colonization of freed Negroes, and a plan for disrupting the social order as little as possible. Lincoln flirted with this concept on several occasions early in his administration. As Senator Browning explained in July 1861, "I should rejoice to see all the States in rebellion return to their allegiance; and if they return, if they lay down the arms of their rebellion and come back to their duties and their obligations, they will be as fully protected, now and at all times hereafter, as they have ever been before, in all their rights, including the ownership, use, and management of slaves."[20]

To Radical sensibilities, Browning's limited agenda was not ordinary prudence; it smacked of timidity and a lack of political will. The only means by which slavery could be eliminated from the American landscape would be to attack it, root and branch, without hesitation or indecision. If such an attack required purging away the institution with blood, as John Brown had prophesied, so be it; the price was not too high. The fact that the Southern states had foolishly brought the issue to a head was welcomed; it presented an opportunity to remake American life absent the blight of human bondage. Moderates who sought to restore the Union as it was before Fort Sumter were squandering a golden opportunity for political, not to mention moral, reform. One man with Radical propensities, Charles Francis Adams, the son and grandson of American presidents, remarked, "We cannot afford to go over this ground more than once. The slave question must be settled this time once and for all."[21]

Lincoln initially agreed with Browning that restoration of the Union was his paramount objective. Having assessed the incoming chief executive as a man easily intimidated and manipulated, the Radicals were determined to change his mind. To achieve this end, they presented the president-elect with a list of suitable candidates to populate the cabinet and thereby ameliorate his natural conservatism and flimsy record of executive leadership. Although Lincoln accepted their mostly unsolicited advice with his usual equanimity, he had his own ideas—appointing his former rival William H. Seward as secretary of state for one.[22]

For many Americans who had read his speeches and knew him through his extensive press coverage, Seward was the quintessential radical, a man who seemed to champion the antislavery cause throughout the North. For true Radical Republicans, however, this popular image was a chimera. In their view, the New York senator was far too willing to compromise his ideals despite his muscular prewar rhetoric. Instead of consistently championing the Radical agenda, Seward appeared to be a political opportunist who constantly shifted his position with the political winds. The Radicals envisioned Secretary of State Seward acting in the Talleyrand-Metternich school of European diplomacy, serving as Lincoln's prime minister and manipulating the outclassed, overmatched presidential pawn with Machiavellian dexterity much as a master chess player will move pieces across a chessboard, dominating a lesser rival.[23]

Seward apparently envisioned such a role for himself as he stepped into his new position in the face of an immediate crisis. In March 1861, only hours after the Lincoln administration came into office, the new president and his cabinet began debating whether to send provisions to Fort Sumter in Charleston Harbor or surrender the fort to South Carolina rebels in hopes of stemming the secessionist movement sweeping through the South. The crisis had commenced the day after Christmas 1860, when Major Robert Anderson, the Union commander at Fort Moultrie across the harbor from the city of Charleston, quietly moved two companies under his command to Fort Sumter after he learned of the existence of the South Carolina Ordinance of Secession. Fort Sumter was easier to defend than Fort Moultrie because it was not surrounded by hostile natives. Yet Sumter was an isolated outpost ensconced in the harbor and would have to be resupplied in the near future.[24]

The new administration faced a deteriorating situation. Everyone recognized that Fort Sumter held little or no strategic value, but the presence of a federal garrison directly across from the Charleston battery was galling to Southerners. President Buchanan, never a steady figure in times of crisis, reluctantly agreed to supply provisions to Anderson's garrison despite the risk that angry Southerners might interpret an effort to hold the fort as a sign of federal aggression. After much waffling, the administration sent a civilian relief ship, the *Star of the West*, but no one notified the South Carolinians of the plan. When the ship appeared unannounced in the harbor on January 9, 1861, a group of cadets from the Citadel, a military school in Charleston, mistook its appearance as an act of aggression and fired on the vessel. Observing the incident from the fort, Major Anderson easily could have fired his own volleys to defend the ship, but he chose not to escalate the confrontation. He withheld fire, the relief ship turned around without reaching the fort, and the crisis momentarily was averted. Much to his relief, James Buchanan could surrender the executive chair to his successor without initiating a bloody war. The Buchanan administration was content to leave Washington, D.C., as it had governed the republic—with a whimper, not a bang.[25]

When Lincoln became president two months after the *Star of the West* confrontation, the question of what to do about Fort Sumter could not be avoided. Major Anderson alerted his superiors that supplies were so low he and his men could not hold out much longer. If Lincoln surrendered the fort, he would avoid a confrontation with the South and probably prevent states in the Upper South as well as the border states from seceding, but his new administration would be wounded, perhaps permanently. Northerners, especially Radicals, would interpret his failure to resupply the fort as weakness. Southerners would see a chief executive too timid to prevent them from acting as they pleased regardless of federal law or constitutional constraints. It was a Hobson's choice however one examined it.

Agonizing over his poor menu of choices throughout the month of March, Lincoln met repeatedly with his cabinet. During these sessions, Secretary of State Seward argued vehemently that the federal forts, especially Fort Sumter and Fort Pickens in Florida, possessed only symbolic value. If the federal government surrendered the forts, the practical effect would be nil, and a confrontation would be averted. Moreover, Southerners' contention that the Lincoln administration was aggressive and hostile toward the South would be effectively rebutted.[26]

Seward's willingness to cede the field to Southern malcontents disgusted the Radicals. They saw his position as cowardice, exactly the sort of unprincipled compromise they loathed. Northern men had kowtowed to the South long enough. Throughout the decade that had passed, from the Compromise of 1850 with its provisions authorizing the offensive Fugitive Slave Act, through the Kansas-Nebraska Act and its ludicrous concept of popular sovereignty, to the wretched *Dred Scott* Supreme Court decision, Northerners had shown little or no intestinal fortitude. Now that the Southern states had undertaken overt, arguably treasonous acts against the government—enacting ordinances of secession and threatening violence against federal forts and installations—the time for hesitation and compromise had passed. The administration must protect federal property. If the rebels fired on the forts, they would be the aggressors and should be punished as traitors to their country.[27]

As the cabinet debated the permutations and combinations of each set of choices throughout March, Seward and the Radicals, for all their doctrinal differences, agreed on one point: Lincoln was not equal to the occasion. The Radicals urged a muscular and immediate response; Seward sought compromise. Watching the administration's indecision from the inside circle, the incoming secretary of state grew frustrated at what he perceived to be Lincoln's vacillation and lack of leadership. The old fellow simply could not make up his mind; he was paralyzed with indecision.

Finally, on April 1, the secretary had reached a breaking point. He directed his son Frederick to deliver a letter to Lincoln titled "Some Thoughts for the President's Consideration." It was a condescending, audacious document, criticizing an administration "without a policy either foreign or domestic." The solution to the lack of leadership, Seward intimated, was for the president to appoint someone in the cabinet to take charge. Seward, naturally, offered to step into the breach as secretary of state, traditionally the senior post in any presidential administration. It was not an altogether unreasonable suggestion; in some administrations the secretary of state had served almost as a copresident, truly a prime minister or first among equals within the cabinet. Despite the existence of historical precedent for this proposed arrangement, the secretary's critics viewed the brazen note as incontrovertible evidence of the machinations they so feared, proof positive of a benign *coup d'état*. Coming so soon in the life of the new administration—before Lincoln and Seward knew each other well—at the very least it was a politically risky move by a presumptuous, possibly egomaniacal, cabinet official.[28]

If the president took umbrage at his secretary of state's presumptuousness, he kept his own counsel. In a patient, understated response, Lincoln explained that as president, he, and he alone, exercised responsibility for developing a policy, which he had already outlined in his inaugural address when he promised to "hold, occupy, and possess the property and places belonging to the government." Consistent with his response to Seward, Lincoln dispatched an unarmed relief ship to resupply Fort Sumter, but he also alerted South Carolinians that the ship was en route. This policy perturbed Seward; the secretary had been confident that his recommendations for evacuating Fort Sumter and resupplying Fort Pickens would prevail. He had even suggested as much to his Southern contacts through back-channel communications. Lincoln's willingness to reject Seward's advice indicated the new president would not be bullied or cowed. It was not the first time he had been underestimated, even by his own cabinet, nor would it be the last.[29]

Seward eventually became one of Lincoln's staunchest allies after he recognized the president's virtues as a wartime leader. Not so with the new secretary of the treasury. Salmon P. Chase was a Radical Republican of the first
order and a political leader whose massive ego blinded him to the strengths
possessed by men he judged to be of lesser ability. Because he found virtually everyone, especially Lincoln, wanting in terms of intellectual prowess or
moral strength of purpose, the imperious Chase projected a haughty public
image that was off-putting to all but the most dyed-in-the-wool Radical Republican.

By the time he joined the cabinet, he already had enjoyed a long, stellar
career as an attorney, senator, and governor of Ohio. Anxious to provide a
countervailing presence to Seward in the cabinet, the Radicals lobbied for
Chase's appointment as the chief financial officer for the government. His
tenure was both a blessing and a curse to the Lincoln administration. To say
Chase was a difficult personality to manage is a gross understatement. He
believed beyond a shadow of a doubt that he, not Lincoln, should occupy the
executive position. Having been elected to the U.S. Senate in 1860, Chase initially was noncommittal when Lincoln offered him the post as treasury secretary, and opposition from some quarters was intense. Nonetheless, Chase was
a man of proven ability and intellect; his appointment to the cabinet was sure
to appease the Radicals, albeit temporarily, while also bringing much-needed
expertise to the Treasury Department at a time when financing the war effort
was a crucial, tricky enterprise.[30]

The debate over appropriate cabinet choices would continue, especially
over the appointment of Simon Cameron as secretary of war, but in the meantime the Confederates' decision to fire on Fort Sumter and Lincoln's call for
troops after the fort capitulated meant that a war had to be fought and won.
Congress convened in a special session on July 4, and the next day Lincoln
sent over a message outlining his war aims. "This is essentially a people's
contest," he explained. "On the side of the Union, it is a struggle for maintaining in the world, that form, and substance of government, whose leading
object is, to elevate the condition of men—to lift artificial weights from
shoulders—to clear the laudable pursuit for all—to afford all, an unfettered
start, and a fair chance in the race of life." He asked for at least four hundred
thousand troops to be mobilized and $400 million to be authorized, "a less
sum per head, than was the debt of our revolution."[31]

Most commentators praised Lincoln's July 4 message, but the Radicals argued he was too tentative in his request for men and materiel. As the Jacobins
installed themselves in powerful positions inside the Congress, especially in
the House of Representatives—with Galusha Grow becoming Speaker of the
House, Thaddeus Stevens assuming the chairmanship of the powerful Ways

and Means Committee, Owen Lovejoy assuming the mantle of chairman of the Agriculture Committee, and James M. Ashley becoming chairman of the Committee on Territories—they agreed that Lincoln should prepare for war by calling up additional troops and asking for the necessary financing. Yet he could have done much more. Tragically, the president's message was silent on slavery—a wasted opportunity in light of the enthusiastic response to his call to arms.

Congress responded by authorizing even more men than Lincoln had requested. They also ratified his previous executive actions except for the suspension of habeas corpus, which they did not mention. If the president had outlined emancipation as a war goal in his message, the Radicals contended, perhaps the goodwill and "rally 'round the flag" sentiments of the nation and the Congress would have won the day, allowing policymakers to endorse a radical departure from the antebellum purposes of the federal government. Abolitionist Wendell Phillips thought he knew why Lincoln failed to act boldly: "We have an honest President, but, distrusting the strength of the popular feeling behind him, he listens overmuch to Seward."[32]

Although they could not convince Lincoln to incorporate emancipation into his war goals at the outset, the Radicals tried to influence national objectives through the legislative process. Congressman Lovejoy introduced a resolution stating, "It is no part of the duty of the soldiers of the United States to capture and return fugitive slaves." If the Confederates were determined to flee the Union through force, they could not rely on provisions of the Fugitive Slave Act to deliver their runaway slaves to them. Building on this foundation, Radicals serving in both houses of Congress introduced measures confiscating the property of anyone taking up arms against the United States. A proposal offered by Samuel Pomeroy of Kansas provided for emancipation in the rebellious states and directed Lincoln to issue a proclamation of "immediate and unconditional emancipation." Pomeroy's proposal resembled Lincoln's subsequent Emancipation Proclamation, but in 1861 an executive proclamation was not yet in the offing.[33]

The cautious, politically astute Lincoln had hoped to marginalize extremists in the North and wait for moderate sensibilities to prevail against extremists in the South; if so, the affair might have reached a satisfactory conclusion regardless of the opening salvos. Despite Lincoln's best efforts, Fort Sumter demonstrated the folly of pursuing a middle course. Reason is a demanding mistress even in placid days; in times of crisis, she becomes a shrew. In the wake of the Confederate firing on Fort Sumter, Lincoln's April 15 call for seventy-five thousand militiamen to a ninety-day term of service, and the

defection of states from the Upper South, the potential for a bloodless reconciliation disappeared. Reason no longer favored negotiation and compromise,
although the president nonetheless refused to consider emancipation as a
policy goal.[34]

Lincoln found he could not resist the Northern public's desire for a quick,
painless, decisive victory. Patriotic fever spread like a contagion, and with
it overconfidence infected the land. In the heated Northern rhetoric of the
day, the rebels were little more than a ragtag group of malcontents similar to
children who exhibited bad behavior because no one had disciplined them. If
an army of sufficient size could be hurled against this sorry band of Southern
rabble-rousers, the disaffected leaders of the so-called Confederate States
of America could be brought to heel in short order. With their leaders out
of commission, the populace would realize it faced the wrath of a superior
Northern army and immediately return to the fold. The whole sordid affair
could be wrapped up in two or three months with minimal disruption to the
social, political, and economic order.[35]

Reality seldom conforms to expectation. The aged warhorse General Winfield Scott, Lincoln's principal military adviser, was far less sanguine than
a majority of the populace. He recognized one indisputable fact of life: the
Federal army, such as it existed after the loss of numerous career military officers to the Confederacy, did not possess adequate personnel or resources to
sustain an offensive overland campaign into enemy territory. In light of this
stark reality, Scott believed that Federal forces must be properly positioned
to gain a strategic advantage. Hence he proposed a scheme disparagingly
referred to as the "Anaconda Plan." As its name suggested, the plan was designed to leverage the North's limited resources, in this case by squeezing the
rebels into submission through a series of naval blockades of Southern ports
coupled with an advance down the Mississippi River.[36]

The strategic merits of Scott's plan, with its dependence on a difficult-
to-enforce blockade, remain debatable. In the hysterical days following
Fort Sumter, the scheme required too much time and patience to implement; the citizenry was anxious for forward motion of almost any kind.
With the public clamoring for action and Treasury Secretary Salmon Chase
urging Lincoln to appoint Chase's protégé, newly promoted Brigadier
General Irvin McDowell, as the commander of the Army of Northeastern
Virginia—later reorganized as the Army of the Potomac—the president
yielded to the pressure. McDowell took to the field in May, although both
he and General Scott were worried that the troops had not been properly
trained. They had little choice; the public outcry for immediate action
would not be denied. Military planning be damned; forward momentum
was the rallying cry of Northern partisans.[37]

Within two months McDowell and his green recruits were on the march toward the new Confederate capital in Richmond. They carried high hopes. On July 21, 1861, after repeated delays, they fought the first major battle of the Civil War against Confederate forces under the command of General P. G. T. Beauregard at Manassas Junction, a small crossroads near the Bull Run River, 28 miles south of Washington, D.C. The ambitious McDowell attempted a flanking maneuver to sweep Southern troops from the field. It almost worked. In retrospect, he should have known that such a complicated plan of attack was beyond the skill of his untested soldiers, but for a time the gamble seemed to pay off. He was in command of the field and the Confederates were on the defensive. If Union men could drive the enemy from the battlefield and give chase to Richmond, the entire war might end, as predicted, in a matter of weeks.[38]

The arrival of Southern reinforcements by railroad in the nick of time changed the course of the battle, tipping the advantage to the rebels. If this sort of *deus ex machina* plot device were employed by a second-rate novelist to resolve a hackneyed tale of battles won and lost, it would be dismissed as unbelievable. Yet it happened at Bull Run. As fresh Confederate troops took up arms, the Federals found themselves driven back. All they had gained through a hard fight was lost. The men were new to unit discipline; they soon panicked and were routed. Washington's elite had traveled by carriage to watch the festivities from nearby fields, but to their dismay they were caught in a chaotic retreat back to the safety of the capital city. A day that started with much promise ended in ignominious defeat for Federal forces and their observers. Although the troops eventually fell back into ranks within the Washington defenses, hyperbolic stories and exaggerated, probably apocryphal eyewitness accounts of the headlong flight from the field of battle only heightened the sense of disappointment, shame, and public hysteria.[39]

By later standards, the first battle of Bull Run (or Manassas, as the Confederates called it) was not a large engagement, but it served notice that the Union could not easily win the war. It also created several indelible legends, such as the advent of the ferocious Rebel Yell and the *nom de guerre* of Confederate General Thomas J. Jackson, thereafter known as "Stonewall" for his performance in the heat of battle. In the short run, Bull Run changed the mood of the Northern public from the unrestrained euphoria of the spring to the grim despondency of the summer to the tenacious determination of the fall. For the administration's many critics, it was yet more evidence that the commander in chief was incompetent, the wrong man in the wrong job at the wrong time. If the president had been firmly in charge, the rebels would have been whipped and the whole awful business of young men fighting and dying would have been concluded once and for all.[40]

As he did often throughout his presidency, Lincoln ignored the firestorm of criticism as best he could and soldiered on despite difficult circumstances. He had little choice but to relieve McDowell of command and search for a suitable replacement in the aftermath of the debacle. Still smarting from the recriminations, Lincoln's initial thought was to turn to General Winfield Scott, the man nicknamed "Old Fuss and Feathers" for his insistence on following military protocol and adhering to strict military discipline. Scott had served as a career army officer as far back as the War of 1812; he was the greatest living military hero in the nation. Unfortunately, his country could no longer rely on him. The Grand Old Man of the Army was too weary and portly to assume active command. The ancient general in chief retained his position for another four months after Bull Run, but ultimately he did not possess the stamina to weather the necessary bureaucratic battles with Congress and his officer corps; he resigned his commission before the year was out.[41]

With few other viable options available to him that July, Lincoln summoned a thirty-four-year-old West Point graduate, George Brinton McClellan, to assume command in McDowell's stead. McClellan eventually succeeded Scott as general in chief in November. In 1861, McClellan seemed an inspired choice. The young officer was a wunderkind who possessed a magic touch. He had enjoyed a stellar career in the antebellum army serving in the Mexican War and observing the Crimean War. Later, he became a prominent railroad executive. After winning several skirmishes in western Virginia in the early months of the conflict, the "Young Napoleon" or "Little Mac," as the diminutive McClellan was nicknamed, appeared to be exactly the caliber of leader the Union needed to push the rebels to their knees.[42]

McClellan brought a level of professionalism to an army that sorely lacked confidence and prestige. He possessed a keen mind, was well versed in military tactics and strategy, and suffered from no want of self-esteem. To restore troop discipline and improve morale, the new general instituted a regimen of constant drilling and instruction in the finer points of military maneuvering. Whatever his later failings, in 1861 George B. McClellan found a disorganized mass of men and shaped it into an effective fighting force.[43]

The Radicals initially welcomed the Young Napoleon. Finally, a man of action was on the scene to arrest the administration's drift toward incoherence as well as correct its indecisiveness and incompetence. Their great fear was that the cabinet and other men of limited ability in Washington would hamper McClellan's effectiveness with too many rules and requirements; thus, the Radicals promised to do all they could to hold needless bureaucracy at bay. For his part, McClellan, never known for his humility, pledged to save the republic in its hour of greatest peril. He was the toast of official Washington in that desperate time.[44]

Would that Little Mac had lived up to his early promise. Unaccustomed to holding a public position of such weight and authority, the young savior became spoiled with heady talk of his military genius. As time marched on and McClellan's troops did not, the young general's self-regard expanded in inverse proportion to his list of accomplishments. History has found him every bit as insufferable as many of his contemporaries did. He can be seen most clearly through letters he wrote to his wife, Ellen, where he allowed his ego to roam free and unfettered. In a note he wrote shortly after he arrived to save the regime, he explained that members of Congress "tell me I am held responsible for the fate of the Nation." The Young Napoleon felt equal to the occasion. "It is an immense task that I have on my hands, but I believe I can accomplish it." In later correspondence, he complained of the incompetence of "wretched politicians" that undermined his efforts and failed to provide him with the resources he needed. Secretary of State Seward was "the meanest of them all" while Secretary of the Navy Gideon Welles "is weaker than the most garrulous old woman." He reserved the most vituperative comments for Lincoln, who "is nothing more than a well meaning baboon."[45]

Aside from his outsized ego and messianic tendencies, Little Mac was the best of commanders and the worst of commanders. As an administrator and military planner, he was brilliant. As a bold, fearless, daring field commander, he was an abysmal failure. McClellan simply could not bring himself to advance and attack the enemy with the alacrity required of a field commander. In fact, on several occasions he allowed the enemy to escape after winning an engagement when an aggressive pursuit might have ended the war or at least taken a decisive step in that direction. A frustrated Lincoln once complained that McClellan's greatest failure was he suffered from "a case of the slows."[46]

Lincoln gradually lost faith in his new general officer, although the president repeatedly allowed Little Mac an opportunity to rehabilitate his reputation. Not everyone shared the commander in chief's well-known patience. Hell hath no fury like a Radical scorned. As McClellan's intransigence and inability or unwillingness to fight became clear, the Radical Republicans rediscovered that the general was a Democrat. With this rediscovery, they realized he was philosophically opposed to emancipation or any genuine remaking of the American republic. McClellan never disguised his ideological opposition to abolitionism, either before or after he assumed command. "I confess to a prejudice in favor of my own race, & can't learn to like the odor of either Billy goats or niggers," he wrote in a letter that reflected his outlook toward persons of color. Had he led the Union army to battlefield victories, such comments, although odious to the Radicals, could have been ignored. But with the general's spotty record of successes, his attitude began to appear traitorous. As 1861 stretched toward 1862, the Radicals barely tolerated Mc-Clellan's bigotry and shortcomings as a battlefield commander. In time, they would turn their full wrath in his direction.[47]

In the meantime, the Radicals had their hands full casting aspersions on their inadequate party leader. Yet another early episode underscored Lincoln's poor leadership skills in the eyes of the Jacobins as well as his lack of commitment to the goal of emancipation. Major General John C. Fremont, the celebrated explorer hailed as the "Pathfinder of the West" and the 1856 Republican presidential nominee, was charged with responsibility for clearing the Missouri frontier of guerrillas loyal to the rebels. On August 30, 1861, using his own initiative, Fremont declared martial law in the state of Missouri and ordered that the slaves of any persons found to have taken up arms against the government of the United States would be freed. The Radicals hailed this edict as the first step toward general emancipation, but the general's proclamation—issued without advance notice to the Lincoln administration—frustrated the president's political goals. Lincoln was anxious to prevent the border states of Missouri, Kentucky, and Maryland from seceding. He feared that an emancipation proclamation would propel ambivalent border state leaders away from a Radical agenda and into the fold of the Southern Confederacy. In a famous and perhaps apocryphal anecdote, Lincoln, when told that God was on the side of the Union cause, reportedly said, "I hope to have God on my side, but I must have Kentucky." Any action that threatened the stability of the border states, no matter how well meaning, could not be allowed.[48]

Determined not to embarrass or compromise the illustrious general, Lincoln wrote "in a spirit of caution, and not of censure," asking that Fremont rescind the proclamation. A self-righteous, politically tone-deaf celebrity accustomed to giving orders but not taking them, Fremont failed to recognize that a subordinate must comply with a superior's orders, no matter how gently they are expressed. In a haughty, arrogant reply, the Pathfinder lectured the president. "If I were to retract it of my own accord, it would imply that I had acted without the reflection which the gravity of the point demanded. But I did not. I acted with deliberation, and upon the certain conviction that it was a measure right and necessary, and I think so still." Lincoln's patience is legendary, but even he could not allow the edict to stand. To the dismay of the Radical Republicans, he countermanded the order.[49]

The frustration the Jacobins felt at the president's decision was captured in a political cartoon published in *Frank Leslie's Illustrated Newspaper* on October 12, 1861. The drawing shows Lincoln adrift in an angry sea wearing a life preserver labeled "Union." To save himself and the Union, he is pushing a black man away, presumably sacrificing him to a watery grave.

A copy of Fremont's proclamation juts from a hat that bobs on the nearby waves. In the background, a ship's mast labeled "Proclamation" is visible; perhaps the ship is sinking or simply moving away. The Lincoln figure calls out, "I'm sorry to have to drop you, Sambo, but this concern won't carry us both!" The doubt the Radicals felt toward Lincoln expressed in the *Vanity Fair* cartoon in 1860, when Lincoln was balancing a black child in a bag while he scampered across a cracking log, had evolved into open mistrust by the fall of 1861.

LINCOLN—*"I'm sorry to have to drop you, Sambo, but this concern won't carry us both!"*

This cartoon from the October 12, 1861, issue of *Frank Leslie's Illustrated Newspaper* expressed the Radical Republicans' fears that Lincoln would sacrifice the goal of emancipation to preserve the Union.

Courtesy of the Library of Congress.

Another episode that fall—the debacle at Ball's Bluff—finally convinced the Radicals they could not stand by idly and allow the Lincoln administration's demonstrated incompetence to destroy the nation. On October 21, 1861, General McClellan ordered Brigadier General Charles Pomeroy Stone to advance across the Potomac River at Harrison's Landing, Virginia, and capture the town of Leesburg, a Confederate transportation hub. Any forward movement at McClellan's behest was to be applauded, but this enterprise was poorly executed. A detachment commanded by Colonel Edward D. Baker received orders to cross the river as part of the Leesburg assault, but a bottleneck developed because the expedition possessed only three boats to transport troops through the water.[50]

After Baker ferried his men across the river, he realized they would have to scale a 100-foot cliff known as Ball's Bluff. The danger inherent in climbing such an edifice and fighting the enemy with no reasonable means of escape should have given Baker pause; nonetheless, he marched on with aplomb, confident he could take Leesburg. Baker was a U.S. senator from Oregon and a friend of Abraham Lincoln, both of which had served him well in his peacetime activities, but they were of little value on a battlefield. He had secured his military commission because it was politically advantageous to appoint him, not because he was deemed the best man for the job. He had served in uniform during the war with Mexico, as had many Civil War officers, but that had been fourteen years earlier. At fifty years of age, his salad days were a distant memory; whatever military talents he had once possessed had deserted him.[51]

As Baker marched his men across an open field toward their objective, they stumbled into an ambush set by four regiments of hidden rebel soldiers. The Confederates sprang the trap and fired into the unsuspecting Northern troops, creating panic in the ranks. The Federal retreat was a disorganized, chaotic free-for-all, with every man for himself. Blinded by fear and fumbling in the brush, scores of wild, desperate men tumbled down the cliffs. Some fellows immediately fell to their deaths while others fractured their limbs or suffered grievous internal injuries. Once on the beach, the hysterical survivors overcrowded the boats, causing them to capsize. Those lucky souls who stayed afloat were picked off by sharpshooters or compelled to surrender on pain of death. In the final analysis, more than two hundred men were wounded or killed, and some seven hundred were captured. Only seven Confederates were lost. Much to Lincoln's horror, his dear friend Colonel Baker numbered among the fallen.[52]

The Northern mood before Ball's Bluff was gloomy; afterward, it was despondent. When news of the fiasco filtered into the capital, the Radicals believed they must act in the best interests of the nation. McClellan, the once-mighty boy general, now appeared as either hopelessly inept or deliberately dragging his heels, perhaps as a sign of his disdain for the Union war effort. Yet while McClellan lost favor, General Stone, the nominal commander at Ball's Bluff, served as a convenient scapegoat. He was later arrested and held in prison for six months without trial or formal charges filed against him.[53]

From a military perspective, Ball's Bluff was a minor setback—humiliating and tragic, to be sure, but not catastrophic. From a political perspective, the consequences were far reaching. Already politically weakened by military losses, the president faced a fresh round of criticism. No relief or solace was in sight. His annual message to Congress, which he delivered to the legislative branch as Congress reconvened in December, further irked the Radicals. Once again, the well-meaning but incompetent president failed to give emancipation its due. Lincoln deliberately skirted the issue because he wanted to call attention to positive developments in Maryland and Kentucky, two border states that had remained loyal to the Union. Although Lincoln would mull over the merits of issuing an emancipation proclamation in 1862, addressing slavery in the annual message would have antagonized the border states at a propitious moment when the president sought to keep those members in the Union.[54]

It had all been too much—the ineptitude at Bull Run, the Fremont episode, the travesty of Ball's Bluff, and now the tepid presidential message. New York congressman Roscoe Conkling introduced a motion to investigate the Ball's Bluff disaster, but something else was needed. A permanent investigatory arm of the Congress would hold the weak president and his bumbling general officers accountable. At the urging of Radical senator Zachariah Chandler, the Thirty-Seventh Congress established the Joint Committee on the Conduct of the War in December 1861 to oversee the administration's wartime policies. The Jacobins controlling the committee urged Lincoln to acknowledge that emancipation was a central administration goal. They desperately wanted him to order McClellan's army, heretofore preoccupied with military drills and stationary activities, to march against the rebels, but they stopped short of usurping executive authority in military activities—for the time being.[55]

From its inception, the committee exercised broad powers and wide discretion to investigate Northern military affairs, "past, present, and future." This expansive goal was crucial because the Radicals disagreed among themselves about whether it was important to rehash the 1861 fiascos or focus on improving military affairs in 1862. Radical senator Henry Wilson explained the committee's central purpose when he remarked, "We should teach men in civil and in military authority that the people expect that they will not make mistakes, and that we shall not be easy with their errors." The administration's helpless flailing about with little or no accountability was at an end. Efforts henceforth would be judged by results, and woe to anyone who offered lame excuses for poor performance. As Wilson thundered, "I want military men to understand that they are not to stand upon technicalities for the preservation of the old Army or the getting up of a new one."[56]

Because the Republican Party controlled the U.S. Congress, the committee comprised five Republicans and two Democrats. From the U.S. Senate, Benjamin F. Wade of Ohio served as the committee chairman. He was joined by another Radical, Senator Chandler of Michigan. Senator Andrew Johnson of Tennessee was the only Democratic senator on the committee and the only representative from a seceding state. Johnson served until March 1862, when he was appointed the new military governor of Tennessee. Joseph Wright, the former governor of Indiana, replaced him. House members on the committee were Radical congressman Julian of Indiana, John Covode of Pennsylvania, and Daniel Gooch of Massachusetts. Moses Fowler Odell from Brooklyn, New York, was the only Democratic House member to serve.[57]

The Thirty-Eighth Congress reappointed the committee with generally the same members in place, although Senate Democrat Benjamin F. Harding of Oregon replaced Joseph Wright. When Harding's Senate term expired in 1865, Charles R. Buckalew of Pennsylvania replaced him. In the House, Republican Benjamin F. Loan replaced John Covode, who had chosen not to sit for reelection to Congress in 1862. Loan, a brigadier general in the Missouri State Militia, was the only committee member who possessed military experience.[58]

The committee's tactics smacked of partisanship and encouraged rancor, reminding critics of the Star Chamber methods in the Old Country. Committee sessions were held in secret—a necessity, members insisted, because they were reviewing military plans best not exposed to the light of day. Republican members typically summoned a witness to be examined behind closed doors without their Democratic colleagues present. With little or no forewarning of what to expect, a witness was peppered with leading questions that left little doubt of the committee's desired outcome. When the necessary information had been gathered to prove the Radicals' point, they moved to a new topic. Seventy-five years before the House Un-American Activities Committee existed, its strategy of partisan political maneuvering was already a staple of politically charged congressional investigations.[59]

Lincoln recognized the committee for what it was—a means for the legislative body to intercede in military affairs. In most instances, the committee was a perpetual thorn in his side, but, on occasion, congressional and executive goals overlapped. In particular, Lincoln shared the Radicals' growing frustration with McClellan, although he did not share their opinion that the Young Napoleon could be goaded into action.

Lincoln had come to know the infuriating general's eccentricities well. In a humiliating incident on November 13, 1861, the president, Secretary of State Seward, and Lincoln's private secretary, John Hay, stopped at McClellan's house to discuss strategy, only to find the general away at a wedding. Never a man to allow ego to dictate matters, Lincoln suggested that he and his party wait for McClellan to return. When Little Mac arrived an hour later and learned that the president of the United States and the secretary of state were waiting to speak with him, he retired for the night without so much as acknowledging their presence. Thirty minutes later, Lincoln reminded McClellan's staff that he, Seward, and Hay were still waiting to see the general. Only then did he learn that McClellan did not deign to descend from his lofty perch. Lesser men might have erupted into anger at this deliberate snub, but Lincoln refused to hold a grudge. If McClellan could propel his armies forward to victory, little else mattered.[60]

The problem was that McClellan was unable or unwilling to move his armies. Each day that passed with no military action was another opportunity lost, and the Radicals would not acquiesce in allowing inertia to substitute for efficacious government policy or forward movement among the troops. While the general was laid up ill with typhoid fever in December, the joint committee held hearings on Bull Run and Ball's Bluff. McClellan had his supporters; they testified to their superior's rare ability to train and motivate his men. Without a doubt, army morale had rebounded markedly since Little Mac had taken the helm after the Bull Run disaster, but improved morale was no longer good enough. The general's opponents were equally well equipped to discuss missed opportunities, wasted time and energy, and hesitation in the face of the enemy.[61]

Armed with committee testimony, a group of Radicals led by Senator Ben Wade confronted the president in the Executive Mansion on the last day of the year. The present state of affairs could not continue. If McClellan did not move soon, he should be relieved of his command. In his typical, blunt fashion, the histrionic Chairman Wade explained, "Mr. President, you are murdering your country by inches in consequence of the inactivity of the military and the want of a distinct policy in regard to slavery."[62]

Wade was the driving force behind the Joint Committee on the Conduct of the War—not only because of his formal position but owing to his intellect and personality. Early in his career, he had been a partner in a law firm with abolitionist Joshua Giddings, and this association colored his worldview for the rest of his life. In the ensuing years, as slavery became an increasingly salient issue, Wade grew ever more radical. During the antebellum era, he came to see the American style of politics and capitalism as detrimental to human freedom and dignity, and he advocated a system that later would be akin to democratic socialism. First elected to the U.S. Senate in 1851, Wade's became a shrill voice in opposition to the Fugitive Slave Act, the Kansas-Nebraska Act, and *Dred Scott.* Whereas the prewar Lincoln had lobbied against extending slavery into the territories, Senator Wade had called for the extinction of slavery wherever it existed. He simply refused to be cowed. When Southerners insisted on preserving their honor with long-winded speeches in Congress or blustery editorials published in the newspapers, Wade matched their flowery language with his own special brand of ornate, overblown prose. It was little wonder he sported the sobriquet "Bluff Ben" Wade. Always eager to demonstrate the logical inconsistencies of his enemies, Wade insisted on denigrating Southern claims to love liberty while simultaneously owning human beings. Moreover, never one to back away from a fight, when an enraged Southerner once challenged Wade to a duel, he accepted. Having called the fellow's bluff, the matter was dropped.[63]

Although he was careful to shield the prickly McClellan from the full brunt of Senator Wade's anger, Lincoln shrewdly used the committee's investigation as the impetus for the army to move into battle sooner rather than later. Writing to McClellan early in January 1862, the president urged his general to move before Congress felt compelled to act in a reckless manner. It was the classic "good cop–bad cop" ruse. Lincoln intimated he was McClellan's friend, but the Radicals were not predisposed to be patient. Forward movement was required as soon as the general regained his health. An exasperated president remarked to another general officer on January 10 of that same year, "The people are impatient; Chase has no money and tells me he can raise no more; the General of the Army has typhoid fever. The bottom is out of the tub. What shall I do?"[64]

Little Mac dragged himself from his sickbed and confronted his detractors during a cabinet meeting on January 13. He had little choice. After learning that his predecessor, General McDowell, had developed a plan and Lincoln, the incompetent baboon, wanted to "borrow" the army to implement the plan, McClellan risked being relegated to the sidelines if he remained immobile. Expressing his fear that someone might leak a detailed plan of attack, he would not reveal his strategy for forward movement to the cabinet, but he promised to meet privately with Lincoln and the new secretary of war, Edwin M. Stanton, in a separate session. Two days later, McClellan repeated his performance in a closed session of the Joint Committee on the Conduct of the War. Because technically he was not a witness, McClellan's testimony was not recorded, although subsequent accounts suggest the general engaged in heated exchanges with several committee members.[65]

After Little Mac was on his feet again, the pressure to commence military operations became unbearable. On January 27, Lincoln issued an order that

McClellan must initiate "a general movement of the land and naval forces" on or before February 22, George Washington's birthday. The president realized that ordering a career military officer to advance on an arbitrary date instead of determining the schedule based on ground conditions and troop readiness was not an optimal method for proceeding, but he had reached the end of his patience. Something had to be done, and soon. Administration critics reacted to Lincoln's order by railing against public knowledge of a specific date for troop movements so that anyone, including the Confederates, could see, but the president felt under enormous pressure to appease the Radicals.[66]

McClellan was not satisfied to submit to the order without offering objections. In an exchange of correspondence with the president, he outlined a scheme to move forces by sea to Urbanna, Virginia, and march them up the Rappahannock River to Richmond. This amphibious turning offensive, McClellan argued, avoided a direct attack against Manassas Junction and could win the war in one dramatic campaign. Yet one problem existed: the ambitious plan might not be ready by February 22. Although Lincoln thought the original idea to move troops overland was superior, he realized the virtues of trusting in the commander on the ground. He never formally rescinded his January 27 order, but he acquiesced to McClellan's plan.[67]

The Radicals were livid. At precisely the moment when the hesitant Lincoln seemed ready and able to demonstrate his resolve, he bowed to the whims of a general already shown to be, at best, overmatched and, at worst, traitorous. Edward Bates, Lincoln's moderate attorney general, confided to his diary, "If we fail to do something effectual in the next thirty days, the administration will be shaken to pieces, the Cabinet will be remodeled, and several of its members must retire."[68]

Whatever its virtues and vices, McClellan's Urbanna plan was obviated by subsequent developments. Confederate general Joseph E. Johnston moved his troops away from their position near Washington, D.C., necessitating a change in Union strategy. Adapting to the change, McClellan modified the plan so that troops would disembark at Fort Monroe, Virginia, and traverse the Virginia Peninsula to Richmond. The Peninsula Campaign was thus conceived. It was the first major movement of what would be a protracted, bloody conflict with numerous peaks and valleys for the Northern war effort. McClellan would lose and regain his command before losing it again. As for Senator Wade's committee, it examined many issues in the coming years, including the administration of specific military departments, contraband trade, government negotiation of ice contracts, the manufacture of heavy ordnance and light draught monitors (small turreted warships), the treatment of Union prisoners of war in Confederate prisons, the controversial peace plan negotiated by General William T. Sherman with Confederate general Joseph E. Johnston, and the massacres at Fort Pillow, Tennessee, and Sand Creek, Colorado. As important as these investigations were, the committee's paramount concern was in examining military battles, especially those that ended in defeat.[69]

In the eyes of many military leaders, the committee adhered to flawed criteria for evaluating military performance. Generally impressed with Northern superiority in money and materiel, committee members were quick to criticize campaigns that failed to produce instant results. The Radicals saw evidence of conspiracies and incompetence in every failure; no commander blundered in the field lest he be part of an anti-Union cabal. Owing to the dearth of military experience among committee members, their second-guessing of battlefield reverses led many frustrated Northern political and military leaders to regard the committee as a perpetual source of delay and unnecessary intrusion into an already muddled fray. Because committee leaders were unabashedly devoted to antislavery ends, members also judged the performance of military leaders in terms of their commitment to the abolitionist cause.[70]

For much of the war, the committee incessantly criticized the Lincoln administration and the army's top officers. During the Thirty-Seventh Congress, the committee devoted a large percentage of its time to having General McClellan removed from command. To that end, during the summer of 1862, Zachariah Chandler delivered a vitriolic rebuke of McClellan before the U.S. Senate that left little doubt of the Radicals' loss of confidence in the Young Napoleon. After McClellan's departure, the committee sponsored several Union generals, including John C. Fremont, John Pope, Ambrose Burnside, and Joseph Hooker. These good Republican men opposed slavery, but their political affiliations did not ensure victories in battle.[71]

During the Thirty-Eighth Congress, the committee focused on the deficiencies of General George Gordon Meade, another leader whose politics were suspect. Although Lincoln was not an ardent supporter of McClellan or Meade, he opposed the committee's efforts to undermine specific generals until more qualified replacements could be identified.[72]

The Joint Committee on the Conduct of the War was created so that the legislative branch could provide a check on the power of the executive. In some ways, the committee served its purpose. Incensed at what they viewed as the president's poor leadership, some committee members supplied popular daily newspapers with secret testimony to sway public opinion in their favor. Unscrupulous committee members made speeches before the House and Senate to advance the committee's point of view at the expense of sound military judgment. Indiana congressman George W. Julian was especially well known for his abrasive speeches. The committee's most notable successes were in the area of wartime propaganda, particularly with the publication of reports on the treatment of Union prisoners of war and the Fort Pillow massacre. Intended to portray the Confederacy as backward and barbaric, these reports laid the groundwork for the "hard peace" championed by the Radical Republicans during Reconstruction.[73]

The committee's record of success was mixed. In some instances, Lincoln met their demands. The reappointment of General Fremont to another command after the emancipation imbroglio late in the summer of 1861 was the most obvious case in point. The arrest and imprisonment of General Stone for alleged disloyalty after Ball's Bluff was another indication of the committee's political power. Moreover, the investigations of light draught monitors, heavy ordnance, and ice contracts exposed no small measure of waste, inefficiency, and bureaucratic red tape. The committee's report on Union prisoners of war and the Fort Pillow massacre improved Northern morale. In any case, committee members may have been motivated by patriotic and humanitarian sentiments, as supporters suggested, but the question remains whether their noble aspirations were eclipsed by the shortcomings of individual committee members.[74]

In many respects, the committee was unable to come to terms with the realities of a civil war. On the issue of appointing commanding generals, the president stood firm and was not bullied by his congressional counterparts. When Lincoln removed General McClellan from command, he did so according to his schedule, not at the committee's insistence. Similarly, when the committee attempted to force the removal of General Meade, Lincoln would not accommodate the group until it suited his purposes to effect a change.

Perhaps the worst aspect of the committee's activities was its contribution to an atmosphere of jealousy and acrimony in the military and among the Northern population. Detractors later argued that the Radical Republicans who controlled the committee interfered with the Union's ability to wage war owing to the collective lack of military knowledge combined with an overly broad grant of congressional authority. Whatever else can be said about the Joint Committee on the Conduct of the War, it marked the ascendancy of the Radical Republicans on the national stage.[75]

The height of their power and influence was yet to come.

Chapter Three

"The Bondsman's Two Hundred and Fifty Years of Unrequited Toil Shall Be Sunk"

Emancipation was a major point of contention—perhaps *the* major point of contention—between Lincoln and the Jacobins during the first eighteen months of his presidency. It lurked beneath every discussion, every criticism, every exchange, however thinly disguised or oblique. Even the administration's supposedly incoherent wartime policies and the frustrations Congress and the president experienced in their dealings with McClellan and other military officers could be surmounted if the ultimate goal was accomplished. For the Radical wing of the president's party, eradicating the peculiar institution would justify the blood and treasure expended on the war. If Lincoln failed to emancipate the slaves, history would excoriate him for allowing a golden opportunity to pass without justifying the hardship and sacrifice endured by a free people.[1]

From the Radicals' perspective, the lumbering, overly cautious Lincoln stubbornly refused to see the light. The man seemed impervious to rational discourse on the question of slavery. As late as the summer of 1862, in public he still insisted that saving the Union was his sole objective in prosecuting the war. Despite his public remarks, however, Lincoln had not been blind to changes occurring in the republic as the war stretched on indefinitely, nor did he ignore the possibility that emancipation might be an effective wartime measure. As so often happened with the president, he trod carefully and mostly kept his own counsel.[2]

His initial lurch toward ending slavery came in the form of a plan for gradual emancipation in the border states. Lincoln also toyed with the idea of freeing slaves when they reached a certain age or compensating slave owners for willingly surrendering their property. Afterward, ex-slaves might be colonized in a foreign nation, perhaps in Haiti or somewhere in Africa or Latin America. All of these plans met with fierce resistance. Border state representatives doggedly defended the peculiar institution; emancipation in any form was out of the question. Radical Republicans vehemently rejected gradual emancipation. Almost no one, it seems, favored colonization. Most blacks who were asked to comment believed it was demeaning and dangerous to depart from the only home they had ever known, and abolitionists thought it betrayed the spirit of individual liberty so central to the American experience. Lincoln's quest to discover middle ground failed.[3]

Momentum built for the president to issue a broad emancipation edict as early as August 1861, when Congress passed the First Confiscation Act allowing the federal government to seize any property, including slaves, used by insurrectionists taking up arms against the Union. Although the act fell short of an emancipation proclamation—it allowed slaves to be seized only if their owners could be shown to have actively assisted the rebellion—it was a first step in a long process that would be the death knell of the peculiar institution.[4]

Another step occurred in April 1862 when Congress enacted a bill providing for compensated emancipation of slaves in the District of Columbia. Under the terms of the bill, each slaveholder in the district would receive $300 for each bondsman set free. Funds were allocated for colonization of the freedmen—provided they consented to the move. Unlike the controversy over whether the federal government possessed authority to free slaves in the states and territories, it was clear that Congress could emancipate slaves in an area under federal jurisdiction. Lincoln signed the measure into law on April 16. "I have never doubted the constitutional authority of Congress to abolish slavery in the district," he said, "and I have ever desired to see the national capital freed from the institution in some satisfactory way."[5]

The Radicals were pleased with their party leader for once, but their bonhomie did not last. A month later, General David Hunter, commander of the Department of the South, which encompassed the states of Georgia, Florida, and South Carolina, issued his own field-level emancipation edict. In General Order No. 11, promulgated on May 9, 1862, Hunter explained that martial law necessitated freeing slaves living in the district under his command. "The three States of Georgia, Florida and South Carolina, comprising the military department of the south, having deliberately declared themselves no longer under the protection of the United States of America, and having taken up arms against the said United States, it becomes a military necessity to declare them under martial law," he declared. "This was accordingly done on the 25th day of April, 1862. Slavery and martial law in a free country are altogether incompatible; the persons in these three States—Georgia, Florida, and South Carolina—heretofore held as slaves, are therefore declared forever free."[6]

Fearing that Lincoln would countermand the edict, exactly as he had done earlier with General Fremont's emancipation order, the Radicals lobbied the commander in chief to support Hunter's action. It was to no avail. On May 19, Lincoln rescinded the order. "No commanding general shall do such a thing, upon my responsibility, without consulting me," he told Secretary of the Treasury Salmon Chase. Although this was a setback for the Radicals, Lincoln left open the possibility of a similar action undertaken at his direction in the near future. The problem with Hunter's proclamation was not necessarily the proclamation itself, but that the general had exceeded his authority. Lincoln told border state representatives that the pressure for emancipation was growing and could not be postponed indefinitely. "You cannot if you would, be blind to the signs of the times," he said.[7]

The signs of the times moved in lockstep with changes in the fortunes of war. By mid-1862, most Americans realized the conflict was not going to be the quick affair everyone thought it would be in the heady days of 1861 before the debacles at Bull Run and Ball's Bluff destroyed the illusion of Northern invincibility. Congress signified changes in the war effort by enacting two new laws on the same day, July 17, 1862. The first measure, the Militia Act, was designed to draft three hundred thousand eligible soldiers. As part of the new law, Congress authorized the president to allow black men to join the Union army for "any war service for which they may be found competent." The problem was that black men were not deemed fit for combat. Their role was strictly limited to manual labor, presumably to free up whites so that men who had worked as laborers could be sent to the front. In recognition of the lower station afforded black soldiers, the statute allowed whites to receive higher pay than blacks for military service. For all of its inequities, the Militia Act recognized black men could perform a service in support of the Union cause; hence, it represented a step toward emancipation, albeit a barely perceptible movement.[8]

The other new law was more important than the Militia Act in advancing the cause of freedom for the enslaved. The Second Confiscation Act punished "traitors" who had taken up arms against the United States government by authorizing seizure of their slaves if the rebels did not surrender within sixty days of the enactment. To clarify the question of whether advancing Union armies were obligated to return slaves found in captured territory, the act declared that slaves who sought refuge behind Union lines were free. The president also was empowered to use blacks to assist in suppressing the insurrection.

The law was the brainchild of Illinois senator Lyman Trumbull and Massachusetts congressman Thomas Eliot, among others. Although Lincoln expressed misgivings about approving the measure, he ultimately did so, another sign of the changing times. He made it clear, however, that Congress must pass resolutions clarifying that the Confiscation Act did not allow for forfeiture of property beyond an individual's natural life and did not violate the Constitution's prohibition on *ex post facto* laws. After Congress complied with his requests, Lincoln was as good as his word, although some of the more aggressive Radicals, especially Ben Wade, were angry at the president's assertion of executive power over Congress.[9]

The act had been debated for months and still contained constitutionally suspect provisions. If the United States claimed to be a republican form of government, how could it justify seizing private property without instituting a judicial proceeding beforehand? The Fifth Amendment guaranteed just compensation when the federal government took private property. Although the act was designed to punish traitorous rebels who presumably had placed themselves beyond the protections of the Constitution when they voluntarily surrendered their membership in the Union, the growth of centralized power under this act could affect federal jurisdiction in other areas by extension. Moreover, it was not always an easy matter to identify who was a traitor and who was not, especially in border states torn apart by family feuds where one faction joined the Union and another aided the Confederacy.

Even as the Confiscation Act snaked its way through Congress, Lincoln mulled over the merits of an emancipation proclamation. It would require all of his considerable political skills to mollify competing factions within the North. On one hand, the conservatives obstinately refused to yield their position that freeing the slaves would prolong the war because it would stiffen Confederate resolve. If the cornerstone of Southern society was slavery, any attempt to remove such an integral feature of the Southern way of life would ensure a fight to the death. On the other hand, the Radicals insisted that the loss of runaway slaves and the decimation of the men and materiel of the South would hasten the end of the war. Confederates could not fight indefinitely if they faced a veritable army of former slaves armed and ready to support the Union cause.[10]

The first fissure in the president's façade of implacability on the slavery issue occurred in June 1862. On June 18, he dined with his vice president, Hannibal Hamlin, at the Soldier's Home, Lincoln's summer getaway from the hustle and bustle of the capital city. Hamlin was an amiable fellow and his relationship with Lincoln was pleasant, yet they were not close friends; the president seldom confided in his deputy. Vice President Hamlin counted himself in the Radical camp, although he was not as strident as Ben Wade or Thaddeus Stevens, the Jacobins' thunderous orators; nonetheless, this political affiliation ensured the president would always hold Hamlin at arm's length. By mid-June 1862, Lincoln recognized an advantage to sharing a secret with the amiable Radical—realizing, of course, that word would circulate through Jacobin circles. Much to Hamlin's surprise, the president intimated that he planned to issue an emancipation proclamation. Lincoln even produced a draft preliminary proclamation and read it to the startled vice president. After listening in shock, Hamlin recovered his composure enough to suggest several revisions. Some historians question whether the June revelation ever occurred or whether it was an apocryphal tale in the Hamlin family lore; nonetheless, the episode illustrates Lincoln's thinking during the summer of 1862.[11]

Lincoln's dinner with Hamlin supposedly was a momentous occasion, but it was hidden from public view. In his public pronouncements, he did not deviate from his standard rhetoric that his sole objective was to preserve the Union. Lincoln met with a group of Progressive Friends on June 20, two days after his discussion with Hamlin, and agreed that emancipation was a worthy goal, but he told them he could not proceed recklessly. The group left the Executive Mansion satisfied that the president sympathized with their position but frustrated with his lack of overt action and unaware he already was considering a radical departure from the status quo. During that same month, Lincoln assured his conservative and moderate friends that he anticipated undertaking no major initiatives in the foreseeable future. Perhaps in this assertion he was deliberately disingenuous, or perhaps he was still wrestling with the costs and benefits of freeing the slaves. In any case, the shrewd politician knew if he decided to move forward with this bold venture, he must unveil his proclamation at an opportune time, when all factions might be placated or at least neutralized.[12]

As the president mulled over the timing of a proclamation, pressure from all sides was unrelenting. During a visit to Harrison's Landing to monitor General McClellan's progress, Lincoln was surprised when Little Mac produced a memorandum on war objectives. Among the purposes outlined in the memorandum, McClellan unequivocally stated, "Military power should not be allowed to interfere with the relations of servitude." Once again, the impudent general had encroached on the political powers of the president. Lincoln read the missive without comment, but already he had moved beyond the limited initiatives that grounded his policies during the early days of the war. If the would-be Napoleon believed he had cause to detest his commander in chief in the past, he would soon find renewed grounds for disagreement.[13]

Conservatives such as McClellan feared Lincoln was moving too fast in undermining the peculiar institution; others feared he was not moving fast enough. Although the Radicals knew the president was evolving, they grew increasingly impatient with his lack of vigor. In July, they increased their pressure for a policy change. Senator Charles Sumner lobbied for a public announcement on July 4 to coincide with Independence Day celebrations. As fitting as such an announcement would have been, Lincoln resisted. The time was not yet ripe. Similarly, he resisted a call from Illinois governor Richard Yates a week later to emancipate slaves as a war measure.[14]

Border state representatives were another matter. During a July 12 meeting at the White House with a group of obdurate Unionist slaveholders, Lincoln explained that the momentum for emancipation was increasing. Referring to slavery, he said, "You prefer that the constitutional relation of the states to the nation shall be practically restored, without disturbance of the institution." In Lincoln's view, if he could accomplish the task of restoring the prewar Union, "my whole duty, in this respect, under the constitution, and my oath of office, would be performed." Because that goal had not been, and could not be, accomplished, a more revolutionary, far-reaching solution was necessary. If slave owners did not realize that a plan for compensated emancipation was the best deal they could get, "the institution in your states will be extinguished by mere friction and abrasion—by the mere incidents of war. It will be gone, and you will have nothing valuable in lieu of it." However clear this blunt assessment appears in retrospect, the representatives would not yield, pronouncing Lincoln's scheme a "radical change in our social system." They sent the president a manifesto the following day explaining their objections.[15]

With his last effort to forge a compromise rebuffed, Lincoln reached his decision. As was often the case, he moved slowly and deliberately, but once he decided on a course of action, he held steadfast to his position unless he could be convinced that reason or circumstances required a change. It was time to inform cabinet members about his new policy. On July 13, the same day he received the border state representatives' manifesto, he first broached the subject with Seward and Welles during a carriage ride to attend the funeral of one of Secretary of War Edwin Stanton's children. As Welles later recorded in his diary, the president described emancipation as "a military necessity absolutely essential for the salvation of the Union." In Lincoln's view, a president possessed emergency powers in wartime he could not exercise in times of peace and tranquility. In the normal course of events, a president could not free the slaves because a prohibition on the domestic slave trade had not been written into the U.S. Constitution. When he must suppress an insurrection, however, a president could take extraordinary steps to preserve the integrity of the nation—even if that meant using authority that otherwise would be denied him.[16]

Eight days later, Lincoln brought the full cabinet, minus the vacationing postmaster general, Montgomery Blair, to a special meeting where he explained that he was "profoundly concerned at the present state of affairs" and therefore "had determined to take some definitive steps in respect to military action and slavery." To that end, he read a series of orders he intended to issue demonstrating a more vigorous prosecution of the war. He asked the gentlemen to return the following day to discuss these matters in greater detail.[17]

On July 22 the cabinet reassembled, this time with Blair attending. Lincoln announced that he had decided to issue an emancipation proclamation. Anticipating objections from conservative cabinet members, he explained that he "had resolved upon this step, and had not called them together to ask their advice." He wanted feedback and suggestions for changing the wording or the manner in which he published the proclamation, but he would entertain no attempts to dissuade him from its issuance.[18]

Montgomery Blair cautioned that emancipation was controversial enough to undermine Republican support in the fall elections and could cost the party control of Congress. Although they were the minority party, the Democrats enjoyed substantial support in the North and had evolved into vocal critics of the Lincoln administration and an effective antiwar party. With increasing casualties and reversals on the battlefield, Lincoln and the Republicans watched public support for their position erode. Salmon Chase, a well-known Radical who had bitterly criticized the president for his lack of alacrity on the slavery issue, curiously blanched at the audacity of Lincoln's proposed proclamation. He suggested that perhaps generals in the field would be better positioned to implement emancipation measures. Although Chase's recommendation was not without merit, the only reasonable explanation for this surprisingly muted reaction was his possible candidacy for the presidency in 1864. If Lincoln issued an emancipation proclamation before the election season commenced, Chase's major platform—a radical change from the plodding, ineffectual leadership of Abraham Lincoln and a call for immediate emancipation—would collapse.[19]

Secretary of State Seward agreed that an emancipation proclamation was needed, but he fretted about the overseas reaction. Echoing Chase's position, he expressed concern that it would be difficult to implement an emancipation proclamation without leaving the particulars to the Union army. He suggested that Lincoln wait "until the eagle of victory takes his flight" so that the edict would not appear to be an act of desperation. A battlefield victory would show that the United States government was not "exhausted" and the proclamation was not "our last shriek, on the retreat," but a thoughtful, deliberate act performed by champions of a victorious republic. Lincoln later said he was struck with the practical force of Seward's last point. "The wisdom of the view of the Secretary of State struck me with very great force. It was an aspect of the case that, in all my thought upon the subject, I had entirely overlooked. The result was that I put the draft of the proclamation aside . . . waiting for a victory."[20]

He would have to wait two months; it was a dry, barren season for Union military successes. During this trying time, Lincoln again struggled to find the right battlefield commander even as Confederate generals Robert E. Lee and Thomas J. "Stonewall" Jackson emblazoned their names in the history books. While he waited, the president read through his draft proclamation, constantly "touching it up here and there, anxiously watching the progress of events."[21]

The progress of events was anything but promising as the administration faced assaults from all quarters by parties favoring emancipation and those opposing a federal edict. Conservatives, especially Democrats, sensing the increasingly incessant clarion call for radical change, repeatedly asked the president to hold off from exacerbating tensions with the South in the dark days of 1862. After battlefield losses that summer, marked departures from the status quo appeared not only unwise, but possibly catastrophic. If Lincoln transformed the war from an essentially conservative struggle to repair the Union into a revolutionary struggle to free blacks and radically alter the American way of life, he would pay dearly at the ballot box. Democratic candidates were already anticipating victory in the fall elections.[22]

The abolitionists and Radicals would entertain no more delay or hesitation. Having already received assurances that change was on the horizon, they pushed the president to get on with it. William Lloyd Garrison pronounced the administration's policies "stumbling, halting, prevaricating, irresolute." The great black abolitionist Frederick Douglass lamented Lincoln's weakness and inability to prevent himself from being used as "the miserable tool of traitors and rebels." During a meeting in Boston, John C. Fremont, the general officer whose field-level emancipation edict had caused Lincoln such headaches a year earlier, publicly called on the president to free the slaves immediately. No one, even the famously resolute Lincoln, could resist such pressure indefinitely.[23]

September 1862 proved to be a propitious time. The president found the justification he needed for emancipation following the battle of Antietam, although it was not the decisive victory he craved. General Robert E. Lee had invaded Maryland in an aggressive push to take the fight to the enemy, as he was wont to do. The ever-cautious McClellan, returned to command after the failure of other generals to prosecute the war with competence, benefited from dumb luck when he acquired a copy of Lee's battle plan ahead of time. Although Little Mac failed to take full advantage of his good fortune—he did not pursue the fleeing Southern forces despite battlefield advantages—he fought the legendary Confederate general to a tactical draw. Despite its inconclusive outcome, many observers deemed Antietam a strategic Union victory because it stopped the Confederate advance into Maryland and pushed Lee's forces back into Virginia. The Lincoln administration had achieved the success it needed for the president to announce the Emancipation Proclamation without appearing desperate. The irony of securing a victory at the hands of the woefully hesitant, supremely bigoted McClellan, thus allowing Lincoln to emancipate slaves in the rebellious states, was not lost on the president or his supporters.[24]

LINCOLN'S LAST WARNING.

"Now, if you don't come down, I'll cut the Tree *from under you*."

This illustration from the October 11, 1862, issue of *Harper's Weekly*, published shortly after Lincoln announced the preliminary Emancipation Proclamation, shows the transformation of the president's position from a year earlier, when he seemed willing to save the Union without affecting slavery.

Courtesy of the Library of Congress.

During a cabinet meeting on September 22, the president began with a reading from the humorist Artemus Ward before turning his attention to the serious business at hand. "I think the time has come," he said. "I wish it were a better time. I wish that we were in a better condition. The action of the army against the rebels has not been quite what I should have best liked." Nonetheless, he felt compelled to move forward. Explaining that he intended to issue the long-awaited proclamation after Lee's army had been driven from Maryland, the president read his revised version of the document and opened the floor for discussion. He made it clear he would not be dissuaded from proceeding with a public announcement of the measure. Seward suggested that Lincoln ensure the government "maintain" the freedom of former slaves rather than leave enforcement of the proclamation ambiguous. After discussing the point, Lincoln agreed.[25]

The preliminary proclamation did not contain the unequivocal call to action or the stirring antislavery rhetoric the Radicals would have preferred. It began with a reiteration of the original purpose of the war, which was "practically restoring the constitutional relation between the United States, and each of the states, and the people thereof." It noted that relations had been "suspended, or disturbed," but not decimated, even though blood had been shed. Having carefully outlined the essentially conservative nature of the Lincoln administration's prosecution of the war, the preliminary proclamation made it clear that the document was not a revolutionary usurpation of the Constitution nor designed to remake the United States of America. It was a war measure that would apply to all states in open rebellion on January 1, 1863. If by that time the rebels in those states had not returned to the fold, their slaves "shall be then, thenceforward, and forever free." Echoing Seward's advice, Lincoln wrote that "the executive government of the United States, including the military and naval authority thereof, will recognize and maintain the freedom of such persons, and will do no act or acts to repress such persons, or any of them, in any efforts they may make for their actual freedom."[26]

When Lincoln published the preliminary proclamation the following day, reaction was mixed. Supporters heralded it as a necessary step in the right direction. One of the president's earliest confidants, Vice President Hannibal Hamlin, predicted the document would "stand as the great act of the age," adding, "God bless you for the great and noble act." A crowd gathered at the White House to serenade the president, and from a window Lincoln told the well-wishers, "I can only trust in God I have made no mistake. It is now for the country and the world to pass judgment on it." Although not completely satisfied with the measure, William Lloyd Garrison recognized it as "an act of immense historic consequence." Frederick Douglass proclaimed, "We shout for joy that we live to record this righteous decree."[27]

Not surprisingly, conservatives, Democrats, and Southerners objected to Lincoln's bold attempt to "render eternal the hatred between the two sections." Although the proclamation was more conservative than it might have been, Northern Democrats argued that this radical departure from the American way of life would demoralize the army as men who had enlisted to fight for their nation were suddenly bleeding and dying in furtherance of "Negro sovereignty." Southerners compared the proclamation to Nat Turner's 1831 rebellion and suggested that Lincoln's incitement to slave insurrection would end the same way: in a violent, bloody race war.[28]

The British press had monitored the course of the sectional conflict and emancipation efforts since the assault on Fort Sumter had been reported. Many British opinion leaders and journalists took stock of Lincoln's proclamation and found it wanting, dismissing the document as a cynical attempt to avoid taking action against slavery in areas where the Federal army controlled the terrain. Because it applied in only the rebellious states and allowed loyal border state slaveholders to retain their property, Lincoln had issued a command affecting people and places where his dominion did not exist. Where he could effectively stop slavery, he did nothing. *Punch*, a British magazine of humor and satire, lambasted Lincoln's efforts with a ditty that included these mocking lines:

> From the Slaves of Southern rebels
> Thus I strike the chain:
> But the slaves of loyal owners
> Still shall slaves remain.
> If their owners like to wop 'em
> They to wop are masters;
> Or if they prefer to swap 'em
> Here are our shin-plasters![29]

The Illustrated London News was equally scathing in its analysis:

The tone of the proclamation, the circumstances under which it was issued, the conditions upon which it is to take effect, and the party views which it is understood to represent, compel us to regard this instrument as having been rather forged for war purposes than fashioned as a basis of national policy—as a weapon against the foes of the United States' government, rather than a frank but tardy exposition of what is just between man and man.[30]

Lincoln had deliberately written the preliminary proclamation in plain language, muting rhetorical flourishes that might evoke a hue and cry from critics. It was a wise move. When General McClellan, certainly one of the

This optimistic drawing (center) depicts the joys of family life after emancipation. Notice that a photograph of Lincoln, the Great Emancipator, hangs on the wall. The scenes to the left (an auction block and whippings) show the brutality of a life in bondage while the scenes at the right (a public school and freedmen drawing a paycheck for their work) express hope for a brighter future.

president's fiercest critics, learned of the document, he confided to his wife that he could not decide whether he would continue to fight under the banner of "servile insurrection." Another army officer, Fitz-John Porter, called it the "absurd proclamation of a political coward." As Montgomery Blair and others had warned, passions were inflamed, and Republicans suffered losses in the fall election, although not as large as feared. If Lincoln had seized on the preliminary proclamation as a forum for gloating or championing radical change, the backlash could have been worse.[31]

—⁂—

Although the war had yet to be won when Lincoln issued the Emancipation Proclamation, he was not satisfied to wait for military victory before he developed a blueprint for reconstructing the fractured Union. The president explored a variety of schemes and measures for addressing the race problem as part of his wartime reconstruction plan. Searching for a moderate approach, he continued to wrestle with the idea of colonizing freed blacks to foreign shores, yet few freedmen evinced a desire to flee their now-native land. Abolitionists decried the effort to discard human beings in so cavalier a fashion. Even whites who bore little affinity for former slaves were reluctant to see a cheap source of labor removed from the landscape. Aside from these philosophical objections, the logistics and expenses associated with colonization imposed almost insurmountable obstacles.[32]

Lincoln never came to terms with the lingering problems of race, but he turned to other reconstruction measures aside from colonization. In his annual message to Congress dated December 8, 1863—less than a year after the Emancipation Proclamation went into effect and approximately sixteen months before Confederate general Robert E. Lee surrendered his army—he unveiled a plan to grant general amnesty to all but the highest-ranking Confederate military and political leaders. As with many of the president's policies, he did not intend for the amnesty plan to be his final word on postwar reconstruction. Moreover, he did not expect Congress to enact legislation or the military to implement the plan without modification. He told his advisers and influential members of Congress that his goal was to initiate reconstruction as expeditiously as possible, but his proposal was merely a starting point; he was open to suggestions on achieving the objective.[33]

In this first tentative step at defining a policy for remaking the nation, Lincoln proposed lenient reconstruction terms: Southerners could rejoin the Union when they swore an oath of allegiance to the United States Constitution and the laws of the nation, including laws outlawing slavery. When the number of citizens affirming the oath in a given state equaled or exceeded 10 percent of the votes cast in the 1860 election, the entire state would be brought back into the Union and allowed to formulate a new government. The proposal was remarkable for its lack of punitive features as well as its low threshold for demonstrating allegiance to the Union. The one nonnegotiable condition was the requirement that Southerners recognize the end of slavery in the reconstructed Union. With this one absolute prerequisite, Lincoln sought to extend the Emancipation Proclamation beyond the exigencies of war.[34]

Lincoln's policy was remarkably forgiving of the South—too forgiving, in the eyes of many Republicans. Southerners had taken up arms against the federal government of the United States. The landscape was scarred; much blood had been shed. Property had been destroyed; the economy was in shambles. To allow traitorous ex-Confederates, many of whom seemed anything but reconstructed or repentant, to reenter the Union without paying a steep price was an open invitation to mischief. New Southern state governments composed of dastardly rebels would soon oppress former slaves and advocate resistance to federal policies. Slavery would be reinstituted in everything but name. If this terrible scenario happened, why had the war been fought?

The Radicals were pleased that the policy unequivocally destroyed the peculiar institution, but, as with so much of what Lincoln did while he occupied the executive office, the plan simply did not go far enough toward ensuring a more perfect Union. In the words of abolitionist Wendell Phillips, the policy's greatest deficiency was that it "frees the slaves and ignores the Negro." Any remaking of the Union without universal suffrage and equality before the law was a task only partially completed. The federal government must ensure that the South did not rise again and resume its former role as an impediment to human progress.[35]

Whatever its deficiencies, Lincoln's plan had its virtues. Language was important: "reconstructing" the Union was not tantamount to "repairing" or "restoring" the Union as it existed before the war. It was making a new Union, an improvement over the old model that had broken apart in 1861. With this modest beginning, details could be added as the plan was implemented.

For all of its leniency and conceptually simple terms and conditions, Lincoln's wartime reconstruction policy proved difficult to implement and enforce. As Federal troops occupied Louisiana, Arkansas, and Mississippi in 1864 and 1865, military officers administered the oath to captured rebels, only to discover widespread, albeit mostly passive, resistance. Captured Confederates faced few options apart from swearing allegiance to a government they did not support. The rebels raised their hands, swore the oath, and bided their time until Federal troops removed to other areas. If they could outlast their oppressors, Southerners believed they could carry on as before. Affirming their allegiance was not tantamount to living up to the oath.[36]

Recognizing this problem, the Radical Republicans proposed more stringent countermeasures. In July 1864, Lincoln's old nemesis, Senator Benjamin Wade of Ohio, along with Congressman Henry Winter Davis of Maryland, introduced H.R. 244, the Wade-Davis Bill, requiring a majority of a state's white males to pledge support for the U.S. Constitution before the state could be readmitted to the Union. Rather than relying on only 10 percent of the population to express allegiance to the United States, the bill was designed to ensure a much greater depth of support before providing former rebels with the benefit of the doubt regarding their good faith toward the Union. After an "ironclad oath" had been administered to at least 50 percent of a state's eligible white males, a state constitutional convention would be scheduled. Southern representatives at the convention would have to guarantee equality before the law as a prerequisite for readmission. Although the bill fell short of calling for Negro suffrage—even the Jacobins realized the time was not ripe and such a provision would engender too much controversy to implement successfully—it took steps in that direction. A crucial ingredient in the Radicals' recipe for reconstruction was that high-ranking Confederate military and civilian leaders were ineligible to swear an oath or participate in a state convention.[37]

Congress enacted H.R. 244 and presented it to Lincoln for his signature before adjourning for the summer. Realizing the bill was a rebuke from the Radicals who "have never been friendly to me," the president refused to sign the measure despite heavy lobbying by several key Jacobins. He was not acting petulantly, although he would be accused of it, nor did he find the bill repugnant. Instead, Lincoln wanted more time to implement and evaluate his wartime reconstruction plan before he agreed to harsh terms that would trigger fierce Southern resistance.[38]

The summer of 1864 was a difficult time for the administration, and no one knew it better than Lincoln. He would stand for reelection in the fall. Many public figures, including more than a few members of his own political party, preferred an alternate candidate. Vetoing the bill was politically risky, yet the president could not bring himself to sign it, either. After Congress adjourned, Lincoln employed the pocket veto, a rarely used presidential power that allowed him to ignore the bill, neither signing nor vetoing it. With Congress out of session, the bill died after ten days. He issued a proclamation explaining he would not object if a particular state adopted the Wade-Davis formula requiring a majority of citizens to pledge the ironclad oath, but he did not think it wise to require every state to adhere to that plan. Stating that he was "unprepared by a formal approval of this bill to be inflexibly committed to any single plan of restoration" as well as "unprepared to declare that the free State constitutions and governments already adopted and installed in Arkansas and Louisiana shall be set aside and held for naught," he was not bound to a specific course of action. Lincoln remained "prepared to give the Executive aid and assistance to any such people so soon as the military resistance to the United States shall have been suppressed in any such State and the people thereof shall have sufficiently returned to their obedience to the Constitution and the laws of the United States."[39]

The Radicals were outraged. The old man of the House of Representatives, Thaddeus Stevens, could not contain himself, nor did he try. "The idea of pocketing a bill & then issuing a proclamation as to how far he will conform to it is matched only by signing a bill and then sending out a veto," he wrote. "How little of the rights of war and the law of nations our President knows!" A month after Lincoln employed the pocket veto, Senator Wade and Congressman Davis issued a public "manifesto," stating, in part, "The President, by preventing this bill from becoming a law, holds the electoral votes of the Rebel States at the dictation of his personal ambition." Lambasting the president's "dictatorial usurpation of power," the incensed legislators charged that "a more studied outrage on the legislative authority of the people has never been perpetrated."[40]

Setting aside the vitriolic hyperbole, the Radicals raised a credible objection. Although the U.S. Constitution designates the president as the "commander in chief" during wartime, it imbues the Congress with authority to "declare war." The delineation of responsibility has never been exact, although clearly the Founders intended for both branches to share responsibility for wartime activities as a check and balance on the other. The Radicals believed that in rejecting the Wade-Davis Bill, Lincoln was circumventing the congressional role in making war by imposing his own brand of reconstruction on the nation without advising and consulting with the legislative branch. The manifesto made it clear the Radicals would not sit by and allow the president to act on his own initiative without risking his political future in the process.[41]

For his part, Lincoln contended that although Congress possessed authority to declare war, it was the president's prerogative, as head of the federal government's executive branch and as commander in chief of the armed forces, to execute the nation's war policies. Part of the execution included developing a plan for reconstructing a nation torn asunder. He knew before he rejected the bill that his action would be unpopular with the Radicals, but Lincoln was nonetheless stung by the criticism. "To be wounded in the house of one's friends is perhaps the most grievous affliction that can befall a man," he remarked to journalist Noah Brooks.[42]

Despite the angry sentiments expressed in the Wade-Davis Manifesto, the president and Congress were not insuperably divided on the terms of reconstruction. Lincoln repeatedly had demonstrated his willingness to compromise and promote flexible policies. Given enough time to work through a nuanced reconstruction plan, he might have come to an accommodation with the Radicals. Yet he did not. No one could have foreseen it as 1864 drew to a close, but time was growing short for the Lincoln presidency.

The administration did not suffer ignominious defeat in the election of 1864, although for much of that year it seemed probable that Lincoln would not win a second term. He initially faced dissent within his own ranks. Former treasury secretary Salmon P. Chase, a perennial presidential candidate, fervently sought the 1864 Republican nomination, and many Radicals favored him over the plodding, conservative Lincoln. The Radicals favored other candidates as well, including Benjamin Butler, a well-known lawyer and Union general and later a congressman, and General John C. Fremont, the Pathfinder of the West and a would-be emancipator. Union general Ulysses S. Grant occasionally garnered attention, but at this stage in his career he professed little interest in the presidency. In the end, Lincoln was simply too strong a candidate to be dislodged as his party's nominee. Always the shrewd politician, his middle approach ensured that the conservatives, the moderates, and the Radicals could not field a candidate with sufficiently broad support to seize the nomination from a wily incumbent, to say nothing of support heading into the fall general election.[43]

And so Lincoln again was the Republican presidential candidate. In November he faced none other than George B. McClellan, the Democratic Party's standard-bearer. After the president finally relieved him of command late in 1862, Little Mac felt ill served by the Lincoln administration. Indeed, his oft-expressed antipathy toward the president was well known throughout the country. With the public announcement of the Emancipation Proclamation, the general had lamented Lincoln's changing objectives for the war. "The preservation of our Union was the sole avowed object for which the war was commenced," he wrote in a public letter released in September 1864. For citizens frustrated by the ineptitude of the current administration, fearful of the Radicals' influence on Lincoln and the as-yet-unknown repercussions of emancipation at war's end, and desirous of attracting the soldier vote, McClellan presented an attractive alternative to the status quo.[44]

As with so much of Little Mac's career, the less one knew about him, the more appealing he appeared. Familiarity bred contempt. He simply did not possess Lincoln's innate political skills, nor was he able to unite his party in opposition to the administration. Aside from the challenges that always occur in confronting an incumbent president at the polls, McClellan's campaign commenced at a severe disadvantage. For all of the fissures and deep disagreements within the Republican Party, the Democrats were hardly a unified group. Many Democrats—especially the "peace at any price" wing derisively labeled "Copperheads"—believed the war to be an abject failure. In their view, negotiation was the only sensible recourse to conclude such a long, divisive, costly, bloody conflict—even if it meant the Union would not be restored and the Confederate States of America would continue to exist.[45]

When the Democrats adopted the Copperhead platform during the 1864 convention, McClellan was placed in a difficult position. He was not a Copperhead. In his September public letter, he confessed as much when he wrote, "I could not look in the face of my gallant comrades of the army and navy who have survived so many bloody battles, and tell them their labors and sacrifices of so many of our slain and wounded brethren have been in vain." With these words, he served notice that he opposed the peace plank of his party's platform. No doubt he sought the soldier's vote with this plaintive statement, but even in this effort he fell short of Lincoln's appeal.[46]

Conventional wisdom dictated that McClellan, as a former general officer who remained popular with the troops, would capture a large majority of the soldier vote. During his tenure in command, Little Mac had won cheers because he transformed a tattered group of men into a well-trained army and restored the pride and morale that were badly damaged after First Bull Run. Had the election been held in 1861 or 1862, conventional wisdom might have carried the day. By 1864, McClellan was no longer in command. Lincoln's steely resolve and his constant efforts to push the army toward victory won great praise from rank-and-file soldiers who longed for a Union victory to provide meaning for their sacrifices. Despite their earlier loyalty to, and high regard for, a revered commander, most soldiers recognized that a vote for McClellan was a vote for peace short of victory. Whatever personal regard soldiers may have felt for their former general officer, they agreed with Lincoln's campaign slogan, "Don't change horses in the middle of a stream."[47]

Lincoln won reelection in November 1864 by a comfortable margin—with 55 percent of the popular vote to 45 percent for McClellan—but it was not a rout. The vote total was 2.18 million to 1.81 million. In the Electoral College, however, Lincoln's dominance was impressive: 212 electoral votes compared with 21 electoral votes for McClellan.[48]

With the triumph of the Lincoln administration in the 1864 election, the war would be prosecuted to a fateful conclusion without compromise or retreat, and with no backtracking on emancipation. Almost four years of bloodshed had produced profound changes in the life of the nation and in the thinking of the nation's chief magistrate. The evolution of Lincoln's wartime aims was most notable in his second inaugural address, which he delivered on the steps of the U.S. Capitol on March 4, 1865:

On the occasion corresponding to this four years ago all thoughts were anxiously directed to an impending civil war. All dreaded it, all sought to avert it. While the inaugural address was being delivered from this place, devoted altogether to *saving* the Union without war, urgent agents were in the city seeking to *destroy* it without war—seeking to dissolve the Union and divide effects by negotiation. Both parties deprecated war, but one of them would *make* war rather than let the nation survive, and the other would *accept* war rather than let it perish, and the war came.[49]

With the war came a mighty tumult, a disruption of the social order, and a change in the objectives of the U.S. government. Before Fort Sumter, "the Government claimed no right to do more than to restrict the territorial enlargement" of slavery, but the rebels sought to "strengthen, perpetuate, and extend this interest," even if their actions "would rend the Union." Although the fighting and the objectives were not limited to a war over slavery, the peculiar institution was the major cause of the fighting, at least in many quarters. "One-eighth of the whole population were colored slaves, not distributed generally over the Union, but localized in the Southern part of it. These slaves constituted a peculiar and powerful interest. All knew that this interest was somehow the cause of the war."[50]

The war had been far too bloody, the sacrifices of blood and treasure far too great. Gone was the old Lincoln, the man who professed an interest in preserving the Union above all else; he had been replaced by a new figure, a righteous redeemer president who would do what he could so "the mighty scourge of war would speedily pass away." Gone was the president's careful movement toward the middle of the political spectrum; now he would make his way into uncharted territory, never ignoring conservative public opinion, but always leading a wary people toward a new life in a remade republic. If he was not quite a Radical or an abolitionist, the new man could not be called a conservative or even a moderate. He was transformed. Gone were the caution and the vacillation the Radicals had railed against in the early days of rebellion; the new approach was to use Federal troops to reconstruct the broken Union.[51]

Lincoln had never been an especially religious man, although he had always professed a belief in the Almighty. He found traditional, organized religion too dogmatic and ideological for his tastes, too focused on emotion and feelings at the expense of reason and judgment. Early in his career, Lincoln faced charges of atheism and faithlessness from his less scrupulous opponents. He attended church because his wife, Mary, pushed him to do so, but Lincoln kept his faith close to his heart, away from his public life and persona. Consequently, his religious feelings seldom permeated his speeches and writings except in an oblique fashion. In the closing months of the war, however, his public pronouncements changed. He began to speak and write of God and redemption. The war, he came to see, might be a price to be paid, a burden to be borne, for the sins of slavery. How strange it was to think God could support the slaveholder and the abolitionist alike, but who could know the inscrutable will of the Lord?[52]

One passage in his second inaugural address reflected the president's new approach to expressions of faith. He referred to Matthew 18:7 in describing the appeal for God's help from combatants on both sides. "It may seem strange that any men should dare to ask a just God's assistance in wringing their bread from the sweat of other men's faces, but let us judge not, that we be not judged," he said. It is little wonder that men are confused about the ways of the Lord, for "the Almighty has His own purposes. 'Woe unto the world because of offenses; for it must needs be that offenses come, but woe to that man by whom the offense cometh.'"[53]

The war between North and South had been transformed into a higher conflict, its purposes no longer limited to salvaging a perpetual Union from despoliation. If Lincoln had not traveled the long road to complete social equality that Radicals such as Thaddeus Stevens and Benjamin Wade desired, he had come most of the way. Unlike many of his ideologically rigid opponents, Lincoln did not claim to possess absolute truth or know in every instance the righteous course of action, but he recognized the distinct possibility that the struggle was a contest required by God:

> If we shall suppose that American slavery is one of those offenses which, in the providence of God, must needs come, but which, having continued through His appointed time, He now wills to remove, and that He gives to both North and South this terrible war as the woe due to those by whom the offense came, shall we discern therein any departure from those divine attributes which the believers in a living God always ascribe to Him? Fondly do we hope, fervently do we pray, that this mighty scourge of war may speedily pass away. Yet, if God wills that it continue until all the wealth piled by the bondsman's two hundred and fifty years of unrequited toil shall be sunk, and until every drop of blood drawn with the lash shall be paid by another drawn with the sword, as was said three thousand years ago, so still it must be said "the judgments of the Lord are true and righteous altogether."[54]

In one of the most often-quoted, eloquent expressions of the task ahead, Lincoln concluded the oration with a pledge to be resolute, yet merciful to both sides. He was remarkably generous to the South, refusing to condemn the rebels for what the Radicals repeatedly labeled "traitorous" behavior. Already some party zealots were calling for a war crimes tribunal and vengeance against the instigators of the conflict. When Lincoln later visited Richmond and heard a Union officer call for Confederate president Jefferson Davis to be hanged, the president responded, "Judge not, that ye be not judged." He expressed this same theme in the second inaugural address. Instead of casting blame and exacting retribution, the president emphasized the need to set aside rancor and division to mend the body politic:

> With malice toward none, with charity for all, with firmness in the right as God gives us to see the right, let us strive on to finish the work we are in, to bind up the nation's wounds, to care for him who shall have borne the battle and for his widow and his orphan, to do all which may achieve and cherish a just and lasting peace among ourselves and with all nations.[55]

History would have been markedly different had Lincoln lived to see the end of the war and the beginning of Reconstruction. It was not to be. On April 11, 1865, in what proved to be his last public appearance, Lincoln stood on the balcony of the White House and spoke to a crowd that had serenaded him the preceding evening. "Let us all join in doing the acts necessary to restoring the proper relations between these states and the Union," he said. He then spoke of his Reconstruction plan for Louisiana. Realizing the Radicals were still upset with his lenient program as well as his pocket veto of the Wade-Davis Bill in 1864, the president suggested he might compromise on the issue of universal manhood suffrage. He recognized the sacrifices of almost two hundred thousand black men who had donned the uniform of the Federal army when he intimated that "very intelligent blacks" might be allowed to vote. Compromise and flexibility, he told the polite but restrained throng, would be crucial to success.[56]

Unbeknownst to Lincoln, an angry young stage actor and Confederate sympathizer, John Wilkes Booth, milled about in the crowd that evening. An egomaniacal, unstable personality, Booth considered himself a fine specimen of a cultured manhood, a Southern gentleman of the first order. Lincoln, in contrast, was a brutish, coarse buffoon who had decimated the South and desecrated her noble ideals. When Lincoln mentioned the possibility of blacks voting, it was all too much for Booth's sensibilities to bear. He turned to a friend and uttered, in disgust, "That means nigger citizenship. Now, by God, I'll put him through. That is the last speech he will ever make."[57]

Booth was true to his word. He had been part of a long-simmering conspiracy to kidnap or possibly kill the president and other high-ranking federal officials as a patriotic service to the Southern Confederacy. It is possible the conspiracy might have dissolved, its goals never coming to fruition, but for Booth's insistence that Lincoln must pay for his sins in the wake of the April 11 speech. On Good Friday, April 14, 1865, the young actor ambushed the president as Lincoln watched a play, *Our American Cousin*, at Ford's Theatre in downtown Washington, D.C. Sneaking up behind his chair as Lincoln sat in the presidential box, Booth fired a bullet point-blank into the president's head. Afterward, the assassin leapt from the rostrum, dramatically proclaiming, "Sic semper tyrannis" ("thus ever to tyrants") before escaping through the back door. A grievously wounded Lincoln slumped in his chair until a group of onlookers carried his enormous frame across the street to a boarding house. He died at 7:22 the following morning, having never regained consciousness.[58]

This drawing, produced in 1865, depicts the apotheosis of Abraham Lincoln. He is welcomed into heaven and adorned with a crown of laurels by none other than George Washington. With his martyrdom, Lincoln ascended into the pantheon of hallowed American statesmen.

Courtesy of the Library of Congress.

The nation was stunned at the news of the president's dramatic death. It was a Greek tragedy sprung to life: On the eve of a mighty victory, Lincoln's life had been brutally snatched away by a vicious miscreant who probably had acted on orders from Jefferson Davis and his dastardly band of ruffians. Although a link between Booth and top Confederate leaders was never demonstrated, the timing of the Confederacy's collapse and the death of the president aroused suspicion among many Americans who saw nefarious plots lurking around every corner. It was little wonder the conspirators in Booth's plot—the so-called vindictive clique of villains—were dispatched to the gallows with unprecedented haste.[59]

From the instant of his death, Lincoln's image was transformed. He was no longer seen as a flesh-and-blood man, an imperfect, harried, occasionally vacillating leader who inched his way painfully, sometimes awkwardly, toward a military resolution of the largest crisis in the nation's history. He ascended to a higher plane in historical memory, becoming an American icon, larger than life, one of the "men of granite" carved onto numerous statues and monuments. A journalist observing the canonization of the dead leader presciently remarked that the assassination "has made it impossible to speak the truth of Abraham Lincoln hereafter."[60]

Looking back at the perilous journey from the opening salvos at Fort Sumter six weeks into the Lincoln administration to Lee's surrender at Appomattox Courthouse and the terrible assassination five days later, Americans gained a new appreciation for the slain president's strengths as a wartime commander in chief. He had navigated a middle course between conservatives who would have negotiated peace with the South at any price and radicals who sought to remake American society from whole cloth into an unrecognizable, alien nation. This man who so often had appeared to be adrift suddenly emerged as a true political genius, perhaps the only public figure of his age able to chart a course forward with flexibility and tenacity. As Secretary of War Edwin Stanton said on Lincoln's deathbed, "Now, he belongs to the ages." Former attorney general Edward Bates expressed the feelings of many who knew the president when he lamented the "calamity which the nation has sustained" and remembered "the mutual sentiments of respect and friendship" he had shared with Lincoln. "I mourn his fall, both for the country and for myself."[61]

The national outpouring of grief was overwhelming, unprecedented except possibly for the mourning that accompanied the death of George Washington. Yet Washington had not fallen victim to an assassin's bullet on the eve of his greatest triumph. Schools and businesses closed in honor of the dead president. Flags flew at half-mast until well into May. When the body was displayed in the East Room of the White House on April 18, an estimated twenty-five thousand people filed in to see their fallen hero one last time.

Some people in the crowd waited up to six hours for the honor. On April 21, the mortal remains of Abraham Lincoln were transferred to a private railcar for the 1,645-mile journey to a quiet piece of ground in Springfield, Illinois, designated as the final resting place for a favorite son of the Prairie State. Mourners lined the tracks for much of the trip.[62]

The famous American poet Walt Whitman was moved to write one of his best-known poems, "O Captain, My Captain," which opened with this stirring stanza:

> O Captain! my Captain! our fearful trip is done;
> The ship has weather'd every rack, the prize we sought is won;
> The port is near, the bells I hear, the people all exulting,
> While follow eyes the steady keel, the vessel grim and daring:
> But O heart! heart! heart!
> O the bleeding drops of red,
> Where on the deck my Captain lies,
> Fallen cold and dead.[63]

The Radicals were as shocked as anyone to learn of the events at Ford's Theatre. Radical congressman George W. Julian wrote to his wife, "Deep sorrow and revenge are almost universal feelings here, and I fear we are on the verge of a new & more terrible war than ever. Humanitarianism, I think, has met with a terrible shock." Even former treasury secretary Salmon P. Chase, whom Lincoln appointed chief justice of the U.S. Supreme Court the preceding year, was distraught when he learned of the murder. Never a strong supporter of a president he believed to be in every way his inferior, Chase could be expected to welcome a change in executive power despite the dramatic circumstances. Yet even he seemed saddened by the swift, savage sword of history. Inadvertently encountering his old enemy Montgomery Blair and Blair's father one day not long after the assassination, an ashen-faced Chase reportedly said, "Mr. Blair, I hope that from this day there will cease all anger & bitterness between us."[64]

When the shock subsided, however, it gave way to optimism among the Jacobins. They had been in the midst of yet another fight with their president when the assassin intervened. Much to the Radicals' consternation, Lincoln had authorized General Geoffrey Weitzel, commander of the Federal forces in Richmond, to permit the Virginia state legislature to convene. Bestowing the imprimatur of the United States government on a Confederate governing body seemed worse than misguided; it threatened to undermine all the country had struggled for, all that men had fought and died for through four long years of heartache and sacrifice. Although the president subsequently rescinded the order, such leniency did not portend a good working relationship between the executive and legislative branches.

With the rebels finally brought to their knees and victory within their grasp, the Radicals were worried that Lincoln had no stomach for punishing the South. His conciliatory words in the second inaugural address disturbed men who believed antebellum Southern culture must be dismantled—with the barrel of a gun if necessary. Extending a hand of friendship and allowing generous terms and conditions for reentering the Union were recipes for disaster. If society was to be remade and an America without slavery was to be realized, a clenched fist would be required. With Lincoln no longer on the scene, perhaps the fist could be wielded by someone less forgiving than this humble prairie lawyer who had ascended far beyond the scope of his talents and abilities. The Radicals could mourn the amiable fellow who had tried his best to do what was right, but now he was gone. It was time to get down to brass tacks and reconstruct a nation.[65]

A fresh start with a new president was exactly what the country needed to ensure the success of Reconstruction. The *New York Times* certainly thought so, reporting on April 17, two days after Lincoln's death, that "the country has a man of courage, of sound judgment and of patriotism which has stood the test of the most terrible trials." The newspaper was referring to Andrew Johnson, a former Jacksonian Democrat and military governor of Tennessee, who sat in the executive chair in Lincoln's stead. True to his contrarian nature, Johnson had been the only Southern senator to declare his support for the Union in the mad, reckless days of secessionist fever in 1860–1861. He also had proved to be a vocal opponent of the Southern charge toward a confederation government, displaying rare moral courage as he turned his back on the section that had nurtured him throughout his life.[66]

Originally appointed to serve as the military governor of eastern Tennessee, Johnson had earned a spot on the national ticket as Lincoln's running mate in the 1864 presidential election. Johnson had not been Lincoln's ideal choice, but the president had acquiesced in the selection when party leaders deigned to choose a Southern Democrat. It had seemed a matter of little consequence, for Lincoln expected his vice president to serve a negligible role in a second term. Thus did amiable Radical Republican Hannibal Hamlin exit stage left and Andy Johnson step into his shoes. The new man was scripted to be a bit player on the national stage, to assume a walk-on role as Lincoln both directed the action and starred in the production while Congress fought to secure a supporting role. The production did not go as planned. Fate had assigned a different role to Andrew Johnson than the minor part originally afforded him. The Tennessee Unionist was not an unknown quantity—he had served on the Joint Committee on the Conduct of the War—but no one knew how he would behave once he shouldered presidential responsibility.[67]

Despite an unpromising start to his executive branch career—he appeared drunk and incoherent when he was sworn in as vice president—Johnson initially made a favorable impression on the Radicals. He had been a target of the Lincoln assassins, but the villain assigned to murder the vice president failed to follow through with the crime. Stepping into his new position seemingly unfazed by his close brush with death, Johnson boldly proclaimed, "Robbery is a crime; rape is a crime; treason is a crime; and crime must be punished. The law provides for it; the courts are open. Treason must be made infamous and traitors punished." As vice president, he had sounded a similar refrain: "Since the world began, there has never been a rebellion of such gigantic proportions, so infamous in character, so diabolical in motive,

Andrew Johnson, pictured here, became president when Lincoln was assassinated in April 1865. Although his promises to punish the Confederates initially met with approval from the Radical Republicans, they came to regard the new president as an enemy.
Courtesy of the National Archives and Records Administration.

so entirely disregardful of the laws of civilized war. It has introduced the most savage mode of warfare ever practiced upon the earth." This muscular rhetoric was a refreshing departure from Lincoln's cautious, generous appeals to reason and mercy for the conquered rebels. The change in tone was music to Jacobin ears.[68]

In the first weeks of the new administration, the president appeared decisive and well suited to his new office. Johnson met with delegations of Radicals and progressives repeatedly. His increasingly tough talk suggested he would brook no dissent when it came to pursuing a firm Reconstruction policy. Ben Wade was an especially willing convert. "Mr. Johnson," he said, "I thank God that you are here. Lincoln had too much of the milk of human kindness to deal with these damned rebels. Now they will be dealt with according to their deserts."[69]

The new president's task was almost as daunting as the burden Lincoln had borne when he ascended to the Executive Mansion. April 1865 was a dark and dangerous time. Although Confederate armed forces surrendered during that month, no one yet knew whether the rebels would disassemble and take to the hills, intent on waging undeclared guerrilla warfare. If Jefferson Davis, Robert E. Lee, and other high-ranking Confederate civilian and military leaders were tried, convicted, and hanged for treason, the Southern reaction might be so bitter and hostile that the nation could never be reconstructed. Even if a nation could emerge, phoenixlike, from the ashes, it would be a long, arduous journey. The Southern states had been decimated by the war; their crops had been depleted and livestock slaughtered by the tens of thousands. The economy lay in ruins. The region's mighty cities resembled the crumbling magnificence of ancient Greco-Roman archaeological sites. Between one-fifth and one-quarter of the Southern white male population of fighting age had perished.[70]

Most challenging of all was the plight of the freedmen, those four million emancipated slaves who now found themselves unencumbered by physical shackles and restraints, yet facing an uncertain future filled with racism and hostility. How could a fractured nation absorb this group into a society that had little use for them? Although the Lincoln administration had focused most of its attention on prosecuting the war, the president had been cognizant of the need to provide for emancipated slaves. At the urging of the Radicals, on March 3, 1865, Congress had enacted a statute establishing the Bureau of Refugees, Freedmen, and Abandoned Lands, also known as the Freedmen's Bureau. Lincoln had eagerly signed the bill. The question facing the new president was how the measure would be implemented and enforced.[71]

Johnson's honeymoon was short lived. As the days and weeks elapsed, he hinted that his actions were not entirely in keeping with his words. Small cracks in the façade grew into fissures that promised a terrible cataclysm. When the Radicals pressed him to discharge Seward as secretary of state and replace him with the more radical Benjamin Butler, Johnson demurred. When they asked about his plans for trying and punishing former Confederate leaders, the president refused to answer their queries. Repeated requests for federal protection of the freedmen seemed to fall on deaf ears. Carl Schurz, a German-American general officer and journalist dispatched by the new president to assess conditions in the South, later reported that he feared the government was too intent on readmitting the former Confederate states without fully appreciating the risks to freedmen if firm guarantees of equality were not put into place. Senator Charles Sumner incessantly lobbied Johnson to ensure "justice to the colored race." For all their hopes that the new administration would prove amenable to remaking society, the Radicals simply had misjudged their man—as they eventually learned to their dismay.[72]

Andrew Johnson was a product of his times. He had been born in North Carolina and raised in Tennessee. He had defended the Union and preached against the evils of secession, but his political philosophy was far removed from the Radicals' position, despite his blustery promises about punishing the rebels. For men of his ilk, expansive federal power was to be feared and avoided if possible. His career before he served as the military governor of eastern Tennessee had been dedicated to limiting government authority. Although he was a nationalist when it came to opposing secession, Johnson was not a proponent of nationalistic policies that undermined state sovereignty.[73]

As for the Radicals' hope that he was "the sincere friend of the Negro," the president soon demonstrated the error of their assumptions. In their zeal to be freed from Lincoln's underlying conservatism, the Jacobins had imagined the new chief executive as a tabula rasa, a blank slate on which they could write a new chapter in this awful business with the rebellious states. They mistook Johnson's antipathy toward Southern slaveholders as a tacit agreement that blacks deserved equal treatment with whites, but ensuring equality of opportunity was never Andrew Johnson's objective.

The president viewed Southern society in terms of class first and race second. He opposed slaveholders because he believed they had controlled Southern society and used their wealth to dominate the nonslaveholding class of white yeomen farmers. Oblivious to the needs of the working classes, the rich planter aristocracy protected its own class at the exclusion of others. In this reading of history, the escalating sectional divide during the 1850s was a morality tale about what happens when the rich elite in a society feels its way of life threatened by outside forces. On the eve of the Civil War, the planter class manipulated the states to declare secession and thereafter convinced poor whites to lay down their lives on hundreds of battlefields to protect the peculiar institution. It was, in the words of that era, "a rich man's war but a poor man's fight."[74]

Despite his opposition to secession, Johnson shared the belief held by many Southern leaders that blacks were innately inferior to whites. Freedmen were not well suited for a world of unfettered capitalism because they possessed neither the native ability nor the disciplined tenacity to thrive in a world of free labor. Apart from engaging in backbreaking agricultural work, what was a former slave suited for in an entrepreneurial system? This perspective never considered the possibility that blacks had been denied educational opportunities across the span of U.S. history, thereby accounting for their relative dearth of intellectual achievements. Nor did it reflect the idea that slaves had never been industrious because their condition of servitude violated a major tenet of capitalism—namely, the sweat of their brow was the basis for the success of their masters and not themselves. For a man so immersed in the prejudices of his era, equality could never be the goal of the war. For Andrew Johnson, the Civil War was fought not to liberate the black man from a white master's yoke, but to restore the Union and liberate poor white yeomen from the rich planter elite's economic imperialism.[75]

The prejudices against blacks were especially devastating to the men of color who had served in the Union army. In many cases, they had sacrificed as much as their white brethren in uniform—and had been paid less money to do so—but they returned to a nation that did not appreciate their service. White Americans could not look beyond race to see the men who had fought, suffered injuries, and sometimes died to support the Union war effort. If the olive branch of peace was extended to white Southerners after Appomattox, what sort of offering would be extended to the black veteran?

The challenge facing black Union veterans was dramatically illustrated in a Thomas Nast cartoon that appeared in *Harper's Weekly* on August 5, 1865. Pointing to a black soldier, the allegorical figure of Columbia, a metaphorical representation of the nation, asks whether white Southerners can be integrated into American society "and not this man?" The Nast cartoon posed an intriguing question. The tragic answer would not be long in coming: blacks continued to face discrimination and hardships in a way that whites, regardless of their sectional affiliation, never would. In *Reforging the White Republic*, historian Eric J. Blum argues that with each passing year after the war—and especially after Reconstruction ended during the 1870s—American society witnessed the evolution of a new white republic as national leaders abandoned the promise of Reconstruction and justified their racial biases based on Protestant Christian values that supplanted the old North-South/slavery-abolitionist schism of the antebellum era. According to Blum, the United States after the war gradually "witnessed Northern white Protestants thoroughly embracing and propagating

This Thomas Nast cartoon from the August 5, 1865, issue of *Harper's Weekly* depicts the allegorical figure of Columbia gesturing sympathetically toward a wounded black soldier. In response to the question of whether she will extend the franchise to Southerners, she asks whether she should offer full citizenship to former Confederates "and not this man?"

an ethnic nationalism that privileged whiteness at the direct expense of the radical civic nationalism of the mid-1860s."[76]

The Jacobins presciently foresaw this movement away from full citizenship for all Americans regardless of race. The question in mid-1865 was whether they could count Andrew Johnson as friend or foe in the struggle to protect citizens of all races. Unfortunately for the Radicals' perspective, if the distinction between their views and Johnson's views was not visible at the outset, it soon became clear.

Throughout April and May 1865, signs began to emerge that Johnson and congressional Republicans did not see eye to eye. When the Joint Committee on the Conduct of the War issued its final reports in May, the authors called for a full-scale program of Negro aid and assistance to ensure the freedmen enjoyed full citizenship rights. In support of the report's conclusions, Radical Republicans inundated the president with letters and visits highlighting the need to implement Reconstruction programs to remake the South. They received a chilly reception. Unlike the politically adroit Lincoln, who occasionally compromised with the Radicals on key measures even when he did not agree, Johnson was temperamentally unable to accept the merits of his opponents' arguments or back away from his own fixed positions. When he made up his mind, Johnson was inflexible—and he had made up his mind on Reconstruction. He was determined to pursue a lenient Reconstruction policy in hopes of restoring the Union as quickly as possible with minimal civil unrest and political strife in the white community of the South. The new president could not be bothered to fret over the tribulations of the freedmen, a group whose problems he neither understood nor cared to understand.[77]

The first public break between the two forces occurred when Johnson issued a proclamation of amnesty on May 29, 1865. Much to the horror of the Jacobins, the measure called for a pardon of all but the highest-ranking Confederate leaders. The plan was even more lenient than Lincoln's 10 percent scheme that had so infuriated the Radicals during the war. Johnson went so far as to appoint pro-Southern provisional state governors to administer the former Confederate states. In the Radicals' view, the president was not engaged in "reconstruction," which implied a reworking of Southern state governments to improve on the deficiencies of an antiquated method of governance; he was "restoring" the old Union as it had existed before hostilities erupted. Numerous slogans of that era captured Johnson's position when they proclaimed the desire for the "Union as it was" and "This is a white man's government."[78]

Johnson's true feelings about the Radicals emerged in the months between the issuance of the May 29 proclamation and the opening of the next congressional session in December. In a letter he wrote to William L. Sharkey, Johnson's appointee as governor of Mississippi, the president assured his man the Radicals could be controlled by extending the franchise to "all persons of color who can read the Constitution of the United States in English and write their names," assuming they owned property worth at least $250. This requirement essentially disenfranchised all freedmen living in Mississippi in 1865, which, of course, was the point. By perpetuating this sham requirement, "you would completely disarm the adversary," Johnson advised. Neutralizing the Jacobins was the most effective way of implementing the president's Reconstruction plans. After erecting a façade of protection for the freedmen, "the radicals, who are wild upon negro franchise, will be completely foiled in their attempts to keep the Southern States from renewing their relations to the Union."[79]

The Radicals supported Johnson as long as they dared, but as the summer of 1865 turned to autumn, they realized a break was in the offing. Many Americans on both sides of the Mason-Dixon Line were weary of the war and its lingering effects. Now that the guns had fallen silent, most citizens wanted nothing more than to return to home and hearth. Johnson's desire to avoid contention and strife in the Southern states therefore received support among much of the populace, a sad fact that outraged the Radicals. The Thirteenth Amendment outlawing slavery had not yet been ratified. Blacks were denied equal opportunity as well as the franchise. If the federal government sought to remake American society, it must not squander this golden opportunity to act.

The Radicals knew then, as historians do now, that far-reaching changes in a nation seldom occur absent wrenching damage to the social fabric. A brief moment in the aftermath of a civil war might afford the president and Congress a chance to move the freedmen from a condition of bondage to a condition of free labor and equal political and civil rights, but the moment would soon recede into the mists of time.

As Congress readied to reconvene in December 1865, the Radicals resolved to push Andrew Johnson into immediate action. If he would not act, they would wrest control over Reconstruction policy from his hands and act in his stead. And if he stood in their way, they would unleash a mighty torrent. Woe to the accidental president should he find himself at odds with the righteous Jacobins.[80]

Chapter Four

"An Ungrateful, Despicable, Besotted Traitorous Man—An Incubus"

The confrontation between President Andrew Johnson and the Radical Republicans in Congress over the course and direction of federal Reconstruction policy has been told many times. Often the tale is presented as an inevitable clash of two opposing forces, reflecting the inherent tension between executive and legislative power in the American political system. Aside from the question of whether a clash between the president and Congress is ever inevitable, the standard portrayal is more or less accurate. Yet such a sterile description ignores the high drama that occurred as the nation's chief magistrate and its principal legislators quarreled over the direction of federal policy. The tragedy is that no one was willing to compromise. Had either side been willing to bargain and negotiate in a spirit of good faith, as Lincoln had demonstrated on innumerable occasions, the outcome might have been far more advantageous to the country, to say nothing of the freedmen who ultimately suffered the ignominious effects of white supremacy and, later, segregation. The intractability and self-righteousness of Johnson and his opponents serve as object lessons on governmental failure and the devastating legacy of poor leadership.

The relationship between President Johnson and congressional leaders in the Republican Party started with much promise but deteriorated throughout the summer and fall of 1865. The president initially held an advantage because he was in office and the Congress was not scheduled to convene until the end of the year. Consequently, he was able to assert his leadership owing to a vacuum of congressional leadership. By the time the Thirty-Ninth Congress convened in December 1865, much of the early work of Reconstruction policy was already in progress. All former states of the Southern Confederacy had complied with Johnson's requirement that they hold state conventions to repudiate Confederate debts, revoke their ordinances of secession, and renounce the peculiar institution of slavery prior to being readmitted to the Union. Eight states were operating reconstructed state governments, and seven Southern states had ratified the Thirteenth Amendment outlawing slavery.[1]

The president's plan to reconstruct the Union, insofar as it rejected the vestiges of slavery that existed in Southern state governments, was not objectionable, but Johnson's rush to restore self-rule was anathema to the Radicals. If the federal government did not carefully provide safeguards to prevent a return to the antebellum status quo, congressional leaders feared the war would have been fought in vain. The freedmen would find themselves trapped in a destructive cycle of poverty, inequality, and racism, all justified in the name of restoring a white man's government. This view of conditions in the Southern states in time would prove to be prescient, but before whites could seize control of state governments, the Radicals fought in the halls of Congress to block the ascendancy of the prewar planter elite and their progeny.[2]

Congressional leaders had formidable legislative tools at their command. Each house of Congress could decide whether it would seat representatives from the offending states and, if so, what preconditions would apply. The Radicals had met in caucus before the opening session of the Thirty-Ninth Congress and developed a strategy for excluding representatives of the Southern states. The clerk of the U.S. House of Representatives—in this case, Edward McPherson, a close friend of Radical Thaddeus Stevens—typically called the roll at the beginning of a new Congress. Generally it was a perfunctory exercise, but not so in 1865. During the roll call before a large crowd of spectators stuffed into the galleries to witness the historic reunion of the states on December 4, McPherson refused to call the names of representatives from the seceded states, a demonstration of congressional brass tacks that was immediately apparent to all. The choreographed pageant was planned in advance, and it achieved the desired effect. When Howard Maynard, a loyal representative from Tennessee, realized his name had been omitted, he leapt to his feet and cried out that he should be included. McPherson did not acknowledge his presence. Maynard's frustration was palpable as he asked, "Does the clerk decline to hear me?"

New York Democrat James Brooks, the House minority leader, entered the fray, objecting to Maynard's exclusion as well. "If Tennessee is not in the Union and has not been in the Union, and is not a loyal state, and the people of Tennessee are aliens and foreigners to the Union," he exclaimed, "by what right does the President of the United States usurp a place in the White House?" When the clerk still would not answer, Brooks pressed the point. "I wish to know when the matter of admitting Southern members will be taken up." Thaddeus Stevens finally spoke. "I have no objections to answering the gentleman. I will press the matter at the proper time." According to some accounts, Stevens also bellowed, "The State of Tennessee is not known to this House nor to Congress."[3]

The first order of business after this exchange was to reelect Schuyler Colfax of Indiana as Speaker of the House. An outspoken Republican who favored harsh reprisals against the traitorous South, Speaker Colfax set forth his agenda at the outset. He explained that he sought to create "a Republican form of government and put the Rebel states anew on such a basis of enduring justice as to guarantee every safeguard and protection to the loyal people." Afterward, the House quickly moved to approve a resolution offered by Congressman Stevens to create a Joint Committee of Fifteen on Reconstruction. The resolution stated: "*Resolved by the House of Representatives*, (the Senate concurring,) That a joint committee of fifteen members shall be appointed, nine of whom shall be members of the House and six members of the Senate, who shall inquire into the condition of the States which formed the so-called confederate States of America, and report whether they, or any of them, are entitled to be represented in either House of Congress, with leave to report at any time by bill or otherwise." Two months later, the House adopted a second resolution: "*Be it resolved by the House of Representatives*, (the Senate concurring,) That in order to close agitation upon a question which seems likely to disturb the action of the Government, as well as to quiet the uncertainty which is agitating the minds of the people of the eleven States which have been declared to be in insurrection, no Senator or Representative shall be admitted into either branch of Congress from any of said States until Congress shall have declared such State entitled to such representation."[4]

With the passage of these resolutions, the Joint Committee of Fifteen on Reconstruction was created to lead congressional efforts to control Reconstruction policy and prevent President Johnson from allowing the rebels to assume control of their Southern state governments prematurely. The committee operated during the Thirty-Ninth Congress before expiring in 1867. During its tenure, the group investigated and heard testimony on conditions in the "late insurrectionary states," often opposing the president's lenient Reconstruction plans. Senator William Pitt Fessenden of Maine served as the committee chairman. James W. Grimes of Iowa, Ira Harris of New York, Jacob M. Howard of Michigan, Reverdy Johnson of Maryland, and George H. Williams of Oregon also served. In the House, eight congressmen in addition to Thaddeus Stevens joined the committee: John A. Bingham of Ohio, Henry T. Blow of Missouri, George S. Boutwell of Massachusetts, Roscoe Conkling of New York, Henry Grider of Kentucky, Justin S. Morrill of Vermont, Andrew J. Rogers of New Jersey, and Elihu B. Washburne of Illinois.[5]

The looming confrontation between the president and Congress in December 1865 was based on fundamental differences in governing philosophy.

Johnson believed he was following Lincoln's precedent when he retained control for establishing federal Reconstruction policies. In his view, the paramount consideration was restoring law and order at virtually any price, even if it meant allowing unrepentant ex-Confederates to resurrect the old style of governance absent the peculiar institution. As he stated in his first annual message to Congress, which he sent to Capitol Hill on December 5, the federal government could not treat the former states of the Southern Confederacy as conquered provinces. If the insurrection had not actually established a new government but was merely a temporary condition of rebellion, as Lincoln repeatedly had argued, the restoration of the Union required minimal disruption to the organs of government. The president already had appointed provisional governments; state conventions had been called; governors and legislators had been elected in the Southern states. A wholesale change in the methods by which state governments interacted with the federal government was inappropriate and unconstitutional. After the offending states ratified the Thirteenth Amendment, the Union would exist as it had operated before the late unpleasantness, save for the institution of slavery. When the amendment eventually was ratified, the federal government would have taken the last step "and thereby complete[d] the work of restoration."[6]

If Johnson ever considered the possibility, indeed, the probability, that restoration of white Southern rule would lead to mischief and abuses almost as inequitable and brutal as those that occurred under the antebellum system of slavery, apparently he was not bothered by it. Several generations of pro-Southern historians of Reconstruction—the so-called Dunning School, named for the Columbia University historian William Archibald Dunning— have supported Johnson's approach, lamenting the failure of presidential Reconstruction and the ascendancy of the Radicals after 1865. Supporters of Professor Dunning argued that the Radicals and their political supporters, in opposing President Johnson's lenient Reconstruction policies, granted license to all manner of corruption and misrule perpetrated by meddling outsiders who neither understood nor sympathized with Southerners facing the almost impossible task of self-governance in a region decimated by war and overrun by lawless, marauding freedmen. In his book *Redemption: The Last Battle of the Civil War*, Nicholas Lemann observes that Dunning and his adherents viewed congressional Reconstruction as "a nightmarish mistake whose horrors exceeded those of the Civil War."[7]

Most modern historians have embraced a strikingly different assessment of presidential Reconstruction than the pro-Johnson view propounded by the Dunning School. Aside from the cruelties practiced against the freedmen under the president's lenient plan, as a philosophical matter Johnson failed to appreciate how his constitutional position differed from that of his predecessor. Because he served during wartime, Lincoln claimed extraordinary presidential powers. After the Confederates surrendered in April 1865, the insurrection collapsed and the president's extraordinary powers were no longer justified. If Johnson had recognized this fundamental change in his position, he might have called Congress into a special session soon after he became president. The seven months during which he developed his policies without consulting with high-ranking members of Congress fostered bitterness and resentment, especially among the Radicals, who came to see the new chief executive's leniency toward the South as infinitely worse than Lincoln's policies had ever been. The Radicals were incensed that Johnson sought to present them with a *fait accompli*. Between the time he became president in April and the opening of the Thirty-Ninth Congress in December, Johnson had moved to marginalize the legislative branch. For all of his numerous faults and infernal hesitation, at least Lincoln had listened to Congress and consulted with them upon occasion.[8]

The battle over the Freedmen's Bureau became a litmus test to differentiate between proponents of presidential Reconstruction and congressional Reconstruction. President Lincoln originally signed the bill establishing the Bureau of Refugees, Freedmen, and Abandoned Lands, also known as the Freedmen's Bureau, in March 1865, but it fell to his successor to implement the measure. The bureau was the brainchild of congressmen and senators who had been struggling as far back as the spring of 1864 to plan for Union victory over the Confederacy. Congress debated several versions of a bill before settling on the measure adopted in 1865. From its inception, the final version ran afoul of critics who fretted over the precedent it created. Because it would apply specifically to freed slaves but not to whites left destitute by the war, detractors argued that it smacked of exactly the sort of racial biases it purported to correct. Moreover, because the bureau would be administered by the War Department after the war officially had ended, critics charged that the bill vested too much power in the hands of the military. The bureau also exercised judicial authority to resolve disputes over labor contracts, land transfers, and other matters involving the freedmen, which led to fears that the agency robbed the judiciary of its constitutionally mandated authority to try civil and criminal cases involving civilians.[9]

Arguably the most controversial provisions in the 1865 Freedmen's Bureau Act concerned the responsibility for allocating land that had been abandoned by fleeing Confederates or confiscated by victorious Union armies. Land-use provisions originally were not included in the bill's major stipulations. They were added in the conference report at the last minute in response to Union general William T. Sherman's Special Field Orders No. 15, issued on January 16, 1865, governing distribution of land from "the islands from Charleston, south, the abandoned rice fields along the rivers for thirty miles back from the sea, and the country bordering the St. Johns River, Florida." Because of the last-minute inclusion of these provisions, the legislative history was almost completely silent on the reasoning; consequently, the land-use plan raised more questions than it answered. The provisions were especially troubling because they allowed the agency only to provide for the use and enjoyment of the land for a period of three years. The act did not allow the bureau to provide clear title to land, which pleased no one. Supporters found the provision to be too weak to establish a free black yeomanry, and critics questioned the validity of the federal government's land confiscation in the first place.[10]

Administration of the Freedmen's Bureau fell to General Oliver O. Howard, a Maine native and graduate of Bowdoin College as well as the U.S. Mil-

General Oliver O. Howard became commissioner of the Freedmen's Bureau in 1865.
Courtesy of the Library of Congress.

itary Academy at West Point. Howard had enjoyed an up-and-down career as a general officer during the war, but his genuine concern for the plight of the freedmen had earned him accolades as the "Christian General." Despite his good intentions and administrative skills, Howard faced an almost impossible task. Assimilating into the fabric of society the newly emancipated slaves, almost all of whom could not read or write and most of whom had no experience working in a free labor system, was unprecedented in American history. Complicating this gargantuan assignment was the realization that Congress had appropriated no funds for the bureau's working, leaving it to General Howard to improvise as best he could. He initially drew personnel from the army to assist in establishing schools and negotiating labor contracts with former slave owners. When he learned of Howard's orders, General Sherman told his colleague, "I fear you have Hercules' task."[11]

The Freedmen's Bureau became a source of widespread controversy during its short life. The Radicals believed it did not possess the requisite legal authority and federal resources to trigger effective change in the lives of the freedmen, and conservatives charged the bureau was rife with cronyism, waste, abuse, and fraud. To some extent, both sides were correct. Whatever its shortcomings, during its brief tenure the bureau distributed twenty-two million rations to people of color who otherwise might have starved. It established forty-five hospitals and clinics to provide much-needed health care for approximately 148,000 former slaves who had suffered mightily at the hands of their masters. The bureau provided transportation for thirty-two thousand people searching for loved ones separated by war or forced sale as well as searching for employment someplace away from their old plantation homes of the antebellum era. More than 9,500 teachers eventually taught blacks to read and write. The bureau itself was responsible, at least in part, for establishing historically black colleges such as Fisk University in Tennessee, Atlanta University in Georgia, and the Hampton Institute in Virginia, among many others. General Howard himself later founded the university that would bear his name.[12]

On May 30, less than two months after he stepped into his new position, Howard announced he would divide former slave states into ten districts that would be administered by assistant Freedmen's Bureau commissioners. The assistant commissioners would be military officers of good standing, which presumably meant they would possess the necessary clout and force of personality to stand up for the freedmen in dangerous or awkward situations where the local citizenry was disinclined to look favorably on the freedmen's plight. Howard intended for the assistant commissioners to lend a helping hand to former slaves struggling to understand the benefits and burdens of life in a free market economy, but Southerners were far from sanguine about the presence of federal agents in their region. If freedmen saw the assistant commissioners as liberators, ex-Confederates viewed representatives of the bureau as little more than an army of occupation.[13]

Most assistant commissioners started out earnestly to administer their districts in an equitable manner. Colonel Eliphalet Whittlesey, a former school superintendent from Ohio who was placed in charge of the North Carolina Freedmen's Bureau, expressed the feelings held by many of his colleagues when he remarked that "the schoolhouse, the spelling book, and the Bible will be found better preservers of peace and good order than the revolver and the bowie knife."[14]

They were noble sentiments, and it was a noble experiment in social engineering unlike anything undertaken before in American history. Unfortunately for the newly emancipated slaves, the endeavor was long on rhetoric and short on a federal commitment of resources. Congress and bureau officials seriously misjudged how long it would take and how many resources would be required to eradicate the centuries of abuse, neglect, and prejudice the freedmen had suffered.

From the outset, additional personnel and funds were sorely lacking. Instead of handling broad, sweeping issues attendant to implementing a new system of free labor in the Southern states, bureau agents found themselves mired in small details, spending much of their time mediating labor disputes between plantation owners anxious to tie laborers to the land for another harvesting season and former slaves with few options but to submit to even the most egregious terms and conditions. With virtually no budget to establish schools for the freedmen and little chance of integrating black children into existing white schools, bureau agents often had to depend on local whites to establish schools, which meant few local resources or high-quality teachers would be available. When throngs of middle-class white women, many of them from New England, arrived to assist in teaching former slaves, they faced appalling treatment and poor conditions that challenged even the most gifted teachers. Forced to live with black families for little pay, ostracized by the white community, and in some cases facing physical danger, white schoolteachers seldom stayed in their positions more than a year or two.[15]

Most bureau agents were dedicated professionals who sought to fulfill their mandate as best they could despite the stark conditions and severe lack of resources they faced. In many cases, they lacked sufficient training and administrative skills to be effective. Sometimes the agents unwisely meddled in local politics and initiated a fierce white backlash. Occasionally, corrupt bureau employees used their positions to enrich themselves. Although the corruption was not as rampant as subsequent urban legends would suggest, enough abuse existed to taint the bureau's reputation in many Southern com-

This racist poster illustrates the anger and hostility that many whites felt toward the Freedmen's Bureau.
Courtesy of the Library of Congress.

munities already embittered over battlefield defeats and the emancipation of slaves. During the congressional debate over enacting the bill, Lazarus Powell, a former governor of Kentucky and U.S. senator known as a vocal critic of emancipation, had predicted that bureau agents would not be men of high quality. According to Powell, the only men who would accept employment under such onerous conditions would be "your broken-down politicians and your dilapidated preachers," men "who are too lazy to work and just a little too honest to steal."[16]

Powell's view of the stereotypical second- or third-rate bureau agent serving a corrupt federal agency was reflected in numerous tracts and posters that circulated throughout the South in 1865 and 1866. A typical example of the opprobrium that many whites felt toward the Freedmen's Bureau can be found on a racist poster protesting the 1866 Pennsylvania gubernatorial election. The poster urged its audience to support white supremacist candidate Hiester Clymer because, unlike his opponent, John W. Geary, he opposed the bureau. The poster explained that the agency's purpose was to "keep the Negro in idleness at the expense of the white man." Reflecting the tenor of the era, it depicted a black man lounging as white men labored in the distance. Despite his strenuous efforts to raise demagoguery to an art form, Clymer lost the election.[17]

Andrew Johnson shared white Southerners' distrust of the Freedmen's Bureau; he, too, feared that federal assistance to any group, no matter how much its members had been oppressed in years past, would encourage a life of indolence in opposition to a free labor ideology. The president's attitude meant the bureau never enjoyed the necessary federal imprimatur it needed to succeed. The agency fell victim to a vicious catch-22: The bureau was viewed as a tainted, failed vehicle for lifting up former slaves so that they could be assimilated into American society. Because it was deemed a failure, the Freedmen's Bureau was denied the resources required to achieve its goals. Absent these resources, the agency's abysmal record became a self-fulfilling prophecy.[18]

Even as the bureau struggled to answer its critics, it was clear by the dawn of 1866 that more help was necessary if former slaves were to have a chance at eking out even a meager existence. Accordingly, congressional Republicans introduced a measure to reauthorize the bureau. Lyman Trumbull's reauthorization bill drew almost universal Republican support even outside of the Radical camp. For that reason, no one expected the president to veto the measure, yet he did.[19]

Johnson justified his veto on constitutional grounds. In his veto message, he repeated the argument that because the bureau exercised authority as a judicial tribunal, it violated Article III of the U.S. Constitution, which vested judicial authority in the courts. In addition, a "system for the support of indigent persons was never contemplated by the authors of the Constitution; nor can any good reason be advanced why, as a permanent establishment, it should be founded for one class or color of our people more than another." The legislative history leading up to passage of the original Freedmen's Bureau Bill indicated that the agency was never intended to serve "as a permanent establishment," but Johnson believed the agency would become a permanent fixture despite assurances to the contrary. In his view, the existence of a federal agency designed to assist freed slaves threatened the traditional arrangement between the federal government and the states because it allowed the former to intercede impermissibly into the affairs of the latter. Moreover, in his explanation that the Constitution was not designed to protect "one class or color of our people more than another," he anticipated the "reverse discrimination" arguments of twentieth-century plaintiffs by more than a century.[20]

As surprising and infuriating as the veto was to congressional Republicans, worse was yet to come. If Johnson had attempted to smooth over relations with key congressional leaders after the veto of the Freedmen's Bureau Bill, he might have escaped the Radicals' full wrath. Yet the president seemed unwilling or incapable of avoiding confrontation, sometimes going out of his way to court controversy. In a speech he delivered on Washington's birthday in February 1866, he unwisely spewed out a vitriolic diatribe that came to be known as "the serenade," or Andrew Johnson's "fatal speech." The screed highlighted Johnson's poor skills as a politician and reflected badly on his character as a man engaged in public affairs. To all but the most obtuse Democrat, he appeared as petulant, bitter, and out of his depth. At one point during an especially turgid section of the speech—as the president presented a litany of self-pitying challenges he had endured during his ten months in office—he compared his suffering to the tribulations of Jesus Christ. "Who has suffered more than I have? I ask the question." Johnson was warming to his plaintive, self-indulgent rhetoric. "I shall not recount the wrongs and the sufferings inflicted on me. It is not the course to deal with a whole people in a spirit of revenge. . . . I have quite as much asperity, and perhaps as much resentment, as a man ought to have, but we must reason regarding man as he is, and must conform our action and our conduct to the example of him who founded our holy religion."[21]

The speech grew progressively worse as the president explained how many in Congress sought to undermine the Union as surely as the secessionists undermined it in previous years. "When the Government has succeeded, there is an attempt now to concentrate all power in the hands of a few at the federal head, and thereby bring about a consolidation of the Republic, which is equally objectionable with its dissolution." Johnson would not stand for this attack on the Constitution or the republic it created: "I am opposed to the Davises, The Toomses, the Slidells and the long list of such [i.e., representing the old slaveholding Southern interests]. But when I perceive on the other hand, men—I care not by what name you call them—still opposed to the Union, I am free to say to you that I am still with the people. I am still for the preservation of these States, for the preservation of the Union, and in favor of this great Government accomplishing its destiny."[22]

The crowd called out for the president to name the men who would destroy the Union as surely as the Southerners he had described. Instead of ignoring such entreaties, he answered the call. "The gentleman calls for three names," he said. "I am talking to my friends and fellow-citizens here. Suppose I should name to you those whom I look upon as being opposed to the fundamental principles of this Government, and as now laboring to destroy them. I say Thaddeus Stevens, of Pennsylvania; I say Charles Sumner, of Massachusetts; I say Wendell Phillips, of Massachusetts." It was all too much. Not only had the new president had the temerity to veto the Freedmen's Bureau Bill, a measure near and dear to Radical hearts, but he had publicly singled out three prominent men and proclaimed them dangerous to the health and success of the American regime. Johnson had thrown down the gauntlet. Wiser heads would have advised the president that the Radicals would never back down from a challenge, but wisdom was in short supply in the Executive Mansion early in 1866.[23]

If the president sought a challenge from the Congress, a challenge he would have. Apart from the well-known abolitionist Wendell Phillips, who did not hold elective office, the other two men Johnson mentioned in his diatribe were among the most gifted and astute legislators ever to serve in the United States Congress. They were not men to be insulted with impunity. By early 1866, Stevens, a congressman from Pennsylvania, physically deformed and weary from his long battles over the evils of slavery, was sliding into the twilight of his life. He would be dead in less than three years. Despite his flagging energy and the diminution of his mental and physical faculties, the man once described as "the Robespierre, Danton, and Marat" of the "Second American Revolution" remained a powerful member of Congress as chairman of the House Ways and Means Committee. "Old Thad," as he was sometimes called, believed former Confederates were so infected with racism and devoted to state rights that they could never be reconstructed. He had been aggravated by Abraham Lincoln's seemingly endless reservoir of patience and goodwill. Treating the rebels with kindness was not an effective strategy, for these wicked men of the South equated kindness with weakness. The path to genuine reconstruction required a boot heel, not the absurd policy of "with malice toward none, with charity for all." In Stevens's view, the best method for returning the Southern states to the Union was to try the Confederate leadership in courts of law and hang those offenders found guilty as traitors. Only by administering the former Confederate States of America as conquered provinces could the United States government make good on its promises to the freedmen and ensure a second secessionist movement did not emerge in coming years. Stevens famously remarked that the Reconstruction Congress must "revolutionize Southern institutions, habits, and manners. The foundations must be broken up and relaid, or all our blood and treasure have been spent in vain." It was little wonder that in the ensuing years and decades, white Southerners would denounce this unyielding champion of equal rights for the freedmen as one of the most dastardly characters to emerge from the Reconstruction era.[24]

Charles Sumner was Old Thad's equal when it came to espousing uncompromising views on reconstructing a new nation from the ashes of the antebellum epoch. Yet the chairman of the influential Senate Foreign Relations Committee was more polished and seemingly sophisticated than his colleague from the Keystone State. If Old Thad's first line of defense was his booming voice and irascible public persona, Sumner's special gift was his penchant for delivering magisterial speeches infused with sardonic oratorical flourishes. A longtime senator who relished the grand traditions and arcane procedural niceties of the upper house of the national legislature, he was a cantankerous, haughty, erudite figure who reveled in verbal repartee and delighted in frequent allusions to classical works of antiquity. A survivor of one of the worst acts of violence ever unleashed inside the halls of Congress, the learned senator from Massachusetts was a living legend. In May 1856, he delivered a long-winded harangue against South Carolina senator Andrew P. Butler, an ardent slavery apologist, denigrating the proud Southern man for supporting the offensive Fugitive Slave Act. Sumner's speech was littered with sexual innuendo—characterizing slavery as a harlot, hence Butler's mistress—and ridiculed the senator's speech impediment and growing infirmity. This incendiary rhetoric was hardly novel, for the houses of Congress reverberated with epithets hurled across the aisle between Northern and Southern representatives in the prewar era. What distinguished the May 1856 episode from other harsh exchanges were the ferocious, unrelenting nature of the verbal attack and the reaction of Congressman Preston Brooks of South Carolina, Butler's cousin. Enraged at the attack on his relative's good name as well as the honor of the state of South Carolina, the hot-tempered young congressman marched into the Senate chamber and confronted Sumner, who was seated at his desk.

"Mr. Sumner, I have read your speech twice over carefully. It is a libel on South Carolina, and Mr. Butler, who is a relative of mine," the congressman declared with barely controlled fury. In response, the senator glanced up at the impudent young man, but he did not have time to respond orally. Wielding a gold-handled cane as a weapon, Brooks gave in to his seething resentment and pummeled Sumner senseless while onlookers gaped at the unexpected scene of gratuitous violence. The seriously injured senator endured a lengthy period of convalescence and eventually returned to the Senate, but he never forgot the violence lurking beneath the Southern façade of gentility. The Charles Sumner who emerged from the war years recognized, as few of his generation could, the need to use an iron hand to force Southerners to accept federal control over Reconstruction.[25]

Messrs. Stevens and Sumner and the other Radicals in Congress wasted no time in marshaling their forces to override the presidential veto of the Freedmen's Bureau Bill. They fell short—the final vote was 30 to 18—but the narrow loss did not deter the president's determined foes. Three months later, Congress passed a similar measure, which Johnson vetoed as well. "I can see no reason for the establishment of the 'military jurisdiction' conferred upon the officials of the Bureau," he explained. This time, the Radicals were ready for him, and they mustered the necessary votes to override the presidential veto. The bureau limped on for several additional years, but the agency never fulfilled its original promise of ensuring fair treatment for newly emancipated slaves and their families.[26]

The battle over reauthorization of the Freedmen's Bureau Bill was not the end of the showdown between the president and Congress over the course of Reconstruction policy. In fact, it was just the beginning. The opening salvos had been fired, but the dispute erupted in full force over the Civil Rights Act of 1866. First set forth as a proposal by Massachusetts senator Henry Wilson in December 1865 "to maintain the freedom of the inhabitants in the States declared in insurrection by the proclamation of the President of the 1st of July 1862," the measure proposed to nullify any law enacted by a state that discriminated on the basis of race, thereby interfering with the civil rights or immunities of any citizen. Enforcement of such a discriminatory state law would be deemed a misdemeanor. Federal officials could not be sued for carrying out their duties unless such cases were removed to federal courts. The bill technically applied to any state in the Union, but in reality it was aimed at curbing abuses in states south of the Mason-Dixon Line. Because the bill antedated enactment of the Thirteenth Amendment outlawing slavery, Wilson's Senate colleague Charles Sumner described the proposal as a necessary step toward abolishing the peculiar institution once and for all in the United States.[27]

On January 5, 1866, Senator Lyman Trumbull formally introduced the Civil Rights Bill of 1866, a slightly modified version of Wilson's proposal. Following ratification of the Thirteenth Amendment on December 18, the Trumbull bill was designed to ensure that the new amendment was implemented effectively. As Trumbull described it, the new law would eliminate the "badge of servitude" that prevented the freedmen from enjoying rights of full citizenship. The terminology was important because the Thirteenth Amendment vested Congress with authority "to enforce this article by appropriate legislation." To that end, the bill defined the rights of American citizenship in no uncertain terms:

> Such citizens, of every race and color, and without regard to any previous condition of slavery or involuntary servitude, . . . shall have the same right in every state and territory in the United States, to make and enforce contracts, to sue, be parties, and give evidence, to inherit, purchase, lease, sell, hold, and convey real and personal property, and to full and equal benefit of all laws and proceedings for the security of person and property, as is enjoyed by white citizens, and shall be subject to like punishment, pains, and penalties, and to none other, any law, statute, ordinance, regulation, or custom to the contrary notwithstanding.[28]

Despite predictable grumblings from Democrats, the bill comfortably passed both houses of Congress. The margin was 33–12 in the Senate and 111–38 in the House of Representatives. As with the bill reauthorizing the Freedmen's Bureau, Johnson vetoed the measure.[29]

The Radicals joined forces with moderates and overrode the president's veto. Fearful that President Johnson would engage in further mischief, they also took additional steps to protect their gains. As a successor to the Joint Committee on the Conduct of the War, the Joint Committee on Reconstruction, created in December 1865, proposed a constitutional amendment to define national citizenship as "all persons born or naturalized in the United States," laying to rest the practice of counting former slaves as three-fifths of white citizens, as had been the case under the Constitution since it was drafted in 1787. Unlike ordinary legislation, which was subject to subsequent tinkering by a Congress that might shy away from its commitment to Reconstruction or succumb to the manipulations of an obstructionist president, a constitutional amendment, if proposed by two-thirds of the Congress and ratified by three-quarters of the states, would be more resistant to subsequent changes.[30]

The proposed amendment proved to be controversial from its first introduction. Republicans argued that an amendment must ensure that citizenship rights, and the protection of those rights, be included as part of the fundamental law of the land. Democrats resisted the interference of the federal government into the affairs of state governments. Victory on the battlefields of the Civil War already had expanded the power of the federal government. Must a new constitutional provision add insult to injury? As the representatives wrangled over the desirability and wording of an amendment, Thaddeus Stevens proposed the language of what would eventually become, with some modifications, the Fourteenth Amendment: "No state shall make or enforce any law which shall abridge the privileges or immunities of citizens of the United States; nor shall any State deprive any person of life, liberty, or property without due process of law; nor deny to any person within its jurisdiction the equal protection of the laws."[31]

As members of Congress debated the measure throughout the spring of 1866, the Radicals proved that despite their collective reputation for intransigence they could compromise when the issue was important and passage was not certain. Even Old Thad, never known for his willingness or ability to bend instead of break, agreed to changes to ameliorate what some Democrats deemed harsh language. Nonetheless, for all of the Republicans' newfound willingness to bargain and negotiate, Southern state officials were angered by what they viewed as the proposed amendment's punitive provisions. In barring pro-Confederate white leaders from holding elective office, the amendment violated Southern notions of a natural white aristocracy.[32]

Johnson was openly hostile to the proposed amendment, but he was severely weakened by his recent confrontations with Congress. Nonetheless, he needlessly threw himself into yet another fight with the Radicals. The proposal that would become the Fourteenth Amendment was hardly the only constitutional change debated that season, and the proposed amendment was not as "radical" as the detractors charged. In fact, it was but one of a flurry of moderate constitutional amendments introduced during the first half of 1866. One proposal repudiated Confederate debt. Another sought to reduce representation in the House of Representatives for any state that sought credit for the addition of newly emancipated slaves without also providing legal protections for the freedmen. These proposals were hardly injurious to the health and welfare of the republic; they represented basic changes for a winning party, the Republicans, anxious to enjoy the fruits of battlefield and electoral successes.[33]

A constitutional amendment did not require presidential approval, yet Johnson expressed his disdain for the amendment. In an open, irreparable break from the Radical camp, the president convened a gathering of his political supporters, the so-called National Union movement, in anticipation of the fall congressional elections. He was a man without a major constituency; only a small group appeared. He had alienated many in the Republican ranks, and most Democrats did not trust the Southern Unionist after he had campaigned as Lincoln's running mate in the 1864 presidential election. Johnson had inadvertently demonstrated how unpopular he was with virtually all factions within the nation.[34]

The congressional debate over the amendment finally culminated on June 13 with a 128–37 victory in the House of Representatives and a 22–11 Senate victory. Two days later, after the two chambers had reconciled variations in the language, the president reluctantly submitted the proposal to the states for ratification. The amendment reached the requisite two-thirds vote two years later, although New Jersey and Ohio attempted to rescind their respective ratifications. Despite these challenges, the Fourteenth Amendment became a part of the Constitution three years after the war, although the Southern states, with the exception of Tennessee, refused to ratify the amendment.[35]

Andrew Johnson was an angry man. In his usual self-pitying manner, he told a group of National Union supporters that "neither the taunts nor jeers of Congress, nor of the subsidized, calumniating press, can drive me from my purpose." To drum up support for his campaign to win support for his mild Reconstruction policies in the fall elections, Johnson embarked on a train tour from August 27 to September 15, 1866. The "swing around the circle"—that is, the effort to take his case to the people and circumvent his congressional opponents—earned its nickname because it moved from Washington, D.C., to New York, to Chicago, to St. Louis through the Ohio River valley, and back to the capital city. It started with great expectations and excitement. An energized president appeared to revel in his interactions with the crowd as he took his case to the people. Secretary of State William Seward and Secretary of the Navy Gideon Welles joined the tour, as did other dignitaries, including war heroes George A. Custer, David Farragut, and the ever-popular Ulysses S. Grant.[36]

The public relations campaign degenerated as hostile Republicans showed up in increasing numbers to jeer at Johnson during rallies. Rather than ignore barbs called out from the Republicans, the president traded insults with hecklers from the crowd, an unseemly exchange that horrified many onlookers, even his supporters, as unbecoming to a president. Informed that his conduct was undignified, the president snapped, "I don't care about my dignity." The remark was widely reported and contributed to a loss of presidential prestige when Johnson desperately needed all the help he could get to gain political support. In a subsequent analysis of the swing, Thaddeus Stevens sardonically commented that "the remarkable circus that traveled through the country . . . cut outside the circle and entered into street brawls with common blackguards." The *New York Tribune* called Johnson an "irritated demagogue."[37]

When the Thirty-Ninth Congress reconvened in December 1866, the problem of how the Southern states would be readmitted into the Union remained a vexing priority. The initial plan had been to welcome the states into the fold upon ratification of the Fourteenth Amendment, but clearly that scheme was unworkable in every Southern state save Tennessee. The Radicals stepped forward to offer a new program. Thaddeus Stevens proposed requiring the Southern states to hold a new convention to replace the Johnson conventions of the previous year. Negro suffrage would be the crucial feature of the conventions along with a prohibition on former Confederates' gaining citizenship for five years. Similarly, Congressman James Ashley offered a substitute plan to undermine all the mechanisms created by the Johnson administration. The proposals, not surprisingly, proved to be controversial; Democrats contended they treated white Southerners as subjugated peoples, hardly the sort of blueprint necessary to reconstruct a nation. After much argument and debate, the measures were referred to the Joint Committee on Reconstruction for further study.[38]

The new bill that emerged from the committee eventually became known as the first Reconstruction Act of 1867. That it remained punitive could not be denied. If the South as it was then constituted would not ratify the Fourteenth Amendment, state governments in the South would have to be reconstituted. The law divided the eleven former states of the Confederate States of America, except Tennessee, into five military districts under the command of a military officer charged with maintaining law and order and holding elections for constitutional conventions. After the new constitutions were developed, they could be submitted to Congress for approval. If a constitution was approved—and approval required ratification of the Fourteenth Amendment—the state could be restored to the Union at the discretion of Congress.[39]

President Johnson rightly viewed the bill as a repudiation of presidential Reconstruction. The preamble was especially offensive: "WHEREAS no legal State governments or adequate protection for life or property now exists in the rebel States of Virginia, North Carolina, South Carolina, Georgia, Mississippi, Alabama, Louisiana, Florida, Texas, and Arkansas," it began, "Be it enacted by the Senate and House of Representatives of the United States of America in Congress assembled, That said rebel States shall be divided into military districts and made subject to the military authority of the United States as hereinafter prescribed." The opening declaration flatly refused to recognize the legitimacy of the state governments the president had established before the Thirty-Ninth Congress convened. The power struggle between the theoretically coequal branches of government had begun in earnest, and the congressional Republicans were determined to win.[40]

Johnson saw the bill as an undisguised attack on the American system of federalism. Article V of the U.S. Constitution allows state legislators to decide whether they will ratify a constitutional amendment, but the Reconstruction Act coerced the Southern states into accepting the Fourteenth Amendment as a precondition for readmission into the Union. Section 5 of the Reconstruction Act read, in part: "When said State, by a vote of its legislature elected under said constitution, shall have adopted the amendment to the Constitution of the United States, proposed by the Thirty-ninth Congress, and known as article fourteen and when said article shall have become a part of the Constitution of the United States said State shall be declared entitled to representation in Congress, and senators and representatives shall be admitted therefrom on their taking the oath prescribed by law."[41]

New York *Evening Post* editor Charles Nordhoff later reported Johnson's angry reaction to the provisions shifting principal responsibility for protecting the freedmen from the executive branch to the legislative branch. According to Nordhoff, the president railed against any legislation that would mistreat white Southerners, who "were trodden under foot 'to protect niggers.'" Not only was Johnson hostile to the freedmen, but he contended that the bill was unconstitutional because it allowed the federal government, though the use of military power after the insurrection had been suppressed, to meddle in state affairs. As a matter of literal constitutional construction, he probably was correct but, once again, the president misjudged the tenor of the times as well as his standing with the Congress. On March 2, 1867, he vetoed the bill, as expected. Anticipating a repeat of the Freedmen's Bureau Bill defeat, congressional Republicans marshaled the necessary two-thirds majority to override the veto.[42]

The confrontation grew in intensity, for March 1867 was a busy month in the national legislature. Congress also enacted the Army Appropriations Act, which, among other things, retroactively validated the actions of Presidents Lincoln, Johnson, and their subordinate commanders for establishing military courts to handle civilian offenses. The measure was passed specifically to answer a U.S. Supreme Court case, *Ex Parte Milligan*, which deemed it unconstitutional to try citizens in military tribunals when civilian courts were still operating. To protect the federal government from citizen suits filed by angry white Southerners who had been subjected to military proceedings and wished to rely on the *Milligan* precedent for recompense, the Appropriations Act retroactively bestowed legal authority on prior executive actions that were, at best, constitutionally suspect.[43]

From Johnson's perspective, the Army Appropriations Act was doubly odious because it included a rider requiring the president to issue all orders to the U.S. military through the general of the army, in this case Ulysses S. Grant. The provision was designed to prevent Johnson from contacting his military governors in the South directly. If Grant could intercede between the president and pro-Confederate military governors, the Radicals might yet limit the damage inflicted by this recalcitrant little man who dared to frustrate Jacobin goals. In addition, the rider made it an impeachable offense for the president to remove, suspend, or relieve the general of the army absent U.S. Senate approval.[44]

Aside from enacting the Reconstruction Act and severely limiting executive power through the Army Appropriations Act, in March 1867 Congress enacted yet another statute to wrest control of Reconstruction from Johnson. Titled the Tenure of Office Act, the measure initiated a fundamental change in a president's relationship with his cabinet. Under Article II of the U.S. Constitution, a president must secure Senate approval to install a cabinet officer, but no such approval is expressly mentioned for a president to dismiss a cabinet officer. Presidents since the beginning of the republic had argued that because the Constitution did not specify Senate approval to remove cabinet officers, these officials must therefore serve at the pleasure of the president. If an executive is to be judged, at least in part, according to how well his administration performs, the president must retain authority to shape his administration as an inherent power of his office. The concern with requiring Senate approval to remove cabinet officers is that an emboldened Senate confronting a weakened executive, as was the case with Andrew Johnson, can force a president to retain officers who are ineffective or disloyal to the administration's core objectives.[45]

The Tenure of Office Act changed the fundamental relationship between the executive and Congress by requiring Senate approval for a president to remove an officer that required Senate approval to take the office. The first section of the measure read:

> That every person holding any civil office to which he has been appointed by and with the advice and consent of the Senate, and every person who shall hereafter be appointed to any such office . . . shall be entitled to hold such office until a successor shall have been in like manner appointed and duly qualified, except as herein otherwise provided: Provided, That the Secretaries of State, of the Treasury, of War, of the Navy, and of the Interior, the Postmaster-General, and the Attorney general, shall hold their offices respectively for and during the term of the President by whom they may have been appointed and for one month thereafter, subject to removal by and with the advice and consent of the Senate.

Fearing yet another congressional usurpation of executive prerogative, Johnson vetoed the Tenure of Office Act. In his view—and the view of many constitutional scholars in subsequent years—such a fundamental change in the U.S. Constitution required a constitutional amendment. Despite the logic of Johnson's position, the Radicals no longer afforded the president the benefit of the doubt when it came to shaping national affairs. They enacted the law despite the president's veto. In time, the Tenure of Office Act would come to haunt Johnson.[46]

In the meantime, the activist Congress still worked at a feverish pace to reconstruct the nation. On March 4, 1867, the day after the Thirty-Ninth Congress adjourned, the Fortieth Congress immediately convened to fine-tune the Reconstruction Act passed only days earlier. The new Congress considered a supplemental bill to provide more detail on implementing the first Reconstruction Act. Once again in opposition to the president, Congress enacted the second Reconstruction Act on March 23, 1867. Aimed at increasing voter rolls without regard to race, the second measure directed district commanders to register eligible voters as a prelude to electing delegates to the state constitutional convention. The success of these efforts depended on the diligence of the commanders and compliance by the local population. In some places, district commanders embraced the status quo and conveniently ignored illegalities. In other areas, they assumed an authoritarian manner befitting a victorious military conqueror. Whatever they did, the commanders were ensured of receiving criticism for acting in a fashion too lenient or too heavy-handed, depending on the predilections of their detractors. The latter requirement also presented a problem because local citizens were reluctant to cooperate with federal authorities.[47]

Within three months, Congress felt compelled to enact a third Reconstruction Act after Attorney General Henry Stanbery narrowly construed the first two Reconstruction acts. Anxious to ensure that no ambiguities existed about the meaning of the statutes, architects of the new law stated that "governments then existing in the rebel States of Virginia, North Carolina, South Carolina, Georgia, Mississippi, Alabama, Louisiana, Florida, Texas, and Arkansas were not legal State governments" and "were to be continued subject in all respects to the military commanders of the respective districts, and to the paramount authority of Congress."[48]

Section 2 of the third Reconstruction Act expressly empowered the commander of a military district, subject to the disapproval of the general of the U.S. Army, "to suspend or remove from office, or from the performance of official duties and the exercise of official powers, any officer or person holding or exercising, or professing to hold or exercise, any civil or military office or duty in such district under any power, election, appointment or authority derived from, or granted by, or claimed under, any so-called State or the government thereof, or any municipal or other division thereof . . . by the detail of some competent officer or soldier of the army, or by the appointment of some other person, to perform the same, and to fill vacancies occasioned by death, resignation, or otherwise."[49]

The president and the Congress had lost all semblances of cooperation and conciliation by this time. In his July 19, 1867, veto message, Johnson explained his latest objection to congressional Reconstruction, namely in the potential for abuse when military officers were vested with civilian authority. "A power that hitherto all the departments of the Federal Government, acting in concert or separately, have not dared to exercise is here attempted to be conferred on a subordinate military officer," Johnson explained. "To him, as a military officer of the Federal Government, is given the power, supported by a sufficient military force, 'to remove every civil officer of the State.' What next?" This blurring of military and civilian authority meant that "an officer or soldier of the Army is thus transformed into a civil officer. He may be made a governor, a legislator, or a judge." Despite these worrisome concerns about crucial constitutional distinctions, the Fortieth Congress overrode the veto and enacted the third Reconstruction Act.[50]

A final Reconstruction Act, passed in March 1868, specified that ratification of new state constitutions "shall be decided by a majority of the votes actually cast," as opposed to 50 percent of registered voters. This lowered threshold ensured that disaffected Southerners who stayed home from the polls would not retard progress toward Reconstruction in recalcitrant states. With this final measure, the Radicals succeeded in wresting much of the control of federal Reconstruction policy away from the president and depositing authority into the hands of a Congress determined to complete the work of remaking the republic.[51]

Yet even as the Radicals emerged ascendant, they blundered by over-reaching. Immutable philosophical principle yielded to temporary political expediency. So great was their distaste for Andrew Johnson, the Jacobins were oblivious to, or disinterested in, the deleterious effects their legislative onslaught wrought on the carefully constructed balance of power under the U.S. Constitution. As a result, a backlash against the Radicals occurred in parts of the North. Men of radical sensibilities had never been popular in the South, but as the 1867 election cycle loomed on the horizon, Republican congressional leaders became convenient targets for detractors who cried out for a return to a normal state of affairs. Continued agitation on Reconstruction frustrated even those Northerners who were not sympathetic to the Southern way of life. The war was over, and citizens longed to return to a less frenetic, less stressful existence. As long as Thaddeus Stevens, Charles Sumner, and their ilk harped on punishing the South and confronting the president, the wounds from the "Late Unpleasantness" refused to heal—or so a significant number of Northerners believed, judging by Democratic gains in state elections in California, Maine, and the Montana territory.[52]

To make matters worse for the Radicals, the intemperate Ben Wade won election as the president *pro tempore* of the U.S. Senate, a mostly honorary position except that it was highly visible and placed him next in line for the presidency should Johnson, who did not have a vice president, leave office before the end of his term. Never one to leave a radical thought unexpressed, Wade delivered a speech in Lawrence, Kansas—site of the violent struggles between antislavery and proslavery forces during the antebellum era of John Brown—promising that "another turn would be given to the screw" if the South failed to adhere to the Reconstruction acts. In that same speech, Wade likened conservatism to hypocrisy and the Radical position to righteousness. It was little wonder that Americans, North and South, who did not share the senator's radical sensibilities found his remarks more than a little off-putting and potentially dangerous.[53]

As early as January 1867, congressional Republicans introduced impeachment resolutions into the U.S. House of Representatives. The measures charged the president with abusing the authority afforded to him by the U.S. Constitution as well as tradition owing to his uses of the veto power, the pardon power, and the appointment power. Even Johnson's most vehement critics recognized these resolutions as partisan ploys designed to intimidate the president or at least influence the vigorous use of presidential prerogatives. When the Judiciary Committee finally recommended impeachment by a 5–4 vote in November 1867, Congressman James Ashley of Ohio explained the core argument leveled against the president was that he refused to work with Congress on developing and implementing Reconstruction policy. Johnson acted "in the interests of the great criminals who carried them into the rebellion, and in such a way as to deprive the people of the loyal States of all chances of indemnity for the past or security for the future, by pardoning their offences, restoring their lands, and hurrying them back—their hearts unrepentant, and their hands yet red with the blood of our people—into a condition where they could once more embarrass and defy, if not absolutely rule the government which they had vainly endeavored to destroy."[54]

Most of the long impeachment resolution focused on what its authors labeled Johnson's "usurpation of power," but which to the dispassionate eye examining the particulars with the clarity of hindsight can be thought of as a litany of political complaints. Even the most jaundiced Republican of the day was hard pressed to show genuine constitutional transgressions of the type envisioned by the Founders when they convened in Philadelphia eighty years earlier. Republican congressman James Wilson of Iowa, a Judiciary Committee member who vigorously dissented from the decision to move out of committee with the impeachment resolution, argued that "a bundle of generalities" did not meet the U.S. Constitution's standard for the "high crimes and misdemeanors" that must be demonstrated to convict a president and remove him from office. The "art of war" sometimes has been defined as "politics by other means"; the same might be said of the art of impeachment in 1867–1868. If the Radicals could not depose their nemesis through the normal channels of political give-and-take, they resolved to seek redress, as with war, by practicing politics by other means.[55]

Despite the zeal for removing an unpopular president, the initial impeachment movement stalled in December 1867 when the House voted against instituting further proceedings. As offensive as this president was to the Republicans, he had not yet taken actions that violated the Constitution's prohibition against engaging in "high crimes and misdemeanors." A prudent chief executive might have accepted this small, razor-thin victory as a clear warning that he should tread carefully in the immediate future, but a prudent chief executive was nowhere to be found. Indeed, for all of the wrangling between Johnson and the Radicals, an additional round of impeachment resolutions probably would not have succeeded had the president not played into the Republicans' hands early in 1868.[56]

The origins of the renewed conflict were predictable. Because he had ascended to the presidency upon the assassination of his predecessor, Johnson had not possessed the time or inclination to vet a new set of advisers; he had retained Lincoln's cabinet although they were not necessarily loyal to him. When it became clear that Secretary of War Edwin M. Stanton, a favorite of the Radicals, repeatedly had undermined the president's Reconstruction policies, Johnson suspended the cabinet secretary on August 12, 1867. The president appointed the ever-popular General Ulysses S. Grant to serve as the interim secretary. In a letter to the president after he learned of his suspension, Stanton grumbled that Johnson had exceeded his authority. Nonetheless, Stanton agreed to step aside—for now. "Under a sense of public duty I am compelled to deny your right under the Constitution and laws of the United States, without the advice and consent of the Senate and without legal cause, to suspend me from office as Secretary of War," he complained. "But inasmuch as the General Commanding the armies of the United States has been appointed *ad interim*, and has notified me that he has accepted the appointment, I have no alternative but to submit, under protest, to superior force." This was an audacious statement, implying, as it did, that Stanton would not have acquiesced in the suspension but for General Grant's willingness to serve as the interim secretary. An ominous, implicit message was delivered as well: if Johnson lost the support of the Union war hero, he could expect no small measure of dissension in the ranks of his own cabinet.[57]

Once again, the president had propelled himself headlong into a confrontation and emerged, if not unscathed, certainly undefeated. Yet he simply would not let the matter rest. He might have worked out an accommodation with his recalcitrant secretary and waited until a more opportune time to discard the offending appendage, but Johnson did not operate that way. He was not a patient man, nor did he care for the give-and-take necessary to appease his congressional critics the way his predecessor had so deftly handled detractors. The Tenure of Office Act now came back to haunt him with all its force and fury. After Johnson removed several military officers from their positions, thereby keeping alive his rupture with Republican legislators, Congress turned its attention to reviewing Secretary Stanton's suspension. With the Radicals leading the charge, the Senate refused to approve Stanton's removal as secretary of war. On January 13, 1868, the Senate voted 35 to 6 to retain the secretary in accordance with the terms of the Tenure of Office Act.[58]

Weakened as he was by recent imbroglios, Johnson should have accepted this rebuke stoically and lived to fight another day despite his opinion that the Tenure of Office Act would not pass constitutional muster. He might have sought vindication in a subsequent court ruling while isolating Stanton from important cabinet decisions, but history is populated with counterfactual ruminations. Not satisfied to back away from a confrontation, the president waded into the battle with his congressional opponents. With full knowledge that his actions would ignite a firestorm of additional criticism, on February

21, 1868, despite his advisers' stern warnings, Johnson sent a terse note to Stanton: "Sir: By virtue of the power and authority vested in me as President by the Constitution and laws of the United States, you are hereby removed from office as Secretary for the Department of War, and your functions as such will terminate upon the receipt of this communication." That same day, he appointed Major General Lorenzo Thomas to serve as secretary of war in an interim capacity after Johnson had experienced a falling out with General Grant. The affair resulted in a comic scene when Thomas confronted Stanton in the latter's office in the War Department and the two men argued over who legitimately served as secretary. After Stanton sent a message to members of Congress that he had been fired, the famously verbose Charles Sumner sent a one-word telegram advising Stanton not to vacate his office: "Stick."[59]

Despite the brief comic interlude, the incident was no laughing matter for anyone involved. The break with Grant, especially, was a propitious development; even the obstinate Johnson recognized its import. The general of the army held no love for his commander in chief but, ever the good soldier, he had obeyed orders and supported his boss because that is what good soldiers do. Over time, Grant's mild antipathy toward the president gradually had soured into something akin to outright disdain. The taciturn, obedient Grant normally kept his opinions to himself, but he had come to see the president as an abject failure, a small, petty, potentially unstable man unequal to the task of rebuilding the nation. As the two men openly quarreled, Johnson simply turned away from his former lieutenant, freezing him out of important meetings and decisions.[60]

Recognizing that a popular war hero was no longer in Johnson's corner, Stanton refused to accede to the president's order; instead, he barricaded himself inside the War Department. In the House of Representatives, the Grand Old Man of the Radical camp, Thaddeus Stevens, saw an opening to again oppose the awful jackal ensconced in the Executive Mansion. Old Thad was heard to bellow, "Didn't I tell you so? What good did your moderation do you? If you don't kill the beast, it will kill you." The most efficacious means of slaying the savage beast was to bring the most potent weapons to bear, in this case impeachment. On February 24, the House did exactly that, commencing impeachment proceedings on a straight party-line vote, 126 to 47.[61]

Leaders in the House of Representatives submitted eleven articles of impeachment, most of which took issue with Johnson's firing of Stanton and the installation of General Thomas as the interim secretary of war. Article 10 inveighed against the president's "inflammatory and scandalous harangues" against Congress. The last article summarized the accusations. The gist of the charges was succinctly captured in this pithy synopsis: "On Monday, February 24, 1868, the House of Representatives of the Congress of the United

States, resolved to impeach Andrew Johnson, President of the United States, of high crimes and misdemeanors, of which, the Senate was apprised and arrangements made for trial."[62]

This development heralded a sea change in American politics. No American president had ever been impeached, although Congress occasionally had threatened to institute such proceedings. Knowing that a trek down this path was fraught with unforeseen perils—not the least of which was the potential damage to the institutional structure of American government by using an unprecedented constitutional remedy in cases that were essentially partisan political disputes—most members of Congress throughout the years had wisely declined to invoke an extreme penalty for actions that fell short of genuinely egregious executive behavior. Article II, Section 4 of the U.S. Constitution requires that a president, vice president, "and all civil Officers of the United States, shall be removed from Office on Impeachment for, and Conviction of, Treason, Bribery, or other high crimes and Misdemeanors." The procedure is that the House of Representatives prepares the articles of impeachment and the Senate, presided over by the chief justice of the U.S. Supreme Court, "shall have the sole Power to try all Impeachments." The constitutional requirement for removing an offending federal official is daunting: two-thirds of the senators present must agree to remove the president from office. If two-thirds cannot agree to convict, the president is acquitted of the charges and remains in office for the duration of his term.[63]

No one on either side of the aisle doubted for a moment that the articles of impeachment were politically motivated, yet hatred for the accidental president was so great that some critics were not bothered by constitutional standards or the lack thereof. *New York Tribune* editor Horace Greeley, always an opportunist when it came to demonizing a vulnerable political opponent, dismissed Johnson as "an aching tooth in the national jaw, a screeching infant in a crowded lecture room." To no one's surprise, the Radicals wholeheartedly agreed, denouncing their presidential foe as "an ungrateful, despicable, besotted traitorous man—an incubus." General William T. Sherman, a man who essentially shared Johnson's narrow views on race, examined his chief's behavior and found it wanting. "He is like a General fighting without an army," he proclaimed.[64]

Seven congressmen—John A. Bingham, George S. Boutwell, Benjamin F. Butler, John A. Logan, Thaddeus Stevens, James F. Wilson, and Thomas Williams—served as impeachment managers to set forth the case against the president in the U.S. Senate. For once, President Johnson did something astute. He assembled a first-rate team of lawyers with extensive experience practicing law in the highest echelons: Henry Stanbery, who had been Johnson's attorney general until he resigned to handle the defense; former Su-

Seven congressmen served as managers of the impeachment case against President Andrew Johnson in 1868. Pictured here, seated from left to right: Benjamin F. Butler of Massachusetts; Thaddeus Stevens of Pennsylvania; Thomas Williams of Pennsylvania; and John A. Bingham of Ohio. Standing, from left to right: James F. Wilson of Iowa; George S. Boutwell of Massachusetts; and John A. Logan III, of Illinois.
Courtesy of the Library of Congress.

preme Court associate justice Benjamin R. Curtis, a dissenter in the infamous *Dred Scott v. Sanford* case; a future attorney general and secretary of state, William M. Evarts; and War Democrats William S. Groesbeck and Thomas A. R. Nelson.[65]

From the beginning, the House impeachment managers faced an arduous task. As much as the Radicals detested the president, it was difficult to fashion a legal case against a man whose greatest offense came in the political realm. Impeaching a chief executive is always a political as well as a legal issue, but in this case the questionable legal bases ensured the matter would be an especially partisan affair.

The opening remarks in the trial, delivered on March 30, fell to Congressman Butler. For all of his public renown, he was not an imposing figure. The former Union general had been execrated during the war as "Beast Butler" for his rough administration of New Orleans and his inflammatory remarks about the city's women as ladies of the evening. He was a passionate opponent of the president, but passion was insufficient to win the day. The cross-eyed, balding, mustachioed Massachusetts representative was once described as "short, broad-shouldered, short-legged, fat, without much neck, but with a good many flaps around the throat, standing as if a trifle bow-legged" as well as sporting "a great cranium of a shining pink color." Another commentator remarked: "Advocate, party-leader, warrior, apostle of an idea, representative; whatever part he essayed, he was at all times and above all the politician." Lacking in charisma or oratorical prowess, he would have to muddle through as best he could on the strength of his convictions.[66]

Worse than his appearance were the Beast's grueling, melodramatic attempts to articulate the president's impeachable offenses with the requisite particularity. Everyone knew he was straining to build a case. He did as well as he could with the shoddy material at his command, but it meant his three-hour opening tirade necessarily ranged over a wide array of complaints culminating in a general summary of Johnson's transgressions. The litany included outrage that the president's "attempt to get the control of the military force of the Government, by the seizing of the Department of War, was done in pursuance his general design if it were possible, to overthrow the Congress of the United States." Exactly how the president would accomplish his underhanded goals deliberately remained unclear, although apparently it required the legislators' acquiescence. "He asks you here, Senators, by your solemn adjudication, to confirm him in that right, to invest him with that power, to be used with the intents and for the purposes which he has already shown." To thwart the overzealous executive, Butler reminded his fellow legislators that "the responsibility is with you; the safeguards of the Constitution against usurpation are in your hands; and the hopes of free institutions wait upon your verdict." The fate of the republic now rested with the U.S. Senate. "The House of Representatives has done its duty. We have presented the facts in the constitutional manner; we have brought the criminal to your bar, and demand judgment at your hands for his so great crimes."[67]

Butler was forced to argue for a technical definition of "an impeachable crime" as "one in its nature or consequences subversive of some fundamental or essential principle of government, or highly prejudicial to the public interest." According to this perspective, Johnson's willful disregard for the Tenure of Office Act met this definition because it was "a violation of the Constitution, of law, of an official oath, or of duty." Relying on an amorphous, malleable understanding of an "impeachable crime," Butler sought to establish a pattern of "abuse of discretionary powers from improper motives, or for any improper purpose." The Beast was not known as a silver-tongued orator, but he was at the height of his histrionic powers this day as he compared Johnson's assault on the legislative branch with Oliver Cromwell's and Napoleon Bonaparte's efforts to engineer a *coup d'état* in their respective nations. Addressing his European counterparts, Butler praised impeachment proceedings as the ultimate safeguard against the machinations of a Cromwell or a Bonaparte: "While your king, Oh, Monarchist, if he becomes a buffoon, or a jester, or a tyrant, can only be displaced through revolution, bloodshed, and civil war," in the United States the rule of law dictates public policy. In this instance, the "rule of law" was a politically motivated impeachment proceeding.[68]

Building to a crescendo of purple prose, Butler concluded his spiel. "Never again, if Andrew Johnson go quit and free this day, can the people of this or any other country by constitutional checks or guards stay the usurpations of executive power. I speak, therefore, not the language of exaggeration, but the words of truth and soberness, that the future political welfare and liberties of all men hang trembling on the decision of the hour."[69]

Impeachment managers James F. Wilson and John A. Bingham followed Butler's opening statement by reading into the record the prosecution's initial evidence as well as the presidential oath of office and a letter Johnson had written explaining why he had removed Secretary Stanton from office. Bingham was especially effective in his role as the chief prosecutor. Generally characterized as a moderate, he had not been an advocate of impeachment. When Speaker of the House Schuyler Colfax appointed him to the team that would present the case to the Senate, the reluctant congressman tackled the chore with his usual tenacity. Bingham enjoyed a reputation as the "Cicero of the Senate" for oratorical skills in the grand tradition of Daniel Webster and the Great Triumvirate of the antebellum era; it was natural that he employ those skills in service of such an important proceeding. The one potential problem in his appointment was that Bingham detested "Beast" Butler. After initially refusing to serve as a prosecutor, he was finally persuaded to set aside his differences with the Massachusetts congressman in the interests of a higher good. Afterward, Bingham went on to play a prominent role in the floor action. If anyone could articulate the case against the president in a forthright, reasonable, eloquent manner, it was John A. Bingham.

The Cincinnati *Commercial* reported that the chief prosecutor read the impeachment articles on the Senate floor with "a firm, measured voice which penetrated to the remotest parts of the chamber." He also delivered the closing argument in the case. According to one commentator, Bingham "was well known as a clever and forcible speaker, overflowing with rhetorical phrases, patriotic appeals and the still warm rallying cries of war." Bingham used his "store of uproarious invective" to outline the case for impeachment as persuasively as anyone could.[70]

After four-and-a-half hours of listening to the case against the president, the senators adjourned for the day. If any drama was to be had in the affair, it was had that first day. Four hot, interminable days followed. The opening sessions had been somewhat exciting as the Senate undertook an unprecedented action against a sitting president of the United States. The gallery was packed with curious gawkers thrilled to be on hand for the beginning of a great historical adventure, but as the trial dragged on throughout the week while the prosecutors presented their evidence, often in mind-numbingly dull and excruciating detail, the spectators thinned out. Most of the interesting facts already had been printed in the daily newspapers, and the rest of the trial involved the drudgery of debating small, technical matters and complicated procedural questions. Disinterested observers recognized with each passing day that the case against the president was collapsing. Castigating an incompetent chief executive from the editorial pages of Republican newspapers, especially an executive as politically tone deaf as Andrew Johnson, was an easy feat; building a constitutional case for removal of that same chief executive by presenting credible evidence of high crimes and misdemeanors in the Senate chamber was a far more difficult task.[71]

The prosecutors watched with increasing dismay as their efforts imploded; they simply did not know how to rehabilitate the case. To make matters worse, the regal chief justice, Salmon P. Chase, for all of his well-known Radical proclivities, tightly controlled the impeachment managers, holding them to strict legalistic interpretations which, coupled with the president's appearance at a dinner party hosted by the chief justice at the outset of the trial, suggested that the impeachment trial had the makings of a debacle.[72]

Benjamin Curtis led for the defense, and he offered a compelling argument that because President Lincoln had appointed Stanton, Johnson was not obliged to retain the services of a counselor he had not chosen. Moreover, the Tenure of Office Act was unconstitutional. In testing its constitutional validity by removing Stanton, Johnson had not committed an impeachable offense. As he summarized the president's position, Curtis implored the senators to consider not simply the effect of the case on current affairs, but on the future of the American system of government. "It must be unnecessary for me to say anything concerning the importance of this case, not only now but in the future," he argued. "It must be apparent to everyone, in any way connected with or concerned in this trial, that this is and will be the most conspicuous instance which ever has been or can ever be expected to be found of American justice or American injustice."[73]

In addition to the inherent legal weaknesses of the case, the impeachment managers discovered that passions had cooled and the public's anger toward the president had faded. For his part, Johnson wisely assumed a low profile throughout the proceedings. In the months preceding impeachment he seemed to relish confrontation, but when the trial commenced he appeared properly chastened. His public face suggested indifference, but privately he fretted over his fate. Each evening at the conclusion of the session, Johnson sought news from William W. Warden, an aide who monitored the trial. "Well," the embattled chief executive would intone in a morbid ritual of quotidian angst, "what are the signs of the zodiac today?"[74]

His political fortune and private mood ebbed and flowed with the news of each day's events. Eventually, the defense team grew optimistic when they realized the tide was turning in their favor. The nation was becoming weary of the tedium of a Senate trial. As the sessions dragged on, the president proactively helped his case by publicly intimating that he would enforce the Reconstruction acts enacted by Congress despite his personal preferences. In agreeing to appoint a moderate, General John Schofield, to succeed Stanton as secretary of war, the president soothed fears that he had abandoned common sense and sound political judgment. No longer did he appear dangerous to moderates. He was hardly anyone's choice as a strong, effective president, but sentiments for driving him from the Executive Mansion before the end of his tenure disappeared.[75]

Even senators who railed against Johnson's policies reluctantly concluded that he was not guilty of impeachable offenses. Poor judgment and political ineptitude were not crimes. Senator William Pitt Fessenden of Maine remarked that if Johnson "were impeached for general cussedness," undoubtedly he would be removed from office, but "that is not the question to be heard." It weighed heavily on senators on both sides of the aisle that if they removed Johnson from office, he had no vice president to succeed him. The presidency would fall to Benjamin Wade, president *pro tempore* of the Senate. For virtually everyone save the Radicals, Wade was as objectionable as Johnson. Many senators also were conscious of the precedent they would establish if they forced Andrew Johnson from office owing to "general cussedness." Future presidents likely would face impeachment proceedings whenever they ran afoul of a recalcitrant Congress awash in partisan bickering. The Founders had reserved the impeachment process for genuinely egregious cases of malfeasance. If the proceedings became routine and purely political, it did not bode well for the constitutional balance of power between the executive and legislative branches.[76]

Senator Fessenden, a moderate, was sometimes characterized as one of the Senate's "doubtful men." While certainly no fan of Andy Johnson, he deemed the whole impeachment business anathema. His well-known aversion to Ben Wade's political excesses meant he would hesitate to take any action that would advance his Radical nemesis into a position of executive authority. With his mind all but made up to vote against impeachment, Fessenden passed his time during the trial playing cards. He told his cousin, "I prefer tar and feathers to lifelong regret." If the impeachment managers could not count on Fessenden's vote, they probably were in trouble with other moderates as well.[77]

Perhaps more troubling for impeachment supporters was the loss of other Senate moderates who might have been expected to support removing the offensive Johnson. Iowa senator James W. Grimes was a harsh critic of the president, berating the man's "many great follies and wickedness," but even he agreed to an acquittal after Johnson assured the senator that political retribution would not be in the offing following the impeachment vote. Eventually, seven moderate Republican senators—Fessenden, Grimes, Edmund Ross, Peter Van Winkle, John B. Henderson, Joseph Fowler, and Lyman Trumbull—agreed to change their votes in favor of the president. The margin proved to be crucial. These "Treacherous Seven" senators eventually faced the verbal wrath of the enraged Radicals, but they held firm. Grimes even suffered a stroke, although he subsequently returned to the Senate after he recuperated.[78]

Closing arguments were set for April 22. Impeachment manager George Boutwell summarized the prosecution's case in a three-hour address. The Massachusetts congressman was not an electrifying orator, and most accounts recollected the boredom that spread throughout the chamber and among spectators in the galleries. Nonetheless, Boutwell's case was thoughtfully and logically presented. The gist of the argument was that if Johnson had sincerely sought to determine the constitutionality of the Tenure of Office Act, he could have tested it in court rather than violating the law. In addition, Boutwell argued that the act applied to Stanton even if the secretary had been selected by Lincoln because the law did not differentiate between cabinet officers appointed by the incumbent and those appointed by his predecessor.[79]

Defense lawyers Thomas Nelson and William S. Groesbeck answered Boutwell's charges and even lobbed a few of their own. In his address, Groesbeck explained that three impeachment managers—Bingham, Stevens, and Logan—were among several Republicans who had sent a letter to the president six weeks earlier lobbying for claimants seeking to secure rights to harness bird guano on the Caribbean island of Alta Vela. The letter was immaterial to the impeachment proceedings, but it embarrassed Republicans who sought to remove Johnson from office even as they solicited him for political favors.[80]

The most eagerly anticipated closing argument came from Old Thad. The ailing Radical was so ill he could barely stand to deliver his speech. The Cincinnati *Commercial* reported that the aging lion's "voice has that dreadful low, grating sound that we hear from deathbeds." Sipping brandy and port as he limped up to the rostrum, the gaunt, hollow-eyed specter of a man explained his task. "During the very brief period which I shall occupy I desire to discuss the charges against the respondent in no mean spirit of malignity or vituperation, but to argue them in a manner worthy of the high tribunal before which I appear and of the exalted position of the accused," he said. "Whatever may be thought of his character of condition, he has been made respectable and his condition has been dignified by the action of his fellow-citizens. Railing accusation, therefore, would ill become this occasion, this tribunal, or a proper sense of the position of those who discuss this question on the one side or the other."[81]

Having professed his intent to avoid the "spirit of malignity or vituperation," Stevens launched into a partisan diatribe that was little more than the "railing accusation" he claimed to eschew. He could not mask his hatred for the little man who occupied the big mansion. In his view, Johnson's transgressions were not limited to a single violation of the Tenure of Office Act; they stretched far beyond that one statute. The president's actions threatened to undermine the possibility, nay the necessity, of change in the country. Johnson's conservative positions and narrow construction of the Constitution would restore the old imperfect Union of the antebellum era, thereby wasting a golden opportunity to form a more perfect Union than the flawed republic created by the American Founders. In squandering his great chance to remake the nation, Johnson was complicit with the rebels who sought to destroy the United States in the war. The victors had "spurned the traitors, and have put the chief of them upon his trial, and demand judgment upon his misconduct. He will be condemned, and his sentence inflicted without turmoil, tumult or bloodshed, and the nation and prosperity without the shedding any further of human blood and with a milder punishment than the world has been accustomed to see, or perhaps than ought now to be inflicted."[82]

Other speeches followed, but with defection of the Treacherous Seven, the die was cast. When the final vote was tallied on May 16, 1868, 35 senators voted for removal and 19 against. The Senate recessed for ten days to consider other articles of impeachment, but the vote remained the same when the senators reconvened. Recognizing they were defeated, the Radicals had no choice but to yield. The Senate adjourned the trial *sine die*, which meant that Andrew Johnson would serve out his term as president of the United States until March 1869. He had escaped removal from office by one vote.[83]

Faced with party leaders' outrage at his vote for acquittal, Fessenden went to great pains to explain his reasons. "The office of President is one of the great coordinate branches of the Government, having its defined powers, privileges, and duties; as essential to the very framework of the Government as any other, and to be touched with as careful a hand," he told his detractors.

"Anything which conduces to weaken its hold upon the respect of the people, to break down the barriers which surround it, to make it the mere sport of temporary majorities, tends to the great injury of our Government, and inflicts a wound upon constitutional liberty."[84]

In a similar vein, Lyman Trumbull, another moderate Republican anxious to justify his position, explained that removing a president from office was a serious business with serious consequences. He argued that "when the excitement of the hour shall have subsided," a precedent would be established, "and no future President will be safe who happens to differ with a majority of the House and two-thirds of the Senate on any measure deemed by them important, particularly if of a political character." The precedent would allow congressional leaders to threaten a president over political differences. "Blinded by partisan zeal, with such an example before them, they will not scruple to remove out of the way any obstacle to the accomplishment of their purposes, and what then becomes of the checks and balances of the Constitution, so carefully devised and so vital to its perpetuity? They are all gone." Whatever the transient view of Andrew Johnson, the long-term damage to the institution of the presidency would be enormous. "In view of the consequences likely to flow from this day's proceedings, should they result in conviction on what my judgment tells me are insufficient charges and proofs, I tremble for the future of my country. I cannot be an instrument to produce such a result."[85]

In the wake of President Johnson's acquittal, both houses of Congress investigated the debacle, although no hidden cabals or conspiratorial shenanigans could be pinpointed. Historians were not long in joining the debate. It seemed virtually impossible that at the apex of their influence in Congress the Radicals should falter in their efforts to remove the object of their scorn and derision. Retrospect affords a dispassionate perspective. For all of the political posturing on both sides, the impeachment case against Andrew Johnson was exceedingly weak. That the Tenure of Office Act could survive close constitutional scrutiny was, at best, dubious. Presidents generally had enjoyed wide latitude to determine who their advisers should be. Denying a president authority to remove cabinet officials and surround himself with loyal men would eviscerate the office. More to the point, allowing the legislative branch to intrude into the detailed workings of the executive branch would upset the delicate structure of checks and balances established by the U.S. Constitution. If the sacred instrument did not explicitly require Senate approval to remove a cabinet officer, an act of Congress could not impose such a constraint. Fundamental changes in the relationship among and between the branches would necessitate a constitutional amendment.[86]

Anti-Johnson forces contended that the delicate structure ought to be upset; Johnson was despoiling the American republic at precisely the moment when the defects in its constitutional system of government could be remedied and the horrific sacrifices of the Civil War could acquire a transcendent meaning. Finally, irrevocably, America could live up to its creed by embracing ideals of equality of opportunity—but for the laggard that accidentally occupied the Executive Mansion. It was a compelling argument, but the president's opponents could not convince two-thirds of U.S. senators to remove the incubus from office in 1868. Sacrificing the freedom of future presidents to resist an encroaching Congress was viewed as too high a price to pay for short-term political gain, especially since Johnson would leave office in less than a year.[87]

Because 1868 was an election year, members of Congress turned their attention to the impending political campaigns immediately after the impeachment trial ended. As a clear sign that the Radicals' political power was on the wane, Ulysses S. Grant and House Speaker Schuyler Colfax emerged as the Republican Party's presidential and vice presidential candidates, respectively. Although earlier in his career Colfax had been an acknowledged friend to the Radical wing, he was not as reliable as Wade, Stevens, or Sumner. As for Grant, he had been close to Johnson before their rift, and even afterward no one in the Republican Party thought him a genuine Radical. He might be characterized as a moderate, but the truth was that the philosophically inconsistent Grant was above all else a political pragmatist. If the Radicals had been asked to rank their preferred candidates on a wish list, Colfax would not have ranked near the top, and Grant would have appeared far lower on the list.[88]

One change in the Radicals' postimpeachment congressional authority was immediate and undeniable. Sepulchral Thaddeus Stevens, the ailing septuagenarian who served as the unofficial grand old man of the Radical cause, had reached the end of his tether as well as his worldly incarnation. It had been obvious to everyone watching the impeachment trial that he was not long for this world, and the doomsayers demonstrated their prescience. Old Thad died on August 11, 1868, less than three months after the final impeachment vote. True to form, the iconoclastic Jacobin willed that his ravaged body be entombed in the black section of a Lancaster, Pennsylvania, cemetery. He died as he had lived—on his own terms.[89]

As for the living Radicals, their decline began the moment the impeachment trial concluded. They had exhausted their political capital and whatever goodwill they possessed. The "golden opportunity" they had spoken of so often would not come to pass, although it would take many years before this failure became evident to most Americans. If the idea that the freedmen could be assimilated into American life and culture had been a tantalizing possibility in 1865, the likelihood receded after 1868. The "revolution" the Radicals had sought would soon falter, triggering a "counterrevolution" beginning around 1868. The burning question for Reconstruction policy at the end of the Johnson administration was whether succeeding presidents were up to the task of holding onto the modest gains of Reconstruction. The future did not appear promising.[90]

Chapter Five

"The Progress of Evolution from President Washington to President Grant Was Alone Evidence Enough to Upset Darwin"

As the 1860s drew to a close, many Americans believed they had survived the most turbulent decade since the creation of the republic. It was difficult to argue with their logic. They had suffered through a bloody, internecine war that had obliterated 2 percent of the nation's population, and still they faced the daunting tasks of rebuilding a country decimated by war and restoring an economy that had not fully recovered. The revolution in customs, manners, and social relations showed no signs of abating. Continued resistance from the South and the patently racist positions of an obdurate chief executive exacerbated tensions, convincing all but the most radical proponents of remaking society that enough was enough. It was time to settle into a less stressful, peaceful life. Citizens can endure only a finite level of uncertainty before they emerge from their fugue to resume their normal lives, whatever "normal" would mean in a postbellum era.[1]

In Congress, the impeachment imbroglio weakened the Radicals' power and imperiled their efforts to push for more aggressive federal Reconstruction policies. The misguided challenge to presidential authority was only one of many changes in the late 1860s and early 1870s signaling the Jacobins' waning influence. Leading Radical Henry Winter Davis, one of the authors of the Wade-Davis Bill during the Lincoln administration, died at the end of 1865. To no one's surprise, the ailing Thaddeus Stevens expired a few months after Johnson's acquittal. Edwin Stanton resigned as secretary of war; although he was appointed to the Supreme Court the following year, he died before he could assume the office. Ben Wade's Senate term ended early in 1869. Charles Sumner lost his chairmanship of the powerful Senate Foreign Relations Committee in March 1871. Whatever presidential ambitions the Radicals harbored, their hour on the national stage was passing, and with it the possibility for realizing their ambitions.[2]

As the Radicals' political power and influence declined, it was natural that mainstream Republicans would turn to Ulysses S. Grant as their standard-bearer. He was a safe bet, a nonideological, middle-of-the-road candidate who was new to politics and not set in his ways. This blank slate was refreshing, for he was seen as honest and straight shooting—a candidate of the people. As Henry Adams, scion of the famous American dynasty, remarked, "Grant represented order. He was a great soldier, and the soldier always represented order. He might be as partisan as he pleased, but a general who had organized and commanded half a million or a million men in the field, must know how to administer."[3]

In many ways, the man born as Hiram Ulysses Grant was exactly what he appeared to be. His early life was not promising. After graduating from West Point, Grant had fought in the war with Mexico prior to leaving the army in the 1850s. He eventually worked with his father in the tanning business before again donning a uniform as civil war erupted. Emerging from the Civil War as a Northern hero, the taciturn Ohio native was the antithesis of the blustering, long-winded politicians of the day; he exuded a quiet confidence that suggested he was above the political fray. This posture of statesmanship, whether genuine or merely a carefully constructed façade, held enormous appeal for citizens searching for stability in turbulent times. Grant had leaned toward the Democratic Party in his early years, but after his break with Johnson it was clear he was entrenched in the Republican camp. The Jacobins thought he retained a "conservative odor," but they had no viable candidate to offer in his stead to carry the Republican banner to electoral victory. Odoriferous or not, Grant unanimously won the nomination when the Republicans held their convention on May 20, 1868, four days after Johnson won an acquittal from the U.S. Senate. Speaker of the House Schuyler Colfax became his running mate.[4]

The Republicans had taken a beating in the 1867 elections as voters deserted Radical candidates and policies devoted to uplifting the freedmen. Grant understood all too well white citizens' fears; as one Ohio Democrat complained, the party was in "the thralldom of niggerism." Anxious to soothe the fears of nervous moderates, the candidate distanced himself from the vituperative rhetoric of the Radicals, although he was careful not to repudiate their position that the South must accede to federal Reconstruction goals. One reason the Grant administration appeared schizophrenic in the years to come—on one hand vigorously protecting the freedmen from Southern abuses while on the other hand ignoring blatant violations of federal law—was because Grant sought to chart a middle course between the excesses of the radical wing of his party and the probusiness, staid policies championed by conservative Republicans. "Let us have peace," his campaign asserted. It was hardly a stirring credo, but the slogan perfectly captured the sentiments of many war-weary Americans.[5]

Former New York governor Horatio Seymour captured the Democratic presidential nomination despite last-minute jockeying by Chief Justice Salmon P. Chase, who returned to the Democratic Party in the nick of time to jostle for a position in the party leadership. Francis Preston Blair Jr. of Missouri, son and namesake of the Blair who had served as part of Andrew Jackson's "kitchen cabinet" and brother of Montgomery Blair, Lincoln's postmaster general, became the vice presidential candidate.

Seymour was a frail, colorless, unimpressive candidate, but Blair proved to be a newspaperman's delight with his penchant for uttering quotable, and politically damaging, phrases. In a notorious letter he wrote to Missouri Unionist James O. Broadhead, Blair remarked, "There is but one way to re-store the Government and the Constitution, and that is for the President-elect to declare [the Reconstruction-era laws] null and void, compel the Army to undo its usurpations at the South, disperse the carpetbag State govern-ments, allow the white people to reorganize their own governments and elect Senators and Representatives." In short, the Democratic ticket was pledged to undo the "mischief" of Reconstruction by abolishing the Freedmen's Bureau, repealing laws that punished the former Confederate states, and ensuring the triumph of white supremacy. With this kind of talk, it was little wonder that the Republican campaign slogan "Scratch a Democrat and you'll find a rebel under his skin" resonated with many voters.[6]

Race played a critical role in the 1868 elections as each side demonized the opponent. Democrats contended that voting for Grant and the Republi-cans was tantamount to allowing blacks and carpetbaggers—that is, Northern whites who interfered in Southern affairs—to exercise dominion over the white race. They also resurrected fears of miscegenation that had proliferated during the 1864 presidential contest, often portraying Republicans as hell bent on continuing the disruption to American life that began with the war and continued with the Radicals' efforts to impeach the president and remake society in an egalitarian image where social parity would exist between the races. Not to be outdone, Republicans matched their opponents' demagogu-ery and added their own flourishes. The more creative Republican ideologues figuratively and literally "waved the bloody shirt," reminding their audiences that the Democrats had opposed the successful prosecution of the war and, in some cases, had actively supported the Southern cause. To vote for Seymour and Blair was to embrace the values of the traitorous South. If Democrats controlled the executive branch, it was only a matter of time before they restored the horrific antebellum conditions that had triggered the war in the first place.[7]

When the election results were tabulated, Grant and Colfax had won, although their victory was hardly the rout it has sometimes been called. Grant claimed slightly more than 3 million votes, or 52.7 percent of the total, while Seymour won 2.7 million votes, or 47.3 percent. Despite the relatively close popular vote, the Republicans enjoyed a distinct advantage in the Electoral College, with 214 electoral votes cast for Grant and Colfax to 80 electoral votes for Seymour and Blair. The Republicans won twenty-six states and the Democrats, eight. Awaiting the returns at a colleague's house, Grant was anything but exuberant even after it was clear he would win the presidency. He seemed almost resigned to bearing the burdens of high office. Returning home in the wee morning hours after learning of his election, he told his wife, "I am afraid I am elected."[8]

He was a career military man. After suffering through numerous failures in his peacetime pursuits, Grant had poured his energies into the army; it was the only endeavor where he had succeeded. He approached his new position in much the same manner as he had approached his career in uniform. As in a military campaign following a victory, the general officer moved to consolidate his gains and plan for the next campaign. President-elect Grant did exactly that; he methodically assembled his cabinet in private, secure in the knowledge that he owed little or nothing to the special interests that often determined the composition and course of a presidential administration. He failed to grasp the beneficial aspects of building coalitions among party leaders and outside interest groups, but those political lessons later would be driven home forcefully as this apolitical man fought on a new type of battlefield.[9]

In his inaugural address, Grant assured his fellow citizens that "when I think it advisable [I] will exercise the constitutional privilege of interposing a veto to defeat measures which I oppose," but for laws that had been duly enacted, they "will be faithfully executed, whether they meet my approval or not." This was a not-so-subtle attempt to distinguish himself from his predecessor, who continually interjected obnoxious opinions with little or no concern for the political consequences. The incoming president also highlighted his lack of indebtedness to special interests as well as his desire to neither punish the South nor promote the region's efforts to denigrate the freedmen:

> The country having just emerged from a great rebellion, many questions will come before it for settlement in the next four years which preceding administrations have never had to deal with. In meeting these it is desirable that they should be approached calmly, without prejudice, hate, or sectional pride, remembering that the greatest good to the greatest number is the object to be attained. This requires security of person, property, and free religious and political opinion in every part of our common country, without regard to local prejudice.

It was not stirring rhetoric—one detractor referred to the address as "a string of platitudes that deserved praise only for its brevity"—but the new president's central message was well received. Most commentators praised the address as the right message delivered at the right time. With a calm, steady hand at the helm, the ship of state might yet navigate the turbulent waters that had roiled the republic of late.[10]

Grant assumed high office armed with conflicting goals. Since the Civil War had transformed him into a hero of the North, he had been mentioned on numerous occasions as a presidential prospect. Yet he was not the typical politician. He did not seek executive power; it sought him. Grant even joked that the extent of his political ambition was to be mayor of his hometown of Galena, Illinois, so that he could finish laying the sidewalk to his house. (Town leaders hastily constructed the sidewalk before he could launch a mayoral

Ulysses S. Grant became the eighteenth president of the United States in March 1869, replacing the much-vilified Andrew Johnson and opening a new chapter in the story of American Reconstruction.
Courtesy of the Library of Congress.

campaign, thus demonstrating that even the threat of running for office sometimes accomplishes one's objectives.) The old general's reluctance to seek the
presidency only heightened his appeal as a statesman who could be trusted to
place the public good ahead of his own private interests.[11]

Throughout the campaign and upon taking office, Grant promised to rise
above the political fray and stop the bickering between Republicans harbor-
ing radical sentiments and the more conservative elements in government.
Therein lay the difficulty that would haunt his administration: he was committed to pursuing a vigorous Reconstruction policy, but at the same time
he recognized the need to ameliorate congressional excesses that proved
too onerous for the public to endorse. He would protect the freedmen, but
he would not alienate the South in the process. These goals, ambitious and
challenging at the outset of a new presidency, would prove to be mutually
exclusive as the 1870s progressed. Eventually, the Grant administration lost
its resolve and all but abandoned Reconstruction.[12]

The compromises and backsliding were in the future when the new president
swore the oath of office early in 1869. Despite the optimism that many Americans felt with Andrew Johnson's departure, the new president faced multiple
challenges as he entered the White House. Perhaps his most immediate problem
was within his own party. Weary of the divisiveness of the war, up-and-coming
Republicans sought to leave behind the bloody battlefields of Antietam and
Gettysburg and embrace policies that would encourage economic development.
For all the later talk of the Republicans as the "party of Lincoln," by the late
1860s many rank-and-file party members were eager to see the enactment of
a protective tariff and government subsidies for business. Eastern Republicans
focused on currency backed by gold as a means of promoting deflation while
westerners longed for easier credit so that more money would circulate in hard
economic times. Although such issues were hardly the stuff of legend or the
policies that men would die for, they reflected the national desire to resume
normal relations in an atmosphere of tranquility. A reluctance to take up arms
again so soon after Appomattox meant that the new administration had to
move cautiously in protecting the freedmen. The president's unwillingness to
challenge the conservative wing of the party, coming on the heels of Johnson's
refusal to champion laws protecting newly emancipated slaves, incensed the
Radicals, but their power was diminishing, and they knew it. If Grant was not
their ideal choice for a champion, he would have to suffice.[13]

He brought with him a strong measure of goodwill, always a useful tool
for a chief executive, but he was also the leader of a political party that had
suffered a blow owing to the impeachment debacle and the perceived over-
reaching by the Radicals. Grant the man had outpolled Grant the party leader,
a clear indication that many voters were growing tired of the infighting in

Washington, D.C., and were weary of Republican policies that seemed punitive toward the South. Indeed, some Northerners believed the work of Reconstruction had been accomplished and it was time to move on to other issues,
such as completing the transcontinental railroad, opening up western lands
for exploration and development, and promoting a sound economy. Realizing
that voters were impatient with Reconstruction policy, Grant urged Congress
to recognize new state governments in Virginia, Texas, and Mississippi.
Readmission for Texas and Mississippi, where Republicans were firmly ensconced in power, was not problematic, but Virginia's readmission was divisive because state leaders had balked at ratifying the Fourteenth Amendment
and appeared reticent to swear an oath of allegiance to the Union.[14]

Violence against Republicans and blacks in Georgia persuaded the president that he must intervene upon occasion to ensure the safety of citizens under attack by reactionary forces. In December 1869, he told Congress that it
must support Governor Rufus Bullock's efforts to disqualify state legislators
who were ineligible to hold office under the Fourteenth Amendment. He also
agreed to allow federal troops to supervise Georgia state government operations. Grant later retreated from his initial commitment to using federal arms
to prop up weak, unpopular Reconstruction governments in the South, but
in the first two years of his administration he moved with alacrity to ensure
that freedmen and their political allies were protected. In another bold step,
he supported ratification of the Fifteenth Amendment, which extended the
franchise to black men.[15]

Southerners were outraged by the Fifteenth Amendment, just as they had
been with previous Reconstruction laws. Less than a decade after the region
had enacted secession ordinances and Alexander Stephens had delivered his
famous cornerstone speech with its well-known philosophy of race for the
newly christened Confederate States of America—"its cornerstone rests,
upon the great truth that the negro is not equal to the white man; that slavery
subordination to the superior race is his natural and normal condition"—the
former rebels were presented with a constitutional amendment allowing
blacks to vote. Democrats proclaimed the amendment the "most revolutionary measure" ever presented to Congress, but the Radicals feared it was too
weak. The amendment did not forbid literacy tests, allow blacks to hold elective office, or require uniform application of voting requirements. Republicans' argument that the black franchise was required for the postwar model
of government administration would eventually yield to Southern objections
to the Fifteenth Amendment. Former Confederates contended that the federal
government must be resisted because "the colored race was its special wards
and favorites." Such objectionable favoritism justified lax or spotty enforcement for critics of the measure.[16]

Historians have called Grant to task for the numerous well-documented failures of his administration, especially during the second term, but despite the administration's shortcomings, the president demonstrated no small measure of intestinal fortitude in supporting ratification of the Fifteenth Amendment. He also proved to be a friend of the freedmen with the appointment of his second attorney general, Amos T. Akerman, in late 1870. It was an inspired choice, especially since the original cabinet members were selected based on their loyalty to the president rather than strictly on their competence for the offices they would inhabit.[17]

Akerman did not fit the original cabinet criteria. The transplanted Southerner was one of the most accomplished cabinet officials to serve the Grant administration and the only former Confederate to hold a high-ranking position during the Reconstruction era. Akerman was that rare public man able to step away from his personal predilections in service of a higher goal. Perhaps his experiences as a resident of both regions afforded him unusual insight into the problems of his day. Born and raised in New Hampshire, Akerman came to live in Georgia after he graduated from Dartmouth College in 1842. When secession fever infected the state, he argued that it was a grave mistake to undermine the Union, but his appeals to reason came to naught. When secession became a *fait accompli*, he reluctantly enlisted in the Confederate army. After the South was defeated four long years later, he joined the Republican Party, a risky decision in the postbellum South. In Akerman's view, after the Union had been preserved and Confederate forces disbanded, survivors were obliged to follow Reconstruction laws even if they did not support the new policies. He was derided as a "scalawag"—a Southern gentleman who supported Republican, hence Northern, policies—but he was not a man easily dissuaded from performing his duty.[18]

Akerman did not share his fellow Southerners' deep-seated prejudice against the freedmen, perhaps because he originally hailed from the North. Whatever his motivations, he encouraged recalcitrant Southerners to acquiesce while the federal government enforced the Reconstruction acts and the Civil War amendments. As head of the newly established U.S. Department of Justice in 1870 and 1871, he led the administration's efforts to suppress white supremacist groups such as the Ku Klux Klan and the White League in Louisiana, although his success was mixed. Akerman and the department managed to curtail the most flagrant abuses, but prejudice was widespread and the public mood shifted. Citizens grew weary of the problems involved with reconstructing the Union and refused to support aggressive law enforcement measures except in the most egregious cases. Throughout the 1870s, Southern states were "redeemed" when whites, many of them former officers in the Confederate army, assumed control of state governments.[19]

Grant watched the gradual dissolution of his administration's Reconstruction policies and searched for a means of arresting the loss of federal control. Despite his lack of well-honed political skills and his willingness to award friends positions in high office even in the face of incompetence, the president shrewdly realized that an effective foreign policy might buttress his administration's record of achievement. Consequently, he looked to the Caribbean island republic of Santo Domingo. The republic already had been the focus of previous administrations; a wide array of influential Americans believed that annexation was in the interests of both nations. Aside from the imperialist advantages of procuring new territory, the island might prove to be a suitable home for "the entire colored population of the United States, should it choose to emigrate." Lincoln had wrestled with the age-old question of whether freed blacks should depart from the United States for more hospitable environs, ultimately deciding that such a scheme was unworkable and undesirable, but Grant was ready to revive the plan in the face of continued Southern opposition to protecting freedmen's rights.[20]

Grant's apologists argue that the president recognized the difficulties in resolving racial problems by shipping off offending personages. According to this view, he was offering freedmen a bargaining tool as they "negotiated" labor contracts with Southern landowners. Because blacks performed so much of the backbreaking agricultural labor in the United States, especially in the South, the loss of workers would decimate the Southern economy, which depended on cotton, tobacco, rice, and indigo, all labor-intensive agricultural products. Because blacks could threaten to immigrate to another country if they were denied favorable employment, they might be able to win concessions that would never be available otherwise.[21]

Assuming that blacks had appreciated the new bargaining chip and could have used it effectively and assuming that whites would have recognized the loss of the labor pool as distinctly possible, the ploy might have worked. Yet logistical problems abounded. Paying for transportation to and from the island was a potential stumbling block, not to mention the question of what would happen to the freedmen once they arrived in their adopted homeland. Since everyone could not leave or might be disinclined to do so, what would happen to the remaining men of color who labored under appalling conditions? These questions were never addressed satisfactorily.[22]

Grant's plans for Santo Domingo demonstrated that his administration recognized a new system of labor relations had arisen in the postwar South. With the loss of the peculiar institution, landowners had to rely on other means of planting and harvesting crops. Their attitudes toward social and political relations had not changed, but their economic reality had. Some whites were embittered by pecuniary losses as well as a blow to their sense of dignity and honor, which compelled them to engage in confrontation and social conflict. Each day they faced labor shortages and little available specie while freed blacks, save those who headed north to escape their former owners, traipsed through the local landscape, reminding whites of their lost social position. For their part, blacks often owned nothing except the ragged clothes they wore and a few meager personal possessions. With little, if any, education or reasonable employment prospects and burdened by seemingly endless racial discrimination, they were virtually destitute.[23]

In the face of this stalemate, a new system of mutual labor dependence developed. The arrangement has been likened to rungs on a ladder. The bottom rung found young men, white and black, who were rootless, possessing little physical or human capital. These men typically toiled for wages and required extensive supervision if they were to labor at full capacity. Wage laborers tended to stay in the community until their impecunious circumstances required them to flee, they indulged a sense of wanderlust, or they moved to the next rung.[24]

Sharecropping was a step up. The system was not administered exactly the same way everywhere in the South, nor was sharecropping hailed as an efficient means of farming. It arose out of mutual necessity and desperation. Landowners possessed acreage but needed workers. Poor men, white and Negro, could work, but they owned no land. Legally, a sharecropper was a wage laborer paid with a share of the crop, but the distinctions frequently blurred. Absent a wage agreement, the arrangement evolved into a *de facto* barter system where workers "shared" the crop in the sense that they could eke out a subsistence living by working the land as farmers with no ownership rights. In a typical arrangement, nonlandowning farmers traded their labor in exchange for livestock, feed and seed, food, clothing, and shelter. Landowners supplied the necessaries on credit with the expectation that the cropper would pay the debt after harvesting the crops.[25]

The system exploited blacks and whites alike, although undoubtedly the former received the worse end of the deal owing to rampant racism. Sharecroppers often were forced to purchase shoddy merchandise and foodstuffs from company stores at exorbitant prices. By the end of the season, they found that repaying the debt to the store and the initial loan left them almost penniless and tied to the land for another year. Landowners found the arrangement hardly ideal, but at least it was workable because the cropper bore the risk of drought, infestation, and falling market prices. A poor crop yield did not relieve the sharecropper from repaying the original debt.[26]

On the next rung of the agricultural ladder, true tenantry meant that a farmer enjoyed some form of ownership rights. The tenant farmer lived and worked on the land, paying rent to the landlord for use of the land, house, and fuel. A share tenant paid rent to the landlord in the form of a share of the crop, which meant a poor harvest hurt the tenant and landlord alike. Cash tenants and standing renters paid a fixed amount regardless of the yield.[27]

Ownership was the top rung of the agricultural ladder. Small yeoman farmers and plantation owners occupied this level. It was difficult, but not impossible, for a determined soul to buy his way up rungs of the ladder. Aside from the difficulties involved in saving money to purchase land while laboring as a cropper, nonlandowning farmers faced daunting challenges in competing with large farms, which tended to be more efficient than smaller concerns.[28]

Regardless of the labor arrangement, blacks almost always fared poorly compared with similarly situated whites. At the end of the war, Negroes thought they would enjoy a measure of prosperity when, in their view, they were promised economic assistance through the Freedmen's Bureau and Northern aid and missionary societies. After the U.S. government returned the confiscated plantations to their original white owners and support for federal Reconstruction policies waned, freedmen recognized, in the words of a Kentucky newspaper reporter, that the slogan "Forty acres and a mule," a well-known shibboleth in the black community, had been supplanted by the harsh epithet of the white landowner, "Work nigger, or starve!"[29]

Even hardy souls who managed to travel north to the "promised land" found the opportunities limited and prejudice widespread. Some former slaves embraced freedom with a shrug of their shoulders. Although technically free to leave, sharecroppers and tenant farmers knew they might starve without a means to support themselves. As one former slave remarked, "Freedom wasn't no difference I knows of. I work for Marse John just the same."[30]

This portrait suggests that freedmen were passive victims of racism and an oppressive society, wholly dependent on the paternalism of enlightened whites, especially those in the federal government, to rescue them from a desperate condition. Negroes unquestionably were victimized by the white power structure and deeply held beliefs about the inherent inferiority of their race; a large number of the downtrodden never surmounted the obstacles placed in their path. Yet many blacks were not satisfied to wallow in self-pity or wait for assistance from benevolent whites. Assertive freedmen hungered for education as a means of moving up from their previously debased condition of servitude, and they paid dearly to attend community schools whenever possible. Whatever obstacles they faced, numerous Negro laborers shouldered incredible burdens and worked diligently to improve their lot. Blacks laboring under the sharecropping system also used their limited free time to forge affective kin relationships that had been denied them when the institution of slavery destroyed families on the auction block. Black croppers and tenants built churches and schools that served as the centerpiece of a restored black community. Some blacks managed to escape tedious agricultural work, travel northward, and become business-men, ministers, teachers, and professionals.[31]

Almost all agricultural workers in the South faced bleak circumstances in the postwar era. Except for the planter elite who managed to finagle their way back into economic and political power after Southern redemption during the 1870s, landowners fared little better than the landless classes. The owner of a small farm had to purchase crops, farm animals, food, clothing, and building materials to operate the farm. Aside from the worries caused by ascendant black culture, white landowners feared the vagaries of the labor force. Disaf-fected croppers might flee in the dark of night, leaving the landowner short-handed and vulnerable at harvesting time. It was possible that sharecroppers and tenants could band together and refuse to work unless conditions changed. A labor shortage was only one possible calamity for the small farmer. If the weather became unfavorable, insects destroyed the crop, the market price dropped, he fell grievously ill, or any other unforeseen mishap occurred, a landowner with a large number of tenants could not pay his mortgage and might lose his farm. In addition, farmers often overplanted cash crops such as cotton, which depleted the soil of nutrients and depressed commodity prices. If he suffered through a loss one season, the desperate landowner, never for-getting the mortgage hanging over his head, planted more of the same cash crop in a frantic attempt to compensate through volume for what he lost in revenue the preceding year. The Southern economy—rooted in agriculture throughout the long antebellum years when the region's leaders denounced industrialization and diversification of the economy—reaped a bitter harvest for what an earlier generation had sown. If the president honestly thought his imperialist policies for a small Caribbean island would affect this rigid sys-tem of labor relations in the South, he was seriously misguided.[32]

Even if Grant's annexation scheme for Santo Domingo had not been logisti-cally problematic, it is doubtful it could have succeeded as a foreign policy initiative. The president did not publicly promote his plan, nor did he devote the necessary time and attention to the strategic planning required to launch such an ambitious, if foolhardy, enterprise. He dispatched his private sec-retary, Orville E. Babcock, to investigate the feasibility of annexation, but the draft treaty that Babcock produced presented political problems for the administration because it appeared to have been the result of nefarious and self-serving negotiations. Even more damaging to the political prospects of ratifying the treaty, Grant and Radical Republican Charles Sumner had a bitter falling out over the annexation issue. The senator rightly pointed out numerous logistical concerns and troubling questions while Grant, sensitive to criticism from the Radical wing, bristled at Sumner's litany of objections. Ratification failed in the U.S. Senate by a 28–28 vote on June 30, 1870, by which time Sumner was frequently lambasting the president from the Senate floor for his flawed, impetuous Santo Domingo policy, among other issues.[33]

The annexation debate was fortuitous for the administration's Reconstruction initiatives. When Southern Republicans demanded that Grant replace his attorney general, Ebenezer Hoar, as the price for their support in the annexation struggle, the president responded by placing Amos Akerman at the helm at precisely the right time for the sake of the freedmen. The rest of the political fallout did not bode so well for the administration's Reconstruction policies. Although part of Grant's self-proclaimed motivation for pursuing annexation was to secure land for blacks departing the United States, the bitter fight among members of his own party highlighted the fissures that had already existed between conservatives, moderates, and Radicals. Upcoming elections would further expose the rifts and undermine the Grant administration's commitment to Reconstruction.[34]

Grant never forgot the first lesson of politics: he must not alienate the voters. No matter how well developed or perspicacious a policy may be, if it is too advanced for the electorate to support or too much out of step with the times, it (and possibly the politician promoting it) will be rejected. This point was driven home to the administration during the 1870 congressional elections. With white Southerners once again participating in the federal electoral process, Democrats captured forty-one seats in the House of Representatives, which narrowed the Republican majority to thirty seats, and in the U.S. Senate, the Democrats won six seats. Prominent Radicals such as George W. Julian, George H. Williams, and John Covode did not return to Congress. The first two suffered defeats at the polls while Covode declined to seek reelection. Julian was especially bitter about his loss, later turning his back on the Radicals. For conservative and even some moderate Republicans, the message was clear: the election results were an unequivocal repudiation of aggressive Reconstruction policies. Blacks had been freed from bondage, the Civil War amendments had been added to the U.S. Constitution, and the Freedmen's Bureau had provided assistance in the early years of the postbellum era. Disenchanted Republicans argued that a 250-year-old debt to black

Americans had been paid in full. It was time to move on and adopt public policies more conciliatory to the Southern states.[35]

Two years later, the call to abandon Reconstruction-era policies was louder than ever. Already the war was receding into memory and a new generation of political leaders was emerging to assume the mantle of the Republican Party. Grant stood at the center of the party factions. For conservatives, he was too wedded to Reconstruction and the Radicals' stated desire to punish

Although President Grant was hardly a Radical, the Southern press often portrayed him that way. In this illustration, the president oversees the disputed election of a Northern "Radical," William Pitt Kellogg, as governor of Louisiana. The illustration shows Kellogg holding the heart he has cut from the subdued female body of Louisiana as the violated woman is restrained by two freedmen. Grant ("Ulysses I") presides over the dastardly ceremony sitting on a throne atop an altar of Radicalism. Grant's attorney general, George Williams, is depicted as a winged demon directing the president's hand, which clutches a sword. At the left, federal officials gleefully watch the operation; at the right, other U.S. states, depicted as women fearing the same fate as Louisiana, watch nervously. A woman labeled "South Carolina" kneels in chains.
Courtesy of the Library of Congress.

the South. The Southern press depicted him as a despot anxious to promote puppet state governments infested with carpetbaggers, those infuriating Northern interlopers who traveled south to wrest political and financial affairs from white natives. To the more radical wing of the party, including the few remaining Jacobins serving in Congress, he was a plodding, cautious, naïve figurehead who surrounded himself with sycophants who manipulated him into supporting unwise policies so that they could enrich themselves at the expense of the freedmen.[36]

Despite criticism from all quarters, the old general remained the standard-bearer; the party ranks yielded no candidate matching Grant's stature to challenge his renomination. When it became clear he would stand for a second term as the Republican presidential nominee, however, the incumbent faced a mutiny of sorts. Self-proclaimed "Liberal Republicans" balked at the thought of another four years under Grant's bland leadership. Unlike the modern conception of a "liberal," which refers to proponents of large government programs championing a level playing field for the disadvantaged and disenfranchised, the Liberal Republicans of 1872 wanted to limit the growth of the federal government and move away from federal Reconstruction policies, which partially explains why Grant wavered in his support for the freedmen as he sought to occupy center ground within his own party.[37]

The irascible Horace Greeley, editor of the *New York Tribune*, was the leader of the Liberal Republican Party, but Charles Francis Adams, a member of the illustrious family that had produced two U.S. presidents, was among the party faithful, as was Carl Schurz, the prominent German-American journalist from Missouri. Another supporter, David Davis, had enjoyed a long friendship with Abraham Lincoln before Lincoln appointed him to the U.S. Supreme Court. Davis later served as a U.S. senator from Illinois. Even Radicals such as Charles Sumner and George W. Julian joined forces with the Liberal Republicans, although in their cases it probably was as much an anti-Grant strategy as an ideological position.[38]

The Liberal Republicans were not a united bunch; their only generally agreed-upon platform called for "the immediate and absolute removal of all disabilities imposed on account of the rebellion." They also viewed "a thorough reform of the civil service as one of the most pressing necessities of the hour." In their opinion, only the establishment of a professional, "merit-based" civil service system ensured that political corruption such as the scandals emerging from inside the Grant administration would not be repeated in coming years.[39]

Carl Schurz was arguably the most vocal proponent of the Liberal Republicans. In numerous speeches and letters, he tried to explain why the Liberal Republican Party had not betrayed Radical Republican principles. According to Schurz, if Southerners would acquiesce in the enforcement of the Civil War amendments and, in return, congressional Republicans would not enact punitive legislation against the region, sectional reconciliation was possible. Amnesty for former Confederates would obviate white Southerners' desire to join vigilante groups such as the Ku Klux Klan because they would not look to outside forces to redress grievances if they could work inside the political system. In colloquial terms, one catches more flies with honey than with vinegar. The first step in instituting this "New Departure" was to set aside the Jacobins' previous policy of punishing the South as conquered territory. What better way to demonstrate good faith than to deny the nomination to the man best known for defeating the South during the war, Ulysses S. Grant?[40]

As the Liberal Republicans came together, many would-be candidates jockeyed for power. The leading contenders were well-known public figures in their day. Schurz might have been a suitable leader, but he was ineligible to serve as president since he was not a "natural born Citizen," as required by Article II of the U.S. Constitution. Despite his illustrious pedigree, Charles Francis Adams never appealed to a broad constituency. Roscoe Conkling was a well-known U.S. senator from New York, but his appeal outside of his home state was limited. Simon Cameron was a former secretary of war in the Lincoln administration, U.S. minister to Russia, and a senator from Pennsylvania, but his reputation was marred by numerous allegations of corruption. Michigan senator Zachariah Chandler held many posts throughout a long, checkered career that smacked of ceaseless chicanery and Machiavellian maneuvering. Each man longed for the big prize, but each ultimately was not electable. Consequently, desperate Liberal Republicans turned to Horace Greeley as the savior of their party during their convention in Cincinnati in May 1872.[41]

Greeley was the foremost newspaperman of his day, although he had never held elective office and could boast of no direct political experience. For decades he had wielded his pen as a sword in the battle for public opinion. During that time, he had enjoyed an up-and-down career that was notable chiefly for its inconsistency. In 1862, Greeley had chided Lincoln for not emancipating the slaves; now, a decade later, he led a wing of the party that urged Republicans to move beyond the struggle for black civil and political rights since, according to the party platform, the issue had been resolved. The call for abandoning the federal government's seven-year-old Reconstruction policies proved irresistible to Democrats who recognized an opportunity to exploit a fissure within the Republican Party and possibly end Reconstruction at the same time. Except for Louisiana and Texas, Democrats throughout the country fused with the Liberal Republicans to champion Greeley's candidacy as an alternative to Grant.[42]

Greeley proved to be a terrible campaigner, an odd character ridiculed by many political commentators, including influential cartoonist Thomas Nast, all of whom chortled at the candidate's support for absurd concepts such as spiritualism, vegetarianism, and human manure as the most efficacious means of improving agricultural production. In a spirited show of defiance, Greeley ignored the long-standing nineteenth-century practice whereby presidential candidates did not campaign directly but left it to surrogates to represent their interests on the stump. The old newspaperman insisted on visibly thrusting himself into the race and campaigning directly for votes. The gamble might have paid off, but he proved to be an uninspiring speaker with a penchant for saying the wrong thing to the wrong audience at the wrong time. Grant's supporters delighted when Greeley made their jobs easier owing to his numerous gaffes and unintentionally hilarious faux pas. One commentator observed that "no two men could look each other in the face and say 'Greeley' without laughing."[43]

In this sarcastic Thomas Nast cartoon published in *Harper's Weekly* on August 24, 1872, Liberal Republican presidential candidate Horace Greeley and Massachusetts senator Charles Sumner, who broke with the Radical Republicans to support Greeley's presidential campaign, try to force a reluctant black man to shake hands with two ominous figures who just slaughtered his family. The ferocious-looking Irish figure on the left represents Tammany Hall, the notoriously corrupt Democratic machine that controlled New York City politics for generations, and the blood-drenched figure on the right represents the Ku Klux Klan. The cartoon insinuates that Liberal Republicans betrayed the freedmen in an unprincipled bid to close ranks with Democrats so that they could wrest the presidency from Grant at all costs.
Courtesy of the Library of Congress.

Despite the widening rift in the Republican ranks in 1872, Grant handily defeated Greeley. When the votes were counted, Grant had garnered 3,598,235 popular votes, or 55.6 percent, to Greeley's 2,834,761 popular votes, or 43.8 percent. The Electoral College vote was even more lopsided, with 286 votes for Grant to 66 for Greeley. Greeley died suddenly on November 29, 1872, after the popular votes had been cast but before the electors met to cast their votes, so his 66 electoral votes were distributed to other candidates. An Ohio Republican explained the results of the popular vote. "That Grant is an Ass, no man can deny, but better an Ass than a mischievous Idiot."[44]

The emergence of the Liberal Republicans diluted the political effectiveness of the Republican Party, which caused, at least in part, the Grant administration to retreat from its Reconstruction policies during the second term. If nothing else, the schism in the party in 1872 sounded warning bells that the end of Reconstruction was in sight because it served notice that even within the "party of Lincoln," support for policies protecting the freedmen was waning. In addition, although Grant won the election, his personal foibles and the administration's scandals had been a point of contention for Liberal Republicans and Democrats. The president and his wing of the party were mortally wounded, and virtually everyone knew it.[45]

Liberal Republicans were incredibly naïve and misguided. Despite the presence of such well-known Radicals as Schurz and Sumner in the ranks, the party's platform was essentially conservative. To think that Southerners would agree to obey odious Reconstruction laws and amendments in hopes of achieving reconciliation with the North so soon after the war was unrealistic. As subsequent events demonstrated, abandoning federal efforts to protect the freedmen in the South was a recipe for encouraging racism and violence. White Southerners had not "learned their lesson." Like many insurgents before and after their time, they realized they could lose the battle and win the war if they waited for Northern resolve, as reflected in the Radical wing of the Republican Party, to grow weary and collapse. The bitter dispute within the ranks dating from the 1872 election, in the words of one historian, "estranged the ideological core of the Republican Party and undermined the political viability of Reconstruction."[46]

Although Grant's vote totals were more impressive in 1872 than they had been in 1868, he entered his second term in a weakened position. When he stepped into the presidency in March 1869, his reputation was at its apex. Except in the South, where inhabitants still seethed with resentment at the battlefield losses inflicted by "Grant the Butcher," he was hailed throughout the land as the hero of Appomattox, the one man who could heal the nation's wounds. Within four years, his reputation declined precipitously as news of his administration's corruption and mismanagement came to light while, at almost the same time, support for Reconstruction all but disappeared. The Ulysses S. Grant who entered his second term was a man bloodied by political losses. He would tread lightly for the remainder of his presidency.[47]

Grant's last four years in office were engulfed in political scandals as well as an economic crisis. In September 1872, shortly before the presidential election, Congressman Oakes Ames of Massachusetts, a member of the committee on railroads and a leading force behind the construction of the transcontinental railroad, was implicated in the Crédit Mobilier bribery scheme. Thus began the unraveling of the Grant administration. Scandals had been hinted at before, but they were nothing compared with the Crédit Mobilier episode, the first of many incidents that came to light during Grant's second term.[48]

The Union Pacific Railroad created Crédit Mobilier in 1864 to oversee construction of the transcontinental railroad project. From its inception, Crédit Mobilier was a fraudulent entity, established so as to appear that Union Pacific's board of directors and principal officers had selected an independent construction management firm to build the transcontinental railroad. In reality, Crédit Mobilier was a shell company that allowed Union Pacific officers to enter into contracts with the supposedly independent firm to build the railroad. Dummy individuals also entered into contracts with Union Pacific, which assigned the contracts to Crédit Mobilier. Afterward, Crédit Mobilier officials used checks issued by Union Pacific to purchase stocks and bonds in the Union Pacific project at par value. Later, Crédit Mobilier sold the stocks and bonds on the open market at high prices. In essence, Union Pacific drove up the price of its own stock by funneling money through a dummy corporation created expressly for the purpose of paying dummy individuals whom Union Pacific had manufactured. The railroad company was guaranteed to realize a huge profit regardless of whether the project was ever completed. Although the corporation eventually succeeded in constructing the transcontinental railroad, it did so at exorbitant prices charged to the federal government.[49]

To ensure the scheme would work, Congressman Ames, who conveniently served as the Crédit Mobilier chairman even as he served in the U.S. House of Representatives—such dual careers for members of Congress were more common in the nineteenth century than in later times—bribed influential members of Congress with cash and reduced stock prices for shares of Crédit Mobilier. Ames opened his records to public scrutiny after he was exposed. When the Grant administration learned that Ames had identified Vice President Colfax as a recipient of bribes, the president agreed that Colfax should be dropped from the ticket in favor of Massachusetts senator Henry Wilson. Although Wilson also was identified as a recipient of Crédit Mobilier bribes, he returned the stocks purchased in his wife's name and eventually was exonerated by a House committee investigating the affair.[50]

Many activities in the Crédit Mobilier fraud occurred during the Johnson years, but the Grant administration bore the brunt of unfavorable public opinion when Ames exposed the plot in 1872. The administration was deeply embarrassed, although Grant himself was never implicated. The matter might have faded from public consciousness had additional scandals not erupted throughout the 1870s. It seemed that every few months a new scheme was exposed to the light of day.[51]

On March 3, 1873, the day before Grant was sworn in for his second term, Congress passed a law to double the salary of the president from $25,000, where it had stood since George Washington's time. The act also affected the salaries of Supreme Court justices and provided members of Congress with a retroactive pay increase amounting to a 50 percent raise. The "salary grab" so incensed the public that Congress subsequently rescinded the act.[52]

In 1874, the public learned of the "Sanborn Incident," a scandal that began when Grant's secretary of the treasury, William A. Richardson, hired a private citizen, John D. Sanborn, to collect back taxes owed to the federal treasury. As part of the deal, Richardson allowed Sanborn to retain half the taxes he collected as compensation. Sanborn ultimately claimed $213,000, of which $156,000 went to his "assistant," Richardson himself. A portion of the funds also wound up in Republican Party campaign coffers.[53]

The following year, a number of criminal enterprises—they were labeled "rings" in the parlance of the day—came to light. They were especially damning because they directly or indirectly implicated administration officials. The Whiskey Ring involved millions of dollars of taxes channeled into a fund from whiskey manufacturers. Orville E. Babcock, the president's close friend and adviser, was named as a ringleader, although he later won an acquittal at trial. The Trading Post Ring involved Secretary of War William Belknap, who accepted extortion funds to allow a trading post agent to remain on duty at Fort Sill, Oklahoma. A House investigative committee discovered that the navy secretary, George M. Robeson, had used $15 million in naval construction appropriations to purchase eighteen home lots in Washington, D.C., in an episode known as the Naval Ring. Interior secretary Columbus Delano resigned in disgrace when he was found to have accepted bribes to provide fraudulent land grants.[54]

Aside from the political corruption that overwhelmed the Grant administration, the Panic of 1873 captured the national attention at a time when support for Reconstruction was on a marked decline. Origins of the panic dated back to the railroad construction boom that began as soon as the war ended in 1865. More than 35,000 miles of track were laid between 1866 and 1873. Anxious to spur economic activity, the federal government under both Johnson and Grant had provided generous grants and subsidies to the railroads. Not only did the construction frenzy create jobs, but new miles of track ensured that the United States would enjoy unprecedented transportation benefits. One of the challenges in governing a geographically large nation was that information, goods, and services required weeks or even months to travel the breadth of the land. Railroads connected Americans and promised a future no longer subject to the tyranny of a large, wide-open land mass. The federal government even helped to rebuild the miles of track destroyed by the Union army in the South.[55]

The furious investment in railroad companies made them the largest employer in the nation outside of the agricultural sector. With each new railroad project, it seemed the expansion would never die. Although large capital investments are inherently risky, citizens came to see the railroads as a sure thing. Speculators willingly accepted the risk of investing funds in clearing land and laying track; in time, the entire infrastructure surrounding the railroads—everything from docks, factories, steel mills, and lumber companies to suppliers of farm animals, among others—was operating at or near capacity. As lucrative as the railroad business was in those booming postwar years, a "bubble" had been created. It could not, and did not, last.[56]

Speculators and banks had invested so much money into railroads and other infrastructure improvements that little capital was available for other projects, especially in the cash-starved South. Delays in acquiring eminent domain rights or title to land, clearing off brush and debris, and blasting through mountains that littered the landscape of large western states meant that little money was available for circulation. The lack of capital was especially burdensome for small farmers who needed loans to purchase seed, equipment, livestock, and day-to-day necessities just to survive until the crops were harvested. National banks stepped into this void and provided ready credit to speculators involved with railroad companies, but they were reluctant to advance funds to farmers when the return on investment seemed tenuous at best. The rise of the banking system came at an especially propitious time; it meant that banks would be ready, willing, and able to fund the expansion of large capital enterprises, but it too often neglected the small entrepreneur.[57]

The federal government was only too happy to accommodate the postwar construction bonanza by enacting a series of laws to establish the modern banking system. The first laws dated from the last two years of the Civil War and required each bank designated as part of the national system to accept one another's notes as legal tender for all debts, public and private. The citizenry was pleased that national public policy was no longer focused merely on vestiges of the war and Reconstruction. Economic expansion and the promise of a larger, more robust economy were wildly popular ideas. If this system of unrestrained expansion triggered inflation—or interfered with treaties signed

with Native Americans as tribal lands were gobbled up at a prodigious rate—
it was a small price to pay for the good times that seemed likely to supplant
wartime years of hardship and scarcity.[58]

By 1869, the first year of the Grant presidency, a few ominous signs appeared on the horizon suggesting that the economic boom was unsustainable
in the long term. On Black Friday, September 24, 1869, financiers Jay Gould
and Jim Fisk attempted to corner the gold market. Only the administration's
decision to release more government gold into the marketplace forestalled a
larger panic. Even so, the collapse of gold prices ruined many speculators and
highlighted weaknesses in the economy. Worse was to come.[59]

In 1873, the United States enacted the Coinage Act, which decreed that
the national currency would no longer be backed with silver and gold. Gold
would be the sole standard. The statute caused an immediate depression in silver prices. Although silver miners and producers were able to make up their
losses by investing in foreign markets, once again the economy experienced
a downturn that caught many speculators by surprise.[60]

The 1870s became a period of economic turmoil for many Americans despite the promising expansion early in the decade. After the Black Friday incident of 1869, a huge fire that destroyed much of Chicago in 1871, an equine
influenza outbreak in 1872, the Coinage Act of 1873, and the administration's
scandals, it seemed that the American way of life preserved during the war
might be on a permanent decline despite the postwar boom. Confidence in
government declined sharply.[61]

The most serious economic crisis occurred in September 1873. The administration finally had begun to worry about inflation after the tremendous
economic growth of the late 1860s and early 1870s. As a result, the federal
government had contracted the money supply. With investment capital tied
up in large-scale infrastructure projects and fewer government notes in circulation, a company strapped for funding was in desperate straits. It was not surprising that an undercapitalized or overextended enterprise would be forced
out of business in those years, but when a major financier was involved, the
consequences were devastating. Jay Cooke & Company, a heavy investor in
railroads, found it could not market millions of dollars of Northern Pacific
Railway bonds. Despite clear signs that an economic downturn was in the
offing, speculators had continued to pour funds into railroads and large-scale
risky enterprises well into 1872 and 1873. Jay Cooke had gambled that a
second transcontinental railroad would repeat the success of the first. Anticipating the millions to be earned, he made plans to inaugurate the new line
after ground was broken near Duluth, Minnesota, in 1870. When he could
not obtain an expected $300 million government loan, however, he could no
longer operate his cash-strapped business. Jay Cooke & Company declared
bankruptcy on September 18, 1873.[62]

With this business failure and its aftershocks, the shaky U.S. financial system collapsed like a poorly constructed house of cards. The demise of Cooke & Company was almost unfathomable before September 1873. The firm was an anchor for much of the banking industry and was thought to be an impregnable fortress of finance. The bankruptcy filing triggered a chain reaction of bank failures throughout the nation's industrial centers. The New York Stock Exchange closed for ten days beginning September 20 to stem the downward spiral. Unfortunately, the damage was done. The United States slipped into a depression as industrial demand declined and factories laid off workers. Unemployment eventually reached 14 percent. During the next two years, eighty-nine of the country's 364 railroads declared bankruptcy and some eighteen thousand business concerns ceased to exist.[63]

Much of the citizenry had expressed faith in Ulysses S. Grant's ability to bring peace and prosperity to the land after the tumult of the war and early Reconstruction under Andrew Johnson. That faith had carried Grant and his party to victory in 1868. He had won reelection in 1872 not because he had amassed a stellar record of victories but because he seemed the lesser of two evils. By the mid-1870s, voters were weary of Republican rule in general and the excesses of the Grant administration in particular, although the president himself remained popular with Americans who appreciated his war record and personal integrity. In the 1874 elections, the Democrats, no longer seen merely as the party of secession, captured the House of Representatives and gained ten seats in the Senate.[64]

As if all these challenges were not enough for the ailing Grant administration to juggle, many members of Congress were determined to win the tug-of-war with the executive over which branch of government should direct national public policy. Grant favored a vigorous chief executive; he refused to go gentle into that good night. As part of his battle with Congress, he fought against the Tenure of Office Act, the statute that served as the ostensible basis for Johnson's impeachment, throughout his term in office. Although he managed to whittle away at the statute's most onerous provisions, it wasn't until 1887, when President Grover Cleveland sat in the Executive Mansion, that the act was finally repealed. In the meantime, the president and Congress continued to butt heads over national priorities, including which branch should control what remained of the nation's Reconstruction program.[65]

Unfortunately for the freedmen, at a time when a counter-Reconstruction movement erupted throughout the South, the Radicals were almost completely eliminated from power, and even moderate Republicans turned away from the problems of civil rights and racial equality. As abolitionist Theodore Tilton wrote in 1871, the Republican Party "has lost the manly mettle of its youth. Its soul is languid. Ceasing to battle for ideas, it now sits down to count figures. It does not sow new seed—it is only garnering its former harvest."[66]

Reconstruction policy was ripe for change when the administration left office in March 1877. Although Grant remained a popular public figure despite his perceived failures as president, numerous detractors agreed with Henry Adams's acerbic assessment of the old general's years as chief executive: "The progress of evolution from President Washington to President Grant was alone evidence enough to upset Darwin."[67]

Chapter Six

"Radicalism Is Dissolving—Going to Pieces, but What Is to Take Its Place Does Not Clearly Appear"

Elias Hill was fifty years old in May 1871. Partially paralyzed since the age of seven and cursed with a dwarflike body, to all appearances he was a wizened, misshapen freak, a danger to no one save perhaps himself. His legs were so tiny they resembled a child's; one arm was locked in a frozen, arthritic claw, virtually a useless appendage. If ever a man faced formidable circumstances in his life, it was Elias Hill. He had been born a slave but had struggled to gain an education, a Herculean task for a black child coming of age in ante-bellum South Carolina. Young Elias's father had purchased his own freedom and eventually saved enough money to free his wife from a life of bondage as well. The slave master saw no point in retaining a disabled child on the premises without the child's parents, so he allowed the boy to accompany his mother into freedom.

Despite his physical deformities, or perhaps because of them, Elias grew to adulthood relatively unscathed by the oppressive atmosphere of the South Carolina Upcountry. Whites gazed at the monstrosity in their midst and dismissed him as harmless. In this case, appearances were deceiving. Hill grew up to be a Baptist minister who possessed a keen, inquisitive mind and a gift for oratory that transformed him into a leader of the black community in York County despite his handicap. Local Negroes paid him to tutor their children and congregated from miles around to hear his fiery sermons. At the dawn of the 1870s, his unabashed support for Union policies and the Grant administration irked white South Carolinians. "I believe the Republican Party advocates what is nearer the laws of God than any other party, and therefore I feel that it is right," he said on one occasion. Although they had been slow to recognize the power of the dwarfish preacher, unreconstructed rebels living in the county eventually decided the "uppity" Negro must be taught a lesson.

It would be an unforgettable lesson taught by brutal taskmasters. Sometime after midnight on May 5, a gang of hoodlums wearing disguises visited the messianic troublemaker under cover of night. Barking dogs and thundering horses heralded their arrival. Elias Hill's brother shared the same property but lived closer to the road; consequently, the mob arrived at his house first. With no hesitation, the ruffians broke down his brother's door and demanded to know where the preacher man was hiding. Listening to his sister-in-law's screams in the next house, Elias knew it was only a matter of time before they came for him.

Within minutes, the assault began. "Someone then hit my door," he later recalled. "It flew open. One ran in the house, and stopping about the middle of the house, which is a small cabin, he turned around, as it seemed to me as I lay there awake, and said, 'Who's here?' Then I knew they would take me, and I answered, 'I am here.' He shouted for joy, as it seemed, 'Here he is! Here he is! We have found him!' and he threw the bedclothes off of me and caught me by one arm, while another man took me by the other and they carried me into the yard between the houses."

York County had been the scene of suspicious fires of late; conventional wisdom suggested that angry blacks had instigated the attacks in retaliation for real or imagined outrages perpetrated against their community. Based on this assumption, the gang screamed at Hill to tell them who was responsible. No one seriously thought the afflicted preacher had started the fires, but they surmised that he had ordered them set. Hill demurred: "I told them it was not me; I could not burn houses; it was unreasonable to ask me. Then they hit me with their fists, and said I did it, I ordered it."

It was not enough to physically beat Elias Hill. He must be humbled, terrorized on pain of death. "They pointed pistols at me all around my head once or twice, as if they were going to shoot me, telling me they were going to kill me; wasn't I ready to die, and willing to die? Didn't I preach?" The men shouted their questions so quickly Hill did not have time to answer. He tried to respond, but he was told to hush. With alarming viciousness, the leader of the group stepped forward and administered the worst beating of the night. "He had a horsewhip, and he told me to pull up my shirt, and he hit me. He told me at every lick, 'Hold up your shirt.' I made a moan every time he cut with the horsewhip. I reckon he struck me eight cuts right on the hip bone; it was almost the only place he could hit my body, my legs are so short—all my limbs drawn up and withered away with pain."

As Hill writhed on the ground in agony, someone threatened to drag him to the river and drown him. Convinced he would be brutally murdered if he defied their orders, he agreed to publish a card in the newspaper renouncing Republicanism. He also agreed not to vote again in York County, agreed to cease talking to a Republican newspaper in Charleston, and promised to quit preaching. His attackers were blunt; they assured their victim they would watch to see whether he complied and "if I did not they would come back the next week and kill me."[1]

Elias Hill had encountered a shadowy paramilitary organization known as the Ku Klux Klan. Of all the counter-Reconstruction efforts in the Southern states, perhaps the most stubbornly persistent problem involved the activities of this and similar extralegal gangs that used violence as a means of terrorizing the freedmen. The attack on this unusual Baptist preacher was notable only because he survived the assault.[2]

Klan violence spread throughout the South during the late 1860s and early 1870s, but nowhere was it as widespread as in the South Carolina Upcountry, the 100-mile swath of land nestled between the Savannah River to the west and the Pee Dee River to the east. By the spring of 1871, the situation had grown so dire that the War Department dispatched a company of the Seventh U.S. Cavalry to restore law and order. Major Lewis Merrill, a West Point graduate and career soldier, commanded ninety men detached from the regiment. He had arrived in York County on March 26, a little more than a month before the attack on Elias Hill. Although the number of incidents had declined since his arrival, Merrill had experienced guerrilla warfare earlier in his career and labored under no illusions; the Klan still controlled the area. Fearing additional nocturnal raids unless he decisively acted, the major called the leading citizens of Yorkville, the county's commercial hub, to his office so that he could lay down the law.[3]

"I came here from Kansas, where I had no knowledge at all of anything connected with these matters, except as one gets in the ordinary reading of the newspapers," he later recalled. "I fully believed that the stories in circulation were enormous exaggerations. When I first came here I was impressed for a number of days with the idea, from my conversation with the principal people here, and from the appearance of things, that there was a probability, and so I reported, of a speedy termination of these acts." Merrill explained why he changed his mind about the stories of Klan activities. "But very soon, from the facts brought to my notice, I had occasion to change my mind, and I became convinced that the Ku-Klux organization was not only a very large one and exceedingly well organized, but a very dangerous one."

He told Yorkville citizens that the U.S. Army would no longer permit vigilante night riders to terrorize the South Carolina Upcountry. Henceforth, the federal government would ensure that domestic tranquility prevailed for the freedmen and their families. Anyone who engaged in violence or aided and abetted the Klan faced immediate arrest and prosecution. The major reminded the citizens that President Grant had taken a personal interest in events unfolding in South Carolina. The outrages must end. Unless community leaders stepped in to restrain the Klansmen, the federal government would intercede by suspending habeas corpus and declaring martial law. He reminded them that recent legislation enacted by Congress authorized the president to use his powers to respond when civil unrest threatened to undermine law and order. Admonishing them that "the choice is yours," Merrill urged Yorkville's white residents to do what they could to suppress the Klan, or outsiders would do it for them.

It was an impressive performance, perhaps a bit theatrical and heavy-handed for some tastes, but effective nonetheless. The message, delivered to fifteen or twenty leading citizens of Yorkville, some of whom undoubtedly were affiliated with the Klan, generated dismay among the townspeople. The extent of Merrill's knowledge of the KKK's inner workings was uncanny. Somehow he had found insiders to "puke"—that is, tell all they knew, as in "spill their guts"—about the group's symbolism and operations. The officer had compiled a massive dossier of information. He spoke tough words. If they were true, from that moment on Kluxers no longer owned the night. They rode at their peril. Only time would tell whether Major Merrill possessed the resources and wherewithal to back up his threats with action.[4]

Almost two-thirds of the citizens of this impoverished agricultural area known as the Piedmont region were Klansmen or sympathizers. It was little wonder. The remnants of the Old South were still in place; traditions and customs stretching back for generations died hard. Many white South Carolinians had been born and bred in the years before the "Late Unpleasantness" to believe that the Negro was not the equal of the white man. Even the lowliest dirt-poor farmer of York County hardscrabble stock found solace in the realization that he was not at the bottom of the social strata. No matter how modest his station in life, he could always look to the Negro as his social inferior. Few York County denizens were genuine members of the planter elite, but each white man had much invested in the racial ethic of the Old South.[5]

Days after the meeting in Merrill's office, a public petition condemning Klan violence appeared. Hundreds of York County citizens signed the petition, including a number of Klansmen who sought to elude detection. As reported in the local newspaper, the *Yorkville Enquirer*, on May 25:

> The undersigned citizens of York County, earnestly desiring the preservation of the public peace and for the purpose of guaranteeing to all citizens the protection of life and liberty, respectfully urge it as a common duty for every citizen to discourage all acts of violence. We do not desire to dictate to others but are convinced that a repetition of violence must disorganize society and result in a spirit of general insubordination, the consequence of which may be deplored when too late to be remedied. As members of the community whose common

interest is imperiled, we pledge our individual efforts and influence to prevent further acts of violence, and will support the civil authorities in bringing offenders to justice. We respectfully solicit a hearty co-operation of our fellow citizens throughout the county in our efforts to preserve the peace and prevent further acts of violence.[6]

The major was not naïve; a petition was a promise secured by nothing more than words, especially if the words were duplicitous. Nonetheless, it was a gesture toward reconciliation, albeit perhaps a hollow one, but preferable to no gesture at all. If the petition was less than totally effective, it suggested the seriousness of the situation and the consequences attendant to engaging in further mayhem. An editorial in the *Yorkville Enquirer* observed that "unless our people at once determine that there will be no further acts of violence in the county, we will soon have occasion to observe the practical operations of the law at its utmost severity, and with all its unpleasant consequences."[7]

Merrill had not merely threatened the white malcontents. He meant what he said. During the time he was stationed in South Carolina, he penetrated the Klan as no other outsider had done. In a report dated June 9, 1871, addressed to his superior officer, General Alfred Terry, he revealed the first public glimpse inside a Ku Klux Klan den. According to informants, an officer known as a grand cyclops headed the South Carolina organization. The grand cyclops was in charge of several chiefs, each of whom commanded a squad of between eight and ten men. Squads communicated with one another through a series of secret signs, codes, and passwords. In extreme cases, a Kluxer could issue a clarion call: "Avalanche!" By whistling two bars of a musical notation, one squad could alert a second squad to attack a particular home. "This signal has been in constant use among them on their night rides and is described by every Negro who has heard it," the major told his commander in the June report.[8]

Merrill and his superiors recognized the Klan's goal was political. The hated Republican Party had prosecuted the war under Abraham Lincoln; afterward, his successors had implemented what white Southerners regarded as draconian Reconstruction policies. Despite the struggles between President Johnson and the Radical Republicans in Congress, the policies that had governed the South for a half-dozen years were primarily the result of Republican victories. As Merrill noted in his report, "Beyond doubt the object of the organization in this vicinity is to terrify the Negroes into obeying the whites in voting or to compel them to stay away from the polls." Negroes voted Republican if they were not prevented from reaching the polls. By terrorizing black community leaders such as Elias Hill and demanding they renounce Republicanism while also eschewing the franchise, Kluxers hoped to strengthen the Democratic Party in the South.[9]

Appalled that such behavior engendered sympathy within the community, Merrill continually sent messages to General Terry and others within the Grant administration warning of a wave of lawlessness washing over the South Carolina Upcountry. The major learned that even he and his men were possible targets of violence. An informant intimated in June that the Klan was planning to slip up on the cavalrymen one night while they patrolled near the little town of Rock Hill. Kluxers intended to fire their rifles into the soldiers' camp—perhaps to frighten the men, perhaps to hit them.[10]

Incensed, Major Merrill again contacted Yorkville's leading citizens. This time, in a written missive, he explained in no uncertain terms that the U.S. Army would not stand for a direct attack by armed hooligans. As part of his preparations, the major ordered additional night patrols and instructed his men to "shoot to kill." Several citizens, including Dr. Rufus Bratton, a reputed Klan leader, visited Merrill and assured him that stories of a planned raid on the soldiers were no more than rumors spread by excitable, misinformed citizens. The major did not believe the assurances, and he said as much. In any event, the attack never occurred. No doubt the Klansmen came to their senses. It was one thing to attack defenseless blacks in the dark. It was almost suicidal to assail well-trained, seasoned, armed, professional soldiers, especially when the soldiers possessed foreknowledge of the scheme. Night riding even declined for a few weeks after Dr. Bratton's discussion with Major Merrill.[11]

Ironically, decreased Klan activity left the Seventh Cavalry in a quandary. Merrill's soldiers were empowered to use necessary force to combat an imminent threat, but a shadowy group hiding in the darkness, biding its time, presented problems. On one hand, if violence ceased while the perpetrators waited patiently, the soldiers eventually would depart. Once they were gone, the Klan could resume normal operations. On the other hand, if the U.S. Army refused to wait for another attack and carried out a sustained campaign to root out Kluxers without carefully identifying the culprits, they risked enraging community members who quietly loathed the Klan. Frustrated with this muddled state of affairs, the major was tempted to round up all community leaders, due process be damned, but he exercised restraint. "It requires great patience and self control to keep one's hands off these infamous cowards," he later remarked.[12]

He knew the importance of gathering evidence, nailing down witnesses and testimony, and assembling a case that could withstand judicial scrutiny. Dramatic speeches delivered to leading citizens and the possibility of armed confrontations were heady, exciting stuff, but Merrill realized it was dull, plodding, methodical preparatory work that would ultimately defeat the Klan. As the days passed and order appeared to return to Yorkville, he instructed his men to comb the countryside for evidence. He held secret meetings with informants and with terrified freedmen who provided additional information on nefarious activities within the county. The major's periodic reports to the War Department built a strong case for increased federal intervention.[13]

On July 22, a three-man congressional subcommittee visited York County to follow up on Merrill's reports. Subcommittee members already had held hearings in Columbia, Union, and Spartanburg, South Carolina, before they arrived. With assistance from local Republican congressman Alexander S. Wallace, the group located eyewitnesses to confirm details the major had previously provided. Their corroboration enhanced Merrill's credibility.[14]

Congressman Wallace was more progressive than most of his constituents, a fact that created tension throughout 1871 and eventually led to his electoral defeat in 1876, the year of the "great redemption" in South Carolina politics. The same evening the subcommittee arrived in Yorkville, Wallace invited the group to dine with him at a local restaurant inside the town's leading hotel. As the members sat down to their meal, a gentleman at a nearby table noticed their arrival. Apparently inebriated, the rowdy fellow loudly announced his low opinion of meddlesome outsiders. Lurching to his feet, he continued his verbal assault, demanding to know which of the men was Congressman Wallace. When Wallace spoke up, the enraged diner reached for a pitcher of cream to splash in the congressman's face.

He might have succeeded in dousing the South Carolina lawmaker were it not for the hotel proprietor, who witnessed the exchange and grabbed the pitcher in midflight. Unfortunately, the tussle sent the contents flying onto Congressman Job Stevenson of Ohio. The scene struck many observers as comical. When Stevenson and Wallace stood and thrust their hands into their pockets to retrieve handkerchiefs, everyone assumed they were reaching for weapons. Such was the custom in York County during that era that violent behavior was acceptable and, indeed, expected. The assailant later apologized to Congressman Stevenson, but for many days afterward he was hailed as a local hero.[15]

A worse episode followed. When they learned of the subcommittee's visit to their community, many York County Negroes were delighted. They appeared in front of the hotel the same evening that the intoxicated restaurant patron hurled his epithets and the pitcher of cream at the congressmen. As blacks stood outside the hotel and serenaded subcommittee members, the local constable, a well-known Klansman, appeared and ordered the crowd to disperse. Although the facts were never clear, some Negroes apparently refused to comply. The constable moved to arrest a black man standing in the crowd, but the fellow defiantly resisted. In the resulting melee, the officer drew his pistol and shot the offender five times in rapid succession. The

scuffle escalated into shouting and fisticuffs; it might have erupted into a
full-fledged riot had Major Merrill and his men not interceded. In the chaotic
aftermath, the white community hailed the constable as a man of courage and
conviction while the black community regarded the brouhaha as but another
dastardly affair in a long series of outrages perpetrated by the ruling class
against the freedmen. To his dismay, Major Merrill was unable to arrest the
sheriff owing to the lack of credible witnesses willing to testify against the
assailant.[16]

The subcommittee remained in Yorkville for six days, but committee
members had seen enough the first evening to appreciate the dangerous circumstances prevailing in the South Carolina Upcountry. The Klan controlled
the machinery of local government in York and surrounding counties, and
it engaged in lawless acts with support from local political leaders. Even in
cases when whites did not approve of the Klan, they dared not speak out for
fear of reprisal. Other citizens expressed passive indifference. As long as the
Klan did not directly bother them, they were satisfied to turn a blind eye to
events destroying their community.[17]

During the summer of 1871, while he waited for the Grant administration to stop vacillating and authorize him to arrest Klansmen terrorizing the
Upcountry, the major presented evidence to the local courts. He faced an
almost impossible battle, and he knew it. York County judge William M.
Thomas explained that an all-white grand jury, which would decide whether
enough evidence existed to move forward with the case, was unlikely to in-
dict KKK suspects any more than an all-white petit jury, which would weigh
the evidence, was likely to convict the defendants. Mindful of the long odds
stacked against him, Merrill pressed on, presenting his evidence to the county
prosecutor in hopes of exposing the Klan to community ridicule. The judge
and the prosecutor argued that the evidence was weak and flimsy, but Merrill
insisted they present the information to the grand jury.[18]

The county grand jury convened in September 1871. Merrill was furious
when he realized that some jury members—perhaps as many as a third—were
Klansmen or their relatives. Even conscientious jurors, in the major's words,
were "browbeaten and overruled by the rest." It was no surprise that the term
of court ended with no indictments issued. Observing the scene with disgust,
Merrill remarked that the court proceedings were "so broad a farce that it was
distasteful to be forced in contact with it."[19]

In the meantime, South Carolina's carpetbagger governor, Robert K. Scott,
was desperate to stop the Ku Klux Klan from interfering with the orderly
operation of state government. A native of Ohio, the transplanted political
leader had served in the U.S. Army during the Civil War and later worked
with the Freedmen's Bureau. He had not sought the governorship; he had

agreed to run only after the South Carolina Republican Party pressed him into service. He remains a controversial figure. Some historians have contended that Scott misused his office to line his own pockets while others have found him to be a well-meaning public servant who was overwhelmed by the violence and ubiquity of the Klan and other Reconstruction-era militia groups. Coupled with Merrill's reports to the War Department, Scott's request for assistance finally pushed Washington to intervene.[20]

The Grant administration had been slow to react to the rising Klan menace, fearing that any military action interpreted as oppressive would trigger additional bloodshed. The Civil War had ended six years earlier, but everyone was mindful that Reconstruction was far from successful in changing hearts and minds. Although the South no longer possessed the resources to engage in full-scale military operations, guerrilla fighting was not out of the question. As a former general officer, President Grant was keenly aware of the destructive potential of a guerrilla campaign, having witnessed such activity in the western theater of the war.[21]

As stories of Klan atrocities reached his office, the president came to realize that he must act decisively. He told his advisers he had hesitated because he did not wish to open old wounds about the legitimacy of federal intervention into state affairs. Congress had enacted several new laws, notably the Civil Rights Act of 1866 and the Enforcement Act of 1870, empowering the federal government to become more involved in state issues; nonetheless, Grant pursued a conservative course. A second Enforcement Act in 1871 placed congressional elections under federal supervision, but the central government remained on the sidelines.[22]

Finally, Grant could no longer wait for white law enforcement officials to restore order in the Southern states. On April 20, 1871, he signed a new federal law—a third Enforcement Act known as the Ku Klux Klan Act of 1871, commonly called the "Force Bill"—which made it a federal offense for any persons to conspire to deny a citizen of the United States the right to participate in political life, own property, vote, or serve on a jury. Despite these provisions, the Force Bill was not as far reaching as it might have been. It fell short of authorizing the imposition of martial law or trying defendants before a military tribunal. Yet the president could intervene into state affairs if, in his view, it was necessary to ensure the "equal protection of the laws" pursuant to the Fourteenth Amendment.[23]

Major Merrill and the Seventh Cavalry had arrived in South Carolina a month before the Ku Klux Klan Act was signed; consequently, their initial orders were limited in scope. It was only at the urging of Grant's second attorney general, Amos Akerman, who had read Merrill's and the subcommittee's reports and had visited South Carolina, that the president finally agreed to use his authority under the Ku Klux Klan Act. On October 12, 1871, partially as a reaction to reports that violence had escalated once again, Grant suspended the writ of habeas corpus in nine South Carolina counties—York, Chester, Lancaster, Fairfield, Spartanburg, Union, Laurens, Newberry, and Chesterfield.[24]

White citizens of the South Carolina Upcountry knew what the president's action meant for their way of life. For the second time in a decade, the Federals had sent armed men into their communities to enforce an edict promulgated by an activist central government. "It is reported that martial law is declared and that the Yankees will commence arresting the men at any time," Mary Davis Brown of the Beersheba Presbyterian Church noted in her diary. "Billy and Caty and John, Lawson and Mag is here tonight, afraid to lie down and go to sleep. Lawson and John left this morning before daylight. I have been down to York today to see what I could hear. They have made no arrests yet but great excitement."[25]

Major Merrill shared the excitement. He finally possessed the authority he needed to take decisive action without having to rely on the civilian court system, which he believed, with good reason, to be under Klan control. He had told Yorkville citizens on May 13 that the federal government would not stand by idly while chaos reigned supreme. Those tough words had not been followed with decisive action in the spring. The delay had cost the young major much prestige, but now things would be different. It was time to demonstrate the power and might of the U.S. Cavalry. Three additional companies of the Seventh arrived by October 19, just in time to round up suspected Kluxers after the president's suspension of habeas corpus. By the end of the month, seventy-nine citizens had been arrested on suspicion of perpetrating or assisting in Klan abuses.[26]

Most Klan leaders already had fled the jurisdiction by October. The jails were crowded mostly with old men, Klan followers, and citizens too impoverished to seek more hospitable environs. Attorney General Akerman arrived to observe the arrests and confer with Major Merrill. "Day after day, for weeks," the major recalled of that time in October 1871, "men came in such numbers that time to hear them confess and means to dispose of or take care of them both failed, and I was powerless to do anything more than secure the persons of those most deeply criminal, and send the rest to their homes on their personal parole to be forthcoming when called for. In some instances, whole Klans, headed by their chief, came in and surrendered together."[27]

Merrill understood the basic tenets of criminal investigations: if a prosecutor could not capture a decision maker in the initial sweep, he could broker a deal with underlings by promising leniency in exchange for information necessary to prosecute higher-ranking members. Using this method, the major discovered information about suspected Klansmen that he had not discovered for himself. By the end of the calendar year, almost two hundred defendants awaited trial.[28]

Of the high-ranking defendants who fled the scene, Dr. Rufus Bratton was the most influential Klansman to abscond. He was among the leading citizens who spoke with Merrill about the need to curb KKK violence in the spring. When the October arrests began, the good doctor no doubt realized the evidence against him was overwhelming and would probably lead to his conviction. He moved to his sister's home in Barnwell, South Carolina, where he hid for several months before fleeing to Selma, Alabama. With federal authorities in hot pursuit, Bratton decided he would be safe only if he left the United States. Sometime around May 22, 1872, he slipped across the border and set up residence in London, Ontario, Canada. Living under an assumed name, "John Simpson," he met with many former York County residents and built a new life as a member of an expatriate community of Klansmen and their sympathizers.

Unfortunately for Dr. Bratton, indefatigable U.S. Secret Service agents tracked him to Ontario. Around 4:00 p.m. on June 4, 1872, two intrepid agents wrestled the fifty-one-year-old physician to the ground and handcuffed him despite his loud protests for onlookers to render assistance. He caused such a furor that eventually the Canadian government learned of the incident. Even as the defendant was formally arrested across the border in Detroit, Canadian officials inquired into the circumstances. Despite later rumors of an international incident owing to the abduction, the scene was hardly confrontational. Exchanges between Canadian and U.S. border officials remained cordial. After Bratton posted $12,000 bail in South Carolina, he escaped again to Canada and set up a medical practice. His wife and children joined him shortly thereafter. The family remained in Ontario until 1876, when they decided to return to South Carolina under the protections afforded by the General Amnesty Act of 1872.[29]

In 1905, novelist Thomas Dixon Jr. loosely modeled the protagonist in his pro-Confederate tract, *The Clansman*, on Dr. Bratton. Dixon's novel was especially important in Southern history because it served as the basis for the first full-length motion picture ever made, D. W. Griffith's histrionic, whitewashed view of history, *The Birth of a Nation*. The film's romanticized view of the Ku Klux Klan led, in part, to the emergence of a second chapter in the history of this extremist organization when several zealous, xenophobic Georgians formed a new group atop Stone Mountain, Georgia, on Thanksgiving Night 1915.[30]

Upcountry Kluxers who lacked Dr. Bratton's resources and contacts in the fall of 1871 soon found themselves stuffed into the Yorkville jail, a dilapidated three-story structure erected near the edge of town. The edifice was not known for its spacious quarters or luxurious amenities. "The ground floor is occupied as a residence of the jailer's family," the *New York Tribune* observed on November 23. "The upper stories are divided into cells and corridors, and now contain more than 100 Ku Klux. The prison is guarded by sentries and is under the charge of Captain Ogden of the 18th Infantry. The prisoners are not confined in the cells, but have limited range of the corridors. They are so closely crowded that there is not much more than room enough on the floor of the cells and corridors for all to lie down at night."[31]

The sudden appearance of four hundred armed soldiers on the Yorkville streets and the incarceration of dozens of male citizens transformed the town into a vista eerily reminiscent of the war. Visiting the town on November 12, a *New York Tribune* reporter was astonished. "The place had the look of a town in war time recently captured by an invading army. There were soldiers everywhere. An infantry camp of clean, white tents, arranged in regular rows, with the alleys between prettily shaded with arbors of green boughs, stood in an oak grove near the station. Everybody but the Negroes and soldiers had the look of excitement and despondency always observable in the inhabitants of a conquered town, and the people I met eyed me suspiciously, as if they feared I might have come to empty some new vial of Government wrath upon their devoted heads."[32]

Even more astonishing than the sight of an occupied territory was the lack of community guilt or outrage at the Klan's activities. The same reporter was dumbstruck by the lack of a "sense of right and wrong, no appreciation of the heinousness of crimes committed upon helpless and offending people." White citizens of York County reserved their righteous indignation for the federal troops who audaciously engaged in "arbitrary arrests" that tore white men from their families with little regard for their civil liberties.[33]

As the number of defendants increased and the jails filled to capacity and beyond, Attorney General Akerman conferred with David T. Corbin, the U.S. attorney for South Carolina, to develop a plan for prosecuting the offenders. The two men agreed that all Kluxers ought to be held accountable for their actions according to their degree of culpability, but the sheer volume of cases precluded mass prosecutions. Akerman explained his thinking in a November 18 letter to Merrill's commanding officer, General Terry. "I feel greatly saddened by this business," he wrote. "It has revealed a perversion of moral sentiment among the Southern whites, which bodes ill to that part of the country for this generation. Without a thorough moral renovation, society there for many years will be—I can hardly bring myself to say savage, but certainly very far from Christian."[34]

Despite this "perversion of moral sentiment" and the possibly "savage" nature of Southern society, Akerman understood that the legal process could not change the citizens' hearts and minds. The best he could expect would be to make examples of Klan leaders in hopes that white South Carolinians would hesitate to support the group. With this end in mind, the attorney general instructed Corbin to focus attention on prosecuting offenders evincing "deep criminality" and leave those men whose "criminality was inferior" for a later date. Other citizens—those persons who did not support the Klan but had tolerated the outrages and reluctantly participated after the fact out of concern for their own safety—were to be released altogether, provided "they bear themselves as good citizens henceforth."[35]

Watching the trial strategy unfold from the sidelines, Major Merrill was incredulous. He had spent more than six months, often at his peril, preparing cases against York County Klansmen. To watch men he personally knew to be guilty released with such light punishment—or no punishment at all apart from the original arrest—was almost more than he could bear. Allowing low-ranking Klansmen to plead to a lesser offense in exchange for testimony against higher-ranking group members was understandable; forgoing prosecution in the name of administrative expediency was unconscionable. Although he understood Akerman's and Corbin's reasons for concentrating on the most promising cases, the major, himself a former military prosecutor, was dismayed. If all his months of methodical investigation were reduced to a handful of prosecutions, he was afraid his labors had been for naught. The U.S. Army could not patrol the nine counties of the South Carolina Piedmont region indefinitely. Merrill feared for the security of the freedmen when the last Union soldier marched away. Blacks would be left at the mercy of their former masters, many of whom remained unreconstructed Confederates and active Kluxers.[36]

The Ku Klux Klan's reign of terror in the South Carolina Upcountry in the early 1870s was by no means the only area where terrorists operated during Reconstruction. White supremacist groups terrorized freedmen in every Southern state and in Northern states as well. The South Carolina episode was illustrative because it demonstrated the scope of resistance to Reconstruction policies in the states of the recently defeated Southern Confederacy. Even when the cavalry literally rode to the rescue, it was no easy matter to suppress a popular insurgency. Identifying, rounding up, and prosecuting perpetrators always presented problems. Modern historians have studied the Upcountry example and concluded that the U.S. Army was instrumental in exposing abuses and penetrating the shadowy world of the Klan, an essential step in destroying the Invisible Empire's cachet for some white Southerners. The tale serves as an object lesson on how federal intervention, as weak and uncoordinated as it was, prevented whites from completely restoring the antebellum way of life during the years before Southerners again controlled state legislatures.[37]

As the most infamous of the white-line groups to emerge during the era, the Ku Klux Klan served as a symbol of many Southerners' determination to restore social relations to "the proper order," which meant the white race would reign over other races and ethnicities. The Klan began sometime late in 1865 or early in 1866—the date varied, depending on the source—when six ex-Confederate soldiers met in Pulaski, Tennessee, to mull over the victory of the Yankees. Bored with the anticlimax of life under Reconstruction after experiencing the excitement of battle, these gentlemen—James Crowe, Richard Reed, Calvin Jones, John Lester, Frank McCord, and John Kennedy—claimed they had formed a social club. Commentator Wyn Craig Wade writes in his history of the group, *The Fiery Cross*, "It has been said that if Pulaski had had an Elks Club, the Klan would never have been born." Later historians have argued that the image of "benign Klan" acting on fraternity pranks in its early days is convenient mythologizing unsupported by facts. According to this interpretation, the Ku Klux Klan never existed as a social club; it was always an outlet for disaffected white Southerners to prevent blacks from asserting their rights as free citizens of the United States. If state governments were controlled by Northern interlopers—despicable "carpetbaggers" who came South with all their belongings packed into a cheap carpetbag, which meant they lacked ties to the community—white Southerners would work outside of the system.[38]

According to most versions of early KKK history, the original members, subsequently christened the "Pulaski Six," wore decorative sheets and conical hats as disguises and shared secrets signs, symbols, and codes. "Kluxers," as they came to be called, deliberately sought to establish a group mythology. The name was a variation on the Greek word *kuklos*, meaning "circle," referring to the circle of friends who met to plan fraternal activities. By dividing out "ku" from the word *kuklos*, changing "klos" to "klux," and adding "klan" as a way of emphasizing the members' Scotch-Irish ancestry, the founders established a secret society with a name that, in their opinion, sounded like "bones rattling together."[39]

The organization's official mythology dictates that the original Ku Klux Klan was devoted solely to "farcical initiations," often staged in a vacant basement of an abandoned house. The Klan "den" assembled while adorned in robes and recruited new members through shenanigans resembling college

Southerners were infuriated by "carpetbaggers," a derisive term denoting Northerners who came to the South to "interfere" with state governments and schools during Reconstruction. This Thomas Nast cartoon from the November 9, 1872, issue of *Harper's Weekly* caricatured Liberal Republican Carl Schurz and his "carpet bag from Wisconsin to Missouri." Nast was upset because Schurz supported Horace Greeley in the 1872 presidential election.
Courtesy of the Library of Congress.

hazing. These silly games may have been the original purpose—the matter cannot be resolved definitively—but in short order, other ex-Confederates joined in the fun. If one accepts this view, the Pulaski Six were co-opted. Whatever the group's origins, within a few short years the Ku Klux Klan was well poised to serve as a domestic terrorist organization. Virtually every credible historian agrees that sometime in 1867 the Klan emerged as a sinister vigilante group, and two prominent Tennesseans led the way. John C. Brown,

During the late 1860s and early 1870s, masked vigilantes such as the Ku Klux Klan roamed the night, terrorizing freedmen throughout the South. This drawing of the "masked sentinel" shows the elaborate costumes and conical hats of the nineteenth-century Klan.

Reprinted from Albion W. Tourgee, *The Invisible Empire.*

president of the Tennessee Coal and Iron Company and later a governor of Tennessee, lent his prestige to the Klan's growth. George Gordon, a boyish former Confederate general and native of Pulaski, penned a prescript, or set of bylaws, for the group. Modeled on a military hierarchy, the prescript established the Klan as a paramilitary organization. From there, it was a short evolution from fraternity-style pranks to patrolling the Southern roadways in the name of "upholding order."[40]

The first recorded Klan visits to the homes of Negroes occurred at night. Hiding beneath strange, elaborate costumes, Kluxers spoke in "awfully sepulchral tones," claiming to be dead Confederates "from another world" killed on the battlefield and roaming the countryside to avenge their deaths. The jejune stunts would have been laughable had the visits not prompted violence against "uppity" freedmen.[41]

The Klan's greatest public relations success occurred when former Confederate general Nathan Bedford Forrest accepted a position as the grand wizard in 1867. A revered, legendary soldier, the former slave trader lent credibility and legitimacy to the group for many white Southerners. As was the case with his unreconstructed brethren, Forrest was troubled by freedmen who were unwilling to accept "their place" in the postbellum South. He was especially fearful of black paramilitary groups such as the Union League. Forrest and men of his ilk learned of the existence of the Union League and, to their way of thinking, it meant a vast conspiracy existed where Southern turncoats (scalawags), Northern interlopers (carpetbaggers), and blacks (freedmen) worked jointly to control corrupt Southern state governments. White Southerners believed that extralegal vigilante groups were the best means of controlling the rampant corruption unleashed by conspirators who sought to trample the noble South under the boot heels of oppression and tyranny.[42]

Forrest served as an inspiration for prospective Kluxers, but after the organization spread beyond Tennessee it took on a life of its own. His affiliation lasted less than two years. Late in January 1869, he announced in "General Order Number One" that he would no longer associate with the Klan because the "honorable and patriotic" club had been hijacked by terrorists who had subverted the noble virtues of the Old South. The general's apologists contend to this day that KKK activities after Forrest's departure degenerated into something entirely different from what he intended, metamorphosing into an outlet for low-class whites to engage in all manner of nefarious activities that in no way reflected the "true" Klan revered in the group's mythology. This argument is disingenuous. John C. Brown, George Gordon, Nathan Bedford Forrest, and other ex-Confederates anxious to protect white supremacy—whatever the cost to the American creed—created an organization that encouraged violence and lent their imprimatur to forces that could not be contained. For his part, Forrest realized he had created a terrorist group he could not control, so he attempted to disavow all knowledge of, or responsibility for, the results. Historical accountability cannot be avoided so easily. He, Brown, Gordon, and the Pulaski Six were the founding fathers of the KKK. The Klan that Major Lewis Merrill encountered in South Carolina in 1871 had matured, it is true, beyond Forrest's original vision, but it was a recognizable offspring.[43]

The offspring was still in its infancy during the 1868 elections, but the Klan's reputation and power grew enormously after that time. By 1869, the "invisible empire" was well known throughout the South, and concern was growing in other parts of the country as well. *Harper's Weekly* and influential national newspapers regularly reported on the group's activities, often characterizing the Klan as a terrorist arm of the Democratic Party. For Southern Democrats, this appellation was a badge of honor. Northern Democrats dismissed tales of Klan outrages as tall tales exaggerated to embarrass the party and based on nothing more than politically motivated urban legends.[44]

President Grant had been reluctant to commit troops to the fight against Klan activities, but Attorney General Akerman, relying mostly on Major Merrill's meticulous dossier, had convinced the president that even the egregious stories generally were accurate. Grant concluded that the Klan was unquestionably a political group committed "by force and terror, to prevent all political action not in accord with the views of the members, to deprive colored citizens of the right to bear arms and of the right of a free ballot, to suppress the schools in which colored children were taught, and to reduce the colored people to a condition closely allied to that of slavery."[45]

The Klan and similar white supremacist groups did not engage in the concerted action of a military campaign; they were far too autonomous and decentralized for that. If the groups shared anything, it was a common goal of electing Democrats to office at all levels of government. Republicans remained firmly in control in most Southern states in the 1868 elections, but as stories of corruption in carpetbagger governments spread, sympathy for the goals of the Klan, if not for its methods, increased. If subsequent observers armed with the benefit of hindsight could dismiss the Ku Klux Klan as cowardly criminals, little more than homegrown terrorists, such opprobrium was not the view of many whites, especially in the South, during the Reconstruction era.[46]

The antipathy that white South Carolinians felt toward Major Merrill and the Seventh Cavalry was typical in the region. The presence of white interlopers, especially those wearing the uniform of the hated Union soldier, infuriated the locals. It was a heart-wrenching burden for former Confederates to contemplate their defeat in the War between the States; to be reminded daily of that loss and to be dictated to by federal officials was excruciating. Moreover, the federal government, intoxicated with victory, had liberated the slaves, thereby destroying the foundation of the Southern economy; now, the infernal Yankees insisted that freedmen must be afforded a status equal to the white man. Southerners still smarting from battlefield losses felt their own pain and indignities to a great degree. They simply could not empathize with the freedmen, whom they believed to be consigned by God and history to toil away at menial work and be satisfied with lower levels of education, wealth, and opportunity. It was the natural order of things: it had always been that way and would always be that way. Anyone who could not see the efficacy of the "Southern way of life" and its caste system was suspect. So great was the disdain that Southerners felt under the yoke of federal intervention that they remained suspicious of centralized authority until the present day. The pattern was repeated throughout the Southern states; the presence of troops and "outsiders" engendered enormous feelings of resentment that lingered for generations.[47]

Regardless of the delusions white Southerners accepted in their view of race relations and the laws of nature, they were factually correct in one respect: the operation of state governments in the 1860s and 1870s satisfied no one. That Reconstruction-era governments were riddled with corruption cannot be doubted. Radicals enjoyed an overwhelming numerical superiority in seven state legislatures well into the 1870s; consequently, all the abuses and corruption were attributed to them despite evidence that malfeasance was not limited to one party or section of the country. It mattered not that many of the scandals involved whites as well as blacks or that Democrats and Republicans alike participated. Conventional wisdom suggested that federal interference with the Southern states was the chief cause.[48]

James S. Pike's widely read account of the abuses in Reconstruction-era South Carolina, *The Prostrate State: South Carolina under Negro Government*, became the template for the polemic masquerading as history. As an antislavery journalist from Maine and former U.S. ambassador to the Netherlands sent to examine South Carolina's state government during the 1870s, Pike could be counted on to assess conditions in a manner favorable to the Union point of view. He had argued vehemently that the franchise should be extended to blacks after the war. Yet his reports, compiled into book form in 1874, surprised observers who were unaware of Pike's racist proclivities before he traveled south. Denouncing "black barbarism" as "ignorant democracy," Pike turned his back on the freedmen, whom he denigrated as "Sambo." "The present government of South Carolina is not only corrupt and oppressive, it is insulting. It denies the exercise of the rights of white communities, because they are white," he wrote. Lest anyone interpret his remarks as wholly inconsistent with his antislavery views of earlier times, Pike explained that his motives were pure. "These remarks are not intended to perpetuate discontent or hostility. They are plain, frank words, addressed to the good sense and intelligence of the reader. They speak to the judgment only. If they have any force, it comes of their truth and justice alone."[49]

Although few Northerners who had witnessed Southern resistance were fooled by the "truth and justice" of Pike's inflammatory rhetoric, white Southerners were delighted with his missive. If a solid pro-Union man such as James Pike could produce an antifreedmen diatribe after observing blacks in political office in South Carolina, it seemed possible that many white Northerners, even staunch Republicans, would follow suit. Coupled with the Lost Cause mythology suggesting that the South may have lost the war but it remained a place of honor and noble traditions, the Southern view of the period was that Radical Republicans, mostly at the behest of power-hungry Jacobins such as Ben Wade, Thaddeus Stevens, and Charles Sumner, imposed their will on conquered Confederates with no regard for the terrible injustices suffered by the populace.[50]

A powerful myth arose in Southern culture. The white South was a virtuous land; its citizens remained faithful to the classical liberalism of the Founders while the corrupt North, smug and self-satisfied with its battlefield victory, was hell bent on infecting other parts of the country with its grubby, avaricious, ultimately decadent factory mentality. Instead of the naturally inferior black race laboring to ensure that whites uplifted society as a whole—which was the Southern view of proper social relations—the Reconstruction era would lead to everyone, white as well as black, laboring away as virtual slaves in factories. If the wages of sin are death, the price to be paid for Northern interference into Southern affairs was the loss of a noble heritage and a betrayal of the ideals of the Declaration of Independence, a kind of death of the American republic. The gradual displacement of family farms by textile plants and manufacturing concerns in the South throughout the rest of the nineteenth century only heightened white Southerners' fears that the Southern way of life was a thing of the past, "gone with the wind," in Margaret Mitchell's subsequent phrasing. The image emerged of uneducated, easily duped blacks being manipulated by cynical Northern whites to support continued federal intervention in Southern affairs. Whites spoke derisively of "the African and his natural protector."[51]

Myths provide a window into the thinking of people in a particular time and place. In the Southern United States during the 1860s and 1870s, white Southerners never considered the possibility that any dishonest soul occupying high office in state governments probably would have taken advantage of lax postwar conditions regardless of race or party. With increasing reliance on government to care for the freedmen, enforce Reconstruction policy, and rebuild the infrastructure damaged during four years of warfare, it was virtually inevitable that unscrupulous characters would abuse the organs of government to some extent, but embittered Southerners were oblivious to such causes and effects. The decline of agriculture as the predominant foundation of the Southern economy and the rise of manufacturing firms owing to the advancement of industrialization inexorably changed Southern life, but white inhabitants were not predisposed to accept such a macroscopic view of history. Human nature and normal societal changes were not problems; Republicans were. If only white Southerners could wrest control of their state governments away from obdurate, meddlesome federal officials, life could return to normal and social relations would exist, except for slavery, as they always had.[52]

Southern whites, especially those who donned disguises and patrolled the highways at night, suffered through depression unlike anything their forbears had known. It seemed as though they would forever be oppressed by the conquerors in Washington. Yet this melancholy, so widespread immediately following Appomattox, eventually gave way to feelings of hope, especially as the Grant administration became immobilized by scandal. By 1872, with a presidential election looming, change was on the horizon. James Pike, Whitelaw Reid, Horace Greeley, and other journalists and political leaders who had been at least moderate Republicans in the past were ready to move past the problems of the freedmen. As moderate Republicans withdrew support for Reconstruction, Democrats, especially white Southerners, recognized an opportunity to capitalize on the national weariness over the problems of the postwar era.[53]

Historians later referred to the backlash against federal Reconstruction policy and the rise of vigilante groups in the period stretching from 1868 until 1877 as the "counter-Reconstruction" or counterrevolution movement. The movement began because for many whites it seemed that radical, or black, Reconstruction overturned the racial structure of Southern society unlike any other development in American history. In reality only South Carolina, Louisiana, and Florida experienced "radical" rule until 1877, the year that most historians have concluded that Reconstruction ended and white Southerners "redeemed" their state governments. Nonetheless, whites believed they were oppressed, and they acted on those feelings.[54]

When Southerners recognized they could not use the legal and political system to achieve their goals in the short term—namely, white supremacy and a return to the "Union as it was"—they moved outside of the system. As Negroes banded together in groups, usually under the auspices of the Union League and similar organizations dedicated to promoting the Republican Party and empowering freedmen to vote, white Southerners feared they would become victims of the same people they had victimized for so long. Rather than surrender the "Southern way of life" to their enemies, they resolved to arm themselves and fight back. If they could not rely on the color of law, they would rally under the dark of night.[55]

From the perspective of white Southerners, the Klan served its purpose in the late 1860s and early 1870s. It reminded blacks of their place in the social hierarchy, and it kept federal officials occupied while Northern attitudes toward Reconstruction gradually changed. Despite the revulsion that some Northerners felt toward the Klan, they began to read and accept stories of oppressive treatment for whites at the hands of carpetbagger governments following publication of *The Prostrate State* and similar works highlighting corruption and mismanagement. Charles Nordhoff, a well-known Republican journalist who wrote for the New York *Evening Post* in the 1860s and later the New York *Herald*, toured the South in 1875 and produced a collection of articles about his experiences, *The Cotton States in the Spring and Summer of 1875*. Nordhoff's assessments echoed Pike's, lending credence to the idea that Reconstruction governments were the problem with, not the solution to, the South's woes. In *The Cotton States*, Nordhoff observed:

> There are no wrongs now in the South which the interference of the Federal Government under the Enforcement Acts can reach. This interference is purely and only mischievous. It has disabled and demoralized the Republican State governments, whose members, sure that they would be maintained by the Federal army everywhere, abandoned their duties, and took to stealing and mal-administration. It has seriously injured the negro, by making him irresponsible to the opinion of his neighbors, and submitting him, in his ignorance, to the mischievous and corrupt rule of black and white demagogues. As a result, it has fostered ill-feeling between the races, from which in the end it is inevitable that the negro must be the greatest sufferer.[56]

As sympathy for white Southerners increased, Northerners tired of the effort to "win the peace." The Grant administration retreated from its commitment to the freedmen while it struggled to operate amid emerging scandals; thus did the scheme of Radical Reconstruction envisioned by the late Thaddeus Stevens and his brethren fall apart. "Radicalism is dissolving—going to pieces," Augustus Summerfield Merrimon, a Democratic U.S. senator from North Carolina, wrote in 1874, "but what is to take its place, does not clearly appear."[57]

Eventually it became clear that federal Reconstruction as it had existed and evolved since the end of the war would not last. To hasten the demise of the status quo, white Southern leaders shrewdly adopted a public façade of reconciliation. If only they were free from oppressive federal policies, these seemingly well-meaning, progressive Southern leaders promised to provide for the freedmen while simultaneously cleaning up corruption in state government.

Mississippi's leading politician, Lucius Quintus Cincinnatus Lamar, went so far as to eulogize the dead Charles Sumner in the U.S. House of Representatives in April 1874 to demonstrate his return to the fold. Such oratory would have been denounced as treacherous in the antebellum era; by the mid-1870s, Southerners understood the wisdom of reconciliation as a means of recapturing state capitals. Fiery speeches delivered by unrepentant rebels had served a purpose for the wounded Southern psyche in the late 1860s, but the 1870s called for more sophisticated, nuanced rhetoric.[58]

Southerners who desired a more activist approach and simply could not bring themselves to champion national unity, even as a public ploy to win Northern sympathy, formed groups similar to the Ku Klux Klan sans strange garb and spooky rituals. "White-line organizations" such as the White League in Louisiana, the White Man's Party in Alabama, the South Carolina Red Shirts, and numerous rifle clubs in small Southern towns were not as clumsy and overtly violent as the Klan, but their goals were similar. They lobbied for white supremacy, but they were satisfied to threaten violence and subtly intimidate freedmen rather than invite undue Northern scrutiny by engaging in nocturnal outrages.[59]

The new, savvy Southern strategy led to the creation of the notorious Mississippi Plan in 1875. Eschewing open invitations to violence, the plan called for whites to "persuade" more than 10 percent of Republican voters—that is, blacks who voted Republican in prior elections—to change their party affiliation. White Southerners moved enough votes out of the Republican column to argue that abusive carpetbagger governments, already rife with corruption and lacking popular support, their edicts enforced only at the end of a bayonet, could no longer be sustained. With subtle intimidation in the face of growing Northern indifference, the Mississippi Plan served as a model for redemption in South Carolina and Louisiana and in time became the inspiration for *de jure* segregation throughout the South.[60]

Chapter Seven

"We Have Been, as a Class, Grievously Wounded, Wounded in the House of Our Friends"

The year 1876 marked a watershed in American history as the nation celebrated its centennial anniversary with an exposition titled the "Progress of the Age" in Philadelphia. One-fifth of the population of the United States—some ten million people—tramped past the exhibits to gawk at new inventions and ponder the promise of a limitless future. The citizenry was weary of the past and ready to move on from present troubles, and no wonder. The economy limped along at a sluggish pace, still reeling from the Panic of 1873. The Grant administration entered its final year marred by a seemingly endless stream of scandals that left the chief executive bloody but unbowed. The most vocal Radical Republicans in Congress were long gone, either victims of electoral defeat or the ravages of time. The war was little more than a decade in the past, yet already it seemed much farther away in time and space. Much had happened since Appomattox—too much in the opinion of many Americans—and sensibilities had changed. The divisiveness that had dominated the political landscape of antebellum America had not altogether disappeared, but the old schisms no longer commanded the attention they had when nullification and secession had been distinct possibilities. Many whites, North and South, were ready to let bygones be bygones and settle down to a less contentious existence. The Centennial Exhibition encouraged a giddy optimism and self-congratulatory aura that were hardly justified by external facts, but the event captured many Americans' longing for a new era of good feeling after the misery of a civil war and the ennui of Reconstruction.[1]

Whites could afford to let bygones be bygones. The waning decades of the nineteenth century held the promise of better times ahead if a man could acquire an education or move west in search of growing opportunities. The small Southern farmer barely eking out a living did not share visions of a rosy future, but a large percentage of more affluent whites saw a new day dawning if the economy would stabilize and government could be set on a slow, steady course that encouraged private-sector growth and safe, conservative fiscal policies.[2]

If anyone in a position of authority or influence had bothered to notice or care, blacks had no cause for jubilation. They were trapped in a subservient role across the nation. They were no longer slaves, it was true, but their condition since emancipation was little better than servitude. Nowhere were the disparities between black and white more apparent than south of the Mason-Dixon Line. Still struggling under the vestiges of slavery, these permanent members of the underclass enjoyed few opportunities for education, employment, or social progress. Reformers were difficult to find. Where the congressional Jacobins once had served as the conscience of the federal government, almost no one in a position of power stepped forward to champion the plight of the freedmen. A void had developed. Blacks once again became the forgotten race. The freedmen had been down so long their position seemed to be part of the natural order of things, their socially constructed inferiority rationalized as a God-given condition. The few hardy souls left over from antebellum times who dared raise a hue and cry risked drowning in a well of enmity or enduring a deluge of ridicule for questioning the established order. By the time the national centennial rolled around, whites had recaptured control of state governments in every Southern state except Louisiana, Florida, and South Carolina. Only 2,800 troops ensured some semblance of federal control over those three states; it was simply a matter of time before the soldiers departed and blacks were left to the mercy of former slaveholders.[3]

Apart from the Centennial Exposition, 1876 generated national attention because it was a presidential election year. Despite his administration's well-documented scandals, the sluggish economy, and the tradition that a president should serve only two terms in office, Ulysses S. Grant had not foreclosed the possibility of seeking a third term. A schism developed in the Republican Party between Grant supporters who advocated another term and those who were weary of the incumbent and vehemently opposed four more years for the scandal-plagued administration. If the president insisted on pursuing an unprecedented course in presidential politics, he risked dividing his party and providing Democrats with the chance they had long awaited to recapture the Executive Mansion.[4]

Many Republicans breathed a sigh of relief when Grant did not stand for reelection. Freed from the albatross of a disgraced incumbent, prominent Republicans vied for the nomination, including Senator James G. Blaine of Maine, Senator Roscoe Conkling of New York, Senator Oliver Morton of Indiana, and Treasury Secretary Benjamin H. Bristow. Blaine was the presumptive favorite as the delegates headed for the Republican convention in Cincinnati in June 1876. When the senator failed to garner the requisite number of delegates on the first ballot, anti-Blaine forces multiplied, and the candidate's appeal waned. The party eventually settled on a dark horse, Ohio governor Rutherford B. Hayes, as the nominee. In the words of historian Henry Adams, Hayes was "a third-rate nonentity whose only recommendation is that he is obnoxious to no one."[5]

Adams's comment, while typical of the acerbic Adams clan and demeaning to Hayes, was not far off the mark. A native of the Buckeye State, Hayes was a Harvard-educated lawyer, former U.S. congressman, and Union veteran. If his résumé sounded impressive on paper, Hayes the man appeared anything but impressive in person. His career was constructed on a foundation of bland inoffensiveness. He was not widely known before 1876, but he had positioned himself as an alternative to the better-known candidates by assiduously avoiding controversy and supporting all the proper Republican policies at the proper time. Immediately following the war, he had opposed President Andrew Johnson and favored punitive Reconstruction policies championed by the Radical Republicans. He was hardly a radical, though. Hayes knew which way the wind blew; his opinions changed as times changed. When the Radicals fell from grace, Hayes could not be found in the progressive camp. As Reconstruction wound down and political support eroded, Governor Hayes argued the merits of forward movement with nary a backward glance. In 1875, he announced support for the scandal-ridden Grant administration despite its well-known ethical, legal, and political deficiencies. When Hayes's presidential prospects suddenly rose during the ensuing year, however, he discovered many differences with Grant's ethics and his policies. In short, as Hayes's political fortunes rose, his support for Reconstruction sank. "I doubt the ultra measures relating to the South," the presidential hopeful declared.[6]

As is often the case, the governor's most attractive feature and the crucial attribute that led to his political ascendancy was his lack of stature and his unwillingness or inability to adhere to fixed political principles. It was neither the first nor the last time a political party would turn away from experienced, controversial men of standing to embrace a bland nonentity to forestall internecine squabbling. During the Republican convention in Cincinnati, Hayes was nominated on the seventh ballot along with Congressman William A. Wheeler of New York as his vice presidential running mate.[7]

Hayes's opponent in the general election was Samuel J. Tilden, a highly regarded reform governor of New York. Nicknamed "Whispering Sammy" for his soft-spoken approach to oratory and "The Great Forecloser" for his ability to get things accomplished, he seemed to outclass his Republican rival. The patrician governor was the opposite of the clichéd politician who chewed tobacco, guzzled liquor on the stump, greeted citizens with a facile, hail-fellow-well-met bravado, and gleefully practiced demagoguery to demonize political opponents. Tilden refused to engage in such silly antics, believing he had an obligation to stand above the murky world of partisan politics. To some detractors, his haughty demeanor came off as arrogance, but Whispering Sammy was unconcerned. If anything, he appeared bemused by his critics as he floated above the brouhaha surrounding the presidential campaign.[8]

In a long, storied career that began during Andrew Jackson's tenure and spanned more than four decades, he had become a revered public figure to many New Yorkers. His squeaky-clean public image was made when, as a state legislator and governor, he risked his popularity by investigating New York City's infamous political machine, the Tweed Ring, as well as the upstate Canal Ring. Even when some Republicans tried to besmirch his name with rumor and innuendo during the 1876 campaign, Tilden's reputation was secure. To citizens of a populist stripe, Tilden appeared aloof and condescending—a fellow who could not be bothered with the problems of the unwashed masses—but this perspective was the minority view.[9]

It was a nasty campaign, to no one's surprise. Presidential politics had become increasingly bitter and partisan since the war. Each side fell back on its standard shibboleths. As they had done in previous campaigns when they "waved the bloody shirt," Republicans harped on the disloyalty of the Democrats as the party that had initiated war in 1861. The oft-heard slogan was "Not every Democrat was a rebel, but every rebel was a Democrat." For their part, Democrats lost no opportunity in decrying the massive corruption associated with the Grant administration as well as the corrupt carpetbagger regimes that ruled some Southern states with an iron grip. Throughout the South, armed paramilitary groups such as the Red Shirts and the White League patrolled the streets drumming up support for Democrats by disrupting Republican meetings and rallies. They also relied on the Mississippi Plan to intimidate black voters. Although each party hurled epithets at the other and claimed the moral high ground, no one had clean hands.[10]

November 7, 1876, was Election Day. At first, all seemed well for the Democrats. When the ballots rolled in and the tallies appeared, Tilden presumably had won a close election. He had carried New York, New Jersey, Connecticut, Indiana, and the entire South, giving him a plurality of about 250,000 popular votes with 203 of the 185 electoral votes needed to win the presidency. Hayes had carried his home state of Ohio, which had been in jeopardy, but his poor showing in other states suggested the Republican Party would finally yield to the Democrats a dozen years after the end of the Civil War.[11]

Despite the Republicans' poor showing, the election was not over. The episode remains muddled to this day, but Election Eve machinations apparently commenced when a disgruntled former Union general and ex-minister to Spain, Daniel Sickles, stopped at Republican National Committee Head-quarters as he returned from the theater. Nicknamed "Devil Dan" for his Machiavellian ways, Sickles was a renowned scoundrel. In 1859, he shot and killed his wife's lover, Philip Barton Key, the son of "Star-Spangled Banner" author Francis Scott Key, in Lafayette Park across the street from the Executive Mansion. During the subsequent trial, Sickles entered a plea of temporary insanity—the first use of such a defense in an American court of law—and won an acquittal. During the Battle of Gettysburg in 1863, Sickles disobeyed orders and lost a leg in the ensuing struggle. Later, while serving as a diplomat in Spain, he gave new meaning to the term *foreign affairs* when he reputedly seduced the deposed queen, Isabella II. If anyone possessed the requisite talent for political maneuvering and the moral relativism to alter election results, Daniel Sickles was a charlatan well equipped for the job.[12]

As the general rifled through arriving dispatches, he was not as disheartened as his crestfallen colleagues. True to his nature, Sickles spotted a path to victory that less malleable personalities might have missed. If the western states of California, Nevada, and Oregon swung into the Republican column, the tide could turn. Hayes would have to capture several Southern states as well, but such an outcome was not beyond the realm of possibility. The scheme depended on quick action undertaken by sympathetic election officials in the hotly contested states. Anxious to implement his plan, Sickles dashed to the telegraph. He was one of several Republican leaders burning up the wires that night. Dispatching an urgent message to Republican leaders in South Carolina, Louisiana, Florida, and Oregon, he echoed other party faithful in advising their Southern brethren to stand fast: "With your state sure for Hayes, he is elected. Hold your state."[13]

Throughout the night, telegrams came and went, as did Republican operatives. Party insider William E. Chandler joined Sickles in sending out messages for a time during the wee morning hours. Eschewing neutrality in the name of partisan politics, John C. Reid, Republican editor of the *New York Times*, also participated, later writing of the "uncertain" election outcome. Around 3:00 a.m., South Carolina governor Daniel H. Chamberlain responded to Sickles's telegram. "All right," the beleaguered carpetbagger wrote. "South Carolina is for Hayes. Need more troops. Communication with the interior cut off by mobs." Representatives from Louisiana, Florida, and Oregon also promised to deliver their respective states for Hayes.[14]

Chandler and Reid grew restless waiting on telegrams to arrive. Pursuing an aggressive strategy, they rushed to Republican National Committee chairman Zachariah Chandler's house for further instructions. They were disappointed in their reception. A heavy drinker, the chairman was difficult to rouse from his drink-induced slumber. The two men eventually gained an audience and outlined their scheme. Groggy and irritated that he had been awakened, Zachariah Chandler listened to his excited colleagues as they babbled about uncertain election returns and the possibility of salvaging a Republican presidential victory. "Do what you think is necessary," he finally said as he fell back into his bed.[15]

Interpreting the chairman's advice as *carte blanche* to press forward with the plan, Chandler and Reid hurried back to party headquarters reassured that their machinations were in keeping with party interests. As expected, vote tallies changed throughout the night, bringing uncertainty where a Tilden victory had seemed all but certain the preceding evening. The Democrat retained an edge in the popular vote, but it was the Electoral College that mattered in American presidential elections. Owing to the efforts of Sickles, Chandler, Reid, and other entrepreneurial Republican leaders, by the morning of November 8 the electoral vote was unclear.[16]

Until all the ballots were counted, a definitive result was impossible to predict; neither candidate could boast of having secured 185 electoral votes. Tilden unquestionably had collected 184 votes, and Hayes had 165. The election would hinge on three contested states: Florida, Louisiana, and South Carolina. In the meantime, an Oregon elector was found to be ineligible because he served as postmaster in Lafayette, Oregon, while also serving as an elector. Under the U.S. Constitution, a person is prohibited from holding public office while he serves as an elector. The conflict seemed little more than a technicality, but technicalities can make a difference in the outcome of a close election.[17]

What followed was arguably the most fiercely contested presidential election until the George W. Bush–Al Gore contest of 2000. The U.S. Constitution requires electoral votes to be counted in the presence of both houses of Congress. In that highly charged atmosphere, however, Democrats and Republicans could not agree on which electors should be recognized and which votes should be counted. When the electors met to cast their votes on December 6, 1876, as required by the Constitution, the results were still disputed. Each side claimed the necessary votes to win the presidency.[18]

The U.S. Constitution normally would be the neutral arbiter of the contest, but dueling, ambiguous provisions only increased the animosity on both sides. On one hand, the Constitution states that "the President of the Senate shall, in presence of the Senate and House of Representatives, open all the [electoral] certificates, and the votes shall then be counted." One interpretation suggested that the president of the Senate possessed authority to count votes and determine which votes were legitimate and which were not. If this interpretation were accepted, members of the House of Representatives and Senate would be spectators. The Democrats naturally rejected this construction since the president *pro tempore* of the Senate, Thomas Ferry, was a Republican and could be expected to proclaim Hayes the victor. (The vice president normally serves as the president of the U.S. Senate, but Vice President Henry Wilson had died of a stroke in November 1875, so his position was vacant. The president *pro tempore* serves in the vice president's stead.) On the other hand, the Twelfth Amendment provides that if no candidate is found to have a majority in the Electoral College, "the House of Representatives shall choose immediately, by ballot, the President. But in choosing the President, the votes shall be taken by states, the representation from each state having one vote." The House of Representatives contained more Democrats than Republicans, so allowing the House to vote probably would have elected Tilden.[19]

The stalemate extended into the new year. In January 1877, Republicans and Democrats resorted to a novel compromise: they appointed an independent electoral commission to decide how the disputed votes would be counted. The commission initially included seven Democrats, seven Republicans, and one independent. At the last minute, the commission's independent member, U.S. Supreme Court justice David Davis, unexpectedly retired and

This Thomas Nast illustration depicts the passions surrounding the disputed presidential election of 1876. The cry of "Tilden or Blood" shows the fear many Democrats harbored that the election would be stolen.

Courtesy of the Library of Congress.

was replaced by a fellow justice, Republican Joseph P. Bradley. The resultant shift in favor of the Republicans did not bode well for Tilden supporters.[20]

The commission commenced counting votes on February 1, 1877, and the laborious process dragged on for a month. As he had so many times before, editorial cartoonist Thomas Nast perfectly captured the national mood. In a cartoon appearing in *Harper's Weekly* on February 17, 1877, while the commission continued counting votes, Nast showed two hands jockeying for position over a pistol. Under the pistol was a note, "Tilden or Blood." Nast titled the cartoon, "A truce—not a compromise, but a chance for high-toned gentlemen to retire gracefully from their very civil declarations of war."[21]

Three days before the new president was scheduled to be sworn into office, the commission announced the results. It was a straight party vote: eight Republicans voted for Hayes and seven Democrats cast their ballots for Til-

Republican Rutherford B. Hayes of Ohio won the disputed election of 1876 and was inaugurated as the nineteenth president of the United States in March 1877.
Courtesy of the Library of Congress.

den. When all was said and done, the commission concluded that Hayes had garnered 50.14 percent of the popular vote to carry twenty-one states and 185 electoral votes, the exact number needed to claim the presidency. According to the commission, Tilden won 49.86 percent of the popular vote, carried seventeen states, and earned 184 electoral votes, one shy of the number required for victory.[22]

That the commission cooked the numbers is not seriously disputed; however, the particulars of the behind-the-scenes political wrangling have long been a point of contention among historians. It was curious that Hayes, standard-bearer for the hated Republican Party, captured South Carolina, Louisiana, and Florida, states anxious to throw off the yoke of Yankee rule. Perhaps he carried those states owing to the continued presence of federal troops, although a more likely explanation is that Hayes's managers cut a "Southern deal" or a "corrupt bargain." Assuming such a bargain existed, its terms were not altogether clear.[23]

Apparently, Hayes and/or his election managers pledged that if the electoral commission included a sufficient number of Republicans to guarantee Hayes's election, the new president would remove federal troops from the statehouses in the disputed states as a reward. The timing and specifics of the *quid pro quo* were difficult to nail down, but Hayes was known to have met with Colonel William H. Roberts, managing editor of the *New Orleans Times*, on December 1, 1876. During the meeting, Roberts claimed to represent the views of L. Q. C. Lamar, Wade Hampton, John B. Gordon, and other prominent white Southerners who sought to understand Hayes's intentions if he were elected. Roberts subsequently recalled telling Hayes that "if we felt that you were friendly to us, we would not make that desperate personal fight to keep you out that we certainly will make if you are not friendly." Understandably, the candidate was deliberately obtuse in characterizing the discussions, remarking only that "in case of my election there will be further conferences, and I hope for good results."[24]

After the Hayes-Roberts exploratory discussions, a deal was finalized through a series of meetings at the Wormley Hotel, a well-known Washington, D.C., hotel owned by prominent black entrepreneur James Wormley. The sessions culminated in a soiree on February 26, 1877. Five Ohio Republicans met with three Louisiana Democrats in the proverbial smoke-filled back room and hammered out a compromise. Congressman James A. Garfield, one of several electoral commission members present, departed before the discussions commenced because he was uncomfortable pledging Hayes's support for an agreement without leaving room for additional negotiations. After Garfield left, the group developed the so-called Wormley Agreements. Republicans agreed to withdraw their support for carpetbag governments in Louisiana and South

Carolina provided that blacks and other Republicans were afforded "proper protection" after the state governments were "redeemed" by white Southerners. The Louisiana state legislature would elect a new Democratic U.S. senator after March 10 so that Hayes would have sufficient time to secure Senate approval for his cabinet nominees without engendering a political backlash. Republicans also pledged to appoint a Southern Democrat to the cabinet to ensure a regional balance.[25]

Whatever the specifics of a Southern deal, the electoral commission accepted the Wormley Agreements. Some historians have questioned the importance of the Southern deal since Reconstruction was all but dead even before the electoral crisis of 1877. In any case, Rutherford B. Hayes was inaugurated as the nineteenth president of the United States on March 5, 1877.[26]

In his inaugural address, the new president heralded the "permanent pacification of the country upon such principles and by such measures as will secure the complete protection of all its citizens in the free enjoyment of all their constitutional rights." This was code for his new policy of harmonious relations with the South. "Many of the calamitous efforts of the tremendous revolution which has passed over the Southern States still remain," he said. "Difficult and embarrassing questions meet us at the threshold of this subject. The people of those States are still impoverished, and the inestimable blessing of wise, honest, and peaceful local self-government is not fully enjoyed."[27]

The message was clear: the federal government must no longer rule over the former states of the Southern Confederacy with a heavy hand. And what of the blacks facing racial discrimination and permanent subservience at the hands of Southern oppressors? Hayes dismissed the idea that Southern state governments would necessarily harm the interests of Negroes:

> With respect to the two distinct races whose peculiar relations to each other have brought upon us the deplorable complications and perplexities which exist in those States, it must be a government which guards the interests of both races carefully and equally. It must be a government which submits loyally and heartily to the Constitution and the laws—the laws of the nation and the laws of the States themselves—accepting and obeying faithfully the whole Constitution as it is.[28]

The words were comforting as long as one assumed the parties would act in good faith. Whether such assurances were naïvely or cynically promised is questionable, but the emphasis on correcting the "evils" afflicting the Southern states—that is, corrupt carpetbag governments—was clear to all.

> The evils which afflict the Southern States can only be removed or remedied by the united and harmonious efforts of both races, actuated by motives of mutual

sympathy and regard; and while in duty bound and fully determined to protect the rights of all by every constitutional means at the disposal of my Administration, I am sincerely anxious to use every legitimate influence in favor of honest and efficient local *self*-government as the true resource of those States for the promotion of the contentment and prosperity of their citizens. In the effort I shall make to accomplish this purpose I ask the cordial cooperation of all who cherish an interest in the welfare of the country, trusting that party ties and the prejudice of race will be freely surrendered in behalf of the great purpose to be accomplished.[29]

The crucial point was that the Southern states would be restored to self-government while "trusting that party ties and the prejudice of race will be freely surrendered." It boggles the mind that Hayes believed such trust would be rewarded in light of past Southern abuses. A less charitable interpretation is that he knew blacks would be mistreated under newly restored Southern white rule, but it was a price worth paying to close the gap between the regions and put the Civil War behind the nation once and for all. The dispassionate observer who regards Hayes's motives warily cannot help but wince at what follows:

Let me assure my countrymen of the Southern States that it is my earnest desire to regard and promote their truest interest—the interests of the white and of the colored people both and equally—and to put forth my best efforts in behalf of a civil policy which will forever wipe out in our political affairs the color line and the distinction between North and South, to the end that we may have not merely a united North or a united South, but a united country.[30]

Wiping out "in our political affairs the color line" would prove to be impossible if, indeed, Hayes actually harbored such intentions. It mattered not whether he sought to be a president of all the people; within a month of taking office, he announced a new Southern policy. As part of the policy, on April 10 the administration ordered federal soldiers to refrain from patrolling the statehouse in Columbia, South Carolina. Exactly two weeks later, the last U.S. troops stationed in any Southern state marched from the city of New Orleans. The Republican Party had irrevocably abandoned its twelve-year-old commitment to Reconstruction.[31]

President Hayes did not view his new policy as an abandonment of Reconstruction. He claimed that it was time to reconcile the nation. By committing the Civil War era to the ash heap of history, he believed he was extending a hand of friendship to the South. Extracting promises of protection for the freedmen and restoring home rule seemed to be wise, efficacious public policy. Time would reveal the defects in his logic and his limited political abilities. As historian Brooks D. Simpson observes, "Hayes had dropped the bloody shirt in his rush to clasp hands across the bloody chasm."[32]

One old-school Radical was left standing at this juncture. In the last year of his life, old Ben Wade, retired from the Senate, took measure of the new chief executive and found him wanting. In a letter he wrote to a prominent journalist, the last of the Jacobins grumbled about the new president:

> During the first month of his administration we find him closeted with two of the worst and most malignant enemies of the colored race that can be found in all that slave-cursed region, and there consulting with these malefactors how best he can put these colored people under the iron heel of their most bitter enemies, and reduce them to a condition infinitely worse than before they were made free. I feel that to have emancipated these people and then to leave them unprotected, would be a crime as infamous as to have reduced them to slavery when they were free; and for Hayes to do this to the men who had, at the hazard of their lives, given him the votes without which he never could have had the power to do this terrible injustice! No doubt he meditates the destruction of the party that elected him. A contemplation of all this fills me with amazement and inexpressible indignation. My only consolation is that history informs me that better men than I ever pretended to be, have, in like manner, been deceived. Some have attempted to excuse him by saying that he "means well," but hell is paved with just such good intentions.[33]

For all of the missteps and blustery rhetoric throughout his public life, Wade's assessment of Hayes proved to be prescient. The new president extended an olive branch to those men who would have dismantled his government a dozen years earlier, and he did so earnestly. Throughout the first year of his tenure, Hayes diligently worked to persuade Southerners that the federal government would not interfere with home rule, and many patronage appointments—the lifeblood of politics, especially in the pre–civil service nineteenth century—went to dyed-in-the-wool Democrats to demonstrate good faith. During a Southern speaking tour in September, President Hayes accompanied South Carolina's Redeemer governor, Wade Hampton, on part of the journey. Such a partnership would have been unthinkable with Hayes's predecessors. As if this association were not symbolic enough to telegraph the president's Southern sympathies, on September 22 he told an Atlanta audience, "I had given that matter some consideration, and now my colored friends, who have thought, or who have been told that I was turning my back upon the men whom I fought for, now listen. After thinking it over, I believe your rights and interests would be safer if this great mass of intelligent white men were left alone by the General Government."[34]

The administration's newfound camaraderie with the South was predicated on reciprocity. White Southern leaders had sworn to enact and enforce laws protecting blacks and support Hayes's policies in exchange for freedom from federal interference. As part of the plan for Southerners to uphold their end of the Wormley Agreements, members of Congress were pledged to support James A. Garfield's election as Speaker of the House. When they failed to provide the required assistance, Republicans were put on notice that the president's faith in white Southern political alliances was ill founded. Republicans who had been fearful of reconciling with the South had acquiesced when Hayes embraced the Democrats. Outraged over the betrayal, Republicans prompted a backlash against internal improvement legislation to assist the South in repairing and modifying its infrastructure. From there, the parties fell out of sorts. When Southern members of Congress sided with western members to pass agrarian legislation, Northern leaders who had been singing the praises of Southern reconciliation suddenly changed their tune.[35]

Old wounds do not always heal; sometimes they fester.

—m—

As the federal government's Reconstruction program passed into the pages of history, so, too, did myriad promises of equality for the black race. A new era of racial discrimination dawned. Freed from the shackles of federal oversight, white Southerners could return to the old ways. "When the bayonets shall depart," one North Carolina Democrat remarked, "then look out for the reaction. Then the bottom rail will descend from the top of the fence." A Kansas Republican echoed this sentiment in a crass but accurate observation: "I think the policy of the new administration will be to conciliate the White men of the South, Carpetbaggers to the rear, and niggers take care of yourselves."[36]

The Redeemers—the top rail now replaced on the top of the fence—subsequently earned the appellation the "Bourbons," presumably referring to the House of Bourbon that forgot nothing of the past and learned few lessons from the tumult of the French Revolution. For their part, the Southern Bourbons, also labeled the "Confederate Brigadiers," were said to have learned nothing from the Civil War. These post-Reconstruction white Southern gentlemen sought to restore the glories of antebellum days to the South of the 1880s. Their task was daunting, for the region had changed after losses on the battlefield and in the marketplace. Agriculture, the backbone of the Cotton South, was the foundation of a nineteenth-century economy even as the twentieth century was rapidly approaching. Industrialization, to some extent, would have to supplant the old ways of earning a living.[37]

They were an eclectic lot, these men of Redemption. Depending on their respective states, they were Confederate veterans, secessionist Democrats and former Whigs, the planter elite, ardent industrialists, or young Turks anxious to move past the unpleasantness of recent years into a glorious future they could not quite see but could imagine on a distant horizon. The South would rise again, and they would be its leaders.[38]

Many Northerners feared that the freedmen would be mistreated by white Southerners if the federal government withdrew troops from the South. After Hayes became president, the last military forces left the Louisiana and South Carolina statehouses, irrevocably ending the period of Reconstruction.

Retrenchment became the mantra in many states. Stories of widespread graft and corruption under the carpetbag governments held a lesson for fiscal conservatives: the purse strings of state governments must be tightened. Prudence necessitated lower taxes and less government intrusion into individual lives. No longer could oppressive state governments trample on civil liberties if the extravagances of Reconstruction and the lingering effects of the Panic of 1873 were to be lessened. Under the "rule of the taxpayer," the motto became a resounding "Spend nothing unless absolutely necessary." The definition of *necessary* depended on time and place, but generally it referred to government salaries and public education. Laissez-faire economics and minimal government became quintessential characteristics of the Southern way of life in the era of Redemption. This minimalist government model also provided a convenient rationale for instituting draconian policies that deprived freedmen of government assistance. If the states were stripped of all but "necessary" authority, blacks would be left to sink or swim on their own.[39]

Measured in terms of reduced state expenditures, retrenchment succeeded. Mississippi slashed expenses in half during the decade following Redemption. Other states reported similar results. Savings were passed to the citizens in the form of lower taxes, although usually the resulting decrease in land levies favored wealthy landowners over less affluent whites who owned little or no land. Poll taxes and licensure fees increased, as did taxes on farm tools and animals. Owing to numerous loopholes and exemptions for wealthy farmers, in time the regressive feature of this new taxation scheme would lead to a schism between lower-class whites and their well-to-do neighbors, but in the short run the rhetoric of "that government is best which governs least" held great appeal for Southerners still smarting from what they believed were oppressive Reconstruction policies.[40]

Whites of all classes came to cherish the mythology of the Lost Cause more than ever during this epoch. If the South could not win the war of the 1860s, it would win the peace of the 1880s. Redeeming corrupt carpetbagger governments and restoring white supremacy was an important first step, but Southerners must be brought together under the aegis of familiar rituals, traditions, and symbols. This period witnessed the deification of Confederacy heroes, especially the triumvirate of Robert E. Lee, Thomas J. "Stonewall" Jackson, and Jefferson Davis. White Southerners venerated the rebels who had struggled for state rights and strict constitutional interpretation as a means of preserving the *status quo ante*. The South may have been defeated on the battlefield by the Butcher Grant with the North's superior technology and the multitude of bodies he threw into the fight, but the noble Southland was a mystical place where the old traditions of honor and chivalry could not be repressed. In the land of cotton, old times there were not forgotten.

If speeches, sermons, pamphlets, memoirs, articles, and books would not preserve the romanticized memories of Confederate valor and perpetuate the new mythology, the erection of monuments and memorials to combatants in the War between the States would.[41]

For all their eclecticism, the Redeemers shared a common purpose: the Reconstruction regime instituted by the hated Federals must be torn down and rebuilt as Southern-friendly, post-Reconstruction governments. This massive makeover required a new breed of white Southern leader to revamp social relations, labor control, and legal mechanisms to ensure whites on top and blacks on bottom. Although it required time and patience to erect this procrustean regime of white supremacy, the Bourbons were a determined lot. Antebellum white Southern leadership had proclaimed the Negro unequal to the white man; the Redeemers would honor these same values.[42]

Post-Reconstruction Confederate hagiography and the installation of Bourbon rule created a societal structure that left blacks hungry for equal treatment. But what could be done? Few outlets existed for people of color to ascend through recognized social, economic, or political channels to prominence in mainstream Southern life and culture. Blacks occasionally held political office even after the death of Reconstruction, but the presence of a black elected official was the exception that proved the rule, and typically a single legislator's influence was minimal or nonexistent. If a black citizen were to achieve prominence as a political leader, a man of letters, or an artist of singular merit, he would have to rise through the black community in the shadow of an oppressive, fiercely racist, white power structure. And the black man who directly challenged a white man risked the loss of his job, his prestige, his family, and perhaps his life.[43]

Proto-Confederate Southern leaders paid lip service to protecting the rights of freedmen and displaced Republicans, but no one misconstrued the new arrangement. In virtually every state south of the Mason-Dixon Line, Democrats exercised one-party control over the machinery of government. One unintentionally candid Tennessee state official, proudly rationalizing his party's gerrymandering, bragged that he sought "to redistrict the State that for the next ten years not a Republican can be elected to the legislature." His point was not subtle. "I believe in the law of revenge," he said. "The Radicals disenfranchised us, and now we intend to disenfranchise them."[44]

This level of candor was usually absent from state action, but the sentiments were commonplace. Because the Redeemers were not required to cavort beneath sheets to mask their identities, they possessed a freedom that Kluxers and other white supremacists of the Reconstruction era had never enjoyed. When practiced in the light of day, disenfranchisement could be accomplished in myriad ways. Sometimes ballot boxes were stuffed. Other times, bribery ensured a certain outcome. Subterfuge was the order of the day, and often the degree and variety of trickery were limited only by the ingenuity of the white power structure. It was not unheard of for a polling station in the black community to be moved with little or no advance notice. Many a freedman showed up to vote only to find the polling place closed for an indefinite period; it would suddenly reopen after the Negroes had departed. Violence was used to keep "uppity" blacks in line upon occasion, but such crass devices were unnecessary if chicanery could be employed in a creative, effective manner.[45]

The rise of the Democratic Party from the ashes of Reconstruction was not without its challenges despite the absence of an effective Republican counterpoint. Some lower-class whites resented upper-class white Redeemers and their policies, which greatly benefited railroads and corporate interests at the expense of the working man. Class resentments that had festered between the planter elite of the low country and upland whites who had never owned slaves or large tracts of land bubbled to the surface in the late 1870s. With blacks effectively marginalized and intimidated, lower-class whites had hoped to enjoy the advantages of white supremacy. To their chagrin, they discovered the same tactics used to control those of a darker hue were also wielded against whites of a smaller purse. Redeemers were not above resorting to deception, ballot-box stuffing, and bribery to protect their interests, no matter the adversary.[46]

The realization that not all whites were afforded equal treatment sparked a movement among the lower classes, especially hill people eking out a subsistence living. In the mid-1870s, the National Grange of the Order of Patrons of Husbandry, commonly known as the Grange, came to the South. This fraternal organization encouraged poor white farmers in different states to work together to ensure that their economic and political interests were protected and advanced. Other disaffected whites banded together under the auspices of formal and informal groups such as the Greenbackers and the Readjusters. Militant populism thus was born and bred. Not all populists were poor, but they shared a deep resentment of white elites who, they believed, patronized them and denigrated their values.[47]

White Redeemers recognized their vulnerability. Fearful of a populist backlash, they promised blacks improved treatment to guard against the rising anger of poor white Grangers. In what initially appeared to be a counterintuitive move, South Carolina's Wade Hampton, a potent symbol of the white political structure, appointed Negroes to minor positions of power during his gubernatorial administration. Redeemers were no friend of the black race, but they understood political expediency. The "fusion principle" was a testament to that understanding: conservative white Redeemers shared their largesse with blacks in the decimated Southern Republican Party in return for a fusion of the two groups to halt populist election victories. It was a curious partnership, but it served both parties well. As vocal opponents of carpetbagger excesses, Redeemers had raised race-baiting and political trickery to an art form, but they ameliorated their vitriolic rhetoric so that they could hold white populists in check. Blacks knew they were being used for political purposes, but they were accustomed to such treatment. Their race entertained no illusions about the depressed value of black skin in a white world. Their decision to uphold the fusion principle was a kind of political expediency as well: if Redeemers would toss them a morsel, however minuscule, it was preferable to the rough treatment blacks would be afforded when white populists, seething with resentment and fiercely racist, finally seized power. The benign paternalism of upper-class whites, even with their narcissistic sense of entitlement and their arrogant air of superiority, was a step above the unvarnished hatred of an angry white farmer who made no pretense of his desire to grind blacks under the boot heels of white supremacy.[48]

In their role as officeholders, Redeemers understood the irony of their position. They had forever banished the evil carpetbaggers and wrested control away from Yankee interlopers. In their view, the abandonment of Reconstruction ought to have solidified the region. Citizens in decades to come would speak of the "Solid South" as though hegemonic dominance became the sole guiding principle in the age of Redemption. Yet the Redeemers of the late 1870s recognized as a new decade dawned that the South was not quite as solid as legend would have it. The Bourbons had become the status quo—only to be assailed by whites frustrated by their own lack of social, political, and economic progress. It was a lesson that many disaffected parties would relearn throughout American history: voicing protest as the party out of power is considerably less challenging than effectively governing as the party in power.[49]

As the 1880s arrived, the South, always a distinctive region, occupied a bizarre space in the American political landscape. Rich whites prospered because they controlled state governments and built large textile mills and industries dependent on cheap, plentiful labor. The vast majority of whites were poor, often laboring in the mills or scratching out a meager existence on small farms. With the decline of cotton prices and another economic downturn at the end of the 1870s, poverty was rampant. State governments refused to spend money on social services or education; therefore, a poor white citizen could harbor no reasonable hope of advancing beyond his lowly station in life.[50]

Negroes, of course, had it even worse; they were simply a forgotten people, mute ghosts dotting the Southern fields and mills. They were seen but seldom heard, like vague, indistinct background figures in the national portrait of nineteenth-century life in the United States. Reconstruction-era Southern governments treated them better than Redemption-era governments, which treated them better than succeeding governments. The myopic, idealistic view of American history suggests that each passing decade represents a cumulative groping toward progress in human affairs, a slow but inexorable lurch toward the light, but the Southern treatment of the Negro demonstrates the naiveté of simplistic historiography. With each passing year of the Gilded Age, a black citizen watched his liberties and security steadily diminish. The only constant was his inferior position in the social strata. If a dirty job needed to be done for low wages, a black would do it. If someone must sacrifice for the good of the whole, a black was offered up as the obvious choice. If a scapegoat were needed to take the blame for social ills, a black was cast as the miscreant—and woe to the man of color who dared raise a disaffected voice in opposition to the established social order.[51]

If blacks of the post-Reconstruction era were no longer bound in a condition of servitude, as they had been before emancipation, and if they were never herded into camps and prearranged ghettos, as occurred under the South African apartheid system, their condition nonetheless could not be characterized as enviable. Lynching and other acts of violence against blacks increased in number and ferocity beginning in the 1880s and extended well into the twentieth century. A black who grumbled about his poor circumstances and limited opportunities risked reprisals too horrible to contemplate, and so he bore his burden silently.

Despite these bleak conditions, Negroes enjoyed one advantage that had been limited during the days of slavery: they could develop a separate society and culture more or less free from white interference. As blacks made gains in literacy and wealth, they created their own cultural traditions, historical celebrations, and privately operated institutions, which were all but invisible to whites. In the world of white America, Negroes were maligned, but in their own enclaves, far away from mainstream Caucasian society, they thrived.[52]

Of the shared values that united white Southerners during the last two decades of the nineteenth century, the most common was the belief that blacks must be kept in their place at the bottom of the social, political, and economic strata. Jim Crow laws ensured that people of color would remain politically impotent. These laws, which legally segregated blacks and whites, were enacted throughout the Southern states beginning in the 1880s. Blacks and whites had self-segregated before that time, but the new laws were far more rigid and brutal than laws and customs previously in place. The eminent historian C. Vann Woodward has argued that new segregation statutes became popular as Redemption governments declined toward the end of that decade. White Redeemers generally were men of affluence; some had been members of the planter elite during antebellum times. After resuming positions of authority in state governments at the end of Reconstruction, they based the legitimacy of the color line on old-school paternalism: blacks were naturally inferior and could not survive if they were not cared for as though they were children or beasts of burden. In infantilizing the freedmen, the Redeemers convinced themselves they were looking out for the best interests of sad, pathetic creatures. Their casual racism generally was not predicated on brutality, although they could be as brutal as circumstances required. They were satisfied to use blacks when it proved politically expedient or leave the dark race to rise or fall in squalor, so far beneath the gaze of the influential white social, political, and economic class as to be invisible. If later generations looked back at the Redeemers with disgust, their contemporaries believed they were acting in accordance with time-tested social mores that probably would never change.[53]

The paternalism of the Redeemers yielded to a ruthless new order. As lower-class whites pushed for greater democratization in the mid- to late 1880s, a new group of leaders emerged. They did not enjoy the status of the planter elite; they were men who had struggled to make something of their lives by overcoming poverty and hardship. Paternalism was not their way. They were accustomed to sharing close quarters with the Negro and held no affection for their black neighbors. Anxious to raise their status and differentiate themselves from the lower classes, they discovered a convenient means of demonstrating their mastery over their dark brethren: a new generation of black codes. Woodward once observed that the "barriers of racial discrimination mounted in direct ratio with the tide of political democracy among whites. In fact, an increase of Jim Crow laws upon the statute books of a state is almost an accurate index of the decline of the reactionary regimes of the Redeemers and triumph of white democratic movements." It was bitterly ironic that increased opportunities for poor white Southerners directly led to decreased opportunities for poor black Southerners.[54]

Although the origins of the term *Jim Crow* remain somewhat obscure, most historians believe the name derived from a popular minstrel song dating from the late 1820s or early 1830s. A self-styled singer-comedian named Thomas Dartmouth Rice—sometimes called "T.D." or "Daddy" Rice—first performed a song, "Jump Jim Crow," adorned in blackface sometime around 1828. A few years later the song appeared in sheet music. "Jump Jim Crow" may have been inspired by a crippled African, Jim Cuff or Jim Crow, who lived in Cincinnati, although some historians dispute this point. In any case,

"Daddy" Rice enjoyed considerable success performing his minstrel show throughout the United States. He was often billed as "Daddy Jim Crow" and proved to be immensely popular as the music and dance were augmented with elements of the broadly farcical commedia dell'arte tradition. Building on Rice's success, other minstrel shows toured the nation, delighting audiences, especially whites who enjoyed snickering at the absurd antics of gullible, moronic Africans, and reinforcing negative racial stereotypes that would linger for generations.[55]

Southern segregation statutes—dubbed "Jim Crow" laws—were prevalent in the waning days of the nineteenth century, but they would have been much more difficult to enact and enforce had the federal government, especially the judiciary, not abandoned the freedmen beginning in the 1870s. By the 1880s, national political leaders had no interest in protecting blacks; a series of weak, ineffectual presidents refused to intercede into state affairs unless forced to do so, and Congress showed little interest in protecting the political rights of a forgotten class. In the meantime, businessmen anxious to promote laissez-faire economic policies at the expense of radical social legislation co-opted the national Republican Party. The "party of Lincoln" became the "party of commerce." According to conservative conventional wisdom, Reconstruction had solved racial issues as well as they could be solved. After Southern state governments had been redeemed, it was time to move on to other, more pressing national issues. Blacks clamoring for protection of their rights were left to their own devices.[56]

In a later time, the U.S. Supreme Court would champion individual rights and civil liberties, especially during the Warren court era of the mid-twentieth century, but in the late nineteenth century the high court closed the door on opportunity and opened the door to segregation. The Fourteenth Amendment might have provided a means for federal intervention, but the court refused to interpret the measure broadly. Section 1 states, "All persons born or naturalized in the United States and subject to the jurisdiction thereof, are citizens of the United States and of the State wherein they reside. No State shall make or enforce any law which shall abridge the privileges or immunities of citizens of the United States; nor shall any State deprive any person of life, liberty, or property, without due process of law; nor deny to any person within its jurisdiction the equal protection of the laws." The purpose of the amendment initially seems straightforward: citizens must be protected from infringements on their constitutional rights. In 1873, the court announced a case, *In Re Slaughterhouse Cases*, that narrowly construed this language.[57]

The facts initially made for an unlikely Fourteenth Amendment challenge. In 1869, Louisiana enacted a law allowing the city of New Orleans to establish a corporation so that all slaughterhouse operations could be centralized in one location. The intent was to protect public health by prohibiting butchers from dumping rotten animal carcasses into the streets. Outraged that the city would intrude into their livelihood by creating a legalized monopoly, twenty-five butchers filed a lawsuit challenging the creation of the corporation. Five of the cases eventually went to the U.S. Supreme Court on appeal. Among the questions raised was whether the due process, equal protection, and privileges and immunities clauses of the Fourteenth Amendment applied at the state level. The high court was divided, but ultimately it ruled in a narrowly tailored, 5–4 decision that the latter clause affected only "national citizenship," not state citizenship. According to Justice Samuel Miller, author of the majority opinion:

> The first section of the fourteenth article, to which our attention is more specially invited, opens with a definition of citizenship—not only citizenship of the United States, but citizenship of the States. No such definition was previously found in the Constitution, nor had any attempt been made to define it by act of Congress. It had been the occasion of much discussion in the courts, by the executive departments, and in the public journals. It had been said by eminent judges that no man was a citizen of the United States, except as he was a citizen of one of the States composing the Union. . . . It is quite clear, then, that there is a citizenship of the United States, and a citizenship of a State, which are distinct from each other, and which depend upon different characteristics or circumstances in the individual.[58]

The court was not satisfied merely to decide the citizenship question. It also limited application of the other clauses to former slaves:

> [O]n the most casual examination of the language of these amendments, no one can fail to be impressed with the one pervading purpose found in them all, lying at the foundation of each, and without which none of them would have been even suggested; we mean the freedom of the slave race, the security and firm establishment of that freedom, and the protection of the newly-made freeman and citizen from the oppressions of those who had formerly exercised unlimited dominion over him. It is true that only the fifteenth amendment, in terms, mentions the negro by speaking of his color and his slavery. But it is just as true that each of the other articles was addressed to the grievances of that race, and designed to remedy them as the fifteenth. We do not say that no one else but the negro can share in this protection. Both the language and spirit of these articles are to have their fair and just weight in any question of construction.[59]

Even when the amendment applied only to freedmen, the court could not see a constitutionally permissible manner for the federal government to interfere with state rights to protect blacks from racial discrimination. For all intents and purposes, the *Slaughterhouse Cases* restricted the practical utility of the Fourteenth Amendment, especially the privileges and immunities clause.[60]

The Supreme Court continued its narrow construction of the Fourteenth and Fifteenth Amendments throughout the remainder of the nineteenth century. With each decision, the high court dealt another blow to black political rights, slowly eroding the early promise of Reconstruction and establishing a firm foundation for legal segregation. Two cases, in particular, *United States v. Reese* and *United States v. Cruikshank*, permitted states to dismantle the remnants of the Reconstruction regime. The former was a voting rights case challenging a Kentucky official's refusal to register a black man to vote in a municipal election. Chief Justice Morrison Waite, writing for a nearly unanimous court, deferred to the state's authority to regulate its own electoral process unencumbered by federal intervention. In reaching this conclusion, Waite allowed state poll taxes and literacy tests to withstand constitutional scrutiny. "The Fifteenth Amendment does not confer the right of suffrage upon anyone," he wrote, essentially vitiating the original intent of the amendment. "It prevents the states, or the United States, however, from giving preference, in this particular, to one citizen of the United States over another on account of race, color, or previous condition of servitude." In the chief justice's opinion, the federal government was not empowered to interfere with a state's decision to implement poll taxes or literacy requirements because such voting requirements affected all voters equally. He was blissfully ignorant of or indifferent to the myriad exemptions afforded whites but not offered to blacks.[61]

The second case, *Cruikshank*, involved one of the most horrific acts of racial violence that occurred during the Gilded Age. On Easter Sunday 1873, a mob of whites set fire to the courthouse in Colfax, Louisiana, where hundreds of blacks had sought refuge following a street battle between freedmen and Southern whites. "Up to the point where the courthouse was set on fire, Colfax was arguably a battleground, and from the start the battle went the whites' way," one prominent historian later observed. "But what was happening now was not a hard military fight but a killing frenzy after the battle was over, after the outcome had been clearly settled, and with the defeated force unarmed." When the smoke finally cleared, scores of blacks lay dead; estimates ranged from seventy to more than three times that number.[62]

In the aftermath of the melee, several white members of the mob were arrested and charged with violating Section 6 the Enforcement Act of 1870, which prohibited conspirators from denying citizens their constitutional rights. Building on the distinctions between the rights of federal and state citizens articulated in the *Slaughterhouse Cases*, the *Cruikshank* court held that the indictments were faulty because the Enforcement Act was a federal statute, but the charges in the case did not involve a denial of federal rights. Writing again for the majority, Chief Justice Waite found that the First Amendment right of assembly and the Second Amendment right to bear arms protected citizens from only federal abuses. Moreover, the due process and equal protection rights mentioned in the Fourteenth Amendment applied only to states, not to individuals. Because individuals perpetrated the massacre and the state imprimatur was never demonstrated, the indictments were invalid. As for a claim that the mob interfered with the victims' right to vote, the court dismissed the complaint because the evidence did not adequately demonstrate that the defendants acted on racial grounds.[63]

If the *Slaughterhouse Cases*, *Reese*, and *Cruikshank* assisted in tearing down the edifice of Reconstruction, the high court's later cases helped construct the segregation regime that took its place. *Hall v. DeCuir* involved a steamboat operator who refused to serve a black patron on the basis of race. At trial, the patron won a civil judgment that was upheld on appeal. The U.S. Supreme Court granted *certiorari* to address the question of whether the steamboat was engaged in interstate commerce—which is regulated by the federal government—or intrastate commerce, which is left to the states. Because the steamboat travelled from New Orleans, Louisiana, to Vicksburg, Mississippi, clearly it involved interstate commerce. In his majority opinion, Chief Justice Waite might have decided that because the federal government possessed authority over interstate commerce and because federal laws prohibited racial discrimination, the defendant was prohibited from discriminating in providing accommodations on a steamboat travelling from one state to another. He chose another route. Using the convoluted reasoning he had come to master, Waite explained that this was a case of a state statute infringing on interstate commerce:

> [I]t may safely be said that state legislation which seeks to impose a direct burden upon interstate commerce or to interfere directly with its freedom does encroach upon the exclusive power of Congress. The statute now under consideration in our opinion occupies that position. . . . On one side of the river or its tributaries he might be required to observe one set of rules, and on the other another. Commerce cannot flourish in the midst of such embarrassments. No carrier of passengers can conduct his business with satisfaction to himself or comfort to those employing him if on one side of a state line his passengers, both white and colored, must be permitted to occupy the same cabin, and on the other be kept separate.[64]

Because the Louisiana statute impeded interstate commerce, the court reversed the case and vacated the judgment in favor of the black patron, essentially allowing commercial carriers to discriminate against customers with impunity in the name of protecting commercial transactions among and between states. A dozen years later, the court further validated racial segregation in public transportation when it held in *Louisville, New Orleans, and Texas Railway Company v. Mississippi* that a state could enact a statute requiring "equal, but separate, accommodation for the white and colored races."[65]

While the U.S. Supreme Court legitimized legal segregation, Congress made one last attempt to provide for equal justice under law. Longtime Radical Charles Sumner, as his last hurrah, championed legislation to guarantee that everyone, regardless of race, color, or previous condition of servitude, would be afforded the same treatment in "public accommodations" such as inns, public conveyances on land or water, theaters, and places of public amusement. Congress enacted the measure the year following Sumner's death as the Civil Rights Act of 1875. When it was clear the act was seldom enforced, Negroes filed suit in state courts to compel state compliance. On appeal, the U.S. Supreme Court agreed to consolidate five lower-court cases and render a decision on the constitutionality of the statute. In the *Civil Rights Cases* of 1883, the justices ruled that the first two sections of the Civil Rights Act of 1875 were unconstitutional because they vested the federal government with too much authority over states. According to C. Vann Woodward, the decision "was only the juristic fulfillment of the Compromise of 1877, and was, in fact, handed down by Justice Joseph P. Bradley, Grant's appointee, who had been a member of the Electoral Commission of 1877." Some observers, unsympathetic to the freedmen, saw the court's opinion as righteous, simply "just retribution to the colored people for their infamous conduct." The convenient practice of blaming the victim would become de rigueur during the Jim Crow era.[66]

If Woodward was correct that the *Civil Rights Cases* fulfilled the Compromise of 1877, the decision in *Williams v. Mississippi* could be said to fulfill the terms of the 1875 Mississippi Plan. A template for black voter intimidation in Southern states at the end of Reconstruction, the Mississippi Plan empowered white Democratic Party leaders to "persuade" black Republicans to switch parties or refrain from registering to vote. The systematic exclusion of Negroes from voting rolls inevitably meant that fewer blacks were eligible for jury service. When a black man was convicted of murder by an all-white jury in Washington County, Mississippi, in 1896, his defense attorney argued that the exclusion of Negroes from the jury pool owing to their disfranchisement under the 1890 Mississippi state constitution and onerous literacy and poll-tax requirements for blacks (and not whites) denied the defendant equal protection of the law under the Fourteenth Amendment.[67]

Once again, the U.S. Supreme Court was blind to the existence of racial discrimination in the judicial system. Quoting the state supreme court, Justice Joseph McKenna, writing for the majority, observed that disparities in voter rolls and jury pools was not because whites discriminated against blacks. Blacks and their behavior were to blame: "By reason of its previous condition of servitude and dependencies, this race had acquired or accentuated certain peculiarities of habit, of temperament, and of character which clearly distinguished it as a race from the whites; a patient, docile people, but careless, landless, migratory within narrow limits, without forethought, and its criminal members given to furtive offenses, rather than the robust crimes of the whites." In the court's opinion, "It cannot be said, therefore, that the denial of the equal protection of the laws arises primarily from the constitution and laws of Mississippi; nor is there any sufficient allegation of an evil and discriminating administration of them."[68]

The long line of court cases retreating from Reconstruction culminated in a landmark 1896 decision, *Plessy v. Ferguson.* A Louisiana statute enacted in 1890 provided for separate accommodations for blacks and whites on railroads if the accommodations were "equal." In reality, segregated railroad accommodations were hardly comparable; the cars reserved for whites were more luxurious than the squalid black section. On June 7, 1892, a light-skinned Creole man who was one-eighth black, Homer Adolph Plessy, stepped into a car of the East Louisiana Railroad. Although he was mostly white, under state law Plessy was deemed "black" and required to move to a segregated car. In a deliberate act of disobedience, he refused to move. As expected, he was arrested and sent to jail for violating state law. When Plessy's case came to trial, he argued that the statute had violated his Thirteenth Amendment rights as well as the equal protection clause of the Fourteenth Amendment. The U.S. Supreme Court ruled against Plessy, holding that although the Thirteenth Amendment abolished slavery, the amendment did not protect blacks from discriminatory state laws. Justice Henry Billings Brown wrote that the "separate but equal" doctrine did not contravene the U.S. Constitution because the state law was not patently unreasonable. "In determining the question of reasonableness," Billings wrote, "it is at liberty to act with reference to the established usages, customs, and traditions of the people, and with a view to the promotion of their comfort, and the preservation of the public peace and good order. Gauged by this standard, we cannot say that a law which authorizes or even requires the separation of the two races in public conveyances is unreasonable, or more obnoxious to the fourteenth amendment than the acts of congress requiring separate schools for colored children in the District of Columbia, the constitutionality of which does not seem to have been questioned, or the corresponding acts of state legislatures."[69]

In one especially execrable passage, Justice Brown attempted to explain why the "separate but equal" stigma was not tantamount to a "badge of inferiority." His justification was hollow and unconvincing:

> We consider the underlying fallacy of the plaintiff's argument to consist in the assumption that the enforced separation of the two races stamps the colored race with a badge of inferiority. If this be so, it is not by reason of anything found in the act, but solely because the colored race chooses to put that construction upon it. The argument necessarily assumes that if, as has been more than once the case, and is not unlikely to be so again, the colored race should become the dominant power in the state legislature, and should enact a law in precisely similar terms, it would thereby relegate the white race to an inferior position. We imagine that the white race, at least, would not acquiesce in this assumption. The argument also assumes that social prejudices may be overcome by legislation, and that equal rights cannot be secured to the negro except by an enforced commingling of the two races. We cannot accept this proposition. If the two races are to meet upon terms of social equality, it must be the result of natural affinities, a mutual appreciation of each other's merits, and a voluntary consent of individuals.[70]

The Supreme Court's appreciation of the state of nineteenth-century race relations was breathtakingly obtuse. The suggestion that feelings of inferiority owing to disparate treatment based on skin color were "solely because the colored race chooses to put that construction upon it" presupposed that some other reasonable construction could explain legal segregation. How else but as a badge of inferiority could a freedman construe the act of being separated from others because his race was unacceptable to the majority? Despite the court's statement to the contrary, the fallacy was the idea that social equality, if it were to exist, would result from "natural affinities, a mutual appreciation of each other's merits, and a voluntary consent of individuals." By legally segregating blacks from whites, natural affinities, mutual appreciation, and voluntary consent to interact would seldom, if ever, occur. In fact, isolating the races so that they would not know each other was precisely the reason segregation laws were enacted in the first place—because the races did not know each other. But they would never know each other if they were subjected to the twisted logic of a "separate but equal" regime. It was a vicious tautology.[71]

Justice John Marshall Harlan, the lone dissenter, called attention to the majority's myopia in an eloquent, passionate dissent. A former slave owner who had repudiated his previous way of thinking, Harlan recognized the deficiencies in the majority opinion. "The white race deems itself to be the dominant race in this country. And so it is, in prestige, in achievements, in education, in wealth, and in power. So, I doubt not, it will continue to be for all time, if it remains true to its great heritage, and holds fast to the principles of constitutional liberty." The problem was that the court's decision in *Plessy* threatened to undermine the nation's great heritage and principles of constitutional liberty because it allowed states to develop a caste system based on race. "Our constitution is color-blind, and neither knows nor tolerates classes among citizens. In respect of civil rights, all citizens are equal before the law. The humblest is the peer of the most powerful. The law regards man as man, and takes no account of his surroundings or of his color when his civil rights as guaranteed by the supreme law of the land are involved. It is therefore to be regretted that this high tribunal, the final expositor of the fundamental law of the land, has reached the conclusion that it is competent for a state to regulate the enjoyment by citizens of their civil rights solely upon the basis of race." They were strong, stirring words, but when written as a dissent, they could not affect current law. Instead, Harlan directed his comments toward the future. "In my opinion, the judgment this day rendered will, in time, prove to be quite as pernicious as the decision made by this tribunal in the *Dred Scott* Case."[72]

Harlan's prognostications would prove to be true, but vindication was more than a half century away when the Supreme Court decided *Plessy*.[73]

As the nineteenth century drew to a close, the Old Man of Abolitionism, Frederick Douglass—one of the few survivors of an age that seemed ever more distant with each passing year—watched the national retreat from the ideals of Reconstruction with disgust. In 1871, he remarked that the "spirit of secession is stronger today than ever." The central problem was continued Southern resistance to Reconstruction and the inability or unwillingness of national leaders to enforce laws protecting the freedmen. As an inevitable consequence of shifting sentiments, white Southerners were enjoying a renaissance of sorts—at the expense of black Americans. The secessionist credo "is now a deeply rooted, cherished sentiment, inseperably identified with the 'lost cause,' which the half measures of the Government towards the traitors has helped to cultivate and strengthen."[74]

If anyone was well suited to assess the state of nineteenth-century race relations, it was Frederick Douglass. He was a living legend, a stark reminder of an age seemingly on the verge of disappearing from collective memory. He had lived at the center of the racial divide for decades; he had liberated himself from slavery and become a symbol of the cruelties of bondage in the antebellum years; he was a proud figure, a vestige of the golden age of abolitionism; he was tangible proof that blacks were not inferior, pathetic creatures

The great civil rights icon of the nineteenth century, Frederick Douglass, feared for the future of black Americans as the Jim Crow era dawned in the South.
Courtesy of the Library of Congress.

lacking a capacity for intellectual growth and self-fulfillment. An eloquent, passionate, dynamic speaker, he had made a name for himself before, during, and after the Civil War as a critic of human bondage and its debasing character. His most famous oration, the July 5, 1852, address assailing the meaning of the Fourth of July for black Americans, had brought him a measure of fame that he had used to good advantage throughout his long career as a public figure. "This Fourth of July is *yours*, not *mine*. *You* may rejoice, I must mourn," he had told his white audience. "Do you mean, citizens, to mock me, by asking me to speak to-day?" It was a question that remained relevant in the aftermath of the war and Reconstruction.[75]

A fierce critic of President Lincoln's limited war aims at the outset of hostilities, Douglass had thrice been a guest at the Executive Mansion. As the war progressed from Fort Sumter to Appomattox, he had been heartened by the Great Emancipator's willingness to issue an emancipation proclamation and distraught when he learned of the assassination. Since Lincoln's passing, Douglass had enjoyed a measure of personal success that did not mirror advances among other blacks. Gray and aged as Reconstruction ended and a new era dawned, he had become the consummate power broker in the black community, serving as president of the Freedmen's Bank, which eventually became insolvent, and marshal of the District of Columbia. For all the accolades he had received, he recognized the limits of his and his race's progress.[76]

The waning days of Douglass's life seemed to be the waning days of the national commitment to black political rights as well. In January 1883, during a banquet to commemorate the twentieth anniversary of the Emancipation Proclamation, he explained the centrality of Lincoln's presidential directive to American history and the need to make further progress between the races. The national narrative could be divided into the period before the proclamation and the period after this singular achievement, he explained. "The day we celebrate affords us an eminence from which we may in a measure survey both the past and the future. It is one of those days which may well count for a thousand years." Be that as it may, more was required of the citizenry if the promises of emancipation were to be realized fully. The Emancipation Proclamation and the Civil War were revolutions of a sort, but as revolutions they were unfinished.[77]

That same year, Douglass read the *Civil Rights Cases* with alarm. He understood intuitively that a full-scale retreat from Reconstruction was in the offing. Addressing a crowd gathered in Washington, D.C., after the opinion was handed down, he remarked, "We have been, as a class, grievously wounded, wounded in the house of our friends." In Douglass's view, the nation had made a commitment to blacks at the end of the Civil War. Promises of equal justice and fair treatment had been given, but those promises were ignored as memories of the war receded. A new class of white leaders did not appreciate the sacrifices blacks had made or the commitment whites had made. The *Civil Rights Cases* were a prime example of the national amnesia. Douglass was confident that "the future historian will turn to the year 1883 to find the most flagrant example of this national deterioration."[78]

As bad as 1883 was for the cause of racial advancement, the situation continued to deteriorate. Five years later, Douglass lamented, "Well the nation may forget. It may shut its eyes to the past, and frown upon any man who may do otherwise, but the colored people of this country are bound to keep the past in lively memory till justice shall be done them."[79]

Justice would be a long time in coming.

Epilogue

"We Wear the Mask That Grins and Lies"

Abolitionist William Lloyd Garrison lived until 1879, long enough to witness the ratification of the Civil War amendments as well as the rise and fall of Reconstruction. He folded *The Liberator* in 1865 and resigned as president of the American Anti-Slavery Society despite objections from some abolitionists, including Wendell Phillips, who argued that emancipation was only part of the goal. Until the freedmen enjoyed equal opportunities with whites, the struggle for freedom would never be completed. The society limped along for another five years, but it did so without Garrison. He turned his attention to the crusade for women's rights and battles over temperance. He later enjoyed a rapprochement with Phillips and occasionally made speeches on the need for equal civil and political rights for all, but Garrison's hour on the national stage had come and gone.[1]

Garrison's death barely preceded the institutionalization of segregation. The 1880s ushered in the dark night of the American Negro—a night so dark and so long that the better part of a century would elapse before sunlight broke through. If justice delayed is justice denied, generations of black Americans were left to dwell in unjust circumstances that can scarcely be imagined in a more enlightened age. Recriminations persist to this day; poor leadership, rampant racism, sour economic circumstances, and a desire to find a convenient scapegoat for social ills in the Old South undoubtedly contributed to the failures of Reconstruction.[2]

For all their noble intentions, the men who struggled to overcome issues of race in the mid-nineteenth century left a mixed legacy. Abraham Lincoln, the Great Emancipator, hailed as arguably the most successful president of his or any era, does not fare well under the harsh light of posterity if judged solely on his record of enlightened racial policy. He comes off far better when placed into the context of his times. Desperate to preserve the Union, anxious to quell disputes among and between the disparate factions of his party as well as with Democrats, and repeatedly challenged to develop a strategy for winning a civil war, he never focused exclusively on the unadulterated problem of race in American life. He did not enjoy that luxury. Had he lived into the postbellum era, Lincoln might have fashioned a workable compromise that succeeded where the Johnson and Grant administrations failed, but no one will ever know what might have been.[3]

The abolitionists and the Radical Republicans seldom receive the same approbation as Lincoln, but their role in fashioning a postwar regime is undeniable. The latter group has been characterized in at least two ways. One extreme view casts the Radicals as power-hungry, would-be demagogues, a perpetual thorn in the side of the benevolent, wise Lincoln. The Radicals constantly pushed him when cooler heads ought to have prevailed, thereby endangering the president's carefully crafted policies. Personally ambitious to a fault and intoxicated with power, these men of extremes were blinded by their own sense of propriety at the exclusion of mainstream public opinion. Were it not for Lincoln's sagacity, whatever modicum of success federal Reconstruction policy achieved likely would never have occurred.[4]

At the opposite extreme, the Radicals are portrayed as principled men who refused to compromise on important moral issues because to do so would have been an act of supreme hypocrisy. More charitable historians have deemed them serious men who courageously confronted the most divisive and significant issues—slavery, race, and political equality—in the nation's history. If the promise of the Declaration of Independence—that "all men are created equal"—was to be realized, fundamental changes would have to be implemented in the regime. According to this perspective, Lincoln was a wise, well-meaning executive, but he was essentially a conservative politician afraid to move boldly and decisively. Accordingly, he was unwilling or unable to use the cataclysm of civil war as a golden opportunity to remake the nation and thereby form a more perfect union. The Radicals gave the president political room to maneuver by creating the extreme left so that he might move from the right into a centrist position. It is one of history's great "what-if" questions to ask whether Abraham Lincoln would have radicalized the war with his Emancipation Proclamation were it not for the political pressure the Radicals brought to bear on the president.[5]

At the same time, the Radical Republicans were rigid, controlling, difficult men. In politics, as in life, compromise is sometimes necessary if one hopes to accomplish important goals. The Radicals were so self-righteous, so absolutely sure of their own moral superiority that they often hurt their cause as much as, perhaps more than, they helped it. Many of their attempts to wrest control of Reconstruction policy from Lincoln during the war were motivated by a thirst for power as much as by a desire to effect positive change in public policy. Stevens, Sumner, Wade, and their brethren could not separate their noble and base motives any more than they could separate feasible and unfeasible policies. Left to their own devices after Lincoln's death, they initially compromised with the moderates to wrest power for directing national reconstruction from the president. It was a fragile recipe for success, and it could not last indefinitely. As long as they banded together with moderates, they succeeded in checking Johnson's power and crafting effective policy over his vetoes, but eventually the Radicals overreached and destroyed their political coalition with the moderates; in doing so, they squandered the very opportunity to change America they had chastised Lincoln and his successors for squandering.[6]

The impeachment of Andrew Johnson is a prime example of the Jacobins' clumsy efforts to advance a radical agenda that was out of step with mainstream public opinion. That Johnson was an ineffective president is generally acknowledged by all but the most pro-Confederate historians, although his detractors and apologists disagree about the reasons for his failure. With a dispassionate, critical eye, it is difficult to assess the Johnson presidency without concluding that, at its core, the collapse occurred owing to the executive's lack of leadership skills. He was a virulent racist who found Lincoln's shoes too big to fill because he could not bring himself to compromise. He courted confrontation when wiser counsel would have dictated a different course. The Radicals reached this conclusion after an uncertain rapprochement in the early days of the new administration. Angered by what they viewed as the new president's treachery, the Jacobins were determined to exact vengeance. Not satisfied to oppose the president through the normal channels of bargaining, negotiation, and trade-offs in the legislative process, they resorted to the last refuge of an angry Congress: impeachment. Their hysteria at Johnson's political opposition blinded them to the damage caused by one branch of government attempting to oust a member of another branch absent clear and incontrovertible evidence of illegality, malfeasance, or treason. It is little wonder the Radicals' political power declined precipitously after Johnson won his acquittal before the U.S. Senate.[7]

From the tortured legacy of civil war, reconstruction, and redemption came the promise of a different America—a land where slavery was a distant memory and race was not the defining characteristic of citizenship and political equality. For all of their faults—and they had many—the Radical Republicans vehemently argued that life in the United States could be better. Lacking Lincoln's superior political skills, they had to be satisfied with the right policy (the abolition of slavery and the extension of full and fair citizenship to all) through the wrong means at the wrong time (impeachment and inopportune legislation lacking popular support). The Radicals pointed toward a way of life not as it existed, but as it could exist in some far-off future.[8]

Into the dark night of the late nineteenth century strode a remarkable man. For Booker T. Washington, born into slavery and coming of age during Reconstruction, the declining prospects of the Negro race were alarming, but they need not be dismaying. He had developed a plan for black advancement. Rather than preach race hatred and advancement through means that would frighten whites or supplant their position in society, he called for gradualism. His was a conservative voice. The pragmatic politician counsels that "something is better than nothing," and Washington learned the lesson from this playbook. "I fear the Negro race lays too much stress on its grievances and not enough on its opportunities," he remarked in a speech at Fisk University in 1895. Rather than lament the sorry state of Negro life in America or threaten to depart for foreign lands, the black man was well advised to recognize that he was inextricably linked to whites.[9]

Elsewhere, he observed:

> The Negro is making progress at the present time as he made progress in slavery times. There is, however, this difference: In slavery the progress of the Negro was a menace to the white man. The security of the white master depended upon the ignorance of the black slave. In freedom the security and happiness of each race depends, to a very large extent, on the education and the progress of the other. The problem of slavery was to keep the Negro down; the problem of freedom is to raise him up. The story of the Negro, in the last analysis, is simply the story of the man who is farthest down; as he raises himself he raises every other man who is above him.[10]

In a well-known address he delivered at the Cotton States and International Exposition in Atlanta, Georgia, on September 18, 1895—some seven months after Fredrick Douglass died—Washington outlined his plan, which became known as the "Atlanta Compromise." In Washington's view, the old adage "If you can't beat 'em, join 'em" contains much wisdom. Blacks would be well advised to appreciate "the importance of cultivating friendly relations with the Southern white man, who is their next-door neighbor." Making the best of a bad situation is the only reasonable course of action: "I would say: 'Cast down your bucket where you are'—cast it down in making friends in every manly way of the people of all races by whom we are surrounded." Rather than threaten whites with the specter of competition between the races, Washington advised Negroes to seek advancement in "agriculture, mechanics, in commerce, in domestic

As a representative of the last generation of black leaders born into slavery, Booker T. Washington argued in a famous 1895 speech that blacks should "concentrate all their energies on industrial education, and accumulation of wealth, and the conciliation of the South." This "go slow" accommodation won Washington support among older blacks and even some whites, but a younger generation of black leaders lambasted the conservative approach.
Courtesy of the Scurlock Studio Records, Archives Center, National Museum of American History, Behring Center, Smithsonian Institution.

service, and in the professions." In a passage that would infuriate subsequent proponents of social equality between the races, he remarked:

The wisest among my race understand that the agitation of questions of social equality is the extremest folly, and that progress in the enjoyment of all the privileges that will come to us must be the result of severe and constant struggle rather than of artificial forcing. No race that has anything to contribute to the markets of the world is long in any degree ostracized. It is important and right that all privileges of the law be ours, but it is vastly more important that we be prepared for the exercise of these privileges. The opportunity to earn a dollar in a factory just now is worth infinitely more than the opportunity to spend a dollar in an opera-house.[11]

Washington's supporters praised his approach as the most effective means of allowing blacks and whites to live together without encouraging warfare between the races. For whites, the bargain was appealing: blacks would willingly undertake the difficult, dirty, demeaning jobs, as befitted their race. For blacks, the proposal allowed them to eke out a living without crossing the color line on fear of their lives. Harmony, to the extent it could ever be promoted, depended on everyone knowing his place and staying within the narrow confines of the agreed-upon boundaries.[12]

As the nineteenth century gave way to the twentieth, life in the United States was an odd bifurcation between blacks and whites as though the two races existed in parallel, and mutually exclusive, worlds. In the instances when worlds collided, the outcome was often violent and almost always disadvantageous to people of color. When the worlds existed separate from each other (but hardly equal), blacks enjoyed a measure of freedom and advancement as Negro churches, schools, financial institutions, small businesses, professions, and sports teams grew and thrived.[13]

As the Jim Crow regime settled over the nation and defined social and economic relations for generations, a healthy Negro middle class arose. Many whites insisted on victimizing blacks and refusing them an equal place in society, but the would-be victims were not satisfied to suffer quietly. They created their own opportunities for advancement. With few leaders openly questioning the wisdom of dual societies existing side by side in the same landscape, blacks accepted the status quo as a welcome opportunity to live free of white violence and degradation. Except for an occasional misfit—a perverse dreamer, or idealistic social philosopher, or revolutionary rabble-rouser, or "misguided" proponent of black outmigration such as the Jamaican Marcus Garvey during the 1920s—few blacks or whites challenged the status quo. No doubt many an introspective soul quietly pondered the inequities that plagued life in the black world, but crossing the color line was as unfathomable as traveling in outer space, and equally as risky.[14]

The Atlanta Compromise made Washington the most revered and influential black leader of his generation. He traveled in circles few men of his era could envision. To have come so far in his life—from impoverished slave to generational leader—transformed him from a flesh-and-blood man into an instantly recognizable icon. To be fair, for all the criticism he would endure from his successors, Washington had accomplished a feat that no one else had—not the abolitionists, not Lincoln, not the Jacobins. He had served as a symbol of Negro empowerment. In a sense, he had secured freedom for the black underclass to exist unmolested, with some noteworthy exceptions, by the white upper class. He had provided breathing room for the rise of the black middle class during the segregationist era. These were mighty accomplishments in that time and place.[15]

Historians might indulge in counterfactual theorizing—what if the Atlanta Compromise had never existed and a race war had ensued?—but Washington's subsequent detractors believed he had betrayed the sentiments of Frederick Douglass and the nineteenth-century abolitionists as well as the Radical Republicans. In assailing Washington's gradualist approach to race relations, a new breed of firebrand refused to compromise, never settling for anything less than total equality. As is so often the case when succeeding generations examine the seemingly timid accomplishments of their predecessors, a younger group of black leaders took Washington, the renowned Wizard of Tuskegee, to task, arguing they would never have been satisfied to be supplicants to whites in exchange for peace and breathing space from the oppression of the Jim Crow regime. Washington's critics believed it was preferable to struggle against oppression, come what may, rather than humbly agree to the terms and conditions dictated by the oppressor.[16]

The most famous and eloquent voice raised against the Atlanta Compromise belonged to W. E. B. Du Bois. A Northern-born and -bred, classically educated man of unusual intellectual gifts, Du Bois had never known slavery. He enjoyed advantages in economic opportunity and social position experienced by few people of any race. A man of letters, social activist, cofounder of the National Association for the Advancement of Colored People (NAACP), and historian of Reconstruction and Redemption, Du Bois was upset by the "cult" surrounding Washington. Anyone who dared to challenge the great man's gradualist approach risked aggravating a bevy of outraged admirers on both sides of the color line.[17]

Du Bois was not a timid fellow; he was willing and able to walk where angels feared to tread. He and a group of like-minded young Turks argued that Washington's accommodationist approach was popular with whites because it ensured that Negroes would always be second-class citizens in the land of their birth. Some black opponents of the Washington plan characterized Negroes who cooperated with Southern whites as "Uncle Toms," a reference to Harriet Beecher Stowe's classic antebellum novel, or "white folks' niggers." Even new black leaders who were disinclined to use such harsh language contended that Negroes would never truly ascend from second-class status as long as legal segregation existed. Limited educational and employment opportunities invariably led to frustrated hopes and dreams as the "talented tenth" necessary for future leadership was not identified.[18]

Du Bois explained his opposition to Washington's ideas in his influential work *The Souls of Black Folk*, first published in 1903. "Mr. Washington came with a simple definite programme at the psychological moment when

The classically educated, Northern-born and -bred W. E. B. Du Bois, pictured here in 1907, criticized Booker T. Washington's accommodationist stance, arguing that blacks should enjoy the same rights and opportunities as whites. In 1909, Du Bois cofounded the National Association for the Advancement of Colored People (NAACP).
Courtesy of the Special Collections Department, W. E. B. Du Bois Library, University of Massachusetts Amherst.

the nation was a little ashamed of having bestowed so much sentiment on Negroes and was concentrating its energies on Dollars," he wrote. "His programme of industrial education, conciliation of the South, and submission and silence as to civil and political rights was not wholly original. . . . But Mr. Washington first indissolubly linked these things; he put enthusiasm, unlimited energy, and perfect faith into this programme, and changed it from a by-path into a veritable Way of Life."[19]

Couching his criticism in respectful terms, Du Bois acknowledged Washington's achievements while simultaneously expressing the wretchedness, indeed the inexorable sadness, of denied opportunities and wasted lives under the Jim Crow regime:

Among his own people, however, Mr. Washington has encountered the strongest and most lasting opposition, amounting at times to bitterness, and even today continuing strong and insistent even though largely silenced in outward expression by the public opinion of the nation. Some of this opposition is, of course, mere envy; the disappointment of displaced demagogues and the spite of narrow minds. But aside from this, there is among educated and thoughtful colored men in all parts of the land a feeling of deep regret, sorrow, and apprehension at the wide currency and ascendancy which some of Mr. Washington's theories have gained.[20]

The Washington–Du Bois exchange in some ways mirrored the exchange between the gradual emancipationists and the radical abolitionists of the antebellum era. A gradual approach to social change assures that the alienation and violence attendant to societal upheaval are minimized, but incremental reform, especially in cases where the inequities are undeniable, can frustrate persons harmed by society's inequities. Whatever their respective merits and drawbacks, conservative and liberal opinions on matters of race and equal treatment echoed across the broad canvas of the twentieth century. Change was a long time in coming, but, when it finally came with the civil rights movement of the 1950s and 1960s, reform was relatively swift.[21]

In the long decades that passed between the death of Reconstruction and the birth of the twentieth-century civil rights movement, blacks were forced into an American version of apartheid. They read the Declaration of Independence with a deep appreciation of the hypocrisy contained in the American credo that "all men are created equal." They did not enjoy the full rights of citizenship guaranteed by the U.S. Constitution. Their sad, hard faces stare from old photographs with a seemingly hopeless acceptance of the ways of the world that proved enervating to all but a handful of intrepid souls who fought their way up from poverty and obscurity. With some noteworthy exceptions, blacks remained nameless and forgotten to mainstream America, human beings who were born, lived, and died with few opportunities to live up to their potential. For much of white America, Negroes were an invisible class with little to offer society.[22]

And if black Americans lost opportunities to engage fully and fairly in national life, what did the country lose as a result of racism and inequality? If a nation is but the sum of its parts, an amalgamation of individuals and their hopes, dreams, and talents, then surely the United States suffered from its legacy of unequal treatment. Untold numbers of great scientists, writers, artists, athletes, political leaders, and philosophers who might have contributed to their country's progress were silenced by the brutal hand of oppression. Forced into a permanent underclass from which few escaped, promising men and women of color could only watch mutely as opportunities to make something of their lives and communities were frittered away, trampled under the feet of Jumpin' Jim Crow. To be sure, extraordinary blacks could point to a solid record of achievement, but the record no doubt would have been more impressive without the suffocating shroud of legal segregation.[23]

They dared not complain until after decades passed, blacks migrated from rural farming communities to large cities in search of improved employment prospects, and their acquired wealth and status empowered them to demand better treatment. Until then, Negroes were forced to grin and bear it, to chase what few opportunities were afforded them in segregated black communities. Over time, their false smiles became a mask, and the mask became a grotesque mockery of the American character. Great black achievements that occurred under the oppressive American regime were all the more precious for their rarity. In most cases, the achievements reflected a subtle, nuanced realization of the circumstances facing the Negro in America. It is no surprise, then, that one of the defining literary expressions of the black experience under segregation, "We Wear the Mask," was penned by a young poet, Paul Laurence Dunbar, who wrote brilliantly of the sorrows of his age. Dunbar captured the plight of his race in lyrical lines that recall a dark and bitter time:

> We wear the mask that grins and lies,
> It hides our cheeks and shades our eyes,—
> This debt we pay to human guile;
> With torn and bleeding hearts we smile,
> And mouth with myriad subtleties.
>
> Why should the world be over-wise,
> In counting all our tears and sighs?
> Nay, let them only see us, while
> We wear the mask.
>
> We smile, but, O great Christ, our cries
> To thee from tortured souls arise.
> We sing, but oh the clay is vile
> Beneath our feet, and long the mile;
> But let the world dream otherwise,
> We wear the mask![24]

Notes

PREFACE AND ACKNOWLEDGMENTS

1. Burton, *The Age of Lincoln.*
2. Fukuyama, *The End of History and the Last Man*, 12; MacKenzie, *The Nineteenth Century*, 513.

PROLOGUE:
"WE HAVE THE WOLF BY THE EAR"

1. Rohrbach, "'Truth Stronger and Stranger than Fiction,'" 727–28.
2. Quoted in Howe, *What Hath God Wrought*, 425.
3. Quoted in Miller, *President Lincoln*, 408–11.
4. Foner, *Forever Free*, 25–26; Hahn, *A Nation under Our Feet*, 55; Horton and Horton, *Slavery and the Making of America*, 103–4; Kraditor, *Means and Ends in American Abolitionism*, 3–10.
5. Howe, *What Hath God Wrought*, 648–53.
6. Howe, *What Hath God Wrought*, 52–61, 432–33.
7. Ford, "Reconfiguring the Old South," 118–21.
8. Horton and Horton, *Slavery and the Making of America*, 37–38, 69–70, 92–95; Wish, "American Slave Insurrections before 1861," 299. For a discussion of the debate surrounding the Vesey conspiracy and whether it was imminent, see especially Johnson, "Denmark Vesey and His Co-Conspirators."
9. Quoted in Horton and Horton, *Slavery and the Making of America*, 112.
10. The story of Nat Turner's rebellion is told in many sources. See, for example, Horton and Horton, *Slavery and the Making of America*, 112–15; Howe, *What Hath God Wrought*, 323–27.
11. Gray, *The Confessions of Nat Turner.*

12. Horton and Horton, *Slavery and the Making of America*, 115.

13. Foner, *Free Soil, Free Labor, Free Men*, 177–78; Whittington, "The Political Constitution of Federalism in Antebellum America," 1–24.

14. Howe, *What Hath God Wrought*, 648–50; Kraditor, *Means and Ends in American Abolitionism*, 6–10.

15. Foner, *Forever Free*, 25–28; Kraditor, *Means and Ends in American Abolitionism*, 26–32.

16. The literature on the multitude of views on slavery is voluminous and far beyond the scope of this book. See, for example, Gates, *Lincoln on Race & Slavery*; Trefousse, *The Radical Republicans*, 112–14; Williams, *Lincoln and the Radicals*, 5–9.

17. Guelzo, "Lincoln and the Abolitionists," 58–63; Williams, *Lincoln and the Radicals*, 6–9; Williams, "Lincoln and the Radicals: An Essay in Civil War History and Historiography," 62.

18. Knowles, "The Constitution and Slavery," 311–13.

19. Quoted in Padover, *Thomas Jefferson on Democracy*, 158. See also Gordon-Reed, *The Hemingses of Monticello*, 536–39.

20. Jefferson, *Notes on the State of Virginia*, 162.

21. Quoted in Davis and Mintz, *The Boisterous Sea of Liberty*, 356. See also Miller, *The Wolf by the Ears*, 2–3; Onuf, "'To Declare Them a Free and Independent People,'" 1–46; Wilentz, "Jeffersonian Democracy and the Origins of Political Antislavery in the United States," 375–401.

22. Cox, *Lincoln and Black Freedom*, 142–84; Foner, "Reconstruction Revisited," 86.

23. Howe, *What Hath God Wrought*, 482; Luse, "Slavery's Champions Stood at Odds," 385–87; McPherson, *The Struggle for Equality*, 136.

24. Ford, "Reconfiguring the Old South," 118–21; Howe, *What Hath God Wrought*, 480–82; Luse, "Slavery's Champions Stood at Odds," 380–87; Sinha, "The Caning of Charles Sumner," 244–50.

25. Bogue, "The Radical Voting Dimension in the U.S. Senate during the Civil War," 450; Cox, *Lincoln and Black Freedom*, ix, 12; Gambill, "Who Were the Senate Radicals?," 237–44; Green, *Freedom, Union, and Power*, 153; Trefousse, *The Radical Republicans*, 4–15.

26. Guelzo, "Lincoln and the Abolitionists," 58–63; Williams, *Lincoln and the Radicals*, 14–16.

27. Quoted in Gates, "AL to Horace Greeley," in *Lincoln on Race & Slavery*, 243–44. See also Cox, *Lincoln and Black Freedom*, x, 183; Foner, *The Fiery Trial*, 228; Yoo, *Crisis and Command*, 219–20.

28. Quoted in Gates, "AL to Horace Greeley," in *Lincoln on Race & Slavery*, 243–44. See also Cox, *Lincoln and Black Freedom*, x; Green, *Freedom, Union, and Power*, 153; White, *A. Lincoln*, 504.

29. Carwardine, *Lincoln: A Life of Purpose and Power*, 218–21; Donald, *Lincoln*, 366–69.

30. Trefousse, *The Radical Republicans*, 280–307.

31. Quoted in Martinez, *Carpetbaggers, Cavalry, and the Ku Klux Klan*, 41. See also Beale, *The Critical Year*, 48–52.

32. Quoted in Means, *The Avenger Takes His Place*, 104–5.

33. Kauffman, *American Brutus*, 328, 342–43; Leonard, *Lincoln's Avengers*, xii–xiv, 10, 63–65.

34. Quoted in Means, *The Avenger Takes His Place*, 208.

35. Beale, *The Critical Year*, 10–19; DeWitt, *The Impeachment and Trial of Andrew Johnson*, 388–90; Henry, *The Story of Reconstruction*, 302–3.

36. Gillette, *Retreat from Reconstruction*, 17–19; Lewinson, *Race, Class, and Party*, 55–57; McFeely, *Grant*, 367–74; Smith, *Grant*, 542.

37. Trefousse, *The Radical Republicans*, 5–15.

38. Williams, *Lincoln and the Radicals*, 373–84.

CHAPTER 1
"THE CRIMES OF THIS GUILTY LAND"

1. Haines, "The Population of the United States, 1790–1920," 143–205; Howe, *What Hath God Wrought*, 477–82; Witcover, *Party of the People*, 47–48.

2. Knowles, "The Constitution and Slavery," 322–24.

3. Howe, *What Hath God Wrought*, 690–98; Kaukiainen, "Shrinking the World," 10–14; Newhall, *The Daguerreotype in America*, 11.

4. Howe, *What Hath God Wrought*, 164–202.

5. Meacham, *American Lion*, xix–xxii, 355–61; Remini, *The Life of Andrew Jackson*, 86–104, 173–74, 194–97; Wilentz, *Andrew Jackson*, 13–16.

6. Meacham, *American Lion*, 302–6; Remini, *The Life of Andrew Jackson*, 338; Yoo, *Crisis and Command*, 161–75.

7. See, for example, Peterson, *The Great Triumvirate*; Remini, *The Life of Andrew Jackson*, 328.

8. Howe, *What Hath God Wrought*, 369–72; Remini, *Daniel Webster*, 27–28.

9. Quoted in Howe, *What Hath God Wrought*, 371. See also McDonald, *States' Rights and the Union*, 104–6.

10. Howe, *What Hath God Wrought*, 147–60; Van Atta, "Western Lands," 633–38.

11. Morrison, *Slavery and the American West*, 96–103.

12. Basinger, "Regulating Slavery," 308–9; Foner, *Forever Free*, 22–23; Foner, *Free Soil, Free Labor, Free Men*, 82–83, 136–38; Horton and Horton, *Slavery and the Making of America*, 148–56.

13. Herzberg, "An Analytic Choice Approach to Concurrent Majorities," 54–58, 78–79; Kuic, "John C. Calhoun's Theory of the 'Concurrent Majority,'" 485–86.

14. Barber, *The Book of Democracy*, 392–93; Bolt, "Founding Father and Rebellious Son," 13–14, 19; Ford, "Reconfiguring the Old South," 118–21.

15. Quoted in Kuic, "John C. Calhoun's Theory of the 'Concurrent Majority,'" 485. For a discussion of how Calhoun's view of liberty contrasted with other views of liberty, especially Lincoln's, see Fischer, *Liberty and Freedom*, 284–89; McDonald, *States' Rights and the Union*, 107.

16. Bolt, "Founding Father and Rebellious Son," 5–8; Howe, *What Hath God Wrought*, 396–97; Wilentz, *Andrew Jackson*, 64–65.

17. Quoted in Meacham, *American Lion*, 135–36. See also Bolt, "Founding Father and Rebellious Son," 19–20; McDonald, *States' Rights and the Union*, 106; Remini, *The Life of Andrew Jackson*, 196–97; Wilentz, *Andrew Jackson*, 65–66; Yoo, *Crisis and Command*, 180–82.

18. Dunning, "Manifest Destiny and the Trans-Mississippi South," 111–27; Hodgson, "Storm over Mexico," 34–35.

19. Quoted in Witcover, *Party of the People*, 180. See also Green, *Freedom, Union, and Power*, 13; Foner, *Free Soil, Free Labor, Free Men*, 60, 152; Witcover, *Party of the People*, 180–81.

20. Griswold del Castillo, *The Treaty of Guadalupe Hidalgo*, 62–63.

21. Borchard, "From Pink Lemonade to Salt River," 24–30; Levine, "Conservatism, Nativism, and Slavery," 455–58, 486–88.

22. Foner, *Free Soil, Free Labor, Free Men*, 81–83; Howe, *What Hath God Wrought*, 832–34; Witcover, *Party of the People*, 164, 183.

23. Brookhiser, *America's First Dynasty*, 124–25; Foner, *Free Soil, Free Labor, Free Men*, 60–61, 81–87, 124–25, 127–29; Levine, "Conservatism, Nativism, and Slavery," 486–87.

24. Gould, *Grand Old Party*, 12–13, 16; Levine, "Conservatism, Nativism, and Slavery," 487–88; Phillips, "'The Crimes against Missouri,'" 72–73.

25. Gienapp, *The Origins of the Republican Party*, 67–69; Harris, *Lincoln's Rise to the Presidency*, 66–67; Kraig, "The Narration of Essence," 238–40.

26. Huston, "Democracy by Scripture versus Democracy by Process," 189–90; Jaffa, "*Dred Scott* Revisited," 207–11; Kraig, "The Narration of Essence," 236–40.

27. Guelzo, *Lincoln and Douglas*, 14–20; Huston, "Democracy by Scripture versus Democracy by Process," 191–200; Jayne, *Lincoln and the American Manifesto*, 152–53; Kraig, "The Narration of Essence," 236–38, 250.

28. Gienapp, *The Origins of the Republican Party*, 104–6; Gould, *Grand Old Party*, 14–15; Green, *Freedom, Union, and Power*, 13; Harris, *Lincoln's Rise to the Presidency*, 66–67; Waugh, *One Man Great Enough*, 225–26.

29. Gienapp, *The Origins of the Republican Party*, 138–39; Levine, "Conservatism, Nativism, and Slavery," 485–88.

30. Gienapp, *The Origins of the Republican Party*, 316–18, 347–48; Gould, *Grand Old Party*, 14–17; Harris, *Lincoln's Rise to the Presidency*, 66; Levine, "Conservatism, Nativism, and Slavery," 485–86.

31. Dred Scott v. John F. A. Sandford, 60 U.S. 393 (1857).

32. Hamilton, "Federalist 78," 465.

33. Baum, *The Supreme Court*, 18–20; Green, *Freedom, Union, and Power*, 14; O'Brien, *Storm Center*, 42–43.

34. Carey, "Political Atheism," 208; Jaffa, "*Dred Scott* Revisited," 201–5; Jayne, *Lincoln and the American Manifesto*, 159–64; Price, "Slavery's Big Victory," 24; Wallance, "The Lawsuit That Started the Civil War," 47–50.

35. Carey, "Political Atheism," 211; Wallance, "The Lawsuit That Started the Civil War," 49; Waugh, *One Man Great Enough*, 241.

36. Allen, "The Political Economy of Blackness," 231–38; Howe, *What Hath God Wrought*, 387–89.

37. Prigg v. the Commonwealth of Pennsylvania, 41 U.S. 539 (1842). See also Carey, "Political Atheism," 210.

38. Moore v. Illinois, 55 U.S. 13, 21 (1852).

39. Strader, Gorman, and Armstrong v. Graham, 51 U.S. 82 (1850).

40. Burns, *Packing the Court*, 59–61; Jaffa, *"Dred Scott* Revisited," 200–204; Mauro, "Taney v. the Missouri Compromise," 52.

41. Allen, "The Political Economy of Blackness," 232–35; Jaffa, *"Dred Scott* Revisited," 210–12; Mauro, "Taney v. the Missouri Compromise," 52; Wallance, "The Lawsuit That Started the Civil War," 50.

42. *Scott*, 60 U.S. 393, 404.

43. Quoted in Wallance, "The Lawsuit That Started the Civil War," 50. See also White, *A. Lincoln*, 236.

44. Quoted in McPherson, *Battle Cry of Freedom*, 176. See also Burns, *Packing the Court*, 61–62; Price, "Slavery's Big Victory," 25.

45. Quoted in Guelzo, *Lincoln and Douglas*, 100. See also Guelzo, "The Lincoln-Douglas Debates: Watch That Finger! Raise Those Arms! Make Your Point!" 60.

46. Quoted in White, *A. Lincoln*, 258.

47. Quoted in Donald, *Lincoln*, 237. See also Carwardine, *Lincoln: A Life of Purpose and Power*, 49–53.

48. Harris, *Lincoln's Rise to the Presidency*, 66–73, 87–88; Jayne, *Lincoln and the American Manifesto*, 159–74; Miller, *President Lincoln*, 131.

49. Harris, *Lincoln's Rise to the Presidency*, 67–68.

50. Quoted in Jayne, *Lincoln and the American Manifesto*, 153.

51. Gates, "Speech at Peoria, Illinois," in *Lincoln on Race & Slavery*, 56–68. See also Harris, *Lincoln's Rise to the Presidency*, 68–72; Jayne, *Lincoln and the American Manifesto*, 153–56; Lincoln, "Speech at Peoria," in *Complete Works of Abraham Lincoln*, Vol. 2, 190–261; White, *A. Lincoln*, 198–203.

52. Guelzo, "Lincoln and the Abolitionists," 60–66, quoted at 60. See also Bromwich, "Lincoln's Constitutional Necessity," 4–6; Foner, *The Fiery Trial*, 63–70; Guelzo, *Lincoln and Douglas*, 32–36.

53. Jayne, *Lincoln and the American Manifesto*, 156–58.

54. Guelzo, "Lincoln and the Abolitionists," 64–70.

55. Guelzo, "Lincoln and the Abolitionists," 65–66; Harris, *Lincoln's Rise to the Presidency*, 86–88; Luse, "Slavery's Champions Stood at Odds," 380–92; McPherson, *The Struggle for Equality*, 136.

56. Lincoln, "Springfield Speech," in *Complete Works of Abraham Lincoln*, Vol. 3, 2. See also Gates, "A House Divided Speech at Springfield Illinois," in *Lincoln on Race & Slavery*, 104; Harris, *Lincoln's Rise to the Presidency*, 91–92.

57. Foner, *The Fiery Trial*, 99–103; Gates, "A House Divided Speech at Springfield Illinois," in *Lincoln on Race & Slavery*, 103–4; Goodwin, *Team of Rivals*, 191–92, 227; Harris, *Lincoln's Rise to the Presidency*, 92–94.

58. Quoted in Harris, *Lincoln's Rise to the Presidency*, 94. See also Blight, "Lincoln on the Moral Bankruptcy of Slavery," 56.

59. Brands, "There Goes the South," 42–43; Bromwich, "Lincoln's Constitutional Necessity," 10–11; Jayne, *Lincoln and the American Manifesto*, 164–65; Waugh, *One Man Great Enough*, 253–54.

60. Lincoln, "Springfield Speech," in *Complete Works of Abraham Lincoln*, Vol. 3, 9–10. See also Foner, *The Fiery Trial*, 101–2; White, *A. Lincoln*, 254.

61. Jayne, *Lincoln and the American Manifesto*, 164–66; Waugh, *One Man Great Enough*, 255.

62. Quoted in Harris, *Lincoln's Rise to the Presidency*, 95. See also Blight, "Lincoln on the Moral Bankruptcy of Slavery," 56; Bromwich, "Lincoln's Constitutional Necessity," 10–11; Guelzo, "Houses Divided," 401; Harris, *Lincoln's Rise to the Presidency*, 94–97; White, *A. Lincoln*, 257–58.

63. Guelzo, "Houses Divided," 408–9.

64. Guelzo, "Houses Divided," 406–9; Guelzo, "The Lincoln-Douglas Debates: Watch That Finger! Raise Those Arms! Make Your Point!" 56, 58; Harris, *Lincoln's Rise to the Presidency*, 106–11.

65. Guelzo, *Lincoln and Douglas*, xiii–xxi; Waugh, *One Man Great Enough*, 260.

66. White, *A. Lincoln*, 264–85.

67. Lincoln and Douglas, "Selections from the Lincoln-Douglas Debates of 1858," 112–13. See also Foner, *The Fiery Trial*, 104–6.

68. Quoted in Gates, "Second Debate with Stephen A. Douglas at Freeport, Illinois," in *Lincoln on Race & Slavery*, 137–42. See also Waugh, *One Man Great Enough*, 270–72.

69. Lincoln and Douglas, "Selections from the Lincoln-Douglas Debates of 1858," 97.

70. Guelzo, "Houses Divided," 412–14; Harris, *Lincoln's Rise to the Presidency*, 122–25.

71. Foner, *The Fiery Trial*, 106–7; Guelzo, *Lincoln and Douglas*, 160–64.

72. Harris, *Lincoln's Rise to the Presidency*, 84–88.

73. Blight, "Lincoln on the Moral Bankruptcy of Slavery," 56–57; Guelzo, "Houses Divided," 414–17; Guelzo, *Lincoln and Douglas*, 160–63, 299; Waugh, *One Man Great Enough*, 73; White, *A. Lincoln*, 287–89. The apocryphal quote can be found in Fehrenbacher and Fehrenbacher, eds., *Recollected Words of Abraham Lincoln*, 533n268.

74. Foner, *Free Soil, Free Labor, Free Men*, 109–10; Kraditor, *Means and Ends in American Abolitionism*, 7–10; Levine, *Black Culture and Black Consciousness*, 67–71.

75. Foner, *Forever Free*, 24–28; Kraditor, *Means and Ends in American Abolitionism*, 4–10.

76. Kraditor, *Means and Ends in American Abolitionism*, 32.

77. Guelzo, "Lincoln and the Abolitionists," 62.

78. Foner, *Free Soil, Free Labor, Free Men*, 303.

79. Basinger, "Regulating Slavery," 308–9; Knowles, "The Constitution and Slavery," 311–12; Phillips, *The Constitution*, 6–7; Waldstreicher, *Slavery's Constitution*, 83–90.

80. Phillips, *The Constitution*, 9.

81. Horton and Horton, *Slavery and the Making of America*, 132–33, 139–41; Howe, *What Hath God Wrought*, 652–53.

82. Horton and Horton, *Slavery and the Making of America*, 132–33; Mitchell, "Notes from the Underground," 43.

83. Catton, *The American Heritage New History of the Civil War*, 28; Howe, *What Hath God Wrought*, 653–54; Sayers, "The Underground Railroad Reconsidered," 438–41.

84. Quoted in Horton and Horton, *Slavery and the Making of America*, 118. See also Horton and Horton, *Slavery and the Making of America*, 137–38.

85. Horton and Horton, *Slavery and the Making of America*, 137; Howe, *What Hath God Wrought*, 653–54; Mitchell, "Notes from the Underground," 45–46.

86. Buccola, "'Each for All and All for Each,'" 400–405; Ramsey, "Frederick Douglass, Southerner," 19–20.

87. Quoted in Buccola, "'Each for All and All for Each,'" 407.

88. Foner, *Forever Free*, 24–28; Kraditor, *Means and Ends in American Abolitionism*, 235–55.

89. Hamilton, "The Strange Career of Uncle Tom," 26; Reynolds, *Mightier than the Sword*, 128.

90. Hamilton, "The Strange Career of Uncle Tom," 23, 26; Hedrick, "'Peaceable Fruits,'" 307; Reynolds, *Mightier than the Sword*, 1–3.

91. Hamilton, "The Strange Career of Uncle Tom," 23, 26; Hedrick, "'Peaceable Fruits,'" 310; Lasser, "Voyeuristic Abolitionism," 109–10; Reynolds, *Mightier than the Sword*, 17–18.

92. Bracher, "How to Teach for Social Justice," 366–68; Hamilton, "The Strange Career of Uncle Tom," 24–25; Lasser, "Voyeuristic Abolitionism," 109–10; Reynolds, *Mightier than the Sword*, 104–7.

93. Hamilton, "The Strange Career of Uncle Tom," 23–26; Horton and Horton, *Slavery and the Making of America*, 154.

94. Quoted in Magdol, *Owen Lovejoy*, 422–23. See also Oates, *To Purge This Land with Blood*, 3–50.

95. DeCaro, *"Fire from the Midst of You,"* 95–99; Oates, *To Purge This Land with Blood*, 26–33; Rowland, "John Brown's Moonlight March," 32.

96. Kraditor, *Means and Ends in American Abolitionism*, 102–8; Matzke, "The John Brown Way," 65–73; McPherson, *Battle Cry of Freedom*, 204; Oates, *To Purge This Land with Blood*, 289; Rowland, "John Brown's Moonlight March," 32–33.

97. Oates, *To Purge This Land with Blood*, 97–106.

98. Phillips, "'The Crime against Missouri,'" 77–81; Von Frank, "John Brown, James Redpath, and the Idea of Revolution," 142–60.

99. Sinha, "The Caning of Charles Sumner," 233–62.

100. Gilbert, "A Behavioral Analysis of John Brown," 113; McGlone, "The 'Madness' of John Brown," 45; Oates, *To Purge This Land with Blood*, 126–37.

101. Catton, *The American Heritage New History of the Civil War*, 37; Horton and Horton, *Slavery and the Making of America*, 166.

102. McPherson, *Battle Cry of Freedom*, 207–8.

103. Gilbert, "A Behavioral Analysis of John Brown," 107–17; McPherson, *Battle Cry of Freedom*, 205–7.

104. Foner, *Forever Free*, 23–24, 32–33; Horton and Horton, *Slavery and the Making of America*, 166; McGlone, "The 'Madness' of John Brown," 46–49.

105. Foner, *Forever Free*, 32–33; Frye, "John Brown's Raid," 265; Horton and Horton, *Slavery and the Making of America*, 161; McPherson, *Battle Cry of Freedom*, 205–6.

106. Frye, "John Brown's Raid," 265; Horton and Horton, *Slavery and the Making of America*, 161–63; McPherson, *Battle Cry of Freedom*, 206.

107. Catton, *The American Heritage New History of the Civil War*, 37; Frye, "John Brown's Raid," 265–66; Horton and Horton, *Slavery and the Making of America*, 163–64.

108. Frye, "John Brown's Raid," 266; Horton and Horton, *Slavery and the Making of America*, 164, 166.

109. Quoted in Frye, "John Brown's Raid," 266.

110. Quoted in McPherson, *Battle Cry of Freedom*, 210. See also: Matzke, "The John Brown Way," 63–67.

111. Quoted in Harris, *Lincoln's Rise to the Presidency*, 180.

112. Quoted in Frye, "John Brown's Raid," 266.

113. Quoted in McPherson, *Battle Cry of Freedom*, 210–11.

114. Quoted in Frye, "John Brown's Raid," 266.

115. Ford, "Reconfiguring the Old South," 118–20; Herzberg, "An Analytic Choice Approach to Concurrent Majorities," 54–55.

116. Foner, *Forever Free*, 15–16; Hahn, *A Nation under Our Feet*, 41; Levine, *Black Culture and Black Consciousness*, 4–6.

117. Genovese, *Roll Jordan Roll*, 4–6; Mallard, *Plantation Life before Emancipation*, 47–48; Stampp, *The Peculiar Institution*, 3–33.

118. Foner, *Forever Free*, 16–20.

119. Mallard, *Plantation Life before Emancipation*, 14–19.

120. Horton and Horton, *Slavery and the Making of America*, 122–23.

121. Foner, *Forever Free*, 16–17; Hahn, *A Nation under Our Feet*, 20–21; Horton and Horton, *Slavery and the Making of America*, 121–22.

122. Foner, *Forever Free*, 18–21; Fox-Genovese, *Within the Plantation Household*, 327–29; Horton and Horton, *Slavery and the Making of America*, 89–90.

123. Horton and Horton, *Slavery and the Making of America*, 115; Howe, *What Hath God Wrought*, 182–85.

124. Fox-Genovese, *Within the Plantation Household*, 103–4.

125. Horton and Horton, *Slavery and the Making of America*, 124; Levine, *Black Culture and Black Consciousness*, 79.

126. Fischer, *Liberty and Freedom*, 274; Genovese, *Roll Jordan Roll*, 5.

127. Horton and Horton, *Slavery and the Making of America*, 118–59; Matzke, "The John Brown Way," 73; Ramsey, "Frederick Douglass, Southerner," 19–36; Sayers, "The Underground Railroad Reconsidered," 435–41.

CHAPTER 2
"MR. PRESIDENT, YOU ARE MURDERING YOUR COUNTRY BY INCHES"

1. Burton, *The Age of Lincoln*, 12–49; McPherson, *Battle Cry of Freedom*, 6–46; Wood, *Empire of Liberty*, 9–10, 37, 519–23.

2. Burton, *The Age of Lincoln*, 22–26; Catton, *The American Heritage New History of the Civil War*, 6–42.

3. Goodwin, *Team of Rivals*, 28–59; Holzer, *Lincoln President-Elect*, 11–14; McPherson, *Battle Cry of Freedom*, 216–21; White, *A. Lincoln*, 325–29.

4. Donald, *Lincoln*, 231–46; Holzer, *Lincoln at Cooper Union*, 206–19.

5. Bromwich, "Lincoln's Constitutional Necessity," 13–15; Carwardine, *Lincoln: A Life of Purpose and Power*, 97–99; Donald, *Lincoln*, 237–40; Egerton, *Year of Meteors*, 128; Foner, *The Fiery Trial*, 136–38; Holzer, *Lincoln at Cooper Union*, 1–6, 239–48; Holzer, "The Photograph That Made Lincoln President," 31–33; Waugh, *One Man Great Enough*, 300–306; White, *A. Lincoln*, 309–14.

6. Fischer, *Liberty and Freedom*, 333–48; White, *A. Lincoln*, 319–39.

7. Brands, "There Goes the South," 42–43; Donald, *Lincoln*, 246–49; Harris, *Lincoln's Rise to the Presidency*, 199–217; McPherson, *Battle Cry of Freedom*, 217–19; White, *A. Lincoln*, 325–29.

8. Egerton, *Year of Meteors*, 140–41; Harris, *Lincoln's Rise to the Presidency*, 202–6; McPherson, *Battle Cry of Freedom*, 216–18.

9. Egerton, *Year of Meteors*, 137–38; McPherson, *Battle Cry of Freedom*, 216–18; White, *A. Lincoln*, 325–26.

10. Burton, *The Age of Lincoln*, 103, 116–17; Gould, *Grand Old Party*, 26–28; Green, *Freedom, Union, and Power*, 15–16; Keegan, *The American Civil War*, 31.

11. Donald, *Lincoln*, 248–50; Egerton, *Year of Meteors*, 137–39; Foner, *The Fiery Trial*, 216; Harris, *Lincoln's Rise to the Presidency*, 202–9; McPherson, *Battle Cry of Freedom*, 218–19; Waugh, *One Man Great Enough*, 321–22; White, *A. Lincoln*, 323–28.

12. Carwardine, *Lincoln: A Life of Purpose and Power*, 72; Fischer, *Liberty and Freedom*, 342–44.

13. Foner, *The Fiery Trial*, 217; Miller, *President Lincoln*, 150–54.

14. Goodwin, *Team of Rivals*, 259–60; Harris, *Lincoln's Rise to the Presidency*, 241–47; Holzer, "Election Day, 1860," 48–50; Williams, "Lincoln and the Radicals: An Essay in Civil War History and Historiography," 47–48; Witcover, *Party of the People*, 205–8.

15. Egerton, *Year of Meteors*, 209–10; Goodwin, *Team of Rivals*, 276–78; Harris, *Lincoln's Rise to the Presidency*, 241–47; Holzer, "Election Day, 1860," 93–96; McPherson, *Battle Cry of Freedom*, 231–33; Waugh, *One Man Great Enough*, 354–58; White, *A. Lincoln*, 350–52.

16. Brands, "There Goes the South," 42–45; Goodwin, *Team of Rivals*, 294–97; Harris, *Lincoln's Rise to the Presidency*, 280–301; Holzer, *Lincoln President-Elect*, 3–7; Waugh, *One Man Great Enough*, 360–66; White, *A. Lincoln*, 350–64.

17. Bogue, "Historians and Radical Republicans," 8–9; Carwardine, *Lincoln: A Life of Purpose and Power*, 137–45; Donald, *Lincoln*, 331–33; Donald, *Lincoln Reconsidered*, 105–9; Trefousse, *The Radical Republicans*, 4–20; Williams, *Lincoln and the Radicals*, 5–9; Williams, "Lincoln and the Radicals: An Essay in Civil War History and Historiography," 43–44.

18. Quoted in Harris, *Public Life of Zachariah Chandler*, 54. See also Bogue, "Historians and Radical Republicans," 9–10; Bogue, "The Radical Voting Dimension in the U.S. Senate during the Civil War," 460–61; Foner, *The Fiery Trial*, 218; Magdol, *Owen Lovejoy*, 320–21; Tap, "Chandler, Zachariah," 398–99; Trefousse,

The Radical Republicans, 5–15; Williams, *Lincoln and the Radicals*, 5–17; Williams, "Lincoln and the Radicals: An Essay in Civil War History and Historiography," 44–45.

19. Donald, *"We Are Lincoln Men,"* 103–39; Stanco, "President Abraham Lincoln and Congress during the Civil War," 25–30; Williams, *Lincoln and the Radicals*, 5–9.

20. Quoted in Williams, *Lincoln and the Radicals*, 9–10. See also Belz, *Reconstructing the Union*, 282–83; Cox, *Lincoln and Black Freedom*, 16, 23–24; Foner, *The Fiery Trial*, 219.

21. Quoted in Williams, *Lincoln and the Radicals*, 10. See also Harris, *Lincoln's Rise to the Presidency*, 5–6; Trefousse, *The Radical Republicans*, 107–10, 218–22; Williams, "Lincoln and the Radicals: An Essay in Civil War History and Historiography," 46–47.

22. Orville H. Browning to Abraham Lincoln, Sunday, February 17, 1861 (Inaugural Address; endorsed by Abraham Lincoln), ALPLC *(Abraham Lincoln Papers at the Library of Congress)*. See also Donald, *Lincoln*, 301–4, 366–69; Goodwin, *Team of Rivals*, 366–70; McPherson, *Battle Cry of Freedom*, 308–12; Weigley, *A Great Civil War*, 90–92.

23. Donald, *Lincoln*, 262–64; Goodwin, *Team of Rivals*, 11–16; Paludan, *The Presidency of Abraham Lincoln*, 37–40; Williams, "Lincoln and the Radicals: An Essay in Civil War History and Historiography," 58–59.

24. Detzer, *Allegiance*, 108–36; Donald, *Lincoln*, 289–92; Goodwin, *Team of Rivals*, 340–43; McPherson, *Battle Cry of Freedom*, 268–71.

25. Winfield Scott to Abraham Lincoln, Tuesday, March 12, 1861 (Report on Fort Sumter), ALPLC. See also Detzer, *Allegiance*, 152–61; McPherson, *Battle Cry of Freedom*, 264–67; Potter, *Lincoln and His Party in the Secession Crisis*, xxv, 268.

26. Edward Bates, Friday, March 29, 1861 (Notes from cabinet meeting on Fort Sumter), ALPLC; Salmon P. Chase, Friday, March 29, 1861 (Notes from cabinet meeting on Fort Sumter), ALPLC. See also Detzer, *Allegiance*, 229–31; McPherson, *Tried by War*, 12–21; Perret, *Lincoln's War*, 13–21; Weigley, *A Great Civil War*, 16–19.

27. Goodwin, *Team of Rivals*, 338–46; Williams, *Lincoln and the Radicals*, 19–22.

28. William H. Seward to Abraham Lincoln, Monday, April 1, 1861 (Memorandum: "Some Thoughts for the President's Consideration"), ALPLC. See also Donald, *Lincoln*, 289–90; Goodwin, *Team of Rivals*, 341–43; McPherson, *Battle Cry of Freedom*, 270–71; Potter, *Lincoln and His Party in the Secession Crisis*, 258; Waugh, *One Man Great Enough*, 410; White, *A. Lincoln*, 404–5.

29. Abraham Lincoln to William H. Seward, Monday, April 1, 1861 (Reply to Seward's "Some Thoughts for the President's Consideration"), ALPLC. See also Goodwin, *Team of Rivals*, 341–43; Keegan, *The American Civil War*, 32–34; McPherson, *Battle Cry of Freedom*, 270–71; Paludan, *The Presidency of Abraham Lincoln*, 58–60; Potter, *Lincoln and His Party in the Secession Crisis*, 363.

30. Salmon P. Chase to Abraham Lincoln, Wednesday, March 6, 1861 (Accepts cabinet post), ALPLC. See also Goodwin, *Team of Rivals*, 29–93; Paludan, *The Presidency of Abraham Lincoln*, 37–39; Trefousse, *The Radical Republicans*, 148–51; Williams, *Lincoln and the Radicals*, 21–22.

31. Abraham Lincoln, [June–July 1861] (Message to Congress, July 4, 1861, Second Printed Draft, with Suggested Changes by William H. Seward), ALPLC. See also Belz, *Reconstructing the Union*, 15; Bromwich, "Lincoln's Constitutional Necessity," 17–21; Donald, *Lincoln*, 301–4; Goodwin, *Team of Rivals*, 367; McPherson, *Battle Cry of Freedom*, 309–10; White, *The Eloquent President*, 112–23; Williams, *Lincoln and the Radicals*, 26.

32. Quoted in Goodwin, *Team of Rivals*, 368. See also Foner, *The Fiery Trial*, 221–24; Magdol, *Owen Lovejoy*, 280; Trefousse, *The Radical Republicans*, 172–73; White, *The Eloquent President*, 123–24; Williams, *Lincoln and the Radicals*, 26.

33. Magdol, *Owen Lovejoy*, 332; Trefousse, *The Radical Republicans*, 204–8; Williams, *Lincoln and the Radicals*, 26–27.

34. Abraham Lincoln, Monday, April 15, 1861 (Proclamation on State Militia), ALPLC. See also Harris, *With Charity for All*, 16–17; McPherson, *Battle Cry of Freedom*, 274–75; Weigley, *A Great Civil War*, 23–24.

35. Goodwin, *Team of Rivals*, 347–51; McPherson, *Battle Cry of Freedom*, 276–82; White, *A. Lincoln*, 411–15.

36. Winfield Scott to William H. Seward, Sunday, March 3, 1861 (Advice on how to handle secession crisis), ALPLC. See also Keegan, *The American Civil War*, 91–92; McPherson, *Battle Cry of Freedom*, 333–35; McPherson, *Tried by War*, 34–36; Paludan, *The Presidency of Abraham Lincoln*, 61; Perret, *Lincoln's War*, 58–60; Weigley, *A Great Civil War*, 30.

37. Abraham Lincoln to Senate, Thursday, February 13, 1862 (Nomination of Irvin McDowell for major general), ALPLC. See also Goodwin, *Team of Rivals*, 370–71; McPherson, *Battle Cry of Freedom*, 335–36, 339; McPherson, *Tried by War*, 38–39; Perret, *Lincoln's War*, 54–60.

38. Donald, *Lincoln*, 307–8; McPherson, *Battle Cry of Freedom*, 335–38; McPherson, *Tried by War*, 38–41; Perret, *Lincoln's War*, 65–69; Weigley, *A Great Civil War*, 58–63; Wert, *The Sword of Lincoln*, 16–19.

39. McPherson, *Battle Cry of Freedom*, 344–45; Perret, *Lincoln's War*, 67–68; Weigley, *A Great Civil War*, 60–61; Wert, *The Sword of Lincoln*, 19–20.

40. Abraham Lincoln, July 23–27, 1861 (Memoranda on Military Policy after Bull Run), ALPLC. See also McPherson, *Battle Cry of Freedom*, 340–48; Paludan, *The Presidency of Abraham Lincoln*, 83; Trefousse, *The Radical Republicans*, 173–75; Williams, *Lincoln and the Radicals*, 30–34.

41. Winfield Scott to Simon Cameron, Friday, August 9, 1861 (Requests placement on retirement list), ALPLC. See also Lesser, *Rebels at the Gate*, 240–41; McPherson, *Battle Cry of Freedom*, 360–61; Perret, *Lincoln's War*, 98–99.

42. Simon Cameron to Abraham Lincoln, Monday, July 29, 1861 (Appointment of generals), ALPLC. See also Goodwin, *Team of Rivals*, 377–79; Keegan, *The American Civil War*, 113–15; Lesser, *Rebels at the Gate*, 15–17, 239–41; McPherson, *Tried by War*, 44–45; Perret, *Lincoln's War*, 71–72; Weigley, *A Great Civil War*, 61–62; Wert, *The Sword of Lincoln*, 28–30.

43. Lesser, *Rebels at the Gate*, 239–41; McPherson, *Battle Cry of Freedom*, 348–49; Paludan, *The Presidency of Abraham Lincoln*, 99–102; Weigley, *A Great Civil War*, 67.

44. Goodwin, *Team of Rivals*, 377–80; Trefousse, *The Radical Republicans*, 175–76; Williams, *Lincoln and the Radicals*, 34–36.

45. Quoted in Goodwin, *Team of Rivals*, 379–84. See also McPherson, *Battle Cry of Freedom*, 358–60; White, *A. Lincoln*, 438–47.

46. Quoted in McPherson, *Tried by War*, 141–42. See also Sears, *George B. McClellan*, 95–124; White, *A. Lincoln*, 480–86.

47. Quoted in Sears, *George B. McClellan*, 116–17. See also McPherson, *Tried by War*, 75–76; Paludan, *The Presidency of Abraham Lincoln*, 104–5; Trefousse, *The Radical Republicans*, 207; Williams, *Lincoln and the Radicals*, 24–27.

48. Quoted in White, *A. Lincoln*, 449. See also Bogue, "Historians and Radical Republicans," 8; Goodwin, *Team of Rivals*, 389–91; McPherson, *Battle Cry of Freedom*, 352–54; Trefousse, *The Radical Republicans*, 175–77; Weigley, *A Great Civil War*, 88–89; Williams, "Lincoln and the Radicals: An Essay in Civil War History and Historiography," 51–52.

49. Abraham Lincoln to Orville H. Browning, Sunday, September 22, 1861 (Fremont's Proclamation), ALPLC; Abraham Lincoln to John C. Fremont, Monday, September 2, 1861 (Fremont's August 30 Proclamation; endorsed by Lincoln, September 3, 1861), ALPLC. See also Belz, *Reconstructing the Union*, 41; Clark, *Decoying the Yanks*, 147–48; Cox, *Lincoln and Black Freedom*, ix, 12; Goodwin, *Team of Rivals*, 392–96; Green, *Freedom, Union, and Power*, 146–47; McPherson, *Battle Cry of Freedom*, 352–54; Nevin, *The Road to Shiloh*, 32; Parrish, "Fremont in Missouri," 8–10; Yoo, *Crisis and Command*, 217.

50. Foner, *The Fiery Trial*, 323–24; Hyman, *The Radical Republicans and Reconstruction*, 163; Morgan, "Ball's Bluff," 31–33; Perret, *Lincoln's War*, 93–94; Weigley, *A Great Civil War*, 66.

51. Goodwin, *Team of Rivals*, 380–81; Morgan, "Ball's Bluff," 32; Perret, *Lincoln's War*, 94–95.

52. George B. McClellan to Abraham Lincoln, Tuesday, October 22, 1861 (Telegram regarding battle at Ball's Bluff), ALPLC. See also McPherson, *Battle Cry of Freedom*, 362–63; Morgan, "Ball's Bluff," 34–38, 56; Paludan, *The Presidency of Abraham Lincoln*, 97; Perret, *Lincoln's War*, 93–97; Weigley, *A Great Civil War*, 66; Wert, *The Sword of Lincoln*, 46–48.

53. Abraham Lincoln to Hannibal Hamlin, Monday, April 28, 1862 (Senate resolution regarding General Charles Stone), ALPLC. See also Hyman, *The Radical Republicans and Reconstruction*, 163; McPherson, *Battle Cry of Freedom*, 363; Morgan, "Ball's Bluff," 34, 56; Tap, *Over Lincoln's Shoulder*, 55–68; Trefousse, *The Radical Republicans*, 187–88; Williams, *Lincoln and the Radicals*, 47, 94–104.

54. Donald, *Lincoln*, 320–21; Goodwin, *Team of Rivals*, 406–8; McPherson, *Battle Cry of Freedom*, 358.

55. Belz, *Reconstructing the Union*, 40; Goodwin, *Team of Rivals*, 425–26; Morgan, "Ball's Bluff," 56; Tap, *Over Lincoln's Shoulder*, 15–24; Trefousse, *The Radical Republicans*, 182–83; Wert, *The Sword of Lincoln*, 58–59; Williams, *Lincoln and the Radicals*, 62–64.

56. Quoted in Williams, *Lincoln and the Radicals*, 63–64. See also McPherson, *Battle Cry of Freedom*, 362–63; Paludan, *The Presidency of Abraham Lincoln*, 104–6; Perret, *Lincoln's War*, 112–13.

57. Harris, *With Charity for All*, 40; Tap, "Inevitability, Masculinity, and the American Military Tradition," 21; Trefousse, *The Radical Republicans*, 182–84; Williams, *Lincoln and the Radicals*, 65–71.

58. Trefousse, *The Radical Republicans*, 245–47.

59. Trefousse, *The Radical Republicans*, 198–201; Williams, *Lincoln and the Radicals*, 72–76.

60. Donald, *Lincoln*, 319–20; Goodwin, *Team of Rivals*, 383–84; McPherson, *Tried by War*, 52–53; Perret, *Lincoln's War*, 110–11.

61. Tap, "Inevitability, Masculinity, and the American Military Tradition," 22–24; Trefousse, *The Radical Republicans*, 184–86; Williams, *Lincoln and the Radicals*, 77–86.

62. Quoted in Donald, *Lincoln*, 332. See also Trefousse, *The Radical Republicans*, 184.

63. Hyman, *The Radical Republicans and Reconstruction*, 4; Perret, *Lincoln's War*, 327–29; Trefousse, *The Radical Republicans*, 7–8, 170–71.

64. Quoted in McPherson, *Tried by War*, 63. See also Belz, *Reconstructing the Union*, 244; Donald, *Lincoln*, 329–31; McPherson, *Battle Cry of Freedom*, 364–68; Trefousse, *The Radical Republicans*, 185–86.

65. George B. McClellan to Abraham Lincoln, Wednesday, January 15, 1862 (Appearance before Joint Committee on Conduct of War), ALPLC. See also Donald, *Lincoln*, 330–31; Williams, *Lincoln and the Radicals*, 84–88.

66. Abraham Lincoln, Monday, January 27, 1862 (Draft of President's General War Order No. 1), ALPLC. See also McPherson, *Tried by War*, 69–70; Perret, *Lincoln's War*, 122–25; Weigley, *A Great Civil War*, 119–20.

67. Abraham Lincoln to George B. McClellan, Monday, February 3, 1862 (Plans to move the army), ALPLC. See also Goodwin, *Team of Rivals*, 425–28; McPherson, *Tried by War*, 73–79; Weigley, *A Great Civil War*, 119–20; Wert, *The Sword of Lincoln*, 60–62.

68. Quoted in Williams, *Lincoln and the Radicals*, 113. See also Trefousse, *The Radical Republicans*, 188–92; Williams, "Lincoln and the Radicals: An Essay in Civil War History and Historiography," 52.

69. McPherson, *Tried by War*, 77–79; Perret, *Lincoln's War*, 122–30; Weigley, *A Great Civil War*, 122–23.

70. Perret, *Lincoln's War*, 329–31; Tap, "Inevitability, Masculinity, and the American Military Tradition," 22–23; Williams, *Lincoln and the Radicals*, 72–75.

71. Tap, "Inevitability, Masculinity, and the American Military Tradition," 21–24, 31–32, 39–42; Williams, *Lincoln and the Radicals*, 267–69.

72. McPherson, *Battle Cry of Freedom*, 362–64; Tap, "Inevitability, Masculinity, and the American Military Tradition," 22–23; Williams, *Lincoln and the Radicals*, 73–75.

73. Belz, *Reconstructing the Union*, 41; Bogue, "Historians and Radical Republicans," 9–10; Hyman, *The Radical Republicans and Reconstruction*, 304; Schneider, "Lincoln and Leadership," 70; Tap, "Inevitability, Masculinity, and the American Military Tradition," 21, 40–42.

74. Tap, "Inevitability, Masculinity, and the American Military Tradition," 42; Williams, *Lincoln and the Radicals*, 17–18, 105–6, 277–78, 344–48.

75. Bogue, "Historians and Radical Republicans," 12–13, 23–27; McPherson, *Battle Cry of Freedom*, 362–64; Perret, *Lincoln's War*, 329–33; Tap, "Inevitability, Masculinity, and the American Military Tradition," 42; Trefousse, *The Radical Republicans*, 5–32; Weigley, *A Great Civil War*, 199–201.

CHAPTER 3
"THE BONDSMAN'S YEARS OF UNREQUITED TOIL SHALL BE SUNK"

1. Guelzo, "Lincoln and the Abolitionists," 68–70; Miller, *President Lincoln*, 181; Trefousse, *The Radical Republicans*, 203–13.

2. Carwardine, *Lincoln: A Life of Purpose and Power*, 205–7; Donald, *Lincoln*, 366–69; Holzer, "A Promise Fulfilled," 32, 34; Williams, "Lincoln and the Radicals: An Essay in Civil War History and Historiography," 53–55.

3. Belz, *Reconstructing the Union*, 282–83; Brands, "Hesitant Emancipator," 56–57; Carwardine, *Lincoln: A Life of Purpose and Power*, 202, 215; Donald, *Lincoln*, 367–68; Livingstone, "The Emancipation Proclamation, the Declaration of Independence, and the Presidency," 205–6.

4. Donald, *Lincoln*, 314, 315; Trefousse, *The Radical Republicans*, 206, 209; White, *A. Lincoln*, 487–88.

5. Abraham Lincoln to Congress, Wednesday, April 16, 1862 (Compensated Emancipation in District of Columbia), ALPLC; Henry Ward Beecher to Abraham Lincoln, April 16, 1862, ALPLC. See also Burton, *The Age of Lincoln*, 162; Carwardine, *Lincoln: A Life of Purpose and Power*, 202; Goodwin, *Team of Rivals*, 460; Green, *Freedom, Union, and Power*, 149; Trefousse, *The Radical Republicans*, 212–13.

6. Quoted in Browne, *Abraham Lincoln and the Men of His Time*, 616. See also Carwardine, *Lincoln: A Life of Purpose and Power*, 203; Livingstone, "The Emancipation Proclamation, the Declaration of Independence, and the Presidency," 206; Paludan, *The Presidency of Abraham Lincoln*, 152–53; Trefousse, *The Radical Republicans*, 213–16; Williams, *Lincoln and the Radicals*, 136–38.

7. Abraham Lincoln, Monday, May 19, 1862 (Proclamation revoking General David Hunter's General Order No. 11 on military emancipation of slaves), ALPLC; Andrew Johnson to Abraham Lincoln, May 22, 1862, ALPLC. See also Cox, *Lincoln and Black Freedom*, ix; Green, *Freedom, Union, and Power*, 155; Guelzo, *Lincoln's Emancipation Proclamation*, 103; McPherson, *Battle Cry of Freedom*, 498–99; Paludan, *The Presidency of Abraham Lincoln*, 152–53; Williams, *Lincoln and the Radicals*, 137–38.

8. Carwardine, *Lincoln: A Life of Purpose and Power*, 255; Donald, *Lincoln*, 380.

9. Belz, *Reconstructing the Union*, 103; Donald, *Lincoln*, 364–65; Goodwin, *Team of Rivals*, 460–61; Perret, *Lincoln's War*, 203; Trefousse, *The Radical Republicans*, 216–22; White, *A. Lincoln*, 492–93; Williams, *Lincoln and the Radicals*, 164–68.

10. Cox, *Lincoln and Black Freedom*, 14; Livingstone, "The Emancipation Proclamation, the Declaration of Independence, and the Presidency," 206–7; Trefousse, *The Radical Republicans*, 222–24; White, *A. Lincoln*, 505, 509–10; Williams, *Lincoln and the Radicals*, 168–70.

11. Donald, *Lincoln*, 363; Guelzo, *Lincoln's Emancipation Proclamation*, 126–27; Trefousse, *The Radical Republicans*, 223.

12. Brands, "Hesitant Emancipator," 56; Carwardine, *Lincoln: A Life of Purpose and Power*, 276–78; Donald, *Lincoln*, 354.

13. Quoted in Goodwin, *Team of Rivals*, 451–52. See also Carwardine, *Lincoln: A Life of Purpose and Power*, 204; Donald, *Lincoln Reconsidered*, 98; Perret, *Lincoln's War*, 180–81; White, *A. Lincoln*, 487–88.

14. Belz, *Reconstructing the Union*, 167; Brands, "Hesitant Emancipator," 56–58; Trefousse, *The Radical Republicans*, 223–24.

15. Border State Congressmen to Abraham Lincoln, July 15, 1862, ALPLC; Donald, *Lincoln*, 362; Gates, "Appeal to Border State Representatives to Favor Compensated Emancipation," in *Lincoln on Race & Slavery*, 233; Abraham Lincoln Address to Border State Representatives, July 12, 1862, ALPLC. See also McPherson, *Tried by War*, 107–8; White, *A. Lincoln*, 493.

16. Brands, "Hesitant Emancipator," 58; Donald, *Lincoln*, 362–63; Goodwin, *Team of Rivals*, 463; Green, *Freedom, Union, and Power*, 155–56; McPherson, *Tried by War*, 108; Trefousse, *The Radical Republicans*, 224; White, *A. Lincoln*, 493.

17. Brands, "Hesitant Emancipator," 58–59; Donald, *Lincoln*, 365; Goodwin, *Team of Rivals*, 463–64.

18. Abraham Lincoln, Tuesday, July 22, 1862 (Preliminary Draft of the Emancipation Proclamation,) ALPLC. See also Brands, "Hesitant Emancipator," 58–59; Donald, *Lincoln*, 365–66; Guelzo, *Lincoln's Emancipation Proclamation*, 4–5, 126; Goodwin, *Team of Rivals*, 464–65; Holzer, "A Promise Fulfilled," 32; Livingstone, "The Emancipation Proclamation, the Declaration of Independence, and the Presidency," 206–7.

19. Donald, *Lincoln*, 366; Gates, "Preliminary Emancipation Proclamation," in *Lincoln on Race & Slavery*, 250–54; Goodwin, *Team of Rivals*, 466–67; Trefousse, *The Radical Republicans*, 224–25.

20. Abraham Lincoln, Tuesday, July 22, 1862 (Preliminary Draft of the Emancipation Proclamation), ALPLC. See also Brands, "Hesitant Emancipator," 58–59; Donald, *Lincoln*, 366; Goodwin, *Team of Rivals*, 464–68; Guelzo, *Lincoln's Emancipation Proclamation*, 155; McPherson, *Battle Cry of Freedom*, 505; White, *A. Lincoln*, 496.

21. Quoted in Goodwin, *Team of Rivals*, 468. See also Burton, *The Age of Lincoln*, 162–64; Donald, *Lincoln*, 366–69; White, *A. Lincoln*, 509.

22. Brands, "Hesitant Emancipator," 59; Donald, *Lincoln*, 369–76; Goodwin, *Team of Rivals*, 477–81.

23. Quoted in McPherson, *Battle Cry of Freedom*, 505. See also McPherson, *Battle Cry of Freedom*, 505–9; Trefousse, *The Radical Republicans*, 226–27.

24. McPherson, *Tried by War*, 123–27; Perret, *Lincoln's War*, 215–19; Wert, *The Sword of Lincoln*, 172–73; White, *A. Lincoln*, 516–18; Yoo, *Crisis and Command*, 218–19.

25. Quoted in Donald, *Lincoln*, 375. See also Fischer, *Liberty and Freedom*, 334; Goodwin, *Team of Rivals*, 481–82; Green, *Freedom, Union, and Power*, 157; Guelzo, *Lincoln's Emancipation Proclamation*, 154–55; White, *A. Lincoln*, 516–19.

26. Abraham Lincoln, Monday, September 22, 1862 (Preliminary Emancipation Proclamation), ALPLC. See also Brands, "Hesitant Emancipator," 59; Cox, *Lincoln*

and Black Freedom, 13; Gates, "Preliminary Emancipation Proclamation," in *Lincoln on Race & Slavery*, 251; Guelzo, *Lincoln's Emancipation Proclamation*, 153–56; Keegan, *The American Civil War*, 169–70; Paludan, *The Presidency of Abraham Lincoln*, 147–58; Trefousse, *The Radical Republicans*, 227–30.

27. Hannibal Hamlin to Abraham Lincoln, September 25, 1862, ALPLC. See also Brands, "Hesitant Emancipator," 59; Donald, *Lincoln*, 377–80; Goodwin, *Team of Rivals*, 483; Livingstone, "The Emancipation Proclamation, the Declaration of Independence, and the Presidency," 208; Trefousse, *The Radical Republicans*, 228; White, *A. Lincoln*, 519–21.

28. Carwardine, "Abraham Lincoln and the Fourth Estate," 20–21; Goodwin, *Team of Rivals*, 483; Livingstone, "The Emancipation Proclamation, the Declaration of Independence, and the Presidency," 208.

29. *Punch*, February 7, 1863. See also Ewan, "The Emancipation Proclamation and British Public Opinion," 15–16.

30. Quoted in Ewan, "The Emancipation Proclamation and British Public Opinion," 16. See also Donald, *Lincoln*, 379; Livingstone, "The Emancipation Proclamation, the Declaration of Independence, and the Presidency," 208; Naveh, "'He Belongs to the Ages,'" 50–51.

31. Brands, "Hesitant Emancipator," 59; Burton, *The Age of Lincoln*, 165–67; Trefousse, *The Radical Republicans*, 228–30; Wert, *The Sword of Lincoln*, 176–77, 211–12.

32. Belz, *Reconstructing the Union*, 282–83; Cox, *Lincoln and Black Freedom*, 16, 23–24; Harris, *With Charity for All*, 54.

33. Currie, "The Civil War Congress," 1215–16; Donald, *Lincoln*, 472–74; Foner, *Reconstruction*, 35–37; Gates, "Annual Message to Congress," in *Lincoln on Race & Slavery*, 292–94; Harris, *With Charity for All*, 143; Hesseltine, *Lincoln's Plan of Reconstruction*, 35–50, 96–97; McPherson, *Battle Cry of Freedom*, 698–713; Waugh, *Re-Electing Lincoln*, 68–71.

34. Abraham Lincoln, Tuesday, December 8, 1863 (Proclamation of Amnesty and Reconstruction), ALPLC. See also Goodwin, *Team of Rivals*, 589–90; Hesseltine, *Lincoln's Plan of Reconstruction*, 35–50; Trefousse, *The Radical Republicans*, 283–86; White, *A. Lincoln*, 613–14; Williams, *Lincoln and the Radicals*, 301–3.

35. Donald, *Lincoln*, 471–73; Gates, "Annual Message to Congress," in *Lincoln on Race & Slavery*, 292–94; Foner, *Reconstruction*, 35–37; Trefousse, *The Radical Republicans*, 283–86.

36. Belz, *Reconstructing the Union*, 198; Donald, *Lincoln*, 472–74; Martinez, *Carpetbaggers, Cavalry, and the Ku Klux Klan*, 31–33; McPherson, *Battle Cry of Freedom*, 698–713.

37. Belz, *Reconstructing the Union*, 224; Carwardine, *Lincoln: A Life of Purpose and Power*, 239–40; Currie, "The Civil War Congress," 1216–17; Donald, *Lincoln*, 510–12; Harris, *With Charity for All*, 186–88; Martinez, *Carpetbaggers, Cavalry, and the Ku Klux Klan*, 33; Trefousse, *The Radical Republicans*, 286–89; Williams, *Lincoln and the Radicals*, 317–20.

38. Quoted in Donald, *Lincoln*, 511. See also Carwardine, *Lincoln: A Life of Purpose and Power*, 240; Goodwin, *Team of Rivals*, 639–40.

39. Quoted in Carwardine, *Lincoln: A Life of Purpose and Power*, 240. See also Currie, "The Civil War Congress," 1218; Flood, *1864: Lincoln at the Gates of History*, 180–83; Goodwin, *Team of Rivals*, 639–40; Harris, *With Charity for All*, 188–89; Hyman, *The Radical Republicans and Reconstruction*, 134; Paludan, *The Presidency of Abraham Lincoln*, 280–81; Peterson, *Lincoln in American Memory*, 38; Trefousse, *The Radical Republicans*, 288–89.

40. Quoted in Trefousse, *The Radical Republicans*, 289–94. See also Carwardine, *Lincoln: A Life of Purpose and Power*, 239–40; Harris, *With Charity for All*, 189–90; Williams, *Lincoln and the Radicals*, 324–27.

41. Carwardine, *Lincoln: A Life of Purpose and Power*, 239–40; Flood, *1864: Lincoln at the Gates of History*, 253; Trefousse, *The Radical Republicans*, 291–94; Williams, *Lincoln and the Radicals*, 324–27; Yoo, *Crisis and Command*, 240–42.

42. Quoted in Goodwin, *Team of Rivals*, 640. See also Flood, *1864: Lincoln at the Gates of History*, 182–83; Trefousse, *The Radical Republicans*, 293–94; Waugh, *Re-Electing Lincoln*, 259–63.

43. Carwardine, *Lincoln: A Life of Purpose and Power*, 290–94; Flood, *1864: Lincoln at the Gates of History*, 130–44, 362–70; Waugh, *Re-Electing Lincoln*, 36–41, 271–72; White, *A. Lincoln*, 632–45; Williams, "Lincoln and the Radicals: An Essay in Civil War History and Historiography," 56–57.

44. Donald, *Lincoln*, 529–30; Flood, *1864: Lincoln at the Gates of History*, 276–78; Goodwin, *Team of Rivals*, 653–54; Paludan, *The Presidency of Abraham Lincoln*, 283–85; Waugh, *Re-Electing Lincoln*, 298–302.

45. Flood, *1864: Lincoln at the Gates of History*, 275–78, 282; Waugh, *Re-Electing Lincoln*, 276–77.

46. Quoted in Flood, *1864: Lincoln at the Gates of History*, 282. See also Waugh, *Re-Electing Lincoln*, 283–92; White, *A. Lincoln*, 638–41.

47. Donald, *Lincoln*, 543–44; Flood, *1864: Lincoln at the Gates of History*, 308–10; Waugh, *Re-Electing Lincoln*, 354–55.

48. Flood, *1864: Lincoln at the Gates of History*, 362–75; Goodwin, *Team of Rivals*, 665–66; Gould, *Grand Old Party*, 38–39; Keegan, *The American Civil War*, 269–71; Waugh, *Re-Electing Lincoln*, 354–55; White, *A. Lincoln*, 644–45.

49. Quoted in Gates, "Second Inaugural Address," in *Lincoln on Race & Slavery*, 311.

50. Abraham Lincoln [March 4, 1865] (Second Inaugural Address; endorsed by Lincoln, April 10, 1865), ALPLC. See also Gates, "Second Inaugural Address," in *Lincoln on Race & Slavery*, 311; Miller, *President Lincoln*, 401–2.

51. Donald, *Lincoln*, 566; Miller, *President Lincoln*, 402–4; White, *A. Lincoln*, 662–63.

52. Miller, *President Lincoln*, 403; White, *The Eloquent President*, 290–96.

53. Lincoln [March 4, 1865] (Second Inaugural Address; endorsed by Lincoln, April 10, 1865), ALPLC. See also Gates, "Second Inaugural Address," in *Lincoln on Race & Slavery*, 311; Miller, *President Lincoln*, 405–7; White, *A. Lincoln*, 663–65; White, *The Eloquent President*, 296.

54. Lincoln [March 4, 1865] (Second Inaugural Address; endorsed by Lincoln, April 10, 1865), ALPLC. See also Gates, "Second Inaugural Address," in *Lincoln*

on Race & Slavery, 311–12; Miller, *President Lincoln,* 407–11; Peterson, *Lincoln in American Memory,* 38–39; White, *The Eloquent President,* 292–96, 298–302.

55. Lincoln [March 4, 1865] (Second Inaugural Address; endorsed by Lincoln, April 10, 1865), ALPLC. See also Currie, "The Civil War Congress," 1226; Donald, *Lincoln,* 567–68; Gates, "Second Inaugural Address," in *Lincoln on Race & Slavery,* 312; Miller, *President Lincoln,* 411–15; White, *A. Lincoln,* 665–66; White, *The Eloquent President,* 301–2.

56. Quoted in Donald, *Lincoln,* 584–85. See also Carwardine, *Lincoln: A Life of Purpose and Power,* 308–9; Harris, *With Charity for All,* 2; Trefousse, *The Radical Republicans,* 300–304.

57. Quoted in Swanson, *Manhunt,* 6. See also Donald, *Lincoln,* 585–88; Kauffman, *American Brutus,* 209–10; White, *A. Lincoln,* 672.

58. Kauffman, *American Brutus,* 3–19, 79; Leonard, *Lincoln's Avengers,* 4–5; Swanson, *Bloody Crimes,* 98–114; Swanson, *Manhunt,* 38–49; White, *A. Lincoln,* 672–75.

59. Kauffman, *American Brutus,* 134–38; Leonard, *Lincoln's Avengers,* 33–65, 67–130.

60. Quoted in Carwardine, *Lincoln: A Life of Purpose and Power,* 319. See also Naveh, "'He Belongs to the Ages,'" 49–50, 53–56; Peterson, *Lincoln in American Memory,* 21; White, *A. Lincoln,* 675–76.

61. Quoted in Donald, *Lincoln,* 599. See also Goodwin, *Team of Rivals,* 744; Naveh, "'He Belongs to the Ages,'" 49–56; Peterson, *Lincoln in American Memory,* 3–4. For a discussion of the controversy over what Stanton actually said—perhaps he said, "Now he belongs to the angels"—see Gopnik, *Angels and Ages,* 24–26.

62. Kauffman, *American Brutus,* 240–41, 278–80; Leonard, *Lincoln's Avengers,* 33; Peterson, *Lincoln in American Memory,* 14; Swanson, *Bloody Crimes,* 183–93, 274–78; Winik, *April 1865,* 355–59.

63. Walt Whitman, "O Captain! My Captain," in Cook, *101 Famous Poems,* 12. See also Peterson, *Lincoln in American Memory,* 138–39.

64. Quoted in Goodwin, *Team of Rivals,* 744. See also Trefousse, *The Radical Republicans,* 305.

65. Harris, *With Charity for All,* 250–53; Leonard, *Lincoln's Avengers,* 176–77; Peterson, *Lincoln in American Memory,* 40; Trefousse, *The Radical Republicans,* 305–7; White, *A. Lincoln,* 669–70; Williams, *Lincoln and the Radicals,* 373–76; Winik, *April 1865,* 208.

66. Quoted in "The Effect of President Lincoln's Death on National Affairs," *New York Times,* April 17, 1865.

67. Calabresi and Yoo, "The Unitary Executive during the Second Half-Century," 738; Henry, *The Story of Reconstruction,* 6–7; Means, *The Avenger Takes His Place,* 4–6; Trefousse, *The Radical Republicans,* 311–19.

68. Quoted in Means, *The Avenger Takes His Place,* 117. See also Beale, *The Critical Year,* 10–16; Calabresi and Yoo, "The Unitary Executive during the Second Half-Century," 738–39.

69. Quoted in Martinez, *Carpetbaggers, Cavalry, and the Ku Klux Klan,* 41. See also Trefousse, *The Radical Republicans,* 307–9; Winik, *April 1865,* 226–27.

70. Calabresi and Yoo, "The Unitary Executive during the Second Half-Century," 738–39; Leonard, *Lincoln's Avengers*, 173–76; Winik, *April 1865*, xi–xvii.

71. Foner, *Reconstruction*, 68–70; Henry, *The Story of Reconstruction*, 59–61; Simkins and Roland, *A History of the South*, 261–62; Winik, *April 1865*, 210–11.

72. Foner, *Reconstruction*, 178–79; Means, *The Avenger Takes His Place*, 117; Trefousse, *The Radical Republicans*, 318.

73. Beale, *The Critical Year*, 10–11; Calabresi and Yoo, "The Unitary Executive during the Second Half-Century," 738; Henry, *The Story of Reconstruction*, 6–7; Means, *The Avenger Takes His Place*, 216–19; Winik, *April 1865*, 268–70.

74. Beale, *The Critical Year*, 11; Means, *The Avenger Takes His Place*, 219–25; Simkins and Roland, *A History of the South*, 255–56.

75. Foner, *Reconstruction*, 176–79; Means, *The Avenger Takes His Place*, 216–19; Simkins and Roland, *A History of the South*, 255.

76. Blum, *Reforging the White Republic*, 7. See also Lears, *Rebirth of a Nation*, 21.

77. Belz, *Reconstructing the Union*, 155–59; Foner, *Reconstruction*, 177–79; Means, *The Avenger Takes His Place*, 216–19; Stampp, *The Era of Reconstruction*, 62; Trefousse, *The Radical Republicans*, 315–17.

78. Calabresi and Yoo, "The Unitary Executive during the Second Half-Century," 739–41; Foner, *Reconstruction*, 183–84; Henry, *The Story of Reconstruction*, 46–48; Hyman, *The Radical Republicans and Reconstruction*, 246–47; Means, *The Avenger Takes His Place*, 201–16; Simkins and Roland, *A History of the South*, 256–58.

79. Quoted in Trefousse, *The Radical Republicans*, 318–19. See also Beale, *The Critical Year*, 36–37; Foner, *Reconstruction*, 221–22; Leonard, *Lincoln's Avengers*, 182–84.

80. Calabresi and Yoo, "The Unitary Executive during the Second Half-Century," 740–41; Foner, *Reconstruction*, 224–27; Simkins and Roland, *A History of the South*, 257–58; Trefousse, *The Radical Republicans*, 325–30.

CHAPTER 4
"AN UNGRATEFUL, DESPICABLE, BESOTTED TRAITOROUS MAN—AN INCUBUS"

1. Burg, "Amnesty, Civil Rights, and the Meaning of Liberal Republicanism," 34; Currie, "The Reconstruction Congress," 385; Foner, *Reconstruction*, 224–27; Simkins and Roland, *A History of the South*, 255–59; Trefousse, *Impeachment of a President*, 7–8.

2. Dunning, *Reconstruction, Political and Economic, 1865–1877*, 52; Foner, *Reconstruction*, 230–31; Henry, *The Story of Reconstruction*, 47–50.

3. Quoted in Trefousse, *The Radical Republicans*, 325–26. See also Beale, *The Critical Year*, 74–75; Currie, "The Reconstruction Congress," 385; Dunning, *Reconstruction, Political and Economic, 1865–1877*, 51–52; Foner, *Reconstruction*, 239; Henry, *The Story of Reconstruction*, 134–35; McKitrick, *Andrew Johnson and Reconstruction*, 258–59; Milton, *The Age of Hate*, 265–68.

4. Clark, "Radicals and Moderates on the Joint Committee on Reconstruction," 79–82; Cong. Globe, 39th Cong., 1st Sess. 31 (December 12 and 13, 1865); Currie, "The Reconstruction Congress," 385–86; Henry, *The Story of Reconstruction*, 135; Kendrick, *The Journal of the Joint Committee of Fifteen on Reconstruction*, 37; McKitrick, *Andrew Johnson and Reconstruction*, 258; Milton, *The Age of Hate*, 267.

5. Calabresi and Yoo, "The Unitary Executive during the Second Half-Century," 741; Kendrick, *The Journal of the Joint Committee of Fifteen on Reconstruction*, 18, 38–39; Lowe, "The Joint Committee on Reconstruction," 55–65; McKitrick, *Andrew Johnson and Reconstruction*, 259–60; Milton, *The Age of Hate*, 267–68; Trefousse, *The Radical Republicans*, 325.

6. Beale, *The Critical Year*, 44–47, 74–75; Henry, *The Story of Reconstruction*, 138–40; Milton, *The Age of Hate*, 268–73; Pierce, *Memoirs and Letters of Charles Sumner*, 268.

7. Lemann, *Redemption*, 194. See also Foner, *Reconstruction*, 236–39; Foner, "Reconstruction Revisited," 82; Simkins and Roland, *A History of the South*, 257–58.

8. Calabresi and Yoo, "The Unitary Executive during the Second Half-Century," 741; Foner, *Reconstruction*, 237–39; Simkins and Roland, *A History of the South*, 256–58.

9. Currie, "The Reconstruction Congress," 390–91; Harrison, "New Representations of a 'Misrepresented Bureau,'" 215–16; Simkins and Roland, *A History of the South*, 261.

10. Quoted in Du Bois, *The Souls of Black Folk*, 22. See also Cox, "The Promise of Land for the Freedmen," 413–40; Harrison, "New Representations of a 'Misrepresented Bureau,'" 216.

11. Quoted in Foner, *Reconstruction*, 143. See also Simkins and Roland, *A History of the South*, 261–62.

12. Harrison, "New Representations of a 'Misrepresented Bureau,'" 219; Henry, *The Story of Reconstruction*, 58–61; Simkins and Roland, *A History of the South*, 261–62.

13. Foner, *Reconstruction*, 153–55; Harrison, "New Representations of a 'Misrepresented Bureau,'" 219; Henry, *The Story of Reconstruction*, 59–60; Simkins and Roland, *A History of the South*, 262.

14. Quoted in Henry, *The Story of Reconstruction*, 60. See also Foner, *Reconstruction*, 142–44; Harrison, "New Representations of a 'Misrepresented Bureau,'" 219; Henry, *The Story of Reconstruction*, 59–60.

15. Foner, *Reconstruction*, 144–47; Harrison, "New Representations of a 'Misrepresented Bureau,'" 218–19; Simkins and Roland, *A History of the South*, 262–63.

16. Quoted in Henry, *The Story of Reconstruction*, 61. See also Foner, *Reconstruction*, 144–47; Harrison, "New Representations of a 'Misrepresented Bureau,'" 218–19; Henry, *The Story of Reconstruction*, 60–62; Simkins and Roland, *A History of the South*, 262; Stampp, *The Era of Reconstruction*, 134–35.

17. Joachim, "Hiester Clymer and the Belknap Case," 24–31.

18. Foner, *Reconstruction*, 144–47; Harrison, "New Representations of a 'Misrepresented Bureau,'" 218–19; Simpson, *The Reconstruction Presidents*, 92–94.

19. Bogue, "The Radical Voting Dimension in the U.S. Senate during the Civil War," 462–64; Calabresi and Yoo, "The Unitary Executive during the Second Half-Century," 741–42; Currie, "The Reconstruction Congress," 392–93; Donald, *The Politics of Reconstruction*, 7–8; Pierce, *Memoirs and Letters of Charles Sumner*, 274–75; Richardson, *West from Appomattox*, 54–56.

20. Quoted in Foner, *Reconstruction*, 248. See also Calabresi and Yoo, "The Unitary Executive during the Second Half-Century," 741–42; Currie, "The Reconstruction Congress," 392–93; Foner, *Reconstruction*, 246–49; Milton, *The Age of Hate*, 287–89; Simkins and Roland, *A History of the South*, 262–63; Trefousse, *The Radical Republicans*, 330–31.

21. Quoted in Castel, *The Presidency of Andrew Johnson*, 69. See also Currie, "The Reconstruction Congress," 390–93; Henry, *The Story of Reconstruction*, 160–62; Trefousse, *The Radical Republicans*, 330–31.

22. Quoted in Trefousse, *The Radical Republicans*, 331–32. See also Castel, *The Presidency of Andrew Johnson*, 69; Calabresi and Yoo, "The Unitary Executive during the Second Half-Century," 741–42; McKitrick, *Andrew Johnson and Reconstruction*, 294.

23. Quoted in Tulis, *The Rhetorical Presidency*, 89. See also Calabresi and Yoo, "The Unitary Executive during the Second Half-Century," 741–42; Henry, *The Story of Reconstruction*, 160–62; McKitrick, *Andrew Johnson and Reconstruction*, 294; Nieman, "Andrew Johnson, the Freedmen's Bureau, and the Problem of Equal Rights, 1865–1866," 399–420; Pierce, *Memoirs and Letters of Charles Sumner*, 281; Schroeder-Lein and Zuczek, *Andrew Johnson: A Biographical Companion*, 337–39; Trefousse, *The Radical Republicans*, 331.

24. Brodie, *Thaddeus Stevens: Scourge of the South*, 231–32; DeWitt, *The Impeachment and Trial of Andrew Johnson*, 24–27; Henry, *The Story of Reconstruction*, 48–49; Klein, "Personality Profile: 'Old Thad' Stevens," 18–23; Murphy, *The Nation Reunited*, 41; Palmer and Ochoa, *The Selected Papers of Thaddeus Stevens*, 184.

25. Quoted in Martinez, *Carpetbaggers, Cavalry, and the Ku Klux Klan*, 39, 41. See also DeWitt, *The Impeachment and Trial of Andrew Johnson*, 32–37; Donald, *Charles Sumner and the Coming of the Civil War*, 278–347; Donald, *Lincoln Reconsidered*, 112–13; Donald, *The Politics of Reconstruction*, 7–8; Green, *Freedom, Union, and Power*, 11–12; Henry, *The Story of Reconstruction*, 48; McKitrick, *Andrew Johnson and Reconstruction*, 268; Sinha, "The Caning of Charles Sumner," 233–62; Stampp, *America in 1857*, 11; Walther, *The Shattering of the Union: America in the 1850s*, 96–100.

26. Quoted in Currie, "The Reconstruction Congress," 393. See also Cong. Globe, 39th Cong., 1st Sess. 943 (February 20, 1866); Palmer and Ochoa, *The Selected Papers of Thaddeus Stevens*, 81.

27. Currie, "The Reconstruction Congress," 393–94; Henry, *The Story of Reconstruction*, 163–64; Simpson, *The Reconstruction Presidents*, 95–96; Trefousse, *The Radical Republicans*, 331–32.

28. Civil Rights Act of 1866 § 1, 14 Stat at 27; Kaczorowski, "Congress' Power to Enforce Fourteenth Amendment Rights," 199–205.

29. Cong. Globe, 39th Cong., 1st Sess. 606–7 (February 2, 1866, House), 1367 (March 13, 1866, Senate); Currie, "The Reconstruction Congress," 398–99; Simpson, *The Reconstruction Presidents*, 96–99.

30. Belz, *Reconstructing the Union*, 304; Foner, *Reconstruction*, 251–52; Henry, *The Story of Reconstruction*, 208–10; Kendrick, *The Journal of the Joint Committee of Fifteen on Reconstruction*, 115; Stampp, *The Era of Reconstruction*, 136–37.

31. Quoted in Henry, *The Story of Reconstruction*, 165. See also Foner, *Reconstruction*, 251–52; Henry, *The Story of Reconstruction*, 164–66; Pierce, *Memoirs and Letters of Charles Sumner*, 283–86; Stampp, *The Era of Reconstruction*, 137–41; Trefousse, *The Radical Republicans*, 345–48.

32. Currie, "The Reconstruction Congress," 401–3; Foner, *Reconstruction*, 254–55; Henry, *The Story of Reconstruction*, 164–65; Trefousse, *The Radical Republicans*, 345–48.

33. Currie, "The Reconstruction Congress," 388–90, 399; Foner, *Reconstruction*, 251–52; Kaczorowski, "To Begin the Nation Anew," 52–55.

34. Foner, *Reconstruction*, 260–61; Trefousse, *The Radical Republicans*, 347–51.

35. Bartley, "The Fourteenth Amendment," 474; Bryant, "Unorthodox and Paradox," 564–65; Currie, "The Reconstruction Congress," 407; Henry, *The Story of Reconstruction*, 332–33; Klarman, *From Jim Crow to Civil Rights*, 19–20; Trefousse, *The Radical Republicans*, 405–8.

36. Quoted in United States Senate, *Trial of Andrew Johnson*, 303. See also Beale, *The Critical Year*, 13; Foner, *Reconstruction*, 264–66; Henry, *The Story of Reconstruction*, 194–96; Mantell, *Johnson, Grant, and the Politics of Reconstruction*, 94; McKitrick, *Andrew Johnson and Reconstruction*, 429; Tulis, *The Rhetorical Presidency*, 87–93.

37. Quoted in Simpson, *The Reconstruction Presidents*, 107; Mantell, *Johnson, Grant, and the Politics of Reconstruction*, 94. See also Beale, *The Critical Year*, 13; DeWitt, *The Impeachment and Trial of Andrew Johnson*, 110–26; Henry, *The Story of Reconstruction*, 194–96; Martinez, *Carpetbaggers, Cavalry, and the Ku Klux Klan*, 43; Tulis, *The Rhetorical Presidency*, 87–93.

38. Currie, "The Reconstruction Congress," 408–9; Foner, *Reconstruction*, 273.

39. Currie, "The Reconstruction Congress," 408–14; Foner, *Reconstruction*, 275–80; Henry, *The Story of Reconstruction*, 219–21.

40. Quoted in Currie, "The Reconstruction Congress," 408–9. See also Foner, *Reconstruction*, 276–77; Henry, *The Story of Reconstruction*, 219–21.

41. Quoted in Currie, "The Reconstruction Congress," 411–12. See also Donald, *The Politics of Reconstruction*, 8; Foner, *Reconstruction*, 276–77; Henry, *The Story of Reconstruction*, 216.

42. Quoted in Foner, *Reconstruction*, 276. See also Currie, "The Reconstruction Congress," 411–12; Henry, *The Story of Reconstruction*, 216; Simpson, *The Reconstruction Presidents*, 113–17; Trefousse, *The Radical Republicans*, 355–61.

43. Ex Parte Milligan, 71 U.S. 2 (1866). See also Currie, "The Reconstruction Congress," 416–18; Henry, *The Story of Reconstruction*, 213–14; Simpson, *Let Us Have Peace*, 172–73.

44. An Act Making Appropriations for the Support of the Army for the Year Ending June Thirtieth, Eighteen Hundred and Sixty-eight, and for Other Purposes § 2, 14 Stat 485, 486–87 (March 2, 1867); Calabresi and Yoo, "The Unitary Executive during the Second Half-Century," 744–46; Castel, *The Presidency of Andrew Johnson*, 113; Currie, "The Reconstruction Congress," 408–14, 416–18; DeWitt, *The Impeachment and Trial of Andrew Johnson*, 201–2; Henry, *The Story of Reconstruction*, 213; Mantell, *Johnson, Grant, and the Politics of Reconstruction*, 78; Simpson, *The Reconstruction Presidents*, 113; Trefousse, *The Radical Republicans*, 361–62.

45. Calabresi and Yoo, "The Unitary Executive during the Second Half-Century," 758–59; Trefousse, *Impeachment of a President*, 116–17; Tulis, "The Two Constitutional Presidencies," 94–101.

46. Quoted in Stewart, *Impeached*, 324. See also Currie, "The Reconstruction Congress," 414–17; Foner, *Reconstruction*, 333; Henry, *The Story of Reconstruction*, 255; Simpson, *The Reconstruction Presidents*, 112–13; Trefousse, *The Radical Republicans*, 356–57.

47. Currie, "The Reconstruction Congress," 422–24; Henry, *The Story of Reconstruction*, 220–21; Milton, *The Age of Hate*, 425–29; Simpson, *The Reconstruction Presidents*, 116–17.

48. Quoted in Currie, "The Reconstruction Congress," 424. See also Simpson, *The Reconstruction Presidents*, 117–18.

49. An Act Supplementary to an Act Entitled "An Act to Provide for the More Efficient Government of the Rebel States," Passed on the Second Day of March, Eighteen Hundred and Sixty-seven, and the Act Supplementary thereto, Passed on the Twenty-third Day of March, Eighteen Hundred and Sixty-seven, 15 Stat 14 (July 19, 1867). See also Currie, "The Reconstruction Congress," 424–25.

50. Quoted in Simpson, *The Reconstruction Presidents*, 117. See also Calabresi and Yoo, "The Unitary Executive during the Second Half-Century," 744–46; Currie, "The Reconstruction Congress," 425–26; Milton, *The Age of Hate*, 445–47.

51. Henry, *The Story of Reconstruction*, 311; Simpson, *Let Us Have Peace*, 239; Simpson, *The Reconstruction Presidents*, 117–18; Trefousse, *The Radical Republicans*, 379.

52. Foner, *Reconstruction*, 313–16; Henry, *The Story of Reconstruction*, 261–67; Trefousse, *The Radical Republicans*, 361–63.

53. Foner, *Reconstruction*, 335; Milton, *The Age of Hate*, 428; Trefousse, *The Radical Republicans*, 361–62.

54. Quoted in Currie, "The Reconstruction Congress," 438–39. See also DeWitt, *The Impeachment and Trial of Andrew Johnson*, 23.

55. Benedict, "From Our Archives," 493–502; Currie, "The Reconstruction Congress," 440; Foner, *Reconstruction*, 333–35; Trefousse, *The Radical Republicans*, 366–69.

56. Currie, "The Reconstruction Congress," 438–43; Simpson, *The Reconstruction Presidents*, 120; Stewart, *Impeached*, 100–113.

57. Edwin M. Stanton to Andrew Johnson, Monday, August 12, 1867, quoted in Calabresi and Yoo, "The Unitary Executive during the Second Half-Century," 751.

See also Henry, *The Story of Reconstruction*, 272; Trefousse, *Impeachment of a President*, 78–84; Trefousse, *The Radical Republicans*, 365–66.

58. Henry, *The Story of Reconstruction*, 272–75; Simpson, *The Reconstruction Presidents*, 120; Trefousse, *The Radical Republicans*, 380–82; Yoo, *Crisis and Command*, 252–53.

59. Stewart, *Impeached*, 135, 332. See also Currie, "The Reconstruction Congress," 443; Simpson, *The Reconstruction Presidents*, 122–23; Stewart, *Impeached*, 134–37; Trefousse, *Impeachment of a President*, 131–36; Trefousse, *The Radical Republicans*, 381–83.

60. Henry, *The Story of Reconstruction*, 273–74; Simpson, *The Reconstruction Presidents*, 120–22; Stewart, *Impeached*, 121–23; Trefousse, *The Radical Republicans*, 381–82.

61. Trefousse, *The Radical Republicans*, 383. See also Currie, "The Reconstruction Congress," 444–45; DeWitt, *The Impeachment and Trial of Andrew Johnson*, 373–74; Stewart, *Impeached*, 148–49; Trefousse, *Impeachment of a President*, 134–45; Trefousse, *The Radical Republicans*, 383–84.

62. Quoted in Stewart, *Impeached*, 340–41. See also Currie, "The Reconstruction Congress," 444–46; Palmer and Ochoa, *The Selected Papers of Thaddeus Stevens*, 352–53; Pierce, *Memoirs and Letters of Charles Sumner*, 350.

63. Calabresi and Yoo, "The Unitary Executive during the Second Half-Century," 755–56; Currie, "The Reconstruction Congress," 451–52; Foner, *Reconstruction*, 334–35; Genovese, *The Power of the American Presidency*, 92–93; Stewart, *Impeached*, 77–81; Thomas, Pika, and Watson, *The Politics of the Presidency*, 256–58; Tulis, *The Rhetorical Presidency*, 90–91; United States Senate, *Proceedings in the Trial of Andrew Johnson*, 1–6.

64. Quoted in Foner, *Reconstruction*, 334. See also Currie, "The Reconstruction Congress," 451–52; Foner, *Reconstruction*, 334; Genovese, *The Power of the American Presidency*, 93; Stewart, *Impeached*, 315–24.

65. Calabresi and Yoo, "The Unitary Executive during the Second Half-Century," 755–56; DeWitt, *The Impeachment and Trial of Andrew Johnson*, 385; Stewart, *Impeached*, 159–62; Trefousse, *The Radical Republicans*, 386–87; United States Senate, *Trial of Andrew Johnson*, 4.

66. Quoted in DeWitt, *The Impeachment and Trial of Andrew Johnson*, 208. See also Lemann, *Redemption*, 38–40; Stewart, *Impeached*, 193–95; United States Senate, *Trial of Andrew Johnson*, 1–87.

67. Quoted in DeWitt, *The Impeachment and Trial of Andrew Johnson*, 408–16. See also Currie, "The Reconstruction Congress," 446–47; Henry, *The Story of Reconstruction*, 306; Stewart, *Impeached*, 193–96; United States Senate, *Trial of Andrew Johnson*, 122.

68. Quoted in DeWitt, *The Impeachment and Trial of Andrew Johnson*, 408–16. See also Beauregard, "The Chief Prosecutor of President Andrew Johnson," 415–16; Henry, *The Story of Reconstruction*, 306–9; Martinez, *Carpetbaggers, Cavalry, and the Ku Klux Klan*, 50–51; Murphy, *The Nation Reunited*, 72–73; Thomas, Pika, and Watson, *The Politics of the Presidency*, 257–58.

69. United States Senate, *Trial of Andrew Johnson*, 122. See also "Impeachment and General Butler," 786; Stewart, *Impeached*, 193–96.

70. Quoted in DeWitt, *The Impeachment and Trial of Andrew Johnson*, 505–6. See also Beauregard, "The Chief Prosecutor of President Andrew Johnson," 419; Calabresi and Yoo, "The Unitary Executive during the Second Half-Century," 755–56; Folsom, "Andrew Johnson and the Constitution," 32–33; Foner, *Reconstruction*, 334–37; Murphy, *The Nation Reunited*, 72–75.

71. Calabresi and Yoo, "The Unitary Executive during the Second Half-Century," 756–57; Currie, "The Reconstruction Congress," 449–52; DeWitt, *The Impeachment and Trial of Andrew Johnson*, 576–96; Folsom, "Andrew Johnson and the Constitution," 32–33; Henry, *The Story of Reconstruction*, 308–9; Martinez, *Carpetbaggers, Cavalry, and the Ku Klux Klan*, 50–51.

72. Currie, "The Reconstruction Congress," 446–47; Stewart, *Impeached*, 196–97.

73. Quoted in DeWitt, *The Impeachment and Trial of Andrew Johnson*, 438. See also Currie, "The Reconstruction Congress," 447–48; DeWitt, *The Impeachment and Trial of Andrew Johnson*, 424–38; Stewart, *Impeached*, 206–10; United States Senate, *Trial of Andrew Johnson*, 414.

74. Quoted in Stewart, *Impeached*, 212. See also DeWitt, *The Impeachment and Trial of Andrew Johnson*, 556–57.

75. Calabresi and Yoo, "The Unitary Executive during the Second Half-Century," 756–57; DeWitt, *The Impeachment and Trial of Andrew Johnson*, 546–49; Stewart, *Impeached*, 317.

76. Quoted in Martinez, *Carpetbaggers, Cavalry, and the Ku Klux Klan*, 50–51. See also Beauregard, "The Chief Prosecutor of President Andrew Johnson," 419; Calabresi and Yoo, "The Unitary Executive during the Second Half-Century," 756–58; Castel, *The Presidency of Andrew Johnson*, 192–93; DeWitt, *The Impeachment and Trial of Andrew Johnson*, 515–96; Folsom, "Andrew Johnson and the Constitution," 32–33; Foner, *Reconstruction*, 336–37; Genovese, *The Power of the American Presidency*, 93; Mantell, *Johnson, Grant, and the Politics of Reconstruction*, 90–96; Klein, "Personality Profile: 'Old Thad' Stevens," 23; Murphy, *The Nation Reunited*, 75; Trefousse, *The Radical Republicans*, 396–98.

77. Quoted in Stewart, *Impeached*, 223. See also Bogue, "The Radical Voting Dimension in the U.S. Senate during the Civil War," 471–72; Currie, "The Reconstruction Congress," 449–50; DeWitt, *The Impeachment and Trial of Andrew Johnson*, 520; Green, *Freedom, Union, and Power*, 11–12; Stewart, *Impeached*, 223–24; Trefousse, *The Radical Republicans*, 392.

78. Henry, *The Story of Reconstruction*, 298–309; Martinez, *Carpetbaggers, Cavalry, and the Ku Klux Klan*, 50–51; Stewart, *Impeached*, 272–74; Trefousse, *The Radical Republicans*, 392–93.

79. DeWitt, *The Impeachment and Trial of Andrew Johnson*, 457–67; Stewart, *Impeached*, 230–31.

80. Beauregard, "The Chief Prosecutor of President Andrew Johnson," 416–18; DeWitt, *The Impeachment and Trial of Andrew Johnson*, 397; Milton, *The Age of Hate*, 534–38; Stewart, *Impeached*, 231–32.

81. Quoted in DeWitt, *The Impeachment and Trial of Andrew Johnson*, 481–83. See also Stewart, *Impeached*, 233–34.

82. Quoted in DeWitt, *The Impeachment and Trial of Andrew Johnson*, 481–83. See also Milton, *The Age of Hate*, 575–76; Stewart, *Impeached*, 233–34.

83. Calabresi and Yoo, "The Unitary Executive during the Second Half-Century," 756–57; Currie, "The Reconstruction Congress," 449; Henry, *The Story of Reconstruction*, 308–9; Pierce, *Memoirs and Letters of Charles Sumner*, 351; Trefousse, *Impeachment of a President*, 172–79.

84. Cong. Globe Supp., 40th Cong., 2nd Sess. 420, 457 (May 7, 1868).

85. Quoted in DeWitt, *The Impeachment and Trial of Andrew Johnson*, 579. See also Currie, "The Reconstruction Congress," 450–51; DeWitt, *The Impeachment and Trial of Andrew Johnson*, 586–89; Milton, *The Age of Hate*, 593–94, 613–14; Stewart, *Impeached*, 280–83.

86. Calabresi and Yoo, "The Unitary Executive during the Second Half-Century," 755–58; Currie, "The Reconstruction Congress," 449–52; DeWitt, *The Impeachment and Trial of Andrew Johnson*, 597–629; Foner, *Reconstruction*, 333–37; Genovese, *The Power of the American Presidency*, 93; Henry, *The Story of Reconstruction*, 308–9; Mantell, *Johnson, Grant, and the Politics of Reconstruction*, 90–96; Stewart, *Impeached*, 284–304.

87. Foner, *Reconstruction*, 334–35; Stewart, *Impeached*, 316–19; Trefousse, *The Radical Republicans*, 388–98.

88. Calabresi and Yoo, "The Unitary Executive during the Second Half-Century," 759; Foner, *Reconstruction*, 336–38; Gould, *Grand Old Party*, 53–58; Simpson, *Let Us Have Peace*, 244–46; Simpson, *The Reconstruction Presidents*, 127–29; Trefousse, *The Radical Republicans*, 399.

89. Bartley, "The Fourteenth Amendment," 478–79; DeWitt, *The Impeachment and Trial of Andrew Johnson*, 597–99; Foner, *Reconstruction*, 343–45; Henry, *The Story of Reconstruction*, 333–34; Klein, "Personality Profile: 'Old Thad' Stevens," 23; Stewart, *Impeached*, 305–6; Trefousse, *Impeachment of a President*, 183; Trefousse, *The Radical Republicans*, 436–37.

90. Foner, *Reconstruction*, 337–38; Gould, *Grand Old Party*, 53–54; Martinez, *Carpetbaggers, Cavalry, and the Ku Klux Klan*, 51–52; Simpson, *The Reconstruction Presidents*, 126–28; Trefousse, *The Radical Republicans*, 399–404.

CHAPTER 5
"THE PROGRESS OF EVOLUTION WAS ALONE EVIDENCE ENOUGH TO UPSET DARWIN"

1. Foner, *Reconstruction*, 11–34; Foote, *The Civil War: A Narrative*. Vol. 3: *From Red River to Appomattox*, 1040; Henry, *The Story of Reconstruction*, 66–73; Trefousse, *The Radical Republicans*, 426–29.

2. Foner, *Reconstruction*, 337–39; Slap, *The Doom of Reconstruction*, 223–24; Stewart, *Impeached*, 305–6; Trefousse, *Impeachment of a President*, 172, 184; Trefousse, *The Radical Republicans*, 402–4.

3. Quoted in Adams, *The Education of Henry Adams*, 260. See also Brookhiser, *America's First Dynasty*, 153–57; Hyman, *The Radical Republicans and Reconstruction*, lx.

4. Gould, *Grand Old Party*, 54–61; Kane, *Facts about the Presidents*, 196–98; Shaw, "Leadership Lessons from the Life of Ulysses S. Grant," 29, 33–34; Simpson, *Let Us Have Peace*, 1–9; Smith, *Grant*, 24, 26–33, 157.

5. Gould, *Grand Old Party*, 54–55; Kane, *Facts about the Presidents*, 197–98; Murphy, *The Nation Reunited*, 76–77; Witcover, *Party of the People*, 234–36.

6. Calabresi and Yoo, "The Unitary Executive during the Second Half-Century," 759; Foner, *Reconstruction*, 337–45; Murphy, *The Nation Reunited*, 76; Simpson, *Let Us Have Peace*, 247–51; Simpson, *The Reconstruction Presidents*, 128–29.

7. Foner, *Reconstruction*, 338–43; Gould, *Grand Old Party*, 54–61; Henry, *The Story of Reconstruction*, 334–35; Simpson, *Let Us Have Peace*, 248–49; Witcover, *Party of the People*, 234–36.

8. Quoted in Simpson, *Let Us Have Peace*, 251. See also Calabresi and Yoo, "The Unitary Executive during the Second Half-Century," 759; Franklin, *Reconstruction after the Civil War*, 82–83; Gould, *Grand Old Party*, 57–58; Witcover, *Party of the People*, 233–36.

9. Calabresi and Yoo, "The Unitary Executive during the Second Half-Century," 759–60; Gould, *Grand Old Party*, 60–61; Smith, *Grant*, 464–66.

10. Quoted in Waugh, *U. S. Grant*, 124; Calabresi and Yoo, "The Unitary Executive during the Second Half-Century," 759–60; Foner, *Reconstruction*, 444–45; Simpson, *The Reconstruction Presidents*, 139; Smith, *Grant*, 466–68.

11. Gould, *Grand Old Party*, 54–55; Murphy, *The Nation Reunited*, 76–77; Simpson, *Let Us Have Peace*, 249–51; Simpson, *The Reconstruction Presidents*, 133–35.

12. Foner, *Reconstruction*, 444–46; Gould, *Grand Old Party*, 58–61; Murphy, *The Nation Reunited*, 76–77.

13. Foner, *Reconstruction*, 449–54; Gould, *Grand Old Party*, 59–60; Trefousse, *The Radical Republicans*, 424–28.

14. Foner, *Reconstruction*, 451–54; Henry, *The Story of Reconstruction*, 375–86; Simpson, *Let Us Have Peace*, 139–41; Trefousse, *The Radical Republicans*, 426–29.

15. Foner, *Reconstruction*, 454; Henry, *The Story of Reconstruction*, 375–76; Simpson, *The Reconstruction Presidents*, 142–44; Trefousse, *The Radical Republicans*, 427–29.

16. Currie, "The Reconstruction Congress," 452–56; Foner, *Reconstruction*, 445–49; McPherson, *Battle Cry of Freedom*, 244–45; Schott, "Cornerstone Speech," 155–56; Simpson, *The Reconstruction Presidents*, 143–45; Valelly, *The Two Reconstructions*, 102–3.

17. Calabresi and Yoo, "The Unitary Executive during the Second Half-Century," 759–60; Gould, *Grand Old Party*, 60–61; Simpson, *The Reconstruction Presidents*, 139–40; Smith, *Grant*, 468–69.

18. Budiansky, *The Bloody Shirt*, 135; Henry, *The Story of Reconstruction*, 284–85; Martinez, *Carpetbaggers, Cavalry, and the Ku Klux Klan*, 63–64; McFeely, *Grant*, 367–74; Smith, *Grant*, 542; Trelease, *White Terror*, 402–3; Wade, *The Fiery Cross*, 87–88; West, *The Reconstruction Ku Klux Klan in York County, South*

Carolina, 1865–1877, 86, 90–91; Williams, *The Great South Carolina Ku Klux Klan Trials, 1871–1872*, 44–46.

19. Budiansky, *The Bloody Shirt*, 142; Everitt, "1871 War on Terror," 27–28; Foner, *Reconstruction*, 457; Hall, "Political Power and Constitutional Legitimacy," 925–26; Martinez, *Carpetbaggers, Cavalry, and the Ku Klux Klan*, 63–64.

20. Donald, *Lincoln*, 343–45; Du Bois, *Black Reconstruction*, 149; McPherson, *Battle Cry of Freedom*, 508–9; Simpson, *The Reconstruction Presidents*, 145–48; Smith, *Grant*, 508–14.

21. Simpson, *The Reconstruction Presidents*, 145–46; Smith, *Grant*, 507–8; Trefousse, *The Radical Republicans*, 452–53.

22. McPherson, *Battle Cry of Freedom*, 508–9; Murphy, *The Nation Reunited*, 44–45; Simpson, *The Reconstruction Presidents*, 146.

23. Ford, "Rednecks and Merchants," 295–318; Gordon, *Sketches of Negro Life and History in South Carolina*, 158–61; Henry, *The Story of Reconstruction*, 362–65; Martinez, *Carpetbaggers, Cavalry, and the Ku Klux Klan*, 109–11.

24. Alston and Kauffman, "Up, Down, and Off the Agricultural Ladder," 266; Ferleger, "Sharecropping Contracts in the Late Nineteenth Century South," 32–33; Ransom and Sutch, *One Kind of Freedom*, 95; Royce, *The Origins of Southern Sharecropping*, 181–82; Shlomowitz, "The Origins of Southern Sharecropping," 557–58; Woodman, "Post-Civil War Southern Agriculture and the Law," 324.

25. Alston and Kauffman, "Up, Down, and Off the Agricultural Ladder," 267; Foner, *Reconstruction*, 106–8, 404–11; Franklin, *Reconstruction after the Civil War*, 179–80; Litwack, *Trouble in Mind*, 128; Murphy, *The Nation Reunited*, 42–46; Reid, "Sharecropping as an Understandable Market Response," 106–8; Reid, "Sharecropping in History and Theory," 427–28; Richardson, *West from Appomattox*, 83; Royce, *The Origins of Southern Sharecropping*, 182; Simkins and Roland, *A History of the South*, 296–97; Woodman, "Post-Civil War Southern Agriculture and the Law," 324–25.

26. Ferleger, "Sharecropping Contracts in the Late Nineteenth Century South," 33; Foner, *Reconstruction*, 106–8; Frederickson, "Masters and Mudsills," 34–48; Murphy, *The Nation Reunited*, 42; Ransom and Sutch, *One Kind of Freedom*, 97–99; Reid, "Sharecropping as an Understandable Market Response," 108; Royce, *The Origins of Southern Sharecropping*, 182–83; Saville, *The Work of Reconstruction*, 137–38; Simkins and Roland, *A History of the South*, 297.

27. Alston and Kauffman, "Up, Down, and Off the Agricultural Ladder," 267; Atack, "Tenants and Yeoman in the Nineteenth Century," 6–7; Ferleger, "Sharecropping Contracts in the Late Nineteenth Century South," 32–33; Ransom and Sutch, *One Kind of Freedom*, 90–91; Woodman, "Class, Race, Politics, and the Modernization of the Postbellum South," 7–8; Woodman, "Post-Civil War Southern Agriculture and the Law," 324–25.

28. Alston and Kauffman, "Up, Down, and Off the Agricultural Ladder," 267; Ransom and Sutch, *One Kind of Freedom*, 87–91, 181; Royce, *The Origins of Southern Sharecropping*, 187–88; Woodman, "Class, Race, Politics, and the Modernization of the Postbellum South," 7–8.

29. Quoted in Murphy, *The Nation Reunited*, 42. See also Du Bois, *Black Reconstruction*, 74–76; Foner, *Reconstruction*, 106–8, 404–11; Henry, *The Story of Reconstruction*, 100–101.

30. Quoted in Murphy, *The Nation Reunited*, 44. See also Foner, *Reconstruction*, 409; Saville, *The Work of Reconstruction*, 138.

31. Brundage, *The Southern Past*, 140–41; Cox, "From Emancipation to Segregation," 307; Foner, "Reconstruction Revisited," 87–88; Litwack, *Been in the Storm So Long*, 500; Litwack, *Trouble in Mind*, 376; McPherson, *The Struggle for Equality*, 134–36; Taylor, *The Negro in South Carolina during the Reconstruction*, 186–88; Taylor, *Travail and Triumph*, viii.

32. Foner, *Reconstruction*, 393–96; Gordon, *Sketches of Negro Life and History in South Carolina*, 158–61; Martinez, *Carpetbaggers, Cavalry, and the Ku Klux Klan*, 109–11; Simkins and Roland, *A History of the South*, 296–97.

33. Foner, *Reconstruction*, 494–96; Simpson, *The Reconstruction Presidents*, 146–48; Smith, *Grant*, 509–12; Trefousse, *The Radical Republicans*, 452–54.

34. Foner, *Reconstruction*, 494; Henry, *The Story of Reconstruction*, 465–66; Simpson, *The Reconstruction Presidents*, 147.

35. Gould, *Grand Old Party*, 63–64; Henry, *The Story of Reconstruction*, 421; Trefousse, *The Radical Republicans*, 439–40; Witcover, *Party of the People*, 239.

36. Gould, *Grand Old Party*, 54–55; Lewinson, *Race, Class, and Party*, 61–62; Scaturro, *President Grant Reconsidered*, 75–76; Smith, *Grant*, 430–33; Trefousse, *The Radical Republicans*, 424–25.

37. Foner, *Reconstruction*, 488–511; Gould, *Grand Old Party*, 61–67; Simpson, *The Reconstruction Presidents*, 158–62; Slap, *The Doom of Reconstruction*, xix–xxv, 126–63.

38. Gould, *Grand Old Party*, 62–63; Trefousse, *The Radical Republicans*, 454–58; Witcover, *Party of the People*, 241–42.

39. Burg, "Amnesty, Civil Rights, and the Meaning of Liberal Republicanism," 43–47; Foner, *Reconstruction*, 488–94; Gould, *Grand Old Party*, 61–63; Slap, *The Doom of Reconstruction*, 199–205; Trefousse, *The Radical Republicans*, 457–60.

40. Burg, "Amnesty, Civil Rights, and the Meaning of Liberal Republicanism," 43–47; Slap, *The Doom of Reconstruction*, 126–31; Trefousse, *The Radical Republicans*, 455–56.

41. Brookhiser, *America's First Dynasty*, 139–40; Foner, *Reconstruction*, 501–3; Gould, *Grand Old Party*, 62–63; Richardson, *Others*, 354–69; Simpson, *The Reconstruction Presidents*, 159–60; Trefousse, *The Radical Republicans*, 454–58.

42. Calabresi and Yoo, "The Unitary Executive during the Second Half-Century," 766–67; Foner, *Reconstruction*, 502–9; Gould, *Grand Old Party*, 66; Simpson, *The Reconstruction Presidents*, 160–61; Slap, *The Doom of Reconstruction*, 150–63; Williams, *Horace Greeley*, 295–96, 301; Witcover, *Party of the People*, 241–43.

43. Quoted in Richardson, *Others*, 369. See also Fitzgerald, *Splendid Failure*, 138–39; Foner, *Reconstruction*, 508–10; Gould, *Grand Old Party*, 66–67; Simpson, *The Reconstruction Presidents*, 160–62; Witcover, *Party of the People*, 242–43.

44. Quoted in Gould, *Grand Old Party*, 67. See also Foner, *Reconstruction*, 509–10; Kane, *Facts about the Presidents*, 200–201; Williams, *Horace Greeley*, 304–6; Witcover, *Party of the People*, 243.

45. Gould, *Grand Old Party*, 67; Simpson, *The Reconstruction Presidents*, 162; Slap, *The Doom of Reconstruction*, 215–21; Witcover, *Party of the People*, 244–45.

46. Quoted in Slap, *The Doom of Reconstruction*, xxv. See also Foner, *Reconstruction*, 510–11; Franklin, *Reconstruction after the Civil War*, 149–50; Murphy, *The Nation Reunited*, 111–12; Simpson, *The Reconstruction Presidents*, 162.

47. Calabresi and Yoo, "The Unitary Executive during the Second Half-Century," 766–67; Simpson, *The Reconstruction Presidents*, 164–65; Smith, *Grant*, 585.

48. Foner, *Reconstruction*, 468; Smith, *Grant*, 560; Trefousse, *The Radical Republicans*, 463; Williams, *Horace Greeley*, 304.

49. Foner, *Reconstruction*, 468; Simpson, *The Reconstruction Presidents*, 164; Smith, *Grant*, 560.

50. Ambrose, *Nothing like It in the World*, 92–93; Gould, *Grand Old Party*, 68; Simpson, *The Reconstruction Presidents*, 164; Smith, *Grant*, 557.

51. Calabresi and Yoo, "The Unitary Executive during the Second Half-Century," 766–67; Shaw, "Leadership Lessons from the Life of Ulysses S. Grant," 33–34; Simpson, *The Reconstruction Presidents*, 164–65; Trefousse, *The Radical Republicans*, 463.

52. Alston, Jenkins, and Nonnenmacher, "Who Should Govern Congress?," 674–75; Foner, *Reconstruction*, 523; Gould, *Grand Old Party*, 68; Smith, *Grant*, 561; Trefousse, *The Radical Republicans*, 463; Witcover, *Party of the People*, 244.

53. Murphy, *The Nation Reunited*, 112, 114; Smith, *Grant*, 586; Trefousse, *The Radical Republicans*, 463.

54. Calabresi and Yoo, "The Unitary Executive during the Second Half-Century," 767–68; Foner, *Reconstruction*, 565–66; Murphy, *The Nation Reunited*, 112, 114–17; Smith, *Grant*, 484, 562, 592–95.

55. Foner, *Reconstruction*, 461–62; Franklin, *Reconstruction after the Civil War*, 176–77; Henry, *The Story of Reconstruction*, 367–68; Murphy, *The Nation Reunited*, 83–86.

56. Foner, *Reconstruction*, 512–13; Murphy, *The Nation Reunited*, 86; Simkins and Roland, *A History of the South*, 321.

57. Foner, *Reconstruction*, 512–17; Richardson, "A Marshall Plan for the South?," 378–87; Simkins and Roland, *A History of the South*, 320–21.

58. Franklin, *Reconstruction after the Civil War*, 185–86; Henry, *The Story of Reconstruction*, 499–500; Murphy, *The Nation Reunited*, 124–25.

59. Calabresi and Yoo, "The Unitary Executive during the Second Half-Century," 763–64; Henry, *The Story of Reconstruction*, 500; Martinez, *Carpetbaggers, Cavalry, and the Ku Klux Klan*, 63; Smith, *Grant*, 496–98.

60. Friedman, "The Crime of 1873," 1159–94; Murphy, *The Nation Reunited*, 124–25; Smith, *Grant*, 480, 590.

61. Foner, *Reconstruction*, 512–13; Henry, *The Story of Reconstruction*, 500; Lubetkin, *Jay Cooke's Gamble*, xv–xvi; Murphy, *The Nation Reunited*, 125; Smith, *Grant*, 583.

62. Foner, *Reconstruction*, 512–13; Lubetkin, *Jay Cooke's Gamble*, 280–82, 288–91; Murphy, *The Nation Reunited*, 125–26; Smith, *Grant*, 583.

63. Fitzgerald, *Splendid Failure*, 174; Franklin, *Reconstruction after the Civil War*, 185–86; Murphy, *The Nation Reunited*, 125–27; Simpson, *The Reconstruction Presidents*, 165.

64. Foner, *Reconstruction*, 549–50; Gould, *Grand Old Party*, 70; Simpson, *The Reconstruction Presidents*, 173–74; Witcover, *Party of the People*, 244.

65. Calabresi and Yoo, "The Unitary Executive during the Second Half-Century," 760–63; Lemann, *Redemption*, 66; Stewart, *Impeached*, 322–24.

66. Quoted in Trefousse, *The Radical Republicans*, 442. See also Foner, *Reconstruction*, 453–54; Henry, *The Story of Reconstruction*, 542–43; Trefousse, *The Radical Republicans*, 441–42.

67. Quoted in Adams, *The Education of Henry Adams*, 266.

CHAPTER 6
"RADICALISM IS DISSOLVING"

1. The episode is recounted in numerous sources. See, for example, Budiansky, *The Bloody Shirt*, 131–32; Martinez, *Carpetbaggers, Cavalry, and the Ku Klux Klan*, 77–78; Trelease, *White Terror*, 371–72; United States Congress, *Report of the Joint Select Committee to Inquire into the Condition of Affairs in the Late Insurrectionary States*, Vol. 5, 1406–15, 1477; West, *The Reconstruction Ku Klux Klan in York County, South Carolina, 1865–1877*, 83.

2. Lester and Wilson, *Ku Klux Klan*, 47–61; Rogers, *The Ku Klux Spirit*, 14–21; Romine and Romine, *A Story of the Original Ku Klux Klan*, 3–17; Rose, *The Ku Klux Klan or Invisible Empire*, 18–19; Shapiro, "The Ku Klux Klan during Reconstruction," 34–55; Simkins, "The Ku Klux Klan in South Carolina," 606–47; Stagg, "The Problem of Klan Violence," 303–18.

3. Budiansky, *The Bloody Shirt*, 115–16; Post, "A Carpetbagger in South Carolina," 40–43; Trelease, *White Terror*, 370–71; United States Congress, *Report of the Joint Select Committee to Inquire into the Condition of Affairs in the Late Insurrectionary States*, Vol. 5, 1464–65; West, *The Reconstruction Ku Klux Klan in York County, South Carolina, 1865–1877*, 80–81; Zuczek, *State of Rebellion*, 93–97.

4. Quoted in United States Congress, *Report of the Joint Select Committee to Inquire into the Condition of Affairs in the Late Insurrectionary States*, Vol. 5, 1482. See also "Arrival of a Cavalry Company," *Yorkville Enquirer*, Yorkville, S.C. (March 30, 1871); Budiansky, *The Bloody Shirt*, 123–24; Trelease, *White Terror*, 372–73; United States Circuit Court, *Proceedings in the Ku Klux Klan Trials at Columbia, S.C., in the United States Circuit Court, November Term, 1871*, 743–48; United States Congress, *Report of the Joint Select Committee to Inquire into the Condition of Affairs in the Late Insurrectionary States*, Vol. 5, 1406–15, 1477, 1482; Wade, *The Fiery Cross*, 95–96.

5. Martinez, *Carpetbaggers, Cavalry, and the Ku Klux Klan*, 133–36; Wade, *The Fiery Cross*, 94–96; West, *The Reconstruction Ku Klux Klan in York County, South Carolina, 1865–1877*, 2–3; Zuczek, *State of Rebellion*, 93–99.

6. "To the Citizens of York County," *Yorkville Enquirer*, Yorkville, S.C. (May 25, 1871).

7. Quoted in United States Congress, *Testimony Taken by the Joint Select Committee to Inquire into the Condition of Affairs in the Late Insurrectionary States*, Vol. 3, 1499.

8. Sefton, *The United States Army and Reconstruction, 1865–1877*, 224–25; Simkins, "The Ku Klux Klan in South Carolina," 611; Wade, *The Fiery Cross*, 96–97; West, *The Reconstruction Ku Klux Klan in York County, South Carolina, 1865–1877*, 84.

9. Quoted in Wade, *The Fiery Cross*, 97. See also United States Congress, *Testimony Taken by the Joint Select Committee to Inquire into the Condition of Affairs in the Late Insurrectionary States*, Vol. 3, 1603–6; West, *The Reconstruction Ku Klux Klan in York County, South Carolina, 1865–1877*, 84.

10. "Arrival of a Cavalry Company," *Yorkville Enquirer*, Yorkville, S.C. (March 30, 1871); Everitt, "1871 War on Terror," 27–28, 30–31; Foner, *Reconstruction*, 454–59; Murphy, *The Nation Reunited*, 98–99; Trelease, *White Terror*, 373–74; United States Congress, *Report of the Joint Select Committee to Inquire into the Condition of Affairs in the Late Insurrectionary States*, Vol. 5, 1464; West, *The Reconstruction Ku Klux Klan in York County, South Carolina, 1865–1877*, 80–83.

11. Martinez, *Carpetbaggers, Cavalry, and the Ku Klux Klan*, 139; Trelease, *White Terror*, 372–73; United States Congress, *Report of the Joint Select Committee to Inquire into the Condition of Affairs in the Late Insurrectionary States*, Vol. 5, 1464; Zuczek, *State of Rebellion*, 94–95.

12. Quoted in United States Congress, *Testimony Taken by the Joint Select Committee to Inquire into the Condition of Affairs in the Late Insurrectionary States*, Vol. 3, 1601. See also Budiansky, *The Bloody Shirt*, 134–35; Simkins, "The Ku Klux Klan in South Carolina," 641; United States Congress, *Testimony Taken by the Joint Select Committee to Inquire into the Condition of Affairs in the Late Insurrectionary States*, Vol. 3, 1601–4.

13. Budiansky, *The Bloody Shirt*, 122–26; Post, "A Carpetbagger in South Carolina," 40–43; Trelease, *White Terror*, 372–73.

14. Budiansky, *The Bloody Shirt*, 128–30; Simkins, "The Ku Klux Klan in South Carolina," 640–41; Trelease, *White Terror*, 374–75; Wade, *The Fiery Cross*, 98–99; West, *The Reconstruction Ku Klux Klan in York County, South Carolina, 1865–1877*, 84–85; Zuczek, *State of Rebellion*, 97.

15. "The Barry-Wallace Difficulty," *Yorkville Enquirer*, Yorkville, S.C. (August 3, 1871); Budiansky, *The Bloody Shirt*, 129; Trelease, *White Terror*, 375; West, *The Reconstruction Ku Klux Klan in York County, South Carolina, 1865–1877*, 85–86.

16. Budiansky, *The Bloody Shirt*, 129–30; Martinez, *Carpetbaggers, Cavalry, and the Ku Klux Klan*, 142–43; Trelease, *White Terror*, 375–76; West, *The Reconstruction Ku Klux Klan in York County, South Carolina, 1865–1877*, 86.

17. Budiansky, *The Bloody Shirt*, 130–34; "The Ku-Klux Committee," *Yorkville Enquirer*, Yorkville, S.C. (July 27, 1871); Simkins, "The Ku Klux Klan in South

Carolina," 640–41; Trelease, *White Terror*, 374–76; West, *The Reconstruction Ku Klux Klan in York County, South Carolina, 1865–1877*, 84–86.

18. Trelease, *White Terror*, 376–77; United States Congress, *Testimony Taken by the Joint Select Committee to Inquire into the Condition of Affairs in the Late Insurrectionary States*, Vol. 3, 1600–1602; Wade, *The Fiery Cross*, 99–100; West, *The Reconstruction Ku Klux Klan in York County, South Carolina, 1865–1877*, 87–88.

19. Quoted in Budiansky, *The Bloody Shirt*, 133. See also "Report of the Grand Jury," *Yorkville Enquirer*, Yorkville, S.C. (October 5, 1871); Trelease, *White Terror*, 376–77; Wade, *The Fiery Cross*, 99–100; West, *The Reconstruction Ku Klux Klan in York County, South Carolina, 1865–1877*, 87–88.

20. Rable, *But There Was No Peace*, 72; Shapiro, "The Ku Klux Klan during Reconstruction," 44–45; Taylor, *The Negro in South Carolina during the Reconstruction*, 192; Trelease, *White Terror*, 377–80; Zuczek, "The Federal Government's Attack on the Ku Klux Klan," 50–52; Zuczek, *State of Rebellion*, 90–92.

21. Calabresi and Yoo, "The Unitary Executive during the Second Half-Century," 765–66; Trelease, *White Terror*, 387–91; Wade, *The Fiery Cross*, 88–91; West, *The Reconstruction Ku Klux Klan in York County, South Carolina, 1865–1877*, 88, 89.

22. Franklin, *Reconstruction after the Civil War*, 164–68; Shapiro, "The Ku Klux Klan during Reconstruction," 44–46; Trelease, *White Terror*, 386–89; Zuczek, *State of Rebellion*, 95–96.

23. Foner, *Reconstruction*, 454–57; Franklin, *Reconstruction after the Civil War*, 167–68; Trelease, *White Terror*, 386–91; Wade, *The Fiery Cross*, 90–92; Williams, "The South Carolina Ku Klux Klan Trials and Enforcement of Federal Civil Rights, 1871–1872," 50–52.

24. Shapiro, "The Ku Klux Klan during Reconstruction," 45; Simkins, "The Ku Klux Klan in South Carolina," 640–41; Taylor, *The Negro in South Carolina during the Reconstruction*, 201–2; Wade, *The Fiery Cross*, 100–101; West, *The Reconstruction Ku Klux Klan in York County, South Carolina, 1865–1877*, 89; Zuczek, *State of Rebellion*, 98–99.

25. Quoted in West, *The Reconstruction Ku Klux Klan in York County, South Carolina, 1865–1877*, 89. See also "Arrests of Citizens," *Yorkville Enquirer*, Yorkville, S.C. (October 26, 1871); Martinez, *Carpetbaggers, Cavalry, and the Ku Klux Klan*, 150–51; Trelease, *White Terror*, 405; West, *The Reconstruction Ku Klux Klan in York County, South Carolina, 1865–1877*, 89–91; Williams, *The Great South Carolina Ku Klux Klan Trials, 1871–1872*, 47–48.

26. "Arrests of Citizens," *Yorkville Enquirer*, Yorkville, S.C. (October 26, 1871); Everitt, "1871 War on Terror," 31–32; Martinez, *Carpetbaggers, Cavalry, and the Ku Klux Klan*, 151; "The Situation," *Yorkville Enquirer*, Yorkville, S.C. (November 2, 1871); Simkins, "The Ku Klux Klan in South Carolina," 641–42; Simkins and Woody, *South Carolina during Reconstruction*, 463; Wade, *The Fiery Cross*, 100–101; West, *The Reconstruction Ku Klux Klan in York County, South Carolina, 1865–1877*, 90–96; Williams, *The Great South Carolina Ku Klux Klan Trials, 1871–1872*, 47–48; Zuczek, *State of Rebellion*, 98–99.

27. Quoted in Trelease, *White Terror*, 404. See also "Arrests of Citizens," *Yorkville Enquirer*, Yorkville, S.C. (October 26, 1871); Everitt, "1871 War on Terror,"

31–32; "The Situation," *Yorkville Enquirer*, Yorkville, S.C. (November 2, 1871); West, *The Reconstruction Ku Klux Klan in York County, South Carolina, 1865–1877*, 89–93; Williams, *The Great South Carolina Ku Klux Klan Trials, 1871–1872*, 47–48; Zuczek, *State of Rebellion*, 98–99.

28. Trelease, *White Terror*, 404; Wade, *The Fiery Cross*, 102–3; West, *The Reconstruction Ku Klux Klan in York County, South Carolina, 1865–1877*, 89–96; Zuczek, *State of Rebellion*, 99–108.

29. Cong. Globe, 42nd Cong., 2nd Sess. 31 3382 (May 13, 1872); Landon, "The Kidnapping of Dr. Rufus Bratton," 330–34; Martinez, *Carpetbaggers, Cavalry, and the Ku Klux Klan*, 193–96; McFeely, *Grant*, 384; Post, "A Carpetbagger in South Carolina," 61; Rawley, "The General Amnesty Act of 1872," 480–84; Simkins, "The Ku Klux Klan in South Carolina," 645; West, *The Reconstruction Ku Klux Klan in York County, South Carolina, 1865–1877*, 126–30; Zuczek, *State of Rebellion*, 119–20.

30. Slide, *American Racist*, 41; Work Projects Administration, *South Carolina: A Guide to the Palmetto State*, 426. See also Martinez, *Carpetbaggers, Cavalry, and the Ku Klux Klan*, 244; Trelease, *White Terror*, 55–56; Wade, *The Fiery Cross*, 119–124; West, *The Reconstruction Ku Klux Klan in York County, South Carolina, 1865–1877*, 130.

31. Quoted in West, *The Reconstruction Ku Klux Klan in York County, South Carolina, 1865–1877*, 92. See also Trelease, *White Terror*, 404–5.

32. Quoted in Trelease, *White Terror*, 405.

33. Quoted in Trelease, *White Terror*, 405. See also Martinez, *Carpetbaggers, Cavalry, and the Ku Klux Klan*, 150–51; Trelease, *White Terror*, 404–5; West, *The Reconstruction Ku Klux Klan in York County, South Carolina, 1865–1877*, 92–93.

34. Quoted in Budiansky, *The Bloody Shirt*, 136–37. See also Rable, *But There Was No Peace*, 108; Trelease, *White Terror*, 406–7; Wade, *The Fiery Cross*, 102–4; Williams, "The South Carolina Ku Klux Klan Trials and Enforcement of Federal Civil Rights, 1871–1872," 51–54.

35. Quoted in Williams, *The Great South Carolina Ku Klux Klan Trials, 1871–1872*, 61. See also Post, "A Carpetbagger in South Carolina," 64–72; Shapiro, "The Ku Klux Klan during Reconstruction," 46; Trelease, *White Terror*, 406–7; Wade, *The Fiery Cross*, 102–4; Williams, "The South Carolina Ku Klux Klan Trials and Enforcement of Federal Civil Rights, 1871–1872," 51–54; Zuczek, "The Federal Government's Attack on the Ku Klux Klan," 56.

36. Shapiro, "The Ku Klux Klan during Reconstruction," 46; Trelease, *White Terror*, 406–8; Wade, *The Fiery Cross*, 103–4; West, *The Reconstruction Ku Klux Klan in York County, South Carolina, 1865–1877*, 97–108; Zuczek, "The Federal Government's Attack on the Ku Klux Klan," 60–62; Zuczek, *State of Rebellion*, 99–100.

37. Blair, "The Use of Military Force to Protect the Gains of Reconstruction," 396–97; Budiansky, *The Bloody Shirt*, 139–45; Sefton, *The United States Army and Reconstruction, 1865–1877*, 224–25; Simkins and Roland, *A History of the South*, 280–82; Trelease, *White Terror*, 401–4; Wade, *The Fiery Cross*, 102–7.

38. Quoted in Wade, *The Fiery Cross*, 33. See also Davis, *Authentic History*, 16–21; Henry, *The Story of Reconstruction*, 222–23; Lester and Wilson, *Ku Klux Klan*,

51–56; Romine and Romine, *A Story of the Original Ku Klux Klan*, 4; Richardson, *Historic Pulaski*, 13–14; Wade, *The Fiery Cross*, 32–33.

39. Avary, *Dixie after the War*, 268; Davis, *Authentic History*, 7–10; Horn, *Invisible Empire*, 9; Jones, "The Rise and Fall of the Ku Klux Klan," 13; Lester and Wilson, *Ku Klux Klan*, 51–56; Parsons, "Midnight Ramblers," 811–15; Richardson, *Historic Pulaski*, 11–16.

40. Horn, *Invisible Empire*, 113; Mitchell, "The Role of General George Washington Gordon in the Ku-Klux Klan," 73–80; Trelease, *White Terror*, 13–14; Wade, *The Fiery Cross*, 38–39.

41. Alexander, "Ku-Kluxism in Tennessee, 1865–1869," 198; Chalmers, *Hooded Americanism*, 2; Lester and Wilson, *Ku Klux Klan*, 73; McWhiney and Simkins, "The Ghostly Legend of the Ku Klux Klan," 109–12; Richardson, *Historic Pulaski*, 29; Romine and Romine, *A Story of the Original Ku Klux Klan*, 10–11; Rogers, *The Ku Klux Spirit*, 16–17; Wade, *The Fiery Cross*, 35–36.

42. Avary, *Dixie after the War*, 275–76; Damer, *When the Ku Klux Rode*, 93–94; Davis, *Authentic History*, 81, 86–87; Foote, *The Civil War: A Narrative*: Vol. 2, *Fredericksburg to Meridian*, 65; Lytle, *Bedford Forrest and His Critter Company*, 382–83; Morton, *The Artillery of Nathan Bedford Forrest's Cavalry*, 338, 343–45; Rable, *But There Was No Peace*, 95; Romine and Romine, *A Story of the Original Ku Klux Klan*, 17; Trelease, *White Terror*, 19–20; Wade, *The Fiery Cross*, 40–41; Warmouth, *War, Politics and Reconstruction*, 70–71.

43. Davis, *Authentic History*, 125–28; Lester and Wilson, *Ku Klux Klan*, 109–13; Romine and Romine, *A Story of the Original Ku Klux Klan*, 24–26; Rose, *The Ku Klux Klan or Invisible Empire*, 71–73; Trelease, *White Terror*, 173–74; Wade, *The Fiery Cross*, 58–60.

44. Cardyn, "Sexualized Racism/Gendered Violence: Outraging the Body Politic in the Reconstruction South," 676–77, 680–83; Trelease, *White Terror*, 28–30, 49–53; Wade, *The Fiery Cross*, 62–64.

45. Quoted in Wade, *The Fiery Cross*, 62. See also Everitt, "1871 War on Terror," 27; Martinez, *Carpetbaggers, Cavalry, and the Ku Klux Klan*, 68–69; Trelease, *White Terror*, 387–91; Zuczek, *State of Rebellion*, 88–93.

46. Everitt, "1871 War on Terror," 26–28; Foner, *Reconstruction*, 425–33; Harcourt, "Who Were the Pale Faces?" 23–66; Wade, *The Fiery Cross*, 82–84.

47. Beatty, *Age of Betrayal*, 156; Foner, *Reconstruction*, 524–29; Franklin, *Reconstruction after the Civil War*, 194–203; Simkins and Roland, *A History of the South*, 281–87.

48. Foner, *Reconstruction*, 603–6; Henry, *The Story of Reconstruction*, 494–97; Lemann, *Redemption*, 67; Simkins and Roland, *A History of the South*, 282–84.

49. Pike, *The Prostrate State*, 9, 61–62.

50. Dray, *Capitol Men*, 135–38; Foner, *Forever Free*, 191–92; Foner, *Reconstruction*, 525–26; Henry, *The Story of Reconstruction*, 496–97; Simkins and Roland, *A History of the South*, 282.

51. Foner, *Forever Free*, 137–39; Foner, *Reconstruction*, 527–29; Franklin, *Reconstruction after the Civil War*, 199–200; Frederickson, "Masters and Mudsills," 43–45; Henry, *The Story of Reconstruction*, 496–97.

52. Foner, *Reconstruction*, 535–37; Franklin, *Reconstruction after the Civil War*, 219–22; Simkins and Roland, *A History of the South*, 320–36.

53. Blum, *Reforging the White Republic*, 7; Foner, *Reconstruction*, 527–28; Simkins and Roland, *A History of the South*, 283–84.

54. Dray, *Capitol Men*, x–xi, 137–39; Foner, *Forever Free*, 192–94; Foner, *Reconstruction*, 527; Franklin, *Reconstruction after the Civil War*, 152–73; Lemann, *Redemption*, 27–29.

55. Dray, *Capitol Men*, 36–37; Foner, *Forever Free*, 130–37; Franklin, *Reconstruction after the Civil War*, 155–58; Simkins and Roland, *A History of the South*, 266–68.

56. Nordhoff, *The Cotton States*, 11–12. See also Foner, *Reconstruction*, 526–27; Henry, *The Story of Reconstruction*, 497; Simkins and Roland, *A History of the South*, 283.

57. Quoted in Foner, *Reconstruction*, 528. See also Franklin, *Reconstruction after the Civil War*; Lemann, *Redemption*, 27–29.

58. Foner, *Forever Free*, 197–98; Foner, *Reconstruction*, 524–29; Franklin, *Reconstruction after the Civil War*, 197–207; Rable, *But There Was No Peace*, 151; Trefousse, *The Radical Republicans*, 465–70.

59. Foner, *Forever Free*, 195–97; Franklin, *Reconstruction after the Civil War*, 155–57; Lemann, *Redemption*, 80–82; Simkins and Roland, *A History of the South*, 284–85.

60. Dray, *Capitol Men*, 180, 336; Foner, *Reconstruction*, 558–63; Henry, *The Story of Reconstruction*, 544–45; Lemann, *Redemption*, 170–209; Lewinson, *Race, Class, and Party*, 85–86; Simkins and Roland, *A History of the South*, 284–86.

CHAPTER 7
"WE HAVE BEEN, AS A CLASS, GRIEVOUSLY WOUNDED"

1. Bruce, *The Century, Its Fruits and Its Festival*, 1–8; Calabresi and Yoo, "The Unitary Executive during the Second Half-Century," 769; Fletcher, *The Centennial Exhibition of 1876*, 3–25; Foner, *Reconstruction*, 564–65.

2. Blum, *Reforging the White Republic*, 7; Foner, *Reconstruction*, 565–69; Simkins and Roland, *A History of the South*, 290–96.

3. Brown, *The Year of the Century: 1876*, 199–200; Hoogenboom, *The Presidency of Rutherford B. Hayes*, 2–3; Martinez, *Carpetbaggers, Cavalry, and the Ku Klux Klan*, 203; Rable, *But There Was No Peace*, 162.

4. Foner, *Reconstruction*, 565–67; Gould, *Grand Old Party*, 70–71; Simpson, *The Reconstruction Presidents*, 184–92; Smith, *Grant*, 585–94; Witcover, *Party of the People*, 244–45.

5. Quoted in Contosta and Muccigrosso, *Henry Adams and His World*, 36. See also Foner, *Reconstruction*, 566–67; Gould, *Grand Old Party*, 71–72; Simpson, *The Reconstruction Presidents*, 189; Witcover, *Party of the People*, 245–46; Young, "The Year They Stole the White House," 1459.

6. Quoted in Martinez, *Carpetbaggers, Cavalry, and the Ku Klux Klan*, 204. See also Gould, *Grand Old Party*, 71–73; Henry, *The Story of Reconstruction*, 554–55; Hoogenboom, *The Presidency of Rutherford B. Hayes*, 11; Logan, *The Betrayal of the Negro*, 13–14; Young, "The Year They Stole the White House," 1459–60.

7. Gould, *Grand Old Party*, 72–73; Kane, *Facts about the Presidents*, 213; Witcover, *Party of the People*, 245–46; Young, "The Year They Stole the White House," 1459.

8. Gould, *Grand Old Party*, 71; Morris, *Fraud of the Century*, 57–68; Rehnquist, *Centennial Crisis*, 33–51, 58–79; Witcover, *Party of the People*, 246–47; Young, "The Year They Stole the White House," 1459.

9. Flick, *Samuel Jones Tilden*, 308–15; Hoogenboom, *The Presidency of Rutherford B. Hayes*, 22–24; Martinez, *Carpetbaggers, Cavalry, and the Ku Klux Klan*, 204–6; Stampp, *The Era of Reconstruction*, 211; Young, "The Year They Stole the White House," 1459–60.

10. Fitzgerald, *Splendid Failure*, 201–2; Flick, *Samuel Jones Tilden*, 303–4; Foner, *Reconstruction*, 567–70; Swint, *Mudslingers*, 79–86; Witcover, *Party of the People*, 246–47; Young, "The Year They Stole the White House," 1459–60.

11. Foner, *Reconstruction*, 575; Gould, *Grand Old Party*, 74–75; Witcover, *Party of the People*, 247; Young, "The Year They Stole the White House," 1460.

12. Foner, *Reconstruction*, 575; Hoogenboom, *The Presidency of Rutherford B. Hayes*, 25; Morris, *Fraud of the Century*, 10–11.

13. Quoted in Gould, *Grand Old Party*, 74. See also Foner, *Reconstruction*, 575; Gould, *Grand Old Party*, 74–75; Polakoff, *The Politics of Inertia*, 202–3; Rehnquist, *Centennial Crisis*, 97.

14. Quoted in Martinez, *Carpetbaggers, Cavalry, and the Ku Klux Klan*, 207. See also Foner, *Reconstruction*, 575; Hoogenboom, *The Presidency of Rutherford B. Hayes*, 26; Polakoff, *The Politics of Inertia*, 202–3; Swint, *Mudslingers*, 82–83; Young, "The Year They Stole the White House," 1460.

15. Quoted in Martinez, *Carpetbaggers, Cavalry, and the Ku Klux Klan*, 207. See also Swint, *Mudslingers*, 82–83; Witcover, *Party of the People*, 247; Young, "The Year They Stole the White House," 1460.

16. Foner, *Reconstruction*, 575–76; Martinez, *Carpetbaggers, Cavalry, and the Ku Klux Klan*, 207–8; Polakoff, *The Politics of Inertia*, 225–27; Simpson, *The Reconstruction Presidents*, 192–93.

17. Calabresi and Yoo, "The Unitary Executive during the Second Half-Century," 769; Kane, *Facts about the Presidents*, 215; Witcover, *Party of the People*, 247; Young, "The Year They Stole the White House," 1460.

18. Foner, *Reconstruction*, 575–76; Gould, *Grand Old Party*, 74–75; Kane, *Facts about the Presidents*, 215; Young, "The Year They Stole the White House," 1460.

19. Foner, *Reconstruction*, 576; Henry, *The Story of Reconstruction*, 581–82; Young, "The Year They Stole the White House," 1460.

20. Calabresi and Yoo, "The Unitary Executive during the Second Half-Century," 769; Foner, *Reconstruction*, 579–80; Gould, *Grand Old Party*, 75; Kane, *Facts about the Presidents*, 215; Witcover, *Party of the People*, 247; Young, "The Year They Stole the White House," 1460–61.

21. "A Truce—Not a Compromise" [Cartoon], *Harper's Weekly*, February 17, 1877, 132; McPherson, *The Abolitionist Legacy*, 86; Young, "The Year They Stole the White House," 1460–61.

22. Beatty, *Age of Betrayal*, 260–61; Calabresi and Yoo, "The Unitary Executive during the Second Half-Century," 769; Foner, *Reconstruction*, 581–82; Gould, *Grand Old Party*, 74–75; Kane, *Facts about the Presidents*, 216; Swint, *Mudslingers*, 84–85; Witcover, *Party of the People*, 249–50; Young, "The Year They Stole the White House," 1461.

23. Foner, *Reconstruction*, 581–82; Martinez, *Carpetbaggers, Cavalry, and the Ku Klux Klan*, 208–10; Young, "The Year They Stole the White House," 1461.

24. Quoted in Young, "The Year They Stole the White House," 1461. See also Foner, *Reconstruction*, 581–82; Kane, *Facts about the Presidents*, 216; Swint, *Mudslingers*, 84–85; Witcover, *Party of the People*, 249–50.

25. Bilhartz and Elliott, *Currents in American History*, 121–23; Foner, *Reconstruction*, 580–82; Franklin, *Reconstruction after the Civil War*, 214; Hoogenboom, *The Presidency of Rutherford B. Hayes*, 46–47; Witcover, *Party of the People*, 249–50; Woodward, *Origins of the New South*, 44–45.

26. Foner, *Reconstruction*, 582; Gould, *Grand Old Party*, 75–76; Henry, *The Story of Reconstruction*, 591–92; Kane, *Facts about the Presidents*, 219; Lears, *Rebirth of a Nation*, 22–23; Richardson, *West from Appomattox*, 176–78; Swint, *Mudslingers*, 84–86; Witcover, *Party of the People*, 251–52; Young, "The Year They Stole the White House," 1461.

27. Quoted in Joint Congressional Committee on Inaugural Ceremonies, *Inaugural Addresses of the Presidents of the United States*, 154–55.

28. Quoted in Joint Congressional Committee on Inaugural Ceremonies, *Inaugural Addresses of the Presidents of the United States*, 155.

29. Quoted in Joint Congressional Committee on Inaugural Ceremonies, *Inaugural Addresses of the Presidents of the United States*, 155–56.

30. Quoted in Joint Congressional Committee on Inaugural Ceremonies, *Inaugural Addresses of the Presidents of the United States*, 156.

31. Blair, "The Use of Military Force to Protect the Gains of Reconstruction," 388, 396; Foner, *Reconstruction*, 582; Gould, *Grand Old Party*, 75–76; Henry, *The Story of Reconstruction*, 591–92; Lewinson, *Race, Class, and Party*, 55–57; Stampp, *The Era of Reconstruction*, 186; Swint, *Mudslingers*, 84–86; Witcover, *Party of the People*, 251–52; Young, "The Year They Stole the White House," 1461.

32. Quoted in Simpson, *The Reconstruction Presidents*, 211. See also Calabresi and Yoo, "The Unitary Executive during the Second Half-Century," 771; Logan, *The Betrayal of the Negro*, 13–16; McPherson, *The Abolitionist Legacy*, 89–90; Rable, *But There Was No Peace*, 183–85.

33. Quoted in Riddle, *The Life of Benjamin F. Wade*, 363. See also Trefousse, *The Radical Republicans*, 468–69.

34. Quoted in Simpson, *The Reconstruction Presidents*, 213. See also Fitzgerald, *Splendid Failure*, 209; Foner, *Reconstruction*, 582–83; Franklin, *Reconstruction after the Civil War*, 214–15; Simpson, *The Reconstruction Presidents*, 213–14; Woodward, *Origins of the New South*, 41–42.

35. Franklin, *Reconstruction after the Civil War*, 216–17; Simpson, *The Reconstruction Presidents*, 213–14; Woodward, *Origins of the New South*, 46–47.

36. Quoted in Foner, *Reconstruction*, 588; Gould, *Grand Old Party*, 75. See also Franklin, *Reconstruction after the Civil War*, 222–23; Gould, *Grand Old Party*, 75–76; Simpson, *The Reconstruction Presidents*, 199–200.

37. Lemann, *Redemption*, 65; Perman, *The Road to Redemption*, 178–80; Simkins and Roland, *A History of the South*, 304–7; Woodward, *Origins of the New South*, 14–15.

38. Simkins and Roland, *A History of the South*, 304–6; Woodward, *Origins of the New South*, 19–22.

39. Perman, *The Road to Redemption*, 143; Simkins and Roland, *A History of the South*, 315–18; Williams, *Beyond Redemption*, 111–12, 146; Woodward, *Origins of the New South*, 58–62.

40. Perman, *The Road to Redemption*, 143–46; Williams, *Beyond Redemption*, 142–45; Woodward, *Origins of the New South*, 58–60.

41. Ayers, *The Promise of the New South*, 27; Coski, *The Confederate Battle Flag*, 61–65; Logan, *The Betrayal of the Negro*, 12; Rable, *But There Was No Peace*, 6; Simkins and Roland, *A History of the South*, 304–6.

42. Foner, *Reconstruction*, 588–89; Lemann, *Redemption*, 185–86; Perman, *The Road to Redemption*, 172–210; Woodward, *Origins of the New South*, 19–22.

43. Dray, *Capitol Men*, 352–55; Foner, *Reconstruction*, 591–92; Franklin, *Reconstruction after the Civil War*, 224–27; Logan, *The Betrayal of the Negro*, 182; Woodward, *The Strange Career of Jim Crow*, 32–35, 82–87.

44. Quoted in Woodward, *Origins of the New South*, 55.

45. Foner, *Reconstruction*, 592–93; Lemann, *Redemption*, 184–85; Simkins and Roland, *A History of the South*, 341; Woodward, *Origins of the New South*, 55–58, 81; Woodward, *The Strange Career of Jim Crow*, 53–54, 82–86.

46. Hild, *Greenbackers, Knights of Labor, and Populists*, 31–32; Simkins and Roland, *A History of the South*, 342–43; Woodward, *Origins of the New South*, 76–82.

47. Ayers, *The Promise of the New South*, 214–16; Foner, *Reconstruction*, 548–49; Hild, *Greenbackers, Knights of Labor, and Populists*, 12–13; Lears, *Rebirth of a Nation*, 150–57; Lewinson, *Race, Class, and Party*, 69–71; Simkins and Roland, *A History of the South*, 341–43; Woodward, *Origins of the New South*, 82–83; Woodward, *The Strange Career of Jim Crow*, 56–59.

48. Hild, *Greenbackers, Knights of Labor, and Populists*, 80–81; Simkins and Roland, *A History of the South*, 341; Woodward, *Origins of the New South*, 103–6; Woodward, *The Strange Career of Jim Crow*, 57–59.

49. Ayers, *The Promise of the New South*, 34–35; Lewinson, *Race, Class, and Party*, 54–55; Simkins and Roland, *A History of the South*, 318–19; Woodward, *Origins of the New South*, 78–86.

50. Ayers, *The Promise of the New South*, 92; Logan, *The Betrayal of the Negro*, 8–11; Simkins and Roland, *A History of the South*, 320–23.

51. Foner, *Reconstruction*, 602–12; Franklin, *Reconstruction after the Civil War*, 222–24; Logan, *The Betrayal of the Negro*, xiii; Woodward, *The Strange Career of Jim Crow*, 69–71.

52. Brundage, *The Southern Past*, 96; Foner, *Forever Free*, 209; Logan, *The Betrayal of the Negro*, 38–39; Woodward, *Origins of the New South*, 208–13.

53. Ayers, *The Promise of the New South*, 434; Litwack, *Trouble in Mind*, 233; Woodward, *Origins of the New South*, 104–6; Woodward, *The Strange Career of Jim Crow*, 54–58.

54. Quoted in Woodward, *Origins of the New South*, 211.

55. Foner, *Forever Free*, 37–38, 208; Woodward, *Origins of the New South*, 211–12, 353–54; Woodward, *The Strange Career of Jim Crow*, 7–8.

56. Foner, *Forever Free*, 207–11; Foner, *Reconstruction*, 602–12; Klarman, *From Jim Crow to Civil Rights*, 10–14; Lears, *Rebirth of a Nation*, 22–23; Logan, *The Betrayal of the Negro*, 12–13, 83; Simkins and Roland, *A History of the South*, 352; Valelly, *The Two Reconstructions*, 117–18.

57. 83 U.S. 36 (1872).

58. 83 U.S. 36, 72, 74.

59. 83 U.S. 36, 72–73.

60. Aynes, "Constricting the Law of Freedom," 632–37; Beatty, *Age of Betrayal*, 134–35; Franklin, *Reconstruction after the Civil War*, 206–7; O'Connor, "Time Out of Mind," 700–705; Woodward, *The Strange Career of Jim Crow*, 70–72.

61. 92 U.S. 214, 217 (1875). See also Goldman, *Reconstruction and Black Suffrage*, 87; Logan, *The Betrayal of the Negro*, 101; Martinez, *Carpetbaggers, Cavalry, and the Ku Klux Klan*, 201; Woodward, *The Strange Career of Jim Crow*, 71.

62. Quoted in Lemann, *Redemption*, 19. See also Keith, *The Colfax Massacre*, xi–xviii; Lemann, *Redemption*, 12–20, 173; Logan, *The Betrayal of the Negro*, 108–10; Rable, *But There Was No Peace*, 127–29.

63. 92 U.S. 542 (1876). See also Beatty, *Age of Betrayal*, 136–40; Goldman, *Reconstruction and Black Suffrage*, 76; Halbrook, *Freedmen, the Fourteenth Amendment, and the Right to Bear Arms*, 169; Kaczorowski, *The Politics of Judicial Interpretation*, 180–91; Keith, *The Colfax Massacre*, 132–52; Lemann, *Redemption*, 22–23, 163; Woodward, *The Strange Career of Jim Crow*, 71.

64. 95 U.S. 485, 488–89, 490 (1878).

65. 133 U.S. 587 (1890).

66. 109 U.S. 3 (1883). Quoted in Woodward, *Origins of the New South*, 216. See also Blight, "'For Something beyond the Battlefield,'" 1159; Dray, *Capitol Men*, 326–32; Klarman, *From Jim Crow to Civil Rights*, 19–20, 49–50; Litwack, *Trouble in Mind*, 392; Woodward, *The Strange Career of Jim Crow*, 71.

67. 170 U.S. 213 (1898). See also Ayers, *The Promise of the New South*, 304; Dray, *Capitol Men*, 343; Lemann, *Redemption*, 170–71; Richardson, *West from Appomattox*, 176–77; Woodward, *The Strange Career of Jim Crow*, 71.

68. 170 U.S. 213, 222.

69. 163 U.S. 537, 550–51 (1896). See also Cooper, "President's Message—The Harlan Standard," 8; Harris, "Symposium," 889–901; Klarman, *From Jim Crow to Civil Rights*, 4; Lears, *Rebirth of a Nation*, 191; Logan, *The Betrayal of the Negro*, 83–84; Woodward, *The Strange Career of Jim Crow*, 54, 71.

70. 163 U.S. 537, 551.

71. Cooper, "President's Message—The Harlan Standard," 8; Dray, *Capitol Men*, 314–27; Foner, *Forever Free*, 207–11.

72. 163 U.S. 537, 559.

73. Cooper, "President's Message—The Harlan Standard," 8; Dray, *Capitol Men*, 327–31; Harris, "Symposium," 881. Vindication came in the landmark case *Brown v. Board of Education*, in which a unanimous U.S. Supreme Court overruled *Plessy v. Ferguson* in 1954.

74. Quoted in Blight, *Frederick Douglass's Civil War*, 229.

75. Quoted in Colaiaco, *Frederick Douglass and the Fourth of July*, 7–11. See also Levine, *Black Culture and Black Consciousness*, 67–71.

76. Dray, *Capitol Men*, 258–63; Stauffer, "Frederick Douglass and the Aesthetic of Freedom," 131–32; Stauffer, *Giants*, 300–301.

77. Quoted in Blight, "'For Something beyond the Battlefield,'" 1158. See also Lears, *Rebirth of a Nation*, 24–25.

78. Quoted in Douglass, *The Life and Times of Frederick Douglass* [1892], 396.

79. Quoted in Blight, "'For Something beyond the Battlefield,'" 1159, 1161.

EPILOGUE:
"WE WEAR THE MASK THAT GRINS AND LIES"

1. Dray, *Capitol Men*, 162–63; Foner, *Reconstruction*, 67; Rohrbach, "'Truth Stronger and Stranger than Fiction,'" 727–55; Simkins and Roland, *A History of the South*, 161.

2. Foner, *Reconstruction*, 604–12; Franklin, *Reconstruction after the Civil War*, 222–27; McPherson, *The Abolitionist Legacy*, 121–22; Trefousse, *The Radical Republicans*, 468–70; Williams, *Lincoln and the Radicals*, xi–xiii.

3. Carwardine, *Lincoln: A Life of Purpose and Power*, 319; Goodwin, *Team of Rivals*, 744; Naveh, "'He Belongs to the Ages,'" 49–50, 53–56; White, *A. Lincoln*, 675–76.

4. Bogue, "The Radical Voting Dimension in the U.S. Senate during the Civil War," 449–50; Cox, *Lincoln and Black Freedom*, 40–42; Donald, *Lincoln Reconsidered*, 105; Foner, *Forever Free*, xx; Hyman, *The Radical Republicans and Reconstruction*, 1, 51; Trefousse, *The Radical Republicans*, 5–15; Williams, *Lincoln and the Radicals*, 373–84; Williams, "Lincoln and the Radicals: An Essay in Civil War History and Historiography," 50–51.

5. Foner, *Forever Free*, xxvii; Foner, *Reconstruction*, 61–62; Harris, *With Charity for All*, 4; McPherson, *Battle Cry of Freedom*, 227–28; Trefousse, *The Radical Republicans*, 5–15.

6. Bogue, "Historians and Radical Republicans," 7–34; Klein, "Personality Profile: 'Old Thad' Stevens," 18–23; Trefousse, *The Radical Republicans*, 468–70; Williams, *Lincoln and the Radicals*, xi–xiii.

7. Foner, *Reconstruction*, 337–38; Gould, *Grand Old Party*, 53–54; Martinez, *Carpetbaggers, Cavalry, and the Ku Klux Klan*, 51–52; Simpson, *The Reconstruction Presidents*, 126–28; Trefousse, *The Radical Republicans*, 399–404.

8. Bogue, "Historians and Radical Republicans," 7–34; Trefousse, *The Radical Republicans*, 468–70; Williams, *Lincoln and the Radicals*, xi–xiii.

9. Quoted in Woodward, *Origins of the New South*, 359. See also McPherson, *The Abolitionist Legacy*, 354–57; Richardson, *West from Appomattox*, 202–4.

10. Washington, *The Story of the Negro*, 399–400.

11. Washington, "The 1895 Atlanta Compromise Speech," 583–87. See also Blackmon, *Slavery by Another Name*, 161; Lears, *Rebirth of a Nation*, 131–32.

12. Ayers, *The Promise of the New South*, 325–26; Foner, *Forever Free*, 211–12; Simkins and Roland, *A History of the South*, 505–6; Woodward, *Origins of the New South*, 357–61.

13. Simkins and Roland, *A History of the South*, 521–22; Woodward, *Origins of the New South*, 354–57; Woodward, *The Strange Career of Jim Crow*, 97–102.

14. Foner, *Forever Free*, 214–17; McPherson, *The Abolitionist Legacy*, 300–301; Simkins and Roland, *A History of the South*, 508–13; Woodward, *Origins of the New South*, 366–68.

15. Foner, *Forever Free*, xxv–xxvi; Logan, *The Betrayal of the Negro*, 344–49; Simkins and Roland, *A History of the South*, 508–13; Woodward, *Origins of the New South*, 366–68.

16. Logan, *The Betrayal of the Negro*, 313; Simkins and Roland, *A History of the South*, 506–7; Woodward, *Origins of the New South*, 367.

17. Ayers, *The Promise of the New South*, 325–27; Lacy, *Cheer the Lonesome Traveler*, 43–45; Lears, *Rebirth of a Nation*, 129–30; Logan, *The Betrayal of the Negro*, 313, 331–32; Woodward, *Origins of the New South*, 367–68.

18. Blackmon, *Slavery by Another Name*, 162; Hahn, *A Nation under Our Feet*, 460; Logan, *The Betrayal of the Negro*, 344–45; Simkins and Roland, *A History of the South*, 507; Woodward, *Origins of the New South*, 367–68.

19. Du Bois, *The Souls of Black Folk*, 41–42.

20. Du Bois, *The Souls of Black Folk*, 45. See also Woodward, *Origins of the New South*, 367–68.

21. Dray, *Capitol Men*, 355–60; Foner, *Forever Free*, 226–37; Logan, *The Betrayal of the Negro*, xv; McPherson, *The Abolitionist Legacy*, 360–61.

22. Foner, *Forever Free*, 214–15; Dray, *Capitol Men*, 352–73; Woodward, *The Strange Career of Jim Crow*, 3–10.

23. Foner, *Forever Free*, 214–15; Klarman, *From Jim Crow to Civil Rights*, 3–4; Simkins and Roland, *A History of the South*, 517–19; Woodward, *Origins of the New South*, 354–56.

24. Paul Laurence Dunbar, "We Wear the Mask," in Adoff, *I Am the Darker Brother*, 134.

Bibliography

Abraham Lincoln Papers at the Library of Congress [Cited as ALPLC]. Washington, D.C.: The Library of Congress, Manuscript Division, American Memory Project. Available at http://memory.loc/gov/ammem/alhtml/alhome.html. Accessed October–November 2009.

Adams, Henry. *The Education of Henry Adams*. Boston: Riverside Press for the Massachusetts Historical Society, 1918.

Adoff, Arnold, ed. *I Am the Darker Brother: An Anthology of Modern Poems by African Americans*. New York: Simon Pulse, 1997.

Alexander, Thomas B. "Ku-Kluxism in Tennessee, 1865–1869." *Tennessee Historical Quarterly* 8, no. 1 (September 1949): 195–219.

Allen, Austin. "The Political Economy of Blackness: Citizenship, Corporations, and Race in *Dred Scott*." *Civil War History* 50, no. 3 (September 2004): 229–60.

Alston, Lee J., Jeffrey A. Jenkins, and Tomas Nonnenmacher. "Who Should Govern Congress? Access to Power and the Salary Grab of 1873." *Journal of Economic History* 66, no. 3 (September 2006): 674–706.

Alston, Lee J., and Kyle D. Kauffman. "Up, Down, and Off the Agricultural Ladder: New Evidence and Implications of Agricultural Mobility for Blacks in the Postbellum South." *Agricultural History* 72, no. 2 (Spring 1998): 263–79.

Ambrose, Stephen E. *Nothing like It in the World: The Men Who Built the Transcontinental Railroad, 1863–1869*. New York: Simon & Schuster, 2000.

Atack, Jeremy. "Tenants and Yeoman in the Nineteenth Century." *Agricultural History* 63, no. 3 (Summer 1988): 6–32.

Avary, Myra Lockett. *Dixie after the War: An Exposition on the Social Conditions Existing in the South, during the Twelve Years Succeeding the Fall of Richmond*. New York: Doubleday, Page & Company, 1906.

Ayers, Edward L. *The Promise of the New South: Life after Reconstruction*. Fifteenth Anniversary Edition. New York and Oxford: Oxford University Press, 2007.

Aynes, Richard L. "Constricting the Law of Freedom: Justice Miller, the Fourteenth Amendment, and the Slaughter-House Cases." *Chicago-Kent Law Review* 70, no. 2 (1994): 627–88.

Balfour, Lawrie. "Unreconstructed Democracy: W. E. B. Du Bois and the Case for Reparations." *American Political Science Review* 97, no. 1 (February 2003): 33–44.

Barber, James David. *The Book of Democracy*. Englewood Cliffs, N.J.: Prentice Hall, 1995.

Bartley, Abel A. "The Fourteenth Amendment: The Great Equalizer of the American People." *Akron Law Review* 36, no. 3 (2003): 473–90.

Basinger, Scott J. "Regulating Slavery: Deck-Stacking and Credible Commitment in the Fugitive Slave Act of 1850." *Journal of Law, Economics, & Organization* 19, no. 2 (October 2003): 307–42.

Baum, Lawrence. *The Supreme Court*. 3rd. ed. Washington, D.C.: Congressional Quarterly Press, 1989.

Beale, Howard K. *The Critical Year: A Study of Andrew Johnson and Reconstruction*. New York: Frederick Ungar, 1958 [1930].

Beatty, Jack. *Age of Betrayal: The Triumph of Money in America, 1865–1900*. New York: Vintage, 2008.

Beauregard, Erving E. "The Chief Prosecutor of President Andrew Johnson." *Midwest Quarterly* 31, no. 3 (Spring 1990): 408–22.

Belz, Herman. *Reconstructing the Union: Theory and Policy during the Civil War*. Ithaca, N.Y.: Cornell University Press, 1969.

Benedict, Michael Les. "From Our Archives: A New Look at the Impeachment of Andrew Johnson." *Political Science Quarterly* 113, no. 3 (Fall 1998): 493–511.

Bilhartz, Terry D., and Alan C. Elliott. *Currents in American History: A Brief History of the United States*. Vol. 2: *From 1861*. Armonk, N.Y.: Sharpe, 2007.

Blackmon, Douglas A. *Slavery by Another Name: The Re-Enslavement of Black Americans from the Civil War to World War II*. New York: Doubleday, 2008.

Blair, William Alan. "The Use of Military Force to Protect the Gains of Reconstruction." *Civil War History* 51, no. 4 (December 2005): 388–402.

Blight, David W. "'For Something beyond the Battlefield': Frederick Douglass and the Struggle for the Memory of the Civil War." *Journal of American History* 75, no. 4 (March 1989): 1156–78.

———. *Frederick Douglass's Civil War: Keeping Faith in Jubilee*. Baton Rouge: Louisiana State University Press, 1989.

———. "Lincoln on the Moral Bankruptcy of Slavery: Inside the Lincoln-Douglass [sic] Debates of 1858." *Magazine of History* 21, no. 4 (October 2007): 56–61.

Blum, Edward J. *Reforging the White Republic: Race, Religion, and American Nationalism, 1865–1898*. Baton Rouge: Louisiana State University Press, 2005.

Bogue, Allan G. "Historians and Radical Republicans: A Meaning for Today." *Journal of American History* 70, no. 1 (June 1983): 7–34.

———. "The Radical Voting Dimension in the U.S. Senate during the Civil War." *Journal of Interdisciplinary History* 3, no. 3 (Winter 1973): 449–74.

Bolt, William K. "Founding Father and Rebellious Son: James Madison, John C. Calhoun, and the Use of Precedents." *American Nineteenth Century History* 5, no. 3 (Autumn 2004): 1–27.

Borchard, Gregory A. "From Pink Lemonade to Salt River: Horace Greeley's Utopia and the Death of the Whig Party." *Journalism History* 32, no. 1 (Spring 2006): 22–33.

Bracher, Mark. "How to Teach for Social Justice: Lessons from *Uncle Tom's Cabin* and Cognitive Science." *College English* 71, no. 4 (March 2009): 363–88.

Brands, H. W. "Hesitant Emancipator: Abraham Lincoln Endured Hours of Personal Anguish Before He Unveiled the Proclamation That Ended Slavery." *American History* 44, no. 2 (June 2009): 54–59.

———. "There Goes the South: President-Elect Abraham Lincoln Remained Strangely Silent as Threats of Secession Became a Reality during the Long Winter before His Inauguration." *American History* 44, no. 1 (April 2009): 40–47.

Brodie, Fawn. *Thaddeus Stevens: Scourge of the South*. New York: Norton, 1959.

Bromwich, David. "Lincoln's Constitutional Necessity." *Raritan* 30, no. 3 (Winter 2001): 1–33.

Brookhiser, Richard. *America's First Dynasty: The Adamses, 1735–1918*. New York: Free Press, 2002.

Brown, Dee. *The Year of the Century: 1876*. New York: Scribner, 1966.

Brown v. Board of Education, 347 U.S. 483 (1954).

Browne, Robert Henry. *Abraham Lincoln and the Men of His Time: His Cause, His Character and True Place in History, and the Men, Statesmen, Heroes, and Patriots Who Formed the Illustrious League about Him*. Chicago: Blakely-Oswald, 1907.

Bruce, Edward C. *The Century, Its Fruits and Its Festival; Being a History and Description of the Centennial Exhibition, with a Preliminary Outline of Modern Progress*. Philadelphia: Lippincott, 1877.

Brundage, William Fitzhugh. *The Southern Past: A Clash of Race and Memory*. Cambridge, Mass., and London: Belknap, 2005.

Bryant, Douglas H. "Unorthodox and Paradox: Revisiting the Ratification of the Fourteenth Amendment." *Alabama Law Review* 53, no. 2 (Winter 2003): 555–81.

Buccola, Nicholas. "'Each for All and All for Each': The Liberal Statesmanship of Frederick Douglass." *Review of Politics* 70, no. 3 (Summer 2008): 400–419.

Budiansky, Stephen. *The Bloody Shirt: Terror after the Civil War*. New York: Plume, 2008.

Burg, Robert W. "Amnesty, Civil Rights, and the Meaning of Liberal Republicanism, 1862–1872." *American Nineteenth Century History* 4, no. 3 (Fall 2003): 29–60.

Burns, James MacGregor. *Packing the Court: The Rise of Judicial Power and the Coming Crisis of the Supreme Court*. New York: Penguin, 2009.

Burton, Orville Vernon. *The Age of Lincoln*. New York: Hill & Wang, 2007.

Calabresi, Steven G., and Christopher S. Yoo. "The Unitary Executive during the Second Half-Century." *Harvard Journal of Law & Public Policy* 26, no. 3 (Summer 2003): 667–801.

Cardyn, Lisa. "Sexualized Racism/Gendered Violence: Outraging the Body Politic in the Reconstruction South." *Michigan Law Review* 100, no. 4 (February 2002): 675–867.

Carey, Patrick W. "Political Atheism: Dred Scott, Roger Brooke Taney, and Orestes A. Brownson." *Catholic Historical Review* 88, no. 2 (April 1988): 207–29.

Carwardine, Richard. "Abraham Lincoln and the Fourth Estate: The White House and the Press during the American Civil War." *American Nineteenth Century History* 7, no. 1 (March 2006): 1–27.

———. *Lincoln: A Life of Purpose and Power*. New York: Knopf, 2003.

Castel, Albert. *The Presidency of Andrew Johnson*. Lawrence: University Press of Kansas, 1979.

Catton, Bruce. *The American Heritage New History of the Civil War*, edited by James M. McPherson. New York: Viking Penguin, 1996.

Chalmers, David M. *Hooded Americanism: The History of the Ku Klux Klan*. 3rd ed. Durham, N.C.: Duke University Press, 1987.

Civil Rights Cases, 109 U.S. 3 (1883).

Clark, Champ. *Decoying the Yanks: Jackson's Valley Campaign*. Alexandria, Va.: Time-Life Books, 1984.

Clark, John G. "Radicals and Moderates on the Joint Committee on Reconstruction." *Mid America* 45, no. 2 (1963): 79–98.

Colaiaco, James A. *Frederick Douglass and the Fourth of July*. New York: Palgrave Macmillan, 2006.

Contosta, Robert, and Robert Muccigrosso. *Henry Adams and His World*. Philadelphia: American Philosophical Society, 1993.

Cook, Roy J., ed. *101 Famous Poems, with a Prose Supplement*. Chicago: Reilly & Lee, 1958.

Cooper, N. Lee. "President's Message—The Harlan Standard: Former Associate Justice Can Teach Us the Value of Reasoned Dissent." *ABA Journal* 83, no. 1 (June 1997): 8.

Coski, John M. *The Confederate Battle Flag: America's Most Embattled Emblem*. Cambridge, Mass., and London: Belknap, 2005.

Cox, LaWanda Fenlason. "From Emancipation to Segregation: National Policy and Southern Blacks." In *Freedom, Racism & Reconstruction: Collected Writings of LaWanda Cox*, edited by Donald G. Nieman, 288–317. Athens: University of Georgia Press, 1997.

———. *Lincoln and Black Freedom: A Study in Presidential Leadership*. Columbia: University of South Carolina Press, 1994.

———. "The Promise of Land for the Freedmen." *Mississippi Valley Historical Review* 45, no. 3 (December 1958): 413–40.

Currie, David P. "The Civil War Congress." *University of Chicago Law Review* 73, no. 4 (2006): 1131–1226.

———. "The Reconstruction Congress." *University of Chicago Law Review* 75, no. 1 (2008): 383–495.

Damer, Eyre. *When the Ku Klux Rode*. Westport, Conn.: Negro Universities Press, 1970 [1912].

Davis, David Brion, and Steven Mintz. *The Boisterous Sea of Liberty: A Document History of America from Discovery through the Civil War*. New York and Oxford: Oxford University Press, 1998.

Davis, Susan L. *Authentic History: Ku Klux Klan, 1865–1877*. New York: American Library Service, 1924.

DeCaro, Louis A. Jr. *"Fire from the Midst of You": A Religious Life of John Brown*. New York: New York University Press, 2002.

Detzer, David. *Allegiance: Fort Sumter, Charleston, and the Beginning of the Civil War*. New York: Harcourt, 2001.

DeWitt, David Miller. *The Impeachment and Trial of Andrew Johnson, Seventeenth President of the United States: A History.* New York: Macmillan, 1903.

Donald, David Herbert. *Charles Sumner and the Coming of the Civil War.* New York: Knopf, 1960.

——. *Lincoln.* New York: Simon & Schuster, 1995.

——. *Lincoln Reconsidered: Essays on the Civil War Era.* 3rd ed. New York: Vintage, 2001.

——. *The Politics of Reconstruction, 1863–1867.* Baton Rouge: Louisiana State University Press, 1965.

——. *"We Are Lincoln Men": Abraham Lincoln and His Friends.* New York: Simon & Schuster, 2003.

Douglass, Frederick. *The Life and Times of Frederick Douglass, Written by Himself: His Early Life as a Slave, His Escape from Bondage, and His Complete History.* London: Christian Age Office, 1882.

Douglass, Frederick. *The Life and Times of Frederick Douglass, Written by Himself: His Early Life as a Slave, His Escape from Bondage, and His Complete History.* New York: Cosimo Classics, 2008 [1892].

Dray, Philip. *Capitol Men: The Epic Story of Reconstruction through the Lives of the First Black Congressmen.* Boston and New York: Houghton Mifflin, 2008.

Dred Scott v. Sandford, 60 U.S. 393 (1857).

Du Bois, W. E. B. *Black Reconstruction, 1860–1880.* New York: Free Press, 1998 [1935].

——. *The Souls of Black Folk: Essays and Sketches.* 8th ed. Chicago: A. C. McClurg, 1909.

Dunning, Mike. "Manifest Destiny and the Trans-Mississippi South: National Laws and the Extension of Slavery into Mexico." *Journal of Popular Culture* 35, no. 2 (Fall 2001): 111–27.

Dunning, William Archibald. *Reconstruction, Political and Economic, 1865–1877.* Vol. 22 of *The American Nation: A History.* New York and London: Harper & Row, 1962 [1907].

Egerton, Douglas R. *Year of Meteors: Stephen Douglas, Abraham Lincoln, and the Election That Brought on the Civil War.* New York: Bloomsbury, 2010.

Everitt, David. "1871 War on Terror." *American History* 38, no. 2 (June 2003): 26–33.

Ewan, Christopher. "The Emancipation Proclamation and Britsh Public Opinion." *Historian* 67, no. 1 (Spring 2005): 1–19.

Ex Parte Milligan, 71 U.S. 2 (1866).

Fehrenbacher, Don E., and Virginia Fehrenbacher, eds. *Recollected Words of Abraham Lincoln.* Palo Alto, Calif.: Stanford University Press, 1996.

Ferleger, Louis. "Sharecropping Contracts in the Late Nineteenth Century South." *Agricultural History* 67, no. 3 (Summer 1993): 31–46.

Fischer, David Hackett. *Liberty and Freedom: A Visual History of America's Founding Ideas.* New York and Oxford: Oxford University Press, 2005.

Fitzgerald, Michael W. *Splendid Failure: Postwar Reconstruction in the American South.* Chicago: Ivan R. Dee, 2008.

Fletcher, Robert Shenk. *The Centennial Exhibition of 1876: What We Saw and How We Saw It.* Philadelphia: S. T. Souder, 1876.

Flick, Alexander Clarence. *Samuel Jones Tilden: A Study in Political Sagacity.* New York: Dodd, Mead, 1939.

Flood, Charles Bracelen. *1864: Lincoln at the Gates of History.* New York: Simon & Schuster, 2009.

Folsom, Burton Jr. "Andrew Johnson and the Constitution." *Ideas on Liberty* 53, no. 8 (September 2003): 32–33.

Foner, Eric. *The Fiery Trial: Abraham Lincoln and American Slavery.* New York and London: Norton, 2010.

———. *Forever Free: The Story of Emancipation and Reconstruction.* New York: Knopf, 2005.

———. *Free Soil, Free Labor, Free Men: The Ideology of the Republican Party before the Civil War.* New York and Oxford: Oxford University Press, 1970.

———. *Reconstruction: America's Unfinished Revolution: 1863–1877.* New York: Francis Parkman Prize Edition, History Book Club, 2005 [1988].

———. "Reconstruction Revisited." *Reviews in American History* 10, no. 4 (December 1982): 82–100.

Foote, Shelby. *The Civil War: A Narrative.* Vol. 2: *From Fredericksburg to Meridian.* New York: Random House, 1974.

———. *The Civil War: A Narrative.* Vol. 3: *From Red River to Appomattox.* New York: Random House, 1974.

Ford, Lacy K. "Reconfiguring the Old South: 'Solving' the Problem of Slavery, 1787–1838." *Journal of American History* 95, no. 1 (June 2008): 95–122.

———. "Rednecks and Merchants: Economic Development and Social Tensions in the South Carolina Upcountry, 1865–1900." *Journal of American History* 71, no. 2 (September 1984): 294–318.

Fox-Genovese, Elizabeth. *Within the Plantation Household: Black & White Women of the Old South.* Chapel Hill: University of North Carolina Press, 1988.

Franklin, John Hope. *Reconstruction after the Civil War.* Chicago and London: University of Chicago Press, 1961.

Frederickson, George M. "Masters and Mudsills: The Role of Race in the Planter Ideology of South Carolina." *South Atlantic Urban Studies* 2, no. 1 (1978): 34–48.

Friedman, Milton. "The Crime of 1873." *Journal of Political Economy* 98, no. 6 (December 1990): 1159–94.

Frye, Dennis E. "John Brown's Raid." In *MacMillan Information Now Encyclopedia: The Confederacy,* edited by Richard N. Current, 265–66. New York: MacMillan Reference USA, 1993.

Fukuyama, Francis. *The End of History and the Last Man.* New York: Free Press, 2006.

Gambill, Edward L. "Who Were the Senate Radicals?" *Civil War History* 11 (September 1965): 237–44.

Gates, Henry Louis Jr., ed. *Lincoln on Race & Slavery.* Princeton, N.J.: Princeton University Press, 2009.

Genovese, Eugene D. *Roll Jordan Roll: The World the Slaves Made.* New York: Vintage, 1976.

Genovese, Michael A. *The Power of the American Presidency, 1789–2000.* New York and Oxford: Oxford University Press, 2001.

Gienapp, William E. *The Origins of the Republican Party, 1852–1856.* New York and Oxford: Oxford University Press, 1987.

Gilbert, James N. "A Behavioral Analysis of John Brown: Martyr or Terrorist?" In *Terrible Swift Sword: The Legacy of John Brown,* edited by Peggy A. Russo and Paul Finkelman, 107–17. Athens: Ohio University Press, 2005.

Gillette, William. *Retreat from Reconstruction, 1869–1879.* Baton Rouge: Louisiana State University Press, 1982.

Goldman, Robert M. *Reconstruction and Black Suffrage: Losing the Vote in Reese and Cruikshank.* Lawrence: University Press of Kansas, 2001.

Goodwin, Doris Kearns. *Team of Rivals: The Political Genius of Abraham Lincoln.* New York: Simon & Schuster, 2005.

Gopnik, Adam. *Angels and Ages: A Short Book about Darwin, Lincoln, and Modern Life.* New York: Random House, 2009.

Gordon, Asa H. *Sketches of Negro Life and History in South Carolina.* 2nd. ed. Columbia: University of South Carolina Press, 1929.

Gordon-Reed, Annette. *The Hemingses of Monticello.* New York: Norton, 2008.

Gould, Lewis L. *Grand Old Party: A History of the Republicans.* New York: Random House, 2003.

Gray, Thomas R. *The Confessions of Nat Turner, the Leader of the Late Insurrection in Southampton, VA as Fully and Voluntarily Made to Thomas R. Gray.* Richmond, Va.: Thomas R. Gray; T. W. White, Printer, 1832.

Green, Michael S. *Freedom, Union, and Power: Lincoln and His Party during the Civil War.* New York: Fordham University Press, 2004.

Griswold del Castillo, Richard. *The Treaty of Guadalupe Hidalgo: A Legacy of Conflict.* Norman: University of Oklahoma Press, 1990.

Guelzo, Allen C. "Houses Divided: Lincoln, Douglas, and the Political Landscape of 1858." *Journal of American History* 94, no. 2 (September 2007): 391–417.

———. *Lincoln and Douglas: The Debates That Defined America.* New York: Simon & Schuster, 2008.

———. "Lincoln and the Abolitionists." *Wilson Quarterly* 24, no. 4 (Autumn 2000): 58–70.

———. "The Lincoln-Douglas Debates: Watch That Finger! Raise Those Arms! Make Your Point!" *America's Civil War* 21, no. 1 (March 2008): 56–61.

———. *Lincoln's Emancipation Proclamation: The End of Slavery in America.* New York: Simon & Schuster, 2006.

Hahn, Steven. *A Nation under Our Feet: Black Political Struggles in the Rural South from Slavery to the Great Migration.* Cambridge, Mass., and London: Belknap, 2005.

Haines, Michael R. "The Population of the United States, 1790–1920." In *The Cambridge Economic History of the United States,* Vol. 2, edited by Stanley L. Engerman and Roger E. Gallman, 143–205. Cambridge and New York: Cambridge University Press, 2000.

Halbrook, Stephen P. *Freedmen, the Fourteenth Amendment, and the Right to Bear Arms, 1866–1876.* Westport, Conn.: Praeger, 1998.

Hall, Kermit L. "Political Power and Constitutional Legitimacy: The South Carolina Ku Klux Klan Trials, 1871–1872." *Emory Law Journal* 33, no. 4 (Fall 1984): 921–51.

Hall v. DeCuir, 95 U.S. 485 (1878).

Hamilton, Alexander, James Madison, and John Jay. *The Federalist Papers,* edited by Clinton Rossiter. New York: New American Library, 1961.

Hamilton, Kendra. "The Strange Career of Uncle Tom." *Black Issues in Higher Education* 19, no. 8 (June 6, 2002): 22–27.

Harcourt, Edward John. "Who Were the Pale Faces? New Perspectives on the Tennessee Ku Klux," *Civil War History* 51, no. 1 (March 2005): 23–66.

Harris, Cheryl I. "Symposium: Race Jurisprudence and the Supreme Court: Where Do We Go from Here? In The Shadow of *Plessy.*" *University of Pennsylvania Journal of Constitutional Law* 7, no. 3 (February 2005): 867–901.

Harris, William C. *Lincoln's Rise to the Presidency.* Lawrence: University Press of Kansas, 2007.

———. *With Charity for All: Lincoln and the Restoration of the Union.* Lexington: University Press of Kentucky, 1999.

Harris, Wilmer Carlyle. *Public Life of Zachariah Chandler, 1851–1875.* Lansing: Michigan Historical Commission, 1917.

Harrison, Robert. "New Representations of a 'Misrepresented Bureau': Reflections on Recent Scholarship on the Freedmen's Bureau." *American Nineteenth Century History* 8, no. 2 (June 2007): 205–29.

Hedrick, Joan D. "'Peaceable Fruits': The Ministry of Harriet Beecher Stowe." *American Quarterly* 40, no. 3 (September 1988): 307–32.

Henry, Robert Selph. *The Story of Reconstruction.* New York: Konecky & Konecky, 1999.

Herzberg, Roberta. "An Analytic Choice Approach to Concurrent Majorities: The Relevance of John C. Calhoun's Theory for Institutional Design." *Journal of Politics* 54, no. 1 (February 1992): 54–81.

Hesseltine, William B. *Lincoln's Plan of Reconstruction.* Chicago: Quadrangle, 1967.

Hild, Matthew. *Greenbackers, Knights of Labor, and Populists: Farmer-Labor Insurgency in the Late-Nineteenth Century South.* Athens: University of Georgia Press, 2007.

Hodgson, Godfrey. "Storm over Mexico." *History Today* 55, no. 3 (March 2005): 34–39.

Holzer, Harold. "Election Day 1860: As Soon as the Returns Were In, the Burdens of the Presidency Weighed upon Abraham Lincoln." *Smithsonian* 39, no. 8 (November 2008): 46–53; 90–96.

———. *Lincoln at Cooper Union: The Speech That Made Abraham Lincoln President.* New York: Simon & Schuster, 2004.

———. *Lincoln President-Elect: Abraham Lincoln and the Great Secession Winter 1860–1861.* New York: Simon & Schuster, 2008.

————. "The Photograph That Made Lincoln President." *Civil War Times* 45, no. 9 (November/December 2006): 24–33.

————. "A Promise Fulfilled." *Civil War Times* 48, no. 6 (December 2009): 28–35.

Hoogenboom, Ari. *The Presidency of Rutherford B. Hayes.* Lawrence: University Press of Kansas, 1988.

Horn, Stanley F. *Invisible Empire: The Story of the Ku Klux Klan, 1866–1871.* Montclair, N.J.: Patterson Smith, 1969.

Horton, James Oliver, and Lois E. Horton. *Slavery and the Making of America.* New York and Oxford: Oxford University Press, 2005.

Howe, Daniel Walker. *What Hath God Wrought: The Transformation of America, 1815–1848.* Oxford and New York: Oxford University Press, 2007.

Huston, James L. "Democracy by Scripture versus Democracy by Process: A Reflection on Stephen A. Douglas and Popular Sovereignty." *Civil War History* 43, no. 3 (September 1997): 189–200.

Hyman, Harold M. *The Radical Republicans and Reconstruction, 1861–1870.* Indianapolis: Bobbs-Merrill, 1967.

"Impeachment and General Butler" [Editorial]. *Harper's Weekly*, December 15, 1866, 786.

In Re Slaughterhouse Cases, 83 U.S. 36 (1872).

Jaffa, Harry V. "*Dred Scott* Revisited." *Harvard Journal of Law and Public Policy* 31, no. 1 (Winter 2008): 197–217.

Jayne, Allen. *Lincoln and the American Manifesto.* Amherst, N.Y.: Prometheus, 2007.

Jefferson, Thomas. *Notes on the State of Virginia.* Edited by William Peden. Chapel Hill and London: University of North Carolina Press, 1954.

Joachim, Walter. "Hiester Clymer and the Belknap Case." *Historical Review of Berks County* 36, no. 1 (Winter 1970–1971): 24–31.

Johnson, Michael P. "Denmark Vesey and His Co-Conspirators." *William and Mary Quarterly* Third Series, 58, no. 4 (October 2001): 915–76.

Joint Congressional Committee on Inaugural Ceremonies. *Inaugural Addresses of the Presidents of the United States.* New York: Cosimo Classics, 2008.

Jones, V. C. "The Rise and Fall of the Ku Klux Klan." *Civil War Times Illustrated* 2, no. 10 (February 1964): 11–17.

Kaczorowski, Robert J. "Congress' Power to Enforce Fourteenth Amendment Rights: Lessons from Federal Remedies the Framers Enacted." *Harvard Journal on Legislation* 42, no. 1 (Winter 2005): 187–283.

————. *The Politics of Judicial Interpretation, the Federal Courts, Department of Justice and Civil Rights, 1866–1876.* Dobbs Ferry, N.Y.: Ocean, 1985.

————. "To Begin the Nation Anew: Congress, Citizenship, and Civil Rights after the Civil War." *American Historical Review* 92, no. 1 (February 1987): 45–68.

Kane, Joseph Nathan. *Facts about the Presidents.* New York: Ace Books, 1976.

Kauffman, Michael W. *American Brutus: John Wilkes Booth and the Lincoln Conspiracies.* New York: Random House, 2004.

Kaukiainen, Yrjo. "Shrinking the World: Improvements in the Speed of Information Transmission." *European Review of Economic History* 5, no. 1 (April 2001): 1–28.

Keegan, John. *The American Civil War: A Military History.* New York: Knopf, 2009.

Keith, LeAnna. *The Colfax Massacre: The Untold Story of Black Power, White Terror, and the Death of Reconstruction.* New York and Oxford: Oxford University Press, 2008.

Kendrick, Benjamin B. *The Journal of the Joint Committee of Fifteen on Reconstruction, 39th Congress, 1865–1867.* Clark, N.J.: Law Book Exchange, 2005 [1914.]

Klarman, Michael J. *From Jim Crow to Civil Rights: The Supreme Court and the Struggle for Equality.* New York and Oxford: Oxford University Press, 2004.

Klein, Frederic Shriver. "Personality Profile: 'Old Thad' Stevens." *Civil War Times Illustrated* 2, no. 1 (February 1964): 18–23.

Knowles, Helen J. "The Constitution and Slavery: A Special Relationship." *Slavery and Abolition* 28, no. 3 (December 2007): 309–28.

Kraditor, Aileen S. *Means and Ends in American Abolitionism: Garrison and His Critics on Strategy and Tactics, 1834–1850.* New York: Vintage, 1969.

Kraig, Robert Alexander. "The Narration of Essence: Salmon P. Chase's Senate Oration against the Kansas-Nebraska Act." *Communication Studies* 48, no. 3 (Fall 1997): 234–53.

Kuic, Vukan. "John C. Calhoun's Theory of the 'Concurrent Majority.'" *American Bar Association Journal* 69, no. 4 (April 1983): 482–86.

Lacy, Leslie Alexander. *Cheer the Lonesome Traveler: The Life of W. E. B. Du Bois.* New York: Dial, 1970.

Landon, Fred. "The Kidnapping of Dr. Rufus Bratton." *Journal of Negro History* 10, no. 3 (July 1925): 330–34.

Lasser, Carol. "Voyeuristic Abolitionism: Sex, Gender, and the Transformation of Antislavery Rhetoric." *Journal of the Early Republic* 28, no. 1 (Spring 2008): 83–114.

Lears, Jackson. *Rebirth of a Nation: The Making of Modern America, 1877–1920.* New York: HarperCollins, 2009.

Lemann, Nicholas. *Redemption: The Last Battle of the Civil War.* New York: Farrar, Straus & Giroux, 2006.

Leonard, Elizabeth D. *Lincoln's Avengers: Justice, Revenge, and Reunion after the Civil War.* New York: Norton, 2004.

Lesser, W. Hunter. *Rebels at the Gate: Lee and McClellan on the Front Line of a Nation Divided.* Naperville, Ill.: SourceBooks, 2004.

Lester, J. C., and D. L. Wilson. *Ku Klux Klan: Its Origin, Growth, and Disbursement.* New York: Da Capo, 1973 [1884].

Levine, Bruce. "Conservatism, Nativism, and Slavery: Thomas R. Whitney and the Origins of the Know-Nothing Party." *Journal of American History* 88, no. 2 (September 2001): 455–88.

Levine, Lawrence W. *Black Culture and Black Consciousness: Afro-American Folk Thought from Slavery to Freedom.* New York and Oxford: Oxford University Press, 1976.

Lewinson, Paul. *Race, Class, and Party: A History of Negro Suffrage and White Politics in the South.* New York: Grosset & Dunlap, 1965.

Lincoln, Abraham. *Complete Works of Abraham Lincoln*. Vols. 2 and 3, edited by John G. Nicolay and John Hay. New York: Thomas-Tandy, 1905.

Lincoln, Abraham, and Stephen A. Douglas. "Selections from the Lincoln-Douglas Debates of 1858." In *The Quest for Justice: Readings in Political Ethics*, 3rd. ed., edited by Leslie G. Rubin and Charles T. Rubin, 95–114. Needham Heights, Mass.: Ginn Press, 1992.

Litwack, Leon F. *Been in the Storm So Long: The Aftermath of Slavery*. New York: Vintage, 1980.

———. *Trouble in Mind: Black Southerners in the Age of Jim Crow*. New York: Knopf, 1998.

Livingstone, David. "The Emancipation Proclamation, the Declaration of Independence, and the Presidency: Lincoln's Model of Statesmanship." *Perspectives on Political Science* 28, no. 4 (Fall 1999): 203–10.

Logan, Rayford W. *The Betrayal of the Negro: From Rutherford B. Hayes to Woodrow Wilson*. Cambridge, Mass.: Da Capo, 1997 [1965].

Louisville, New Orleans, and Texas Railway Company v. Mississippi, 133 U.S. 587 (1890).

Lowe, Richard. "The Joint Committee on Reconstruction—Some Clarifications." *Southern Studies: An Interdisciplinary Journal of the South* 3, no. 1 (Spring 1992): 55–65.

Lubetkin, M. John. *Jay Cooke's Gamble: The Northern Pacific Railroad, the Sioux, and the Panic of 1873*. Norman: University of Oklahoma Press, 2006.

Luse, Christopher A. "Slavery's Champions Stood at Odds: Polygenesis and the Defense of Slavery." *Civil War History* 53, no. 4 (December 2007): 379–412.

Lytle, Andrew. *Bedford Forrest and His Critter Company*. New York: McDowell, Obolensky, 1960.

MacKenzie, Robert. *The Nineteenth Century: A History*. 16th ed. London: Thomas & Sons, 1909.

Magdol, Edward. *Owen Lovejoy: Abolitionist in Congress*. New Brunswick, N.J.: Rutgers University Press, 1967.

Mallard, R. Q. *Plantation Life before Emancipation*. Richmond: Whittett & Shepperson, 1892.

Mantell, Martin E. *Johnson, Grant, and the Politics of Reconstruction*. New York and London: Columbia University Press, 1973.

Martinez, J. Michael. *Carpetbaggers, Cavalry, and the Ku Klux Klan: Exposing the Invisible Empire during Reconstruction*. Lanham, Md.: Rowman & Littlefield, 2007.

Matzke, Jason P. "The John Brown Way: Frederick Douglass and Henry David Thoureau on the Use of Violence." *Massachusetts Review* 46, no. 1 (Spring 2005): 62–75.

Mauro, Stephen. "Taney v. the Missouri Compromise." *Civil War Times* 45, no. 2 (March/April 2006): 52.

McDonald, Forrest. *States' Rights and the Union: Imperium in Imperio, 1776–1876*. Lawrence: University Press of Kansas, 2000.

McFeely, William S. *Grant: A Biography*. New York: Norton, 1981.

McGlone, Robert E. "The 'Madness' of John Brown." *Civil War Times* 48, no. 5 (October 2009): 42–49.

McKitrick, Eric L. *Andrew Johnson and Reconstruction*. New York and Oxford: Oxford University Press, 1988 [1960].

McPherson, James M. *The Abolitionist Legacy: From Reconstruction to the NAACP*. Princeton, N.J.: Princeton University Press, 1976.

———. *Battle Cry of Freedom: The Civil War Era*. New York: Ballantine, 1988.

———. *The Struggle for Equality: Abolitionists and the Negro in the Civil War and Reconstruction*. Princeton, N.J.: Princeton University Press, 1964.

———. *Tried by War: Abraham Lincoln as Commander in Chief*. New York: Penguin, 2008.

McWhiney, Grady H., and Francis Butler Simkins. "The Ghostly Legend of the Ku Klux Klan." *Negro History Bulletin* 14, no. 4 (February 1951): 109–12.

Meacham, Jon. *American Lion: Andrew Jackson in the White House*. New York: Random House, 2008.

Means, Howard. *The Avenger Takes His Place: Andrew Johnson and the 45 Days That Changed the Nation*. New York: Harcourt, 2006.

Miller, John Chester. *The Wolf by the Ears: Thomas Jefferson and Slavery*. New York: Free Press, 1977.

Miller, William Lee. *President Lincoln: The Duty of a Statesman*. New York: Knopf, 2008.

Milton, George Fort. *The Age of Hate: Andrew Johnson and the Radicals*. New York: Coward-McCann, 1930.

Mitchell, Enoch L. "The Role of General George Washington Gordon in the Ku-Klux Klan." *Western Tennessee Historical Society Papers* 1, no. 1 (1947): 73–80.

Mitchell, Robert B. "Notes from the Underground: Passengers on This 'Railroad' Never Forgot Their Life or Death Journey from Bondage." *America's Civil War* 23, no. 2 (May 2010): 42–49.

Morgan, James A. III. "Ball's Bluff: 'A Very Nice Little Military Chance.'" *America's Civil War* 18, no. 5 (November 2005): 30–38; 56.

Moore v. Illinois, 55 U.S. 13 (1852).

Morris, Roy Jr. *Fraud of the Century: Rutherford B. Hayes, Samuel Tilden, and the Stolen Election of 1876*. New York: Simon & Schuster, 2003.

Morrison, Michael A. *Slavery and the American West: The Eclipse of Manifest Destiny*. Chapel Hill: University of North Carolina Press, 1997.

Morton, John Watson. *The Artillery of Nathan Bedford Forrest's Cavalry*. Marietta, Ga.: R. Bemis, 1995.

Murphy, Richard W. *The Nation Reunited: War's Aftermath*. Alexandria, Va.: Time-Life Books, 1987.

Naveh, Eyal. "'He Belongs to the Ages': Lincoln's Image and the American Historical Consciousness." *Journal of American Culture* 16, no. 4 (Winter 1993): 49–57.

Nevin, David. *The Road to Shiloh: Early Battles in the West*. Alexandria, Va.: Time-Life Books, 1983.

Newhall, Beaumont. *The Daguerreotype in America*. 3rd ed. Mineola, N.Y.: Dover, 1976.

Nieman, Donald G. "Andrew Johnson, the Freedmen's Bureau, and the Problem of Equal Rights, 1865–1866." *Journal of Southern History* 44, no. 3 (August 1978): 399–420.

Nordhoff, Charles. *The Cotton States in the Spring and Summer of 1875*. New York: D. Appleton, 1876.

Oates, Stephen B. *To Purge This Land with Blood: A Biography of John Brown*. 2nd. ed. Amherst: University of Massachusetts Press, 1984.

O'Brien, David M. *Storm Center: The Supreme Court in American Politics*. New York: Norton, 1986.

O'Connor, Michael P. "Time Out of Mind: Our Collective Amnesia about the History of the Privileges or Immunities Clause." *Kentucky Law Journal* 93, no. 3 (2004/2005): 659–735.

Onuf, Peter S. "'To Declare Them a Free and Independent People': Race, Slavery, and National Identity in Jefferson's Thought." *Journal of the Early Republic* 18, no. 1 (Spring 1998): 1–46.

Padover, Saul K., ed. *Thomas Jefferson on Democracy*. New York: New American Library, 1939.

Palmer, Beverly Wilson, and Holly Byers Ochoa, eds. *The Selected Papers of Thaddeus Stevens*. Vol. 2: April 1865–August 1868. Pittsburgh, Pa.: University of Pittsburgh Press, 1998.

Paludan, Phillip Shaw. *The Presidency of Abraham Lincoln*. Lawrence: University Press of Kansas, 1994.

Parrish, William E. "Fremont in Missouri." *Civil War Times Illustrated* 17, no. 1 (April 1978): 4–10.

Parsons, Elaine Frantz. "Midnight Ramblers: Costume and Performance in the Reconstruction-Era Ku Klux Klan." *Journal of American History* 92, no. 3 (December 2005): 811–36.

Perman, Michael. *The Road to Redemption: Southern Politics, 1869–1879*. Chapel Hill: University of North Carolina Press, 1984.

Perret, Geoffrey. *Lincoln's War: The Untold Story of America's Greatest President as Commander in Chief*. New York: Random House, 2004.

Peterson, Merrill D. *The Great Triumvirate: Webster, Clay, and Calhoun*. New York and Oxford: Oxford University Press, 1988.

———. *Lincoln in American Memory*. New York and Oxford: Oxford University Press, 1995.

Phillips, Christopher. "'The Crime against Missouri': Slavery, Kansas, and the Cant of Southernness in the Border West." *Civil War History* 48, no. 1 (March 2002): 60–81.

Phillips, Wendell. *The Constitution: A Pro-Slavery Compact. Selections from the Madison Papers, Etc*. New York: American Anti-Slavery Society, 1844, 1856. Reprint, New York: Negro Universities Press, 1969.

Pierce, Edward Lillie, ed. *Memoirs and Letters of Charles Sumner*. Vol. 2. Boston: Roberts Brothers, 1877.

Pike, James S. *The Prostrate State: South Carolina under Negro Government.* Ann Arbor: Scholarly Publishing Office, University of Michigan Library, 2006 [1874].

Plessy v. Ferguson, 163 U.S. 537 (1896).

Plutarch. *Plutarch's Lives.* Vol. 1, translated and edited by John Langhorne, D.D., and William Langhorne, A.M., 84–92. Cincinnati: Applegate, Pounsford, 1872.

Polakoff, Keith Ian. *The Politics of Inertia: The Election of 1876 and the End of Reconstruction.* Baton Rouge: Louisiana State University Press, 1973.

Post, Louis F. "A Carpetbagger in South Carolina." *Journal of Negro History* 10, no. 1 (January 1925): 10–79.

Potter, David Morris. *Lincoln and His Party in the Secession Crisis.* New York: AMS Press, 1979 [1942].

Price, Sean. "Slavery's Big Victory: In the 1857 *Dred Scott* Case, the Supreme Court Sowed the Seeds of War." *New York Times Upfront* 133, no. 11 (February 5, 2001): 23–25.

Prigg v. the Commonwealth of Pennsylvania, 41 U.S. 539 (1842).

Rable, George C. *But There Was No Peace: The Role of Violence in the Politics of Reconstruction.* Athens: University of Georgia Press, 1984.

Ramsey, William M. "Frederick Douglass, Southerner." *Southern Literary Messenger* 40, no. 1 (Fall 2007): 19–38.

Ransom, Roger L., and Richard L. Sutch. *One Kind of Freedom: The Economic Consequences of Emancipation.* 2nd. ed. Cambridge and New York: Cambridge University Press, 2001.

Rawley, James A. "The General Amnesty Act of 1872: A Note." *Mississippi Valley Historical Review* 47, no. 3 (December 1960): 480–84.

Rehnquist, William H. *Centennial Crisis: The Disputed Election of 1876.* New York: Knopf, 2004.

Reid, Joseph D. Jr. "Sharecropping as an Understandable Market Response." *Journal of Economic History* 33, no. 1 (March 1973): 106–30.

———. "Sharecropping in History and Theory." *Agricultural History* 49, no. 2 (April 1975): 426–40.

Remini, Robert V. *Daniel Webster: The Man and His Time.* New York: Norton, 1997.

———. *The Life of Andrew Jackson.* New York: Harper & Row, 1988.

Reynolds, David S. *Mightier than the Sword: Uncle Tom's Cabin and the Battle for America.* New York: Norton, 2011.

Richardson, Darcy C. *Others: Third Party Politics from the Nation's Founding Fathers to the Rise and Fall of the Greenback-Labor Party.* Bloomington, Ind.: iUniverse, 2004.

Richardson, Heather Cox. "A Marshall Plan for the South? The Failure of Republican and Democratic Ideology during Reconstruction." *Civil War History* 51, no. 4 (December 2005): 378–87.

———. *West from Appomattox: The Reconstruction of America after the Civil War.* New Haven, Conn.: Yale University Press, 2007.

Richardson, W. T. *Historic Pulaski: Birthplace of the Ku Klux Klan; Scene of Execution of Sam Davis.* Pulaski, Tenn.: Author, 1913.

Riddle, Albert Gallatin. *The Life of Benjamin F. Wade.* Cleveland, Ohio: Williams, 1888.

Rogers, J. A. *The Ku Klux Spirit*. Baltimore, Md.: Black Classic Press, 1980 [1923].

Rohrbach, Augusta. "'Truth Stronger and Stranger than Fiction': Reexamining William Lloyd Garrision's *Liberator*." *American Literature* 73, no. 4 (December 2001): 727–55.

Romine, W. B., and Mrs. W. B. Romine. *A Story of the Original Ku Klux Klan*. Pulaski, Tenn.: Pulaski Citizen, 1934.

Rose, Mrs. S. E. F. *The Ku Klux Klan or Invisible Empire*. New Orleans, La.: L. Graham, 1914.

Rowland, Tim. "John Brown's Moonlight March." *America's Civil War* 22, no. 4 (September 2009): 29–35.

Royce, Edward. *The Origins of Southern Sharecropping*. Philadelphia: Temple University Press, 1993.

Rubenzer, Steven J., and Thomas R. Faschingbauer. *Personality, Character, & Leadership in the White House: Psychologists Assess the Presidents*. Dulles, Va.: Brassleys, 2004.

Saville, Julie. *The Work of Reconstruction: From Slave to Wage Laborer in South Carolina, 1860–1870*. Cambridge and New York: Cambridge University Press, 1994.

Sayers, Daniel O. "The Underground Railroad Reconsidered." *Western Journal of Black Studies* 28, no. 3 (Fall 2004): 435–43.

Scaturro, Frank J. *President Grant Reconsidered*. Lanham, Md.: University Press of America, 1998.

Schneider, Thomas E. "Lincoln and Leadership." *Perspectives in Political Science* 36, no. 2 (Spring 2007): 69–72.

Schott, Thomas E. "Cornerstone Speech." In *MacMillan Information Now Encyclopedia: The Confederacy*, edited by Richard N. Current, 155–56. New York: MacMillan Reference USA, 1993.

Schroeder-Lein, Glenna, and Richard Zuczek. *Andrew Johnson: A Biographical Companion*. Santa Barbara, Calif.: ABC-CLIO, 2001.

Sears, Stephen W. *George B. McClellan: The Young Napoleon*. Cambridge, Mass.: Da Capo, 1988.

Sefton, James E. *The United States Army and Reconstruction, 1865–1877*. Westport, Conn.: Greenwood Press, 1967.

Shapiro, Herbert. "The Ku Klux Klan during Reconstruction: The South Carolina Episode." *Journal of Negro History* 49, no. 1 (January 1964): 34–55.

Shaw, Robert B. "Leadership Lessons from the Life of Ulysses S. Grant." *Leader to Leader* 42, no. 1 (October 2006): 29–35.

Shlomowitz, Ralph. "The Origins of Southern Sharecropping." *Agricultural History* 53, no. 3 (July 1979): 557–75.

Simkins, Francis Butler. "The Ku Klux Klan in South Carolina." *Journal of Negro History* 12, no. 4 (October 1927): 606–47.

Simkins, Francis Butler, and Charles Pierce Roland. *A History of the South*. 4th ed. New York: Knopf, 1972.

Simkins, Francis Butler, and R. H. Woody. *South Carolina during Reconstruction*. Chapel Hill: University of North Carolina Press, 1932.

Simpson, Brooks D. *Let Us Have Peace: Ulysses S. Grant and the Politics of War and Reconstruction, 1861–1868*. Chapel Hill: University of North Carolina Press, 1991.

———. *The Reconstruction Presidents*. Lawrence: University Press of Kansas, 1998.

Sinha, Manisha. "The Caning of Charles Sumner: Slavery, Race, and Ideology in the Age of the Civil War." *Journal of the Early Republic* 23, no. 2 (Summer 2003): 233–62.

Slap, Andrew L. *The Doom of Reconstruction: The Liberal Republicans in the Civil War Era*. Bronx, N.Y.: Fordham University Press, 2006.

Slide, Anthony. *American Racist: The Life and Films of Thomas Dixon*. Lexington: University Press of Kentucky, 2004.

Smith, Jean Edward. *Grant*. New York: Simon & Schuster, 2001.

Stagg, J. C. A. "The Problem of Klan Violence: The South Carolina Up-Country, 1868–1871." *Journal of American Studies* 8, no. 3 (December 1974): 303–18.

Stampp, Kenneth M. *America in 1857: A Nation on the Brink*. New York and Oxford: Oxford University Press, 1990.

———. *The Era of Reconstruction, 1865–1877*. New York: Knopf, 1965.

———. *The Peculiar Institution: Slavery in the Ante-Bellum South*. New York: Vintage, 1989.

Stanco, William. "President Abraham Lincoln and Congress during the Civil War." *Capitol Dome* 46, no. 1 (Spring 2009): 25–30.

Stauffer, John. "Frederick Douglass and the Aesthetics of Freedom." *Raritan* 25, no. 1 (Summer 2005): 114–36.

———. *Giants: The Parallel Lives of Frederick Douglass and Abraham Lincoln*. New York: Twelve/Hachette, 2008.

Stewart, David O. *Impeached: The Trial of President Andrew Johnson and the Fight for Lincoln's Legacy*. New York: Simon & Schuster, 2009.

Strader, Gorman, and Armstrong v. Graham, 51 U.S. 82 (1850).

Sundstrom, Ronald. "Fredrick Douglass's Longing for the End of Race." *Philosophia Africana* 8, no. 2 (August 2005): 143–70.

Swanson, James L. *Bloody Crimes: The Chase for Jefferson Davis and the Death Pageant for Lincoln's Corpse*. New York: Morrow, 2010.

———. *Manhunt: The 12-Day Chase for Lincoln's Killer*. New York: Morrow, 2006.

Swint, Kerwin C. *Mudslingers: The Top 25 Negative Political Campaigns of All Time—Countdown from No. 25 to No. 1*. Westport, Conn.: Praeger, 2006.

Tap, Bruce. "Chandler, Zachariah (1813–1879)." In *Encyclopedia of the American Civil War: A Political, Social, and Military History*, edited by David Stephen Heidler and Jeanne T. Heidler, 398–99. New York: Norton, 2002.

———. "Inevitability, Masculinity, and the American Military Tradition: The Committee on the Conduct of the War Investigates the American Civil War." *American Nineteenth Century History* 5, no. 2 (Summer 2004): 19–46.

———. *Over Lincoln's Shoulder: The Committee on the Conduct of the War*. Lawrence: University Press of Kansas, 1998.

Taylor, Alrutheus Ambush. *The Negro in South Carolina during the Reconstruction*. Washington, D.C.: Association for the Study of Negro Life and History, 1924.

Taylor, Arnold H. *Travail and Triumph: Black Life and Culture in the South since the Civil War*. Westport, Conn.: Greenwood Press, 1976.

Taylor, Michael J. C. "'A More Perfect Union': *Ableman v. Booth* and the Culmination of Federal Sovereignty." *Journal of Supreme Court History* 28, no. 2 (2003): 101–15.

Thomas, Norman C., Joseph A. Pika, and Richard A. Watson. *The Politics of the Presidency*. 3rd. ed. Washington, D.C.: Congressional Quarterly Press, 1994.

Tourgee, Albion W. *The Invisible Empire: Part I—A New, Illustrated, and Enlarged Edition of a Fool's Errand, by One of the Fools; The Famous Historical Romance of Life in the South Since the War; Part II—A Concise Review of Recent Events, Showing the Elements on Which the Tale Is Based, with Many Thrilling Personal Narratives and Other Startling Facts and Considerations, Including an Account of the Rise, Extent, Purpose, Methods, and Deeds of the Mysterious Ku-Klux Klan; All Fully Authenticated*. New York: Fords, Howard & Hulbert, 1879.

Trefousse, Hans L. *Impeachment of a President: Andrew Johnson, the Blacks, and Reconstruction*. Bronx, N.Y.: Fordham University Press, 1999.

———. *The Radical Republicans: Lincoln's Vanguard for Racial Justice*. New York: Knopf, 1969.

Trelease, Allen W. *White Terror: The Ku Klux Klan Conspiracy and Southern Reconstruction*. Baton Rouge: Louisiana State University Press, 1971.

"A Truce—Not a Compromise" [Cartoon]. *Harper's Weekly*, February 17, 1877, 132.

Tulis, Jeffrey K. *The Rhetorical Presidency*. Princeton, N.J.: Princeton University Press, 1987.

———. "The Two Constitutional Presidencies." In *The Presidency and the Political System*, 3rd. ed., edited by Michael Nelson, 85–115. Washington, D.C.: Congressional Quarterly Press, 1990.

United States Circuit Court [Fourth Circuit]. *Proceedings in the Ku Klux Klan Trials at Columbia, S.C., in the United States Circuit Court, November Term, 1871*. Columbia, S.C.: Republican Printing Company, State Printers, 1872.

United States Congress. *Report of the Joint Select Committee to Inquire into the Condition of Affairs in the Late Insurrectionary States. The Ku Klux Klan Conspiracy*. Vol. 5. Washington, D.C.: Government Printing Office, 1872. Reprint. New York: AMS Press, 1968.

———. *Testimony Taken by the Joint Select Committee to Inquire into the Condition of Affairs in the Late Insurrectionary States*. Vol. 3. Washington, D.C.: Government Printing Office, 1872. Reprint. New York: AMS Press, 1968.

United States Senate. *Proceedings in the Trial of Andrew Johnson*. Washington, D.C.: U.S. Government Printing Office, 1869.

———. *Trial of Andrew Johnson, President of the United States, before the Senate of the United States, on Impeachment by the House of Representatives for High Crimes and Misdemeanors*. Vol. 1. Washington, D.C.: U.S. Government Printing Office, 1868.

United States v. Cruikshank, 92 U.S. 542 (1876).

United States v. Reese, 92 U.S. 214 (1875).

Valelly, Richard M. *The Two Reconstructions: The Struggle for Black Enfranchisement*. Chicago and London: University of Chicago Press, 2004.

Van Atta, John R. "Western Lands and the Political Economy of Henry Clay's American System, 1819–1832." *Journal of the Early American Republic* 21, no. 4 (Winter 2001): 633–65.

Von Frank, Albert J. "John Brown, James Redpath, and the Idea of Revolution." *Civil War History* 52, no. 2 (June 2006): 142–60.

Wade, Wyn Craig. *The Fiery Cross: The Ku Klux Klan in America*. New York and Oxford: Oxford University Press, 1987.

Waldstreicher, David. *Slavery's Constitution: From Revolution to Ratification*. New York: Hill and Wang, 2009.

Wallance, Gregory J. "The Lawsuit That Started the Civil War." *Civil War Times* 45, no. 2 (March/April 2006): 46–52.

Walther, Eric H. *The Shattering of the Union: America in the 1850s*. Wilmington, Del.: SR Books, 2004.

Warmouth, Henry C. *War, Politics and Reconstruction: Stormy Days in Louisiana*. New York: Macmillan, 1930.

Washington, Booker T. "The 1895 Atlanta Compromise Speech." In *The Booker T. Washington Papers*, Vol. 3, edited by Louis R. Harlan, 583–87. Urbana: University of Illinois Press, 1974.

———. *The Story of the Negro: The Rise of the Race from Slavery*. Vol. 2. New York: Doubleday, Page, 1909.

Waugh, Joan. *U. S. Grant: American Hero, American Myth*. Chapel Hill: University of North Carolina Press, 2009.

Waugh, John C. *One Man Great Enough: Abraham Lincoln's Road to Civil War*. Boston and New York: Houghton Mifflin, 2007.

———. *Re-Electing Lincoln: The Battle for the 1864 Presidency*. New York: Crown, 1997.

Weigley, Russell F. *A Great Civil War*. Bloomington and Indianapolis: Indiana University Press, 2000.

Wert, Jeffrey D. *The Sword of Lincoln*. New York: Simon & Schuster, 2005.

West, Jerry L. *The Reconstruction Ku Klux Klan in York County, South Carolina, 1865–1877*. Jefferson, N.C.: McFarland, 2002.

White, Ronald C. Jr. *A. Lincoln: A Biography*. New York: Random House, 2009.

———. *The Eloquent President: A Portrait of Lincoln through His Words*. New York: Random House, 2005.

Whittington, Keith. "The Political Constitution of Federalism in Antebellum America: The Nullification Debate as an Illustration of Informal Mechanisms of Constitutional Change." *Publius* 26, no. 2 (Spring 1996): 1–24.

Wilentz, Sean. *Andrew Jackson*. New York: Times Books/Henry Holt, 2005.

———. "Jeffersonian Democracy and the Origins of Political Antislavery in the United States: The Missouri Crisis Revisited." *Journal of the Historical Society* 4, no. 3 (September 2004): 375–401.

Williams, Lou Falkner. *The Great South Carolina Ku Klux Klan Trials, 1871–1872*. Athens: University of Georgia Press, 1996.

———. "The South Carolina Ku Klux Klan Trials and Enforcement of Federal Civil Rights, 1871–1872." *Civil War History* 39, no. 1 (March 1993): 47–66.

Williams, Patrick G. *Beyond Redemption: Texas Democrats after Reconstruction.* College Station: Texas A & M University Press, 2007.

Williams, Robert C. *Horace Greeley: Champion of American Freedom.* New York: New York University Press, 2006.

Williams, T. Harry. *Lincoln and the Radicals.* Madison and Milwaukee: University of Wisconsin Press, 1965.

———. "Lincoln and the Radicals: An Essay in Civil War History and Historiography." In *The Selected Essays of T. Harry Williams,* with a biographical introduction by Estelle Williams, 43–62. Baton Rouge: Louisiana State University Press, 1983.

Williams v. Mississippi, 170 U.S. 213 (1898).

Winik, Jay. *April 1865: The Month That Saved America.* New York: HarperCollins, 2001.

Wish, Harvey. "American Slave Insurrections before 1861." *Journal of Negro History* 22, no. 3 (July 1937): 299–320.

Witcover, Jules. *Party of the People: A History of the Democrats.* New York: Random House, 2003.

Wood, Gordon S. *Empire of Liberty: A History of the Early Republic, 1789–1815.* Oxford and New York: Oxford University Press, 2009.

Woodman, Harold D. "Class, Race, Politics, and the Modernization of the Postbellum South." *Journal of Southern History* 63, no. 1 (February 1997): 3–22.

———. "Post-Civil War Southern Agriculture and the Law." *Agricultural History* 53, no. 1 (January 1979): 319–37.

Woodward, C. Vann. *Origins of the New South, 1877–1913.* Baton Rouge: Louisiana State University Press, 1951.

———. *The Strange Career of Jim Crow.* 2nd. ed. Oxford and New York: Oxford University Press, 1966.

Work Projects Administration of the State of South Carolina. *South Carolina: A Guide to the Palmetto State.* American Guide Series. New York: Oxford University Press, 1941.

Yoo, John. *Crisis and Command.* New York: Kaplan, 2009.

Young, Rowland L. "The Year They Stole the White House." *American Bar Association Journal* 62, no. 11 (November 1976): 1458–61.

Zuczek, Richard. "The Federal Government's Attack on the Ku Klux Klan: A Reassessment." *South Carolina Historical Magazine* 97, no. 1 (January 1, 1996): 47–64.

———. *State of Rebellion: Reconstruction in South Carolina.* Columbia: University of South Carolina Press, 1996.

Index

About the Author

J. Michael Martinez began his career in the private practice of law. He later earned a PhD in political science and a second PhD in public administration. Today, he works as corporate counsel with a manufacturing company in Monroe, Georgia. He also teaches political science, criminal justice, and public administration courses as a part-time faculty member at Kennesaw State University, the University of South Dakota, and the University of Georgia, respectively. His recent books include *Life and Death in Civil War Prisons* (2004) and *Carpetbaggers, Cavalry, and the Ku Klux Klan* (2007). Visit him on the Internet at www.jmichaelmartinez.com.